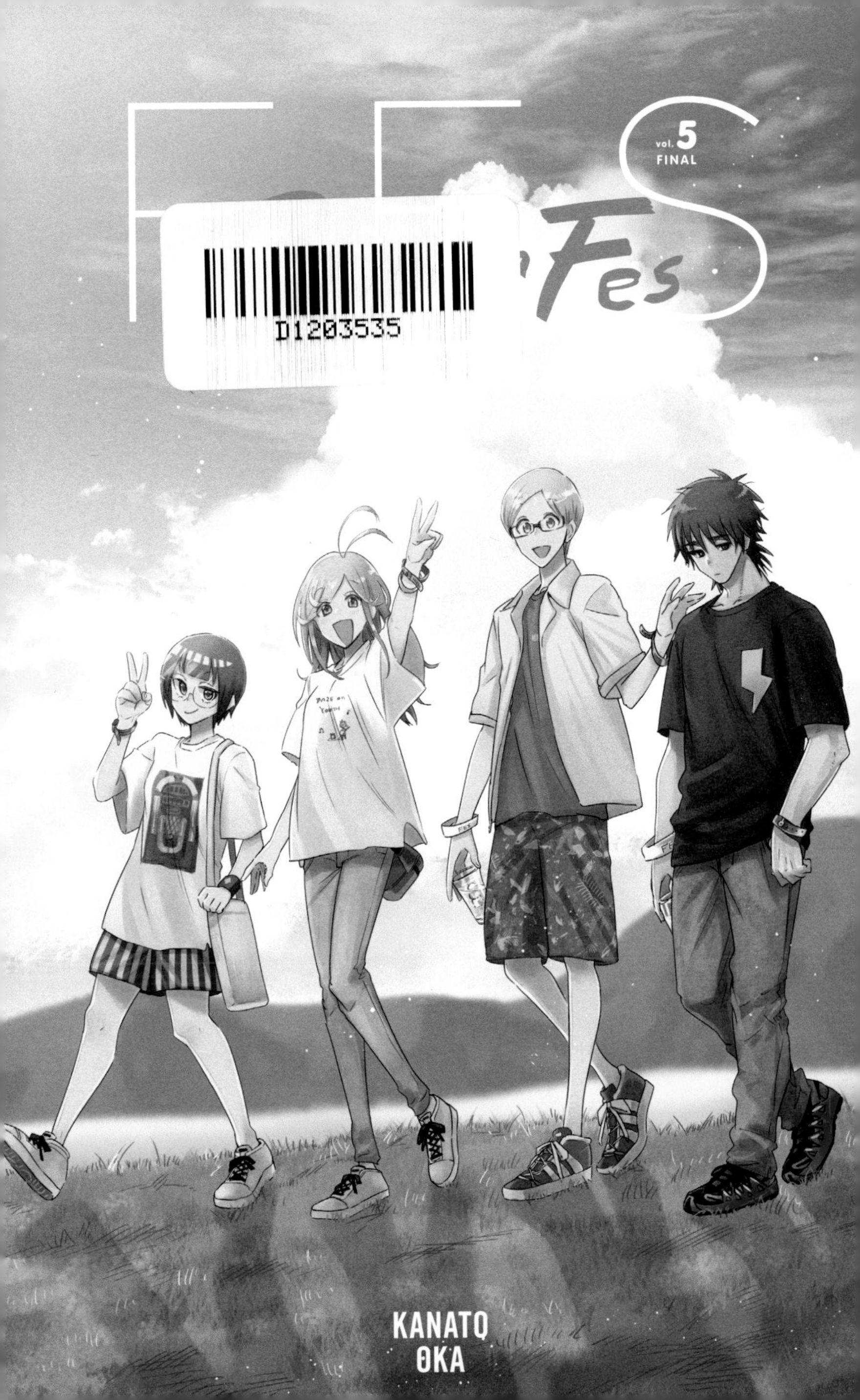

Fes
vol. 5
FINAL
KANATO OKA

FES

Days on Fes

contents

SIDE STAGE | MAIN STAGE

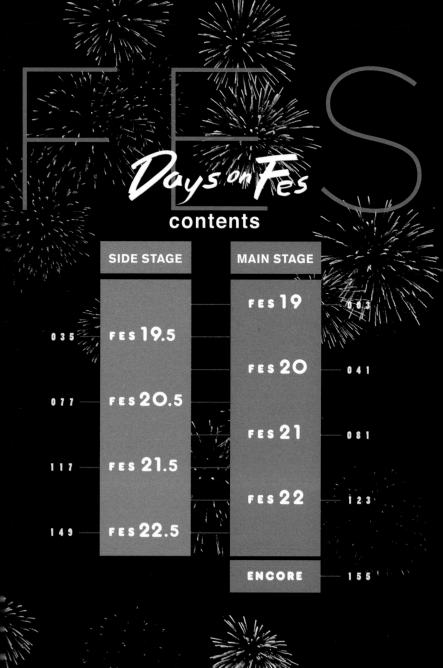

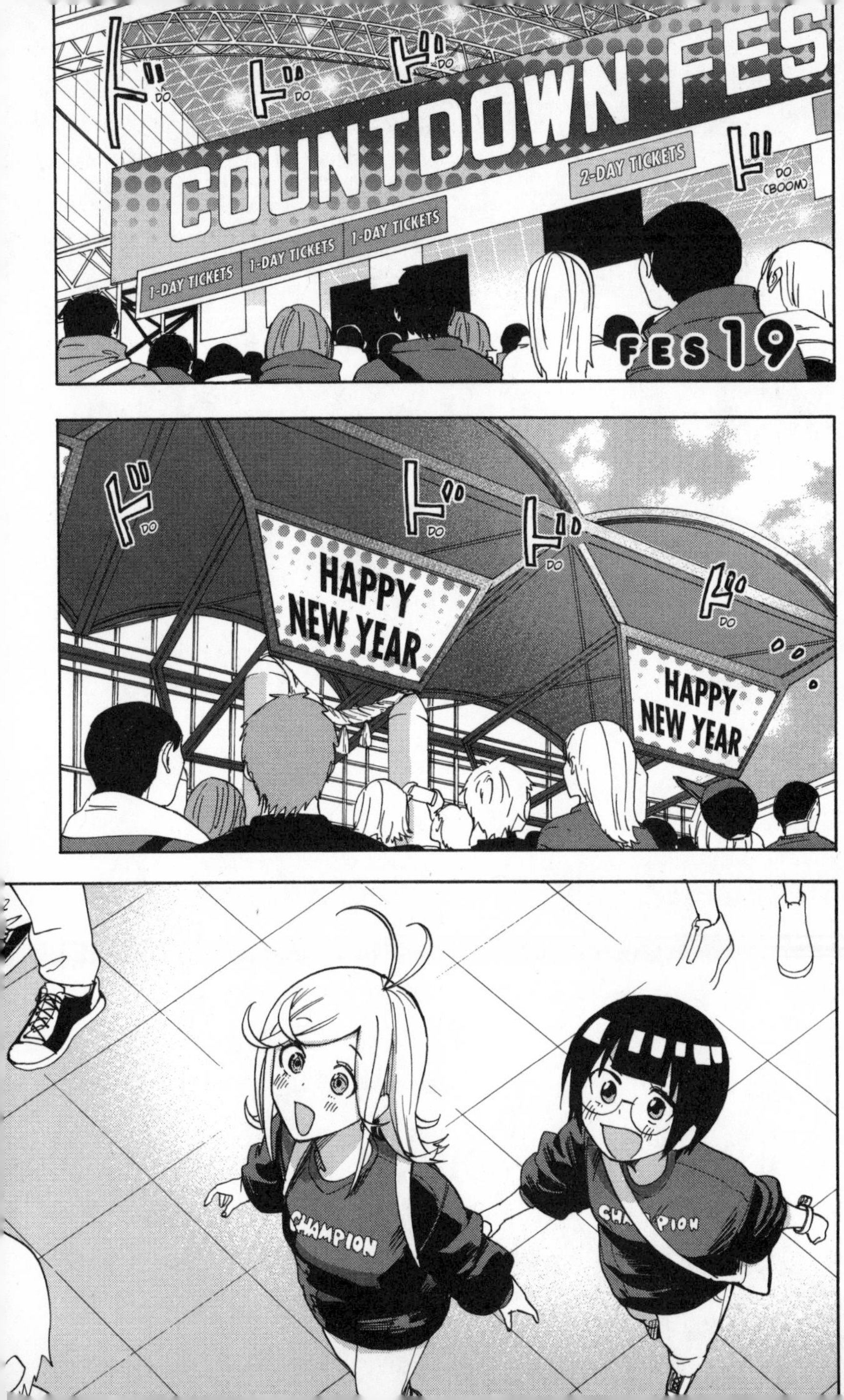
COUNTDOWN FES
DO (BOOM)
DO
DO
DO
2-DAY TICKETS
1-DAY TICKETS
1-DAY TICKETS
1-DAY TICKETS
FES 19
DO
DO
DO
DO
HAPPY NEW YEAR
HAPPY NEW YEAR
CHAMPION
CHAMPION

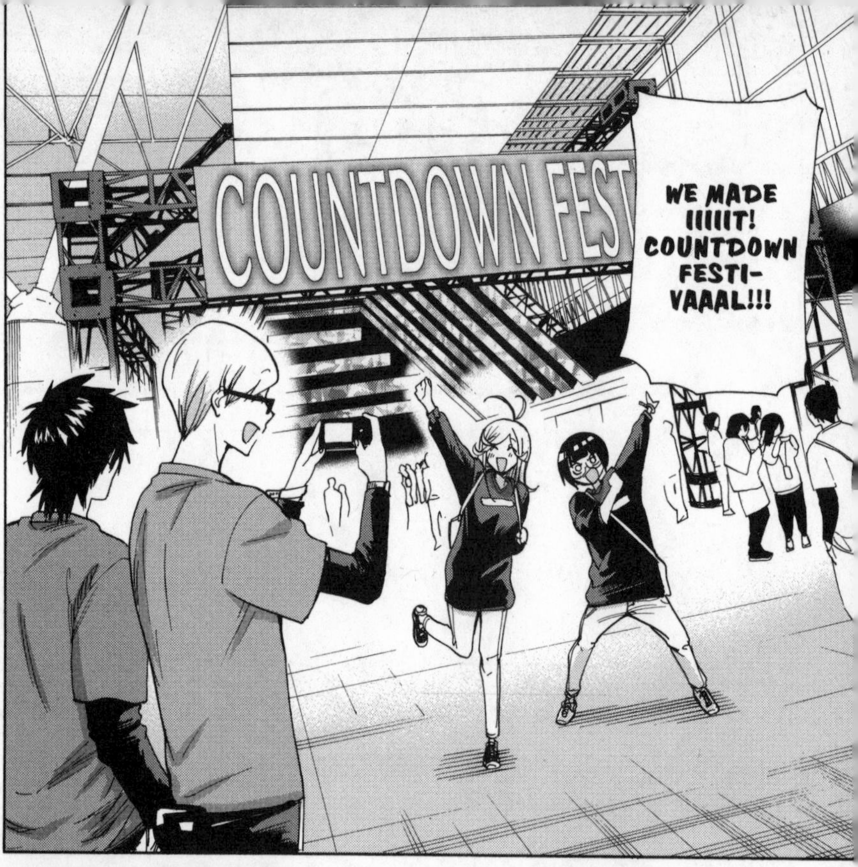
COUNTDOWN FEST
WE MADE IIIIIIT! COUNTDOWN FESTI-VAAAL!!!

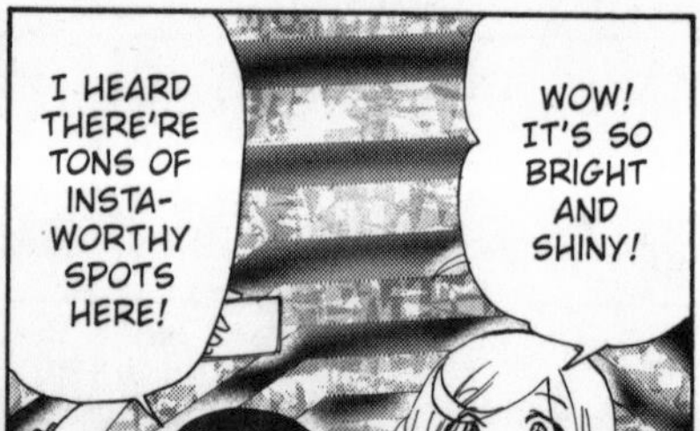
WOW! IT'S SO BRIGHT AND SHINY!
I HEARD THERE'RE TONS OF INSTA-WORTHY SPOTS HERE!
CHAMPION
CHAMPION

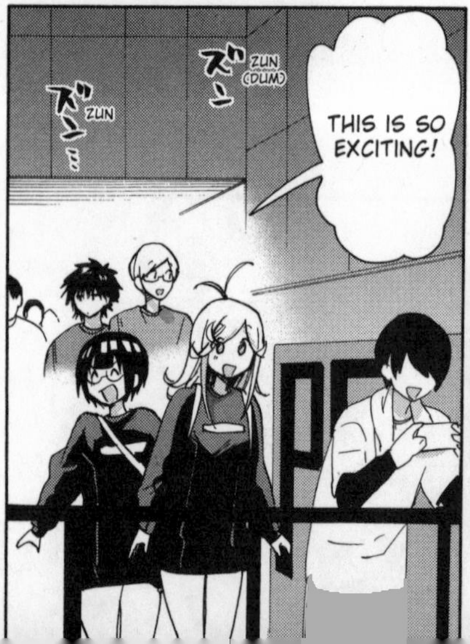
ZUN (DUM)
ZUN
THIS IS SO EXCITING!

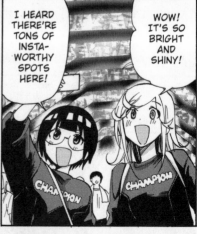

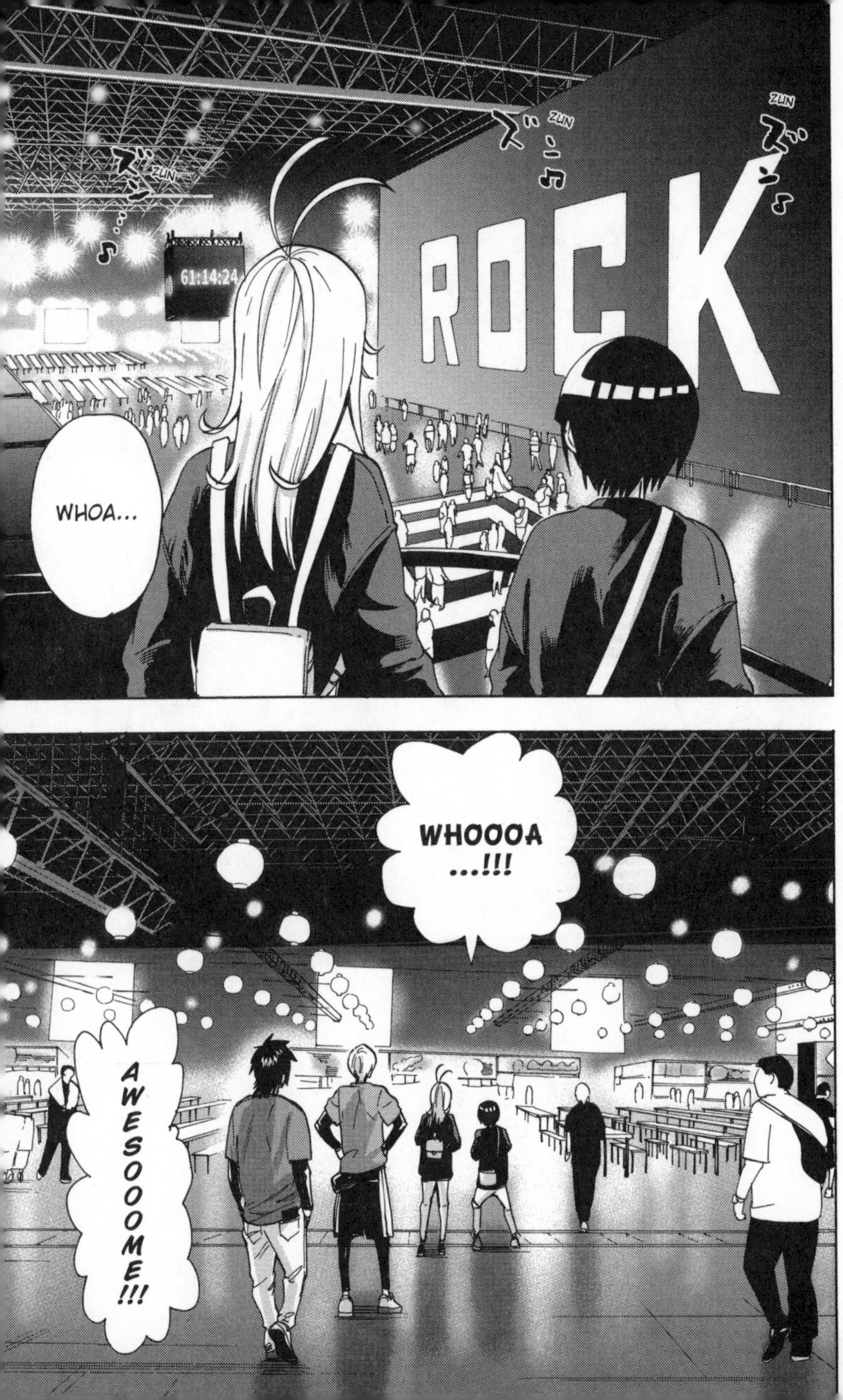
ZUN
ZUN
ROCK
ZUN
61:14:24
WHOA...
WHOOOA ...!!!
AWESOOOOME!!!

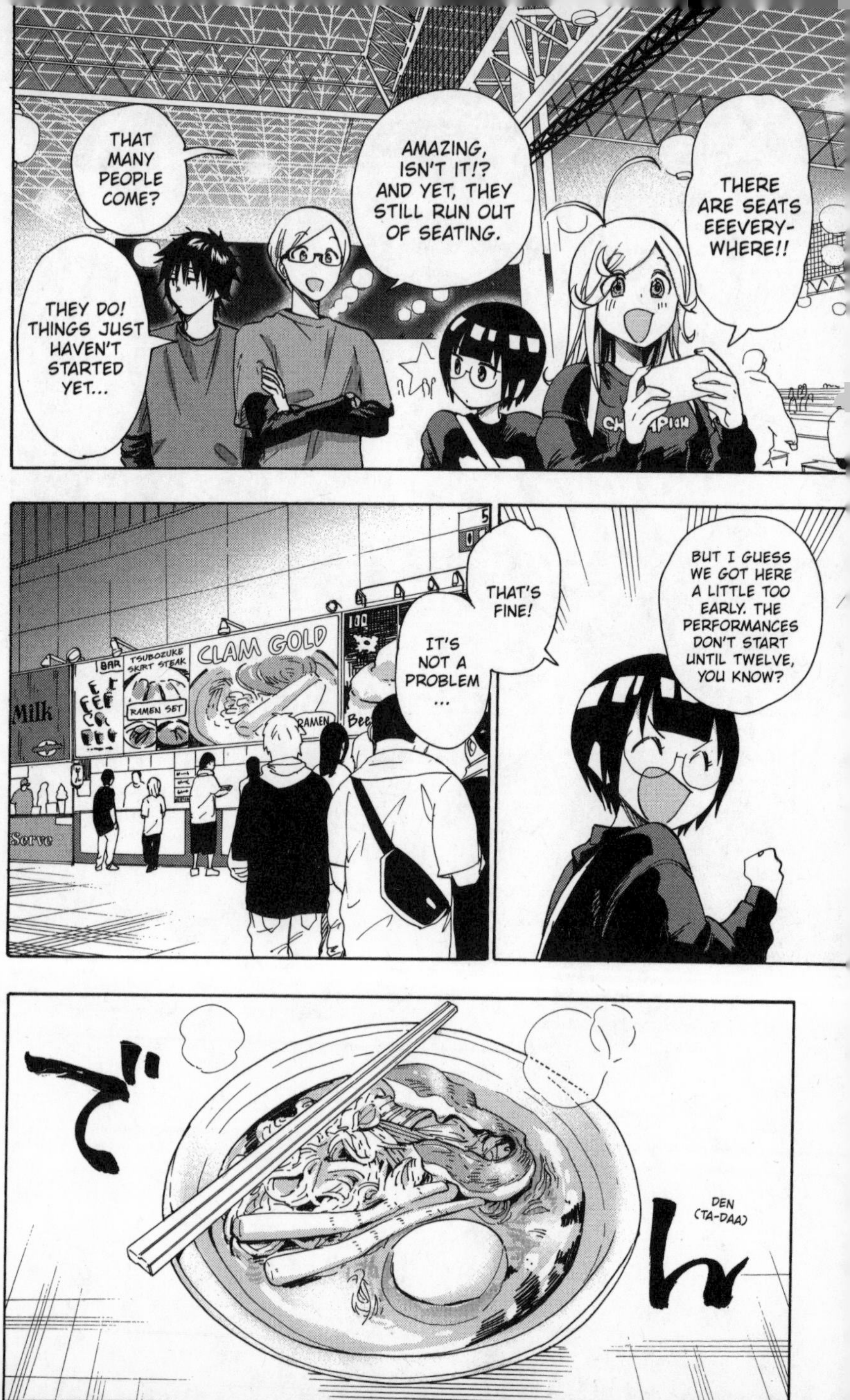
THERE ARE SEATS EEEVERY-WHERE!!
AMAZING, ISN'T IT!? AND YET, THEY STILL RUN OUT OF SEATING.
THAT MANY PEOPLE COME?
THEY DO! THINGS JUST HAVEN'T STARTED YET...
BUT I GUESS WE GOT HERE A LITTLE TOO EARLY. THE PERFORMANCES DON'T START UNTIL TWELVE, YOU KNOW?
THAT'S FINE!
IT'S NOT A PROBLEM ...
CLAM GOLD
TSUBOZUKE SKIRT STEAK
RAMEN SET
BAR
Milk
RAMEN
Serve
でん
DEN (TA-DAA)

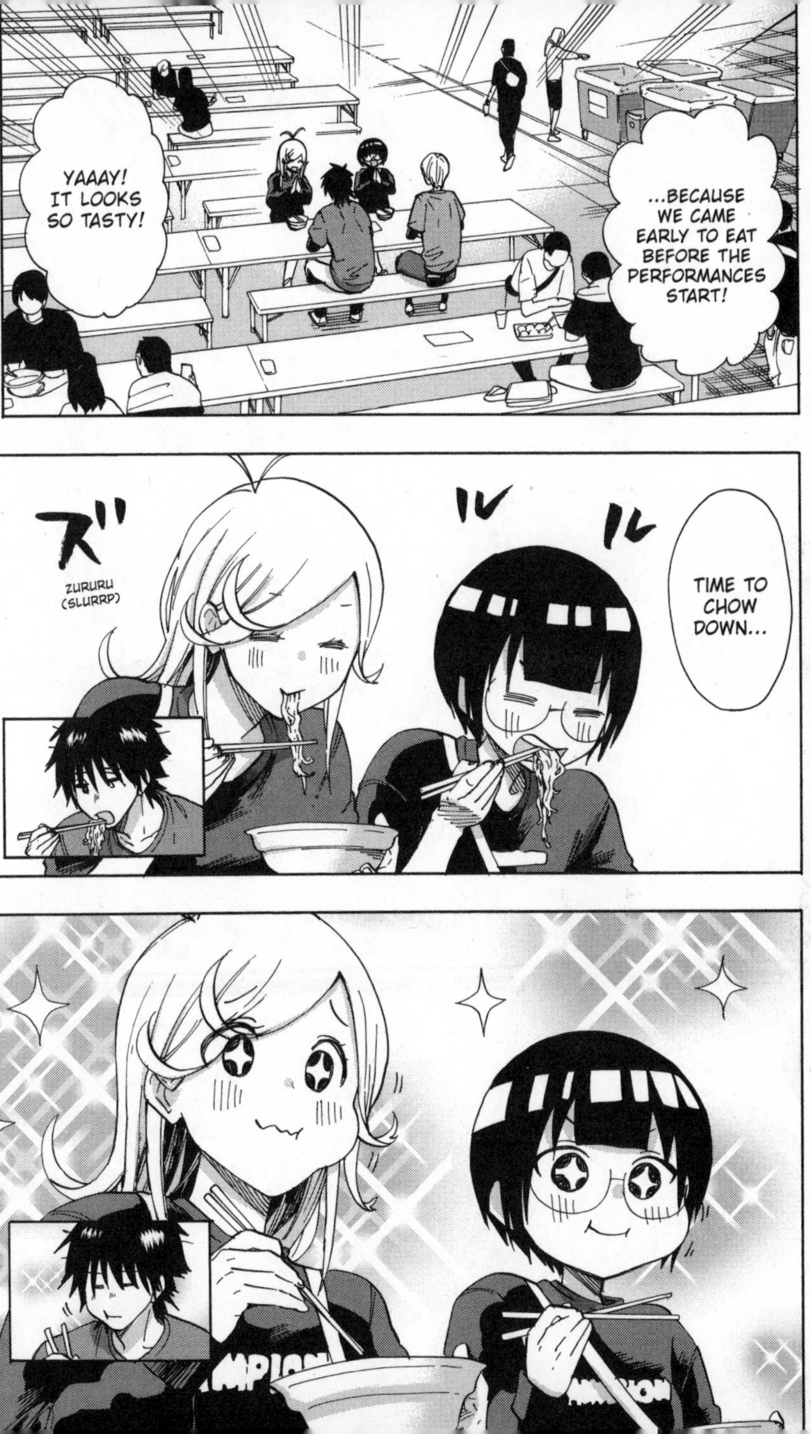
...BECAUSE WE CAME EARLY TO EAT BEFORE THE PERFORMANCES START!
YAAAY! IT LOOKS SO TASTY!
TIME TO CHOW DOWN...
ズルル
ZURURU (SLURRP)

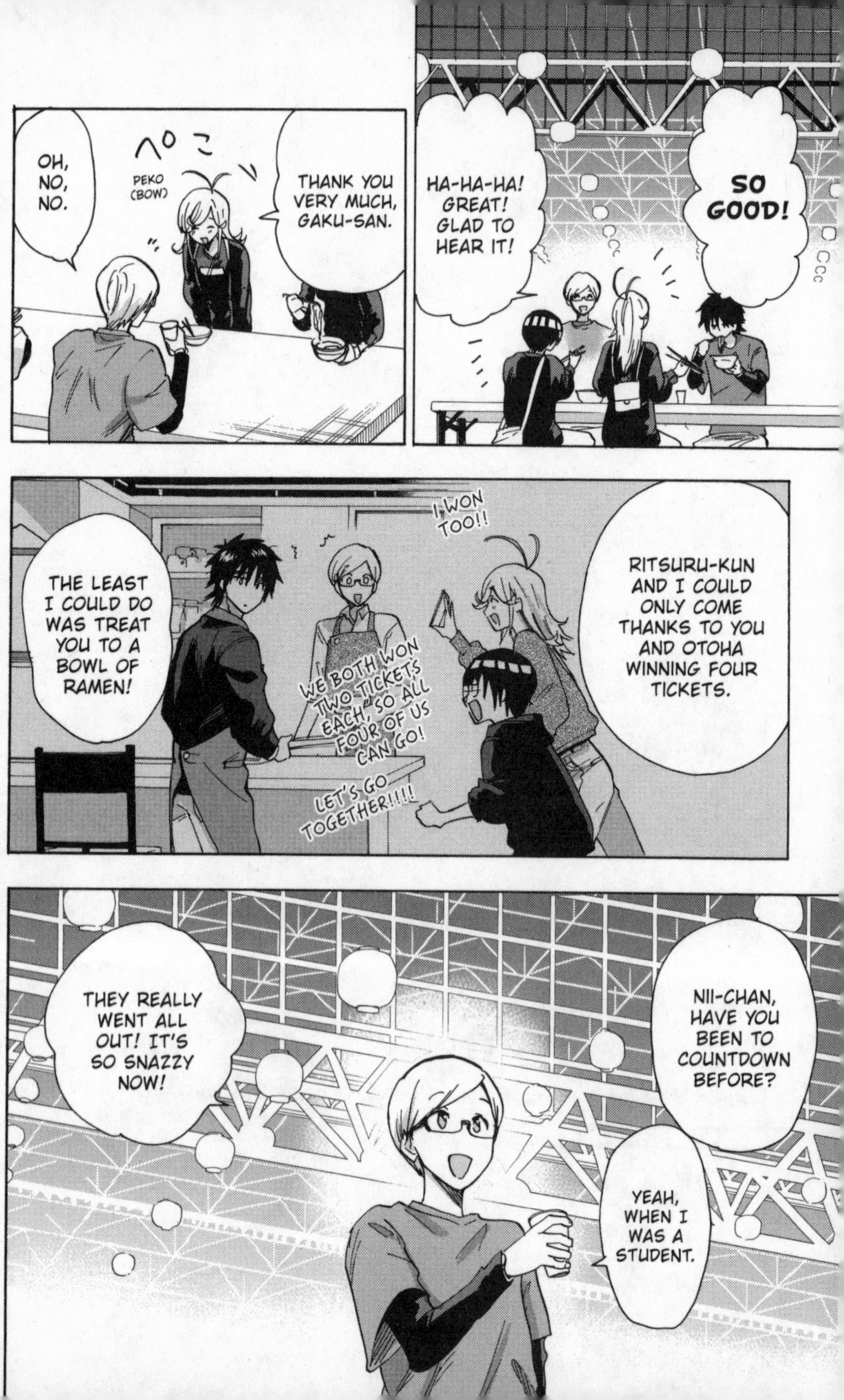
SO GOOD!
HA-HA-HA! GREAT! GLAD TO HEAR IT!
THANK YOU VERY MUCH, GAKU-SAN.
ぺこ
PEKO (BOW)
OH, NO, NO.
RITSURU-KUN AND I COULD ONLY COME THANKS TO YOU AND OTOHA WINNING FOUR TICKETS.
I WON TOO!!
WE BOTH WON TWO TICKETS EACH, SO ALL FOUR OF US CAN GO!
LET'S GO TOGETHER!!!!
THE LEAST I COULD DO WAS TREAT YOU TO A BOWL OF RAMEN!
NII-CHAN, HAVE YOU BEEN TO COUNTDOWN BEFORE?
THEY REALLY WENT ALL OUT! IT'S SO SNAZZY NOW!
YEAH, WHEN I WAS A STUDENT.

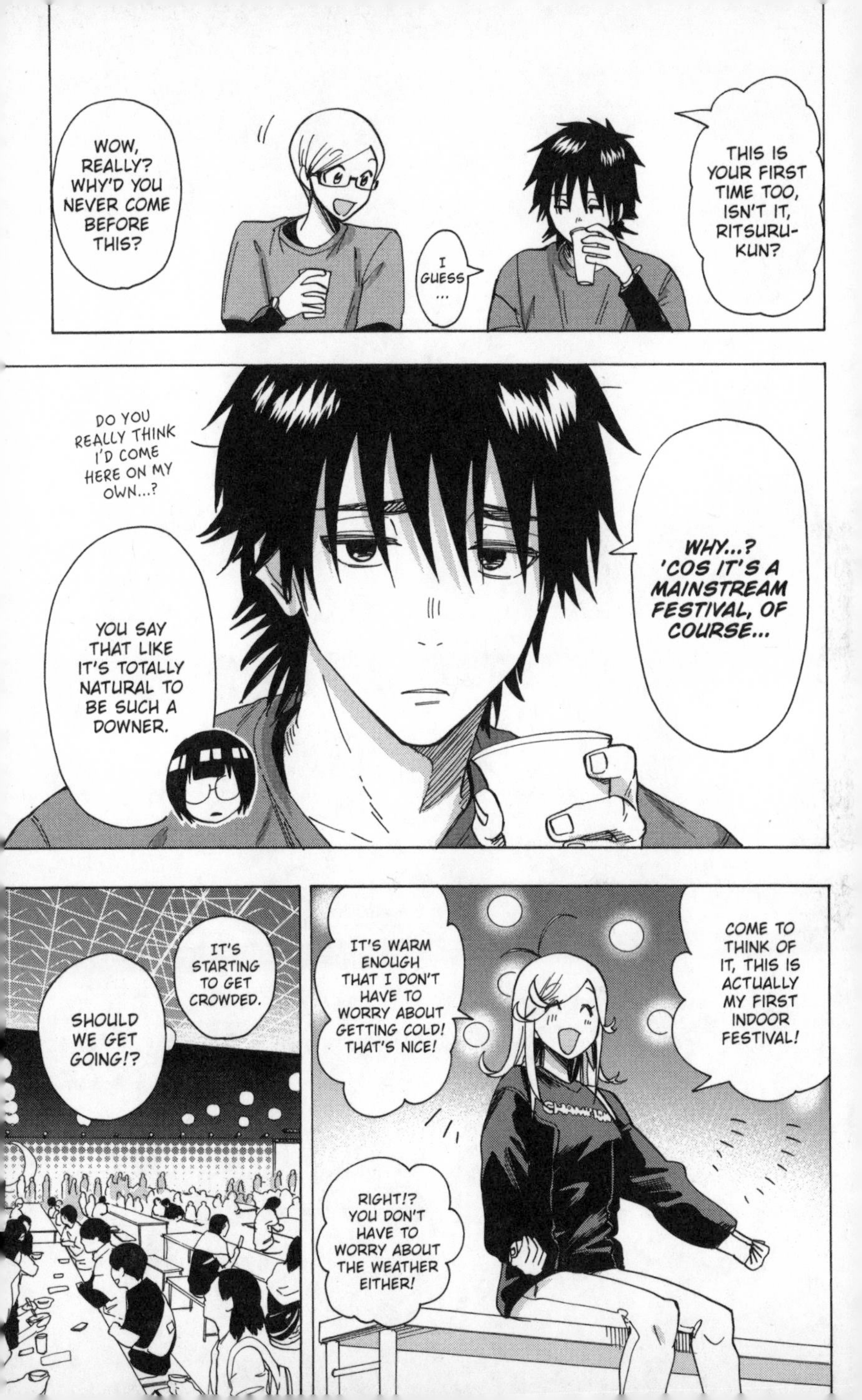
THIS IS YOUR FIRST TIME TOO, ISN'T IT, RITSURU-KUN?
I GUESS...
WOW, REALLY? WHY'D YOU NEVER COME BEFORE THIS?
WHY...? 'COS IT'S A MAINSTREAM FESTIVAL, OF COURSE...
DO YOU REALLY THINK I'D COME HERE ON MY OWN...?
YOU SAY THAT LIKE IT'S TOTALLY NATURAL TO BE SUCH A DOWNER.
COME TO THINK OF IT, THIS IS ACTUALLY MY FIRST INDOOR FESTIVAL!
IT'S WARM ENOUGH THAT I DON'T HAVE TO WORRY ABOUT GETTING COLD! THAT'S NICE!
RIGHT!? YOU DON'T HAVE TO WORRY ABOUT THE WEATHER EITHER!
IT'S STARTING TO GET CROWDED.
SHOULD WE GET GOING!?

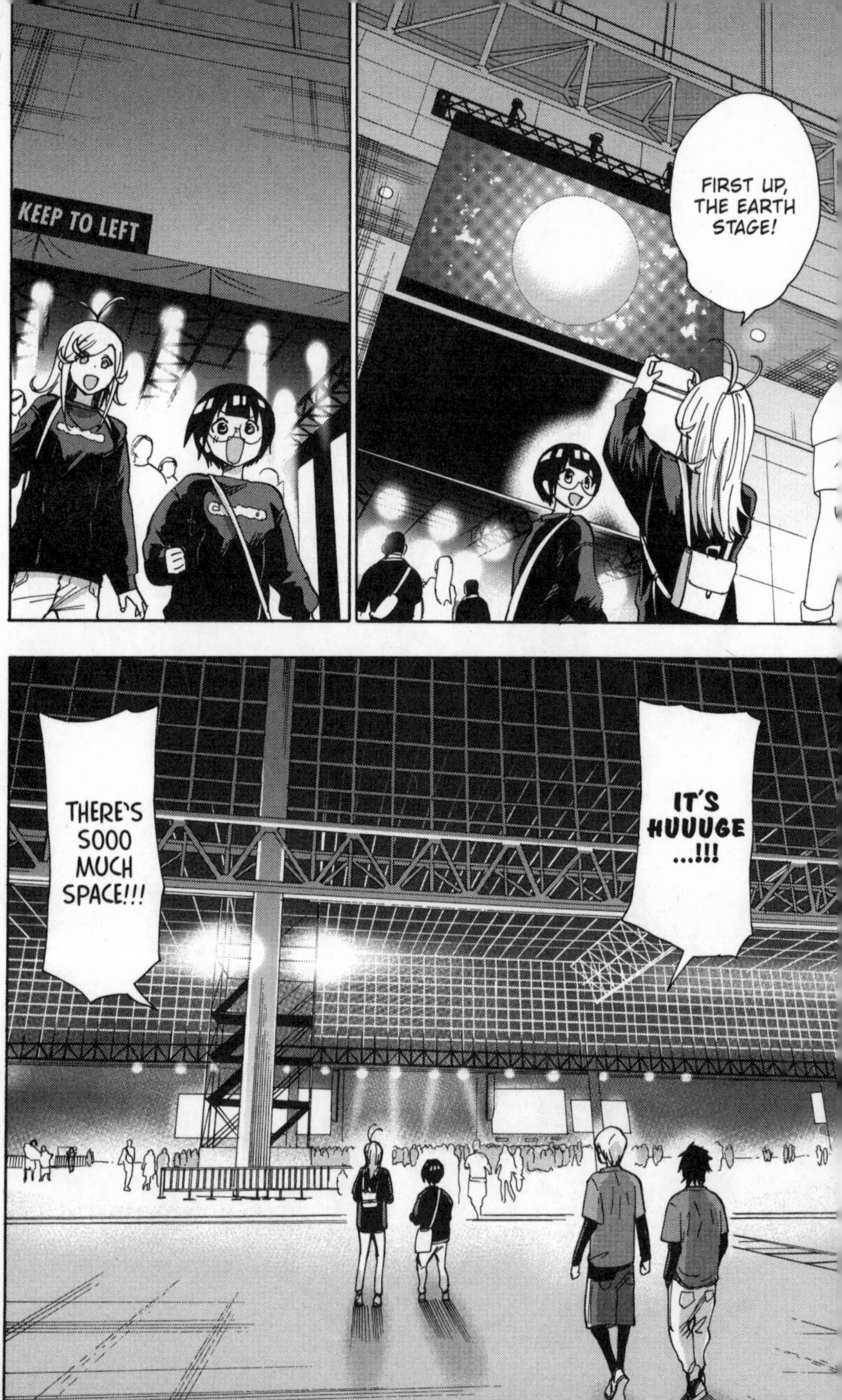
FIRST UP, THE EARTH STAGE!
KEEP TO LEFT
IT'S HUUUGE ...!!!
THERE'S SOOO MUCH SPACE!!!

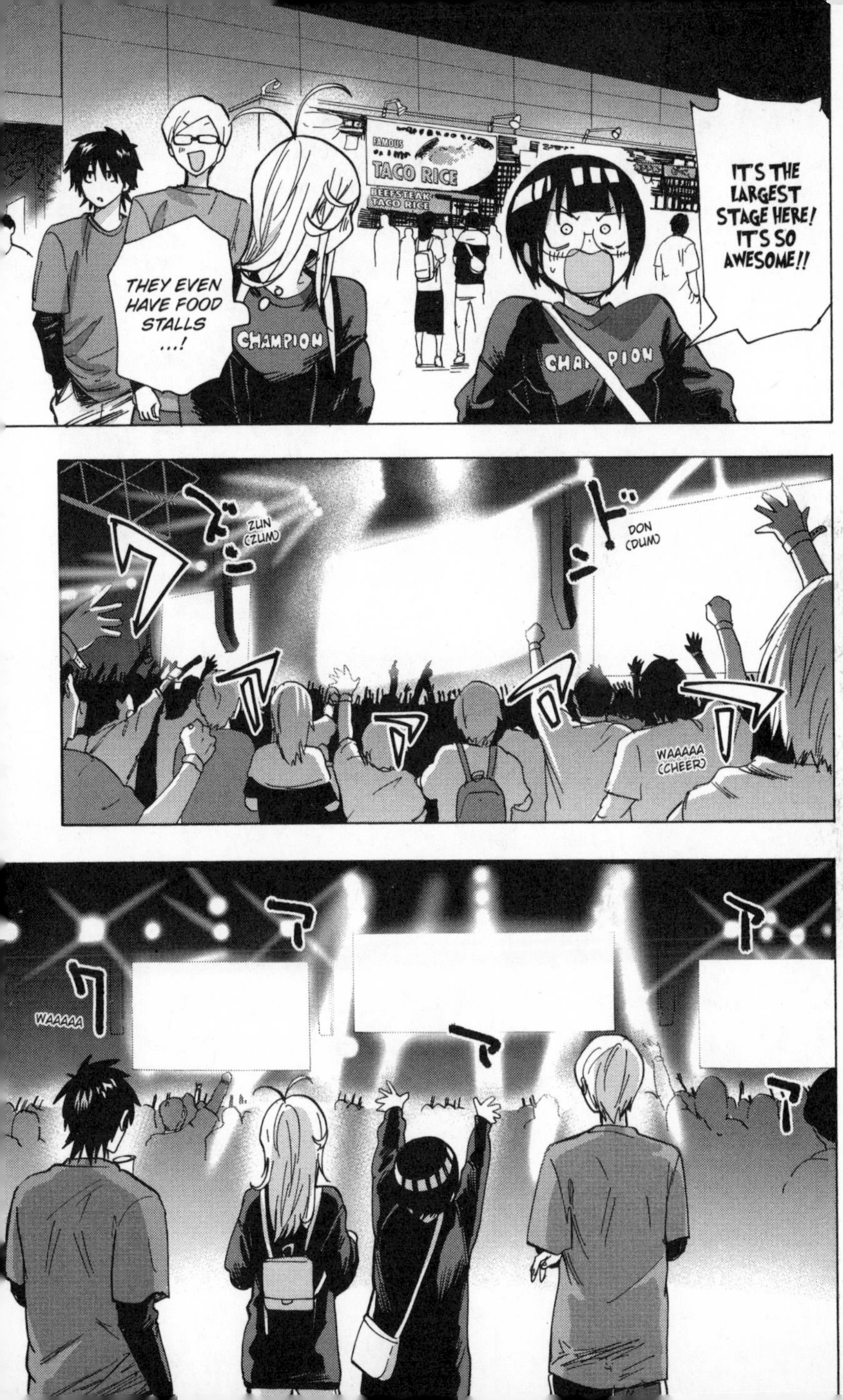
IT'S THE LARGEST STAGE HERE! IT'S SO AWESOME!!
FAMOUS TACO RICE
BEEFSTEAK TACO RICE
CHAMPION
CHAMPION
THEY EVEN HAVE FOOD STALLS ...!
DON (DUM)
ZUN (ZUM)
WAAAAA (CHEER)
WAAAAA

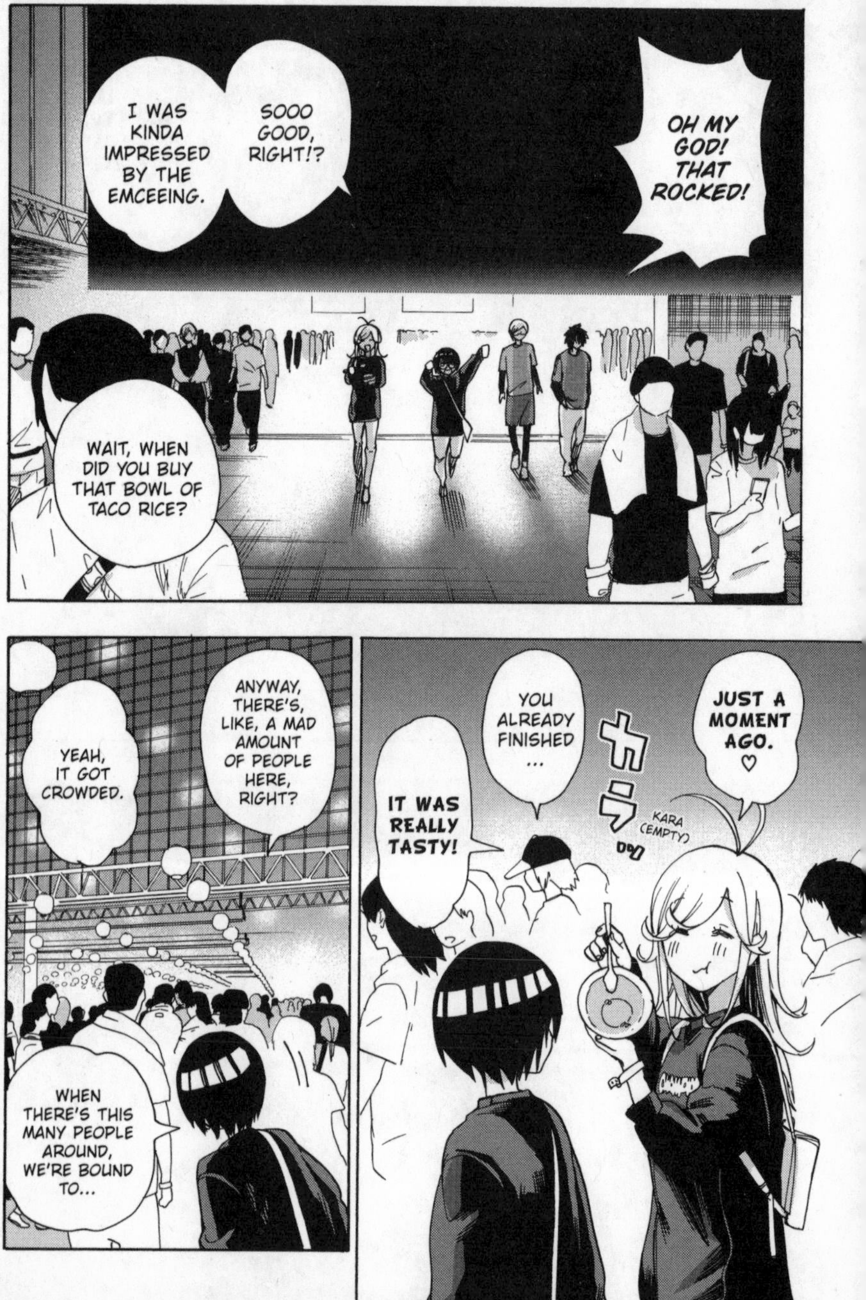
OH MY GOD! THAT ROCKED!
SOOO GOOD, RIGHT!?
I WAS KINDA IMPRESSED BY THE EMCEEING.
WAIT, WHEN DID YOU BUY THAT BOWL OF TACO RICE?
JUST A MOMENT AGO. ♡
カラ
KARA (EMPTY)
YOU ALREADY FINISHED...
IT WAS REALLY TASTY!
ANYWAY, THERE'S, LIKE, A MAD AMOUNT OF PEOPLE HERE, RIGHT?
YEAH, IT GOT CROWDED.
WHEN THERE'S THIS MANY PEOPLE AROUND, WE'RE BOUND TO...

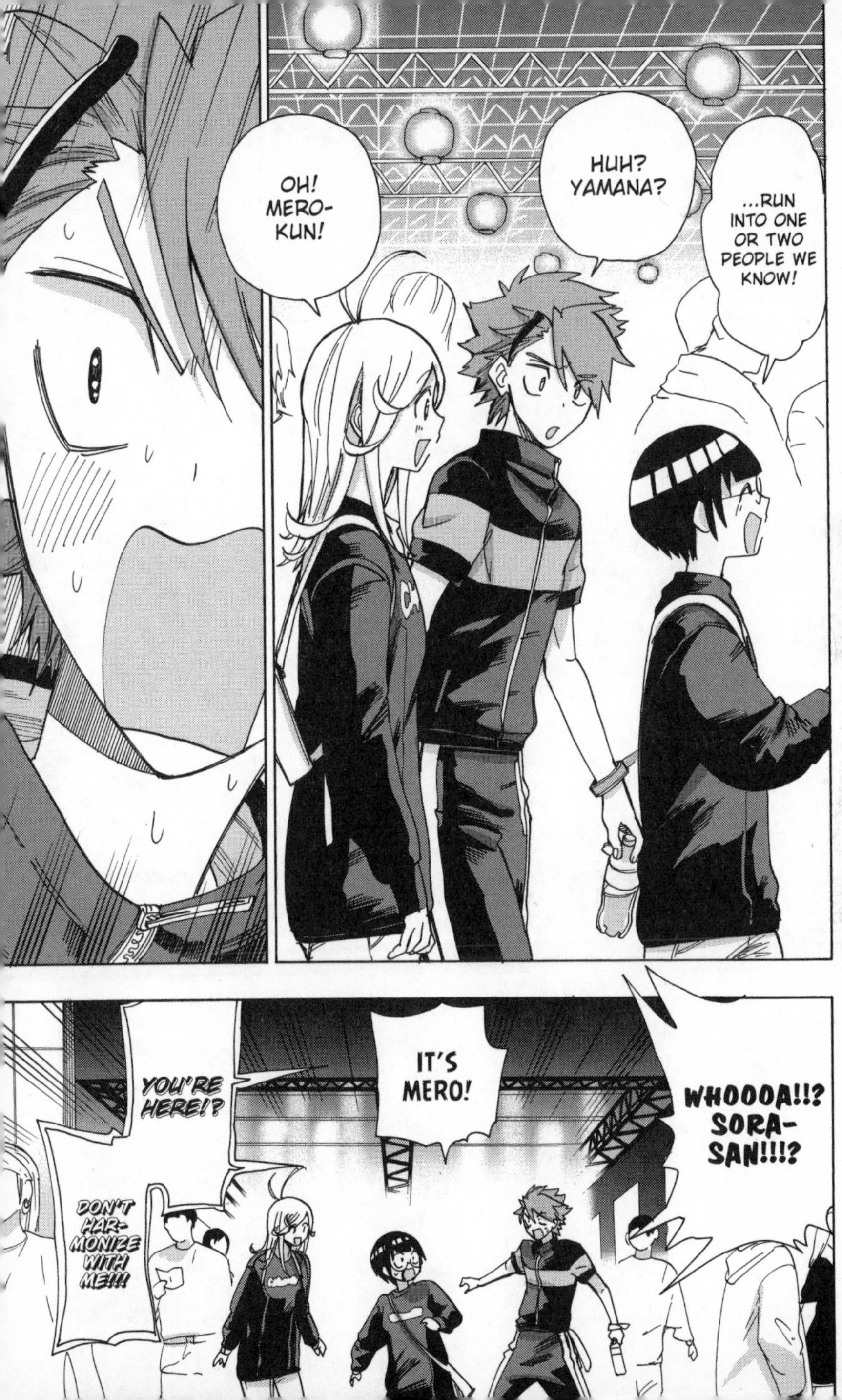
...RUN INTO ONE OR TWO PEOPLE WE KNOW!
HUH? YAMANA?
OH! MERO-KUN!
WHOOOA!!? SORA-SAN!!!?
IT'S MERO!
YOU'RE HERE!?
DON'T HAR-MONIZE WITH ME!!!

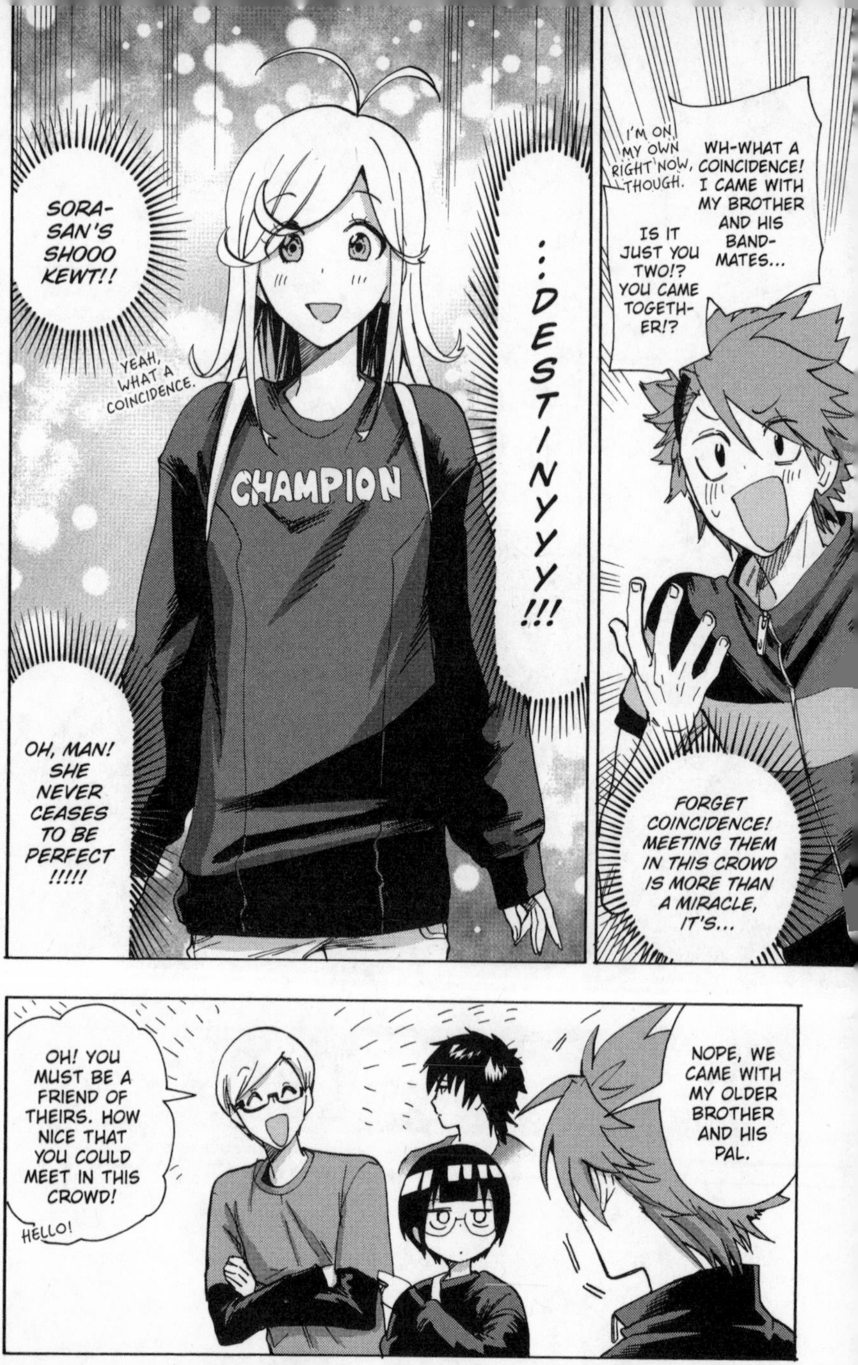
WH-WHAT A COINCIDENCE! I CAME WITH MY BROTHER AND HIS BAND-MATES...
I'M ON MY OWN RIGHT NOW, THOUGH.
IS IT JUST YOU TWO!? YOU CAME TOGETH-ER!?
FORGET COINCIDENCE! MEETING THEM IN THIS CROWD IS MORE THAN A MIRACLE, IT'S...
...DESTINYYY!!!
SORA-SAN'S SHOOO KEWT!!
YEAH, WHAT A COINCIDENCE.
OH, MAN! SHE NEVER CEASES TO BE PERFECT!!!!!
NOPE, WE CAME WITH MY OLDER BROTHER AND HIS PAL.
OH! YOU MUST BE A FRIEND OF THEIRS. HOW NICE THAT YOU COULD MEET IN THIS CROWD!
HELLO!

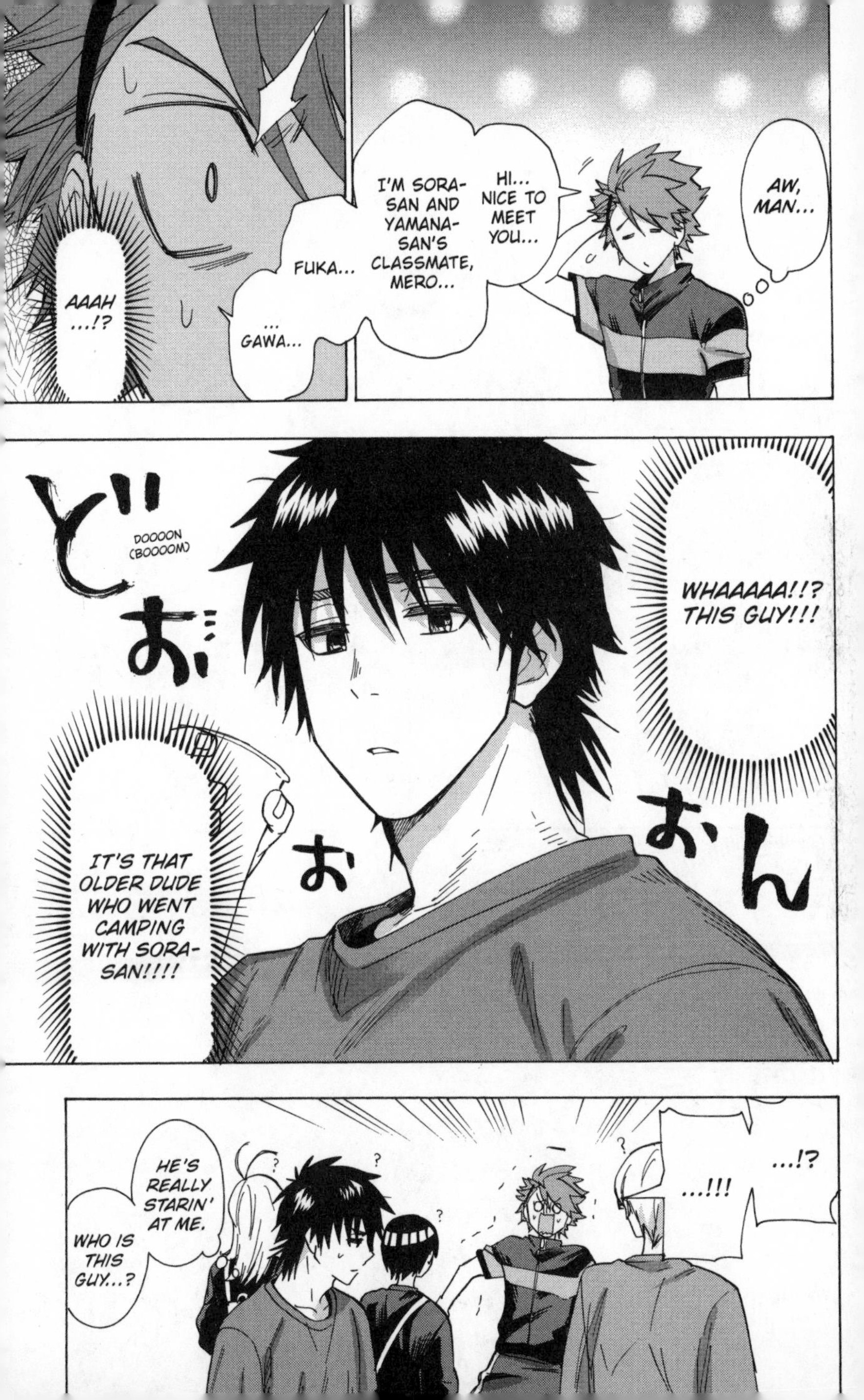
AW, MAN...
HI... NICE TO MEET YOU...
I'M SORA-SAN AND YAMANA-SAN'S CLASSMATE, MERO...
FUKA...
...GAWA...
AAAH ...!?
WHAAAAA!!? THIS GUY!!!
どおおおん
DOOOON (BOOOOM)
IT'S THAT OLDER DUDE WHO WENT CAMPING WITH SORA-SAN!!!!
...!?
...!!!
HE'S REALLY STARIN' AT ME.
WHO IS THIS GUY...?

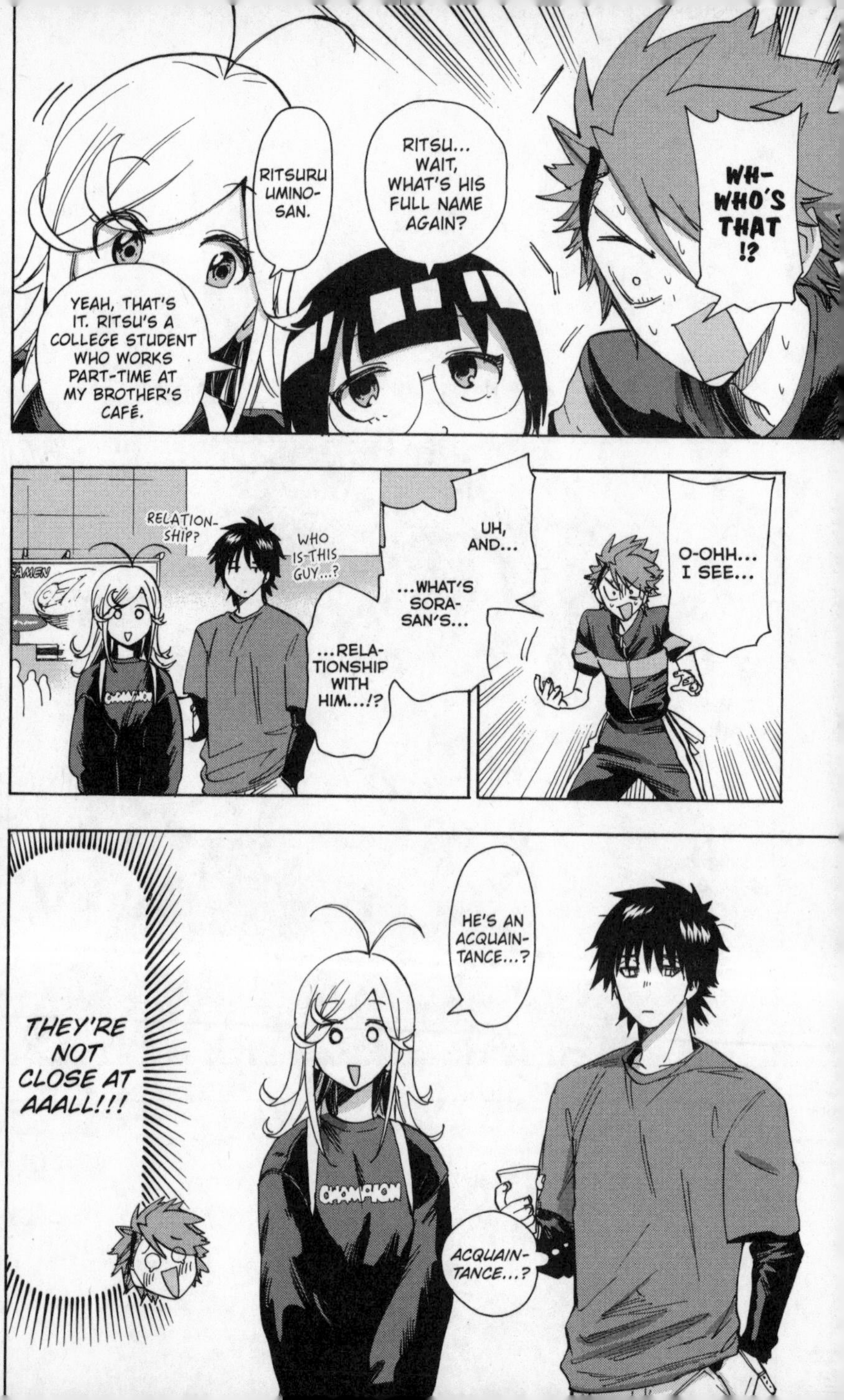
WH-WHO'S THAT!?
RITSU... WAIT, WHAT'S HIS FULL NAME AGAIN?
RITSURU UMINO-SAN.
YEAH, THAT'S IT. RITSU'S A COLLEGE STUDENT WHO WORKS PART-TIME AT MY BROTHER'S CAFÉ.
O-OHH... I SEE...
UH, AND...
...WHAT'S SORA-SAN'S...
...RELATIONSHIP WITH HIM...!?
WHO IS THIS GUY...?
RELATIONSHIP?
HE'S AN ACQUAINTANCE...?
THEY'RE NOT CLOSE AT AAALL!!!
ACQUAINTANCE...?

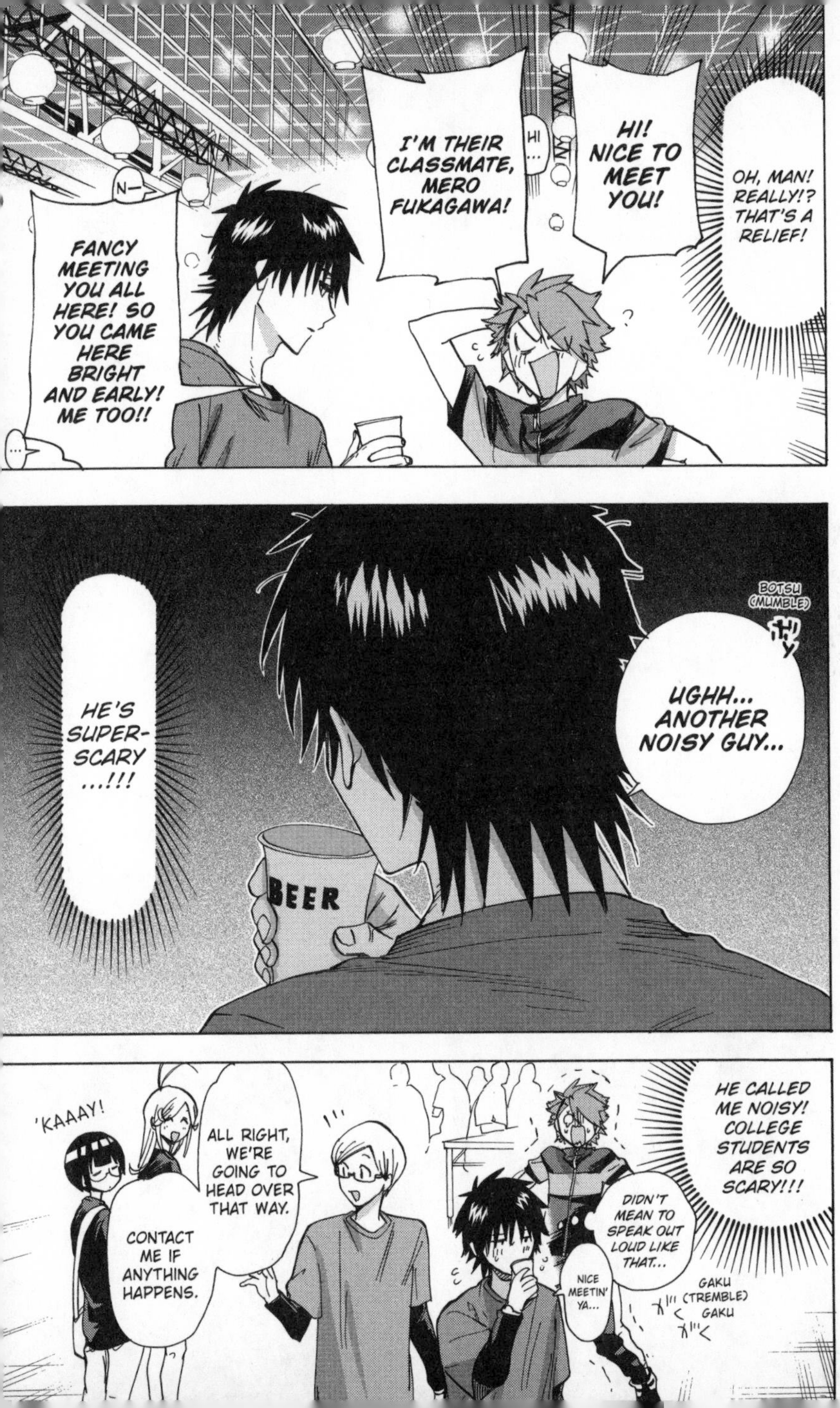
OH, MAN! REALLY!? THAT'S A RELIEF!
HI! NICE TO MEET YOU!
HI...
I'M THEIR CLASSMATE, MERO FUKAGAWA!
N—
FANCY MEETING YOU ALL HERE! SO YOU CAME HERE BRIGHT AND EARLY! ME TOO!!
...
BOTSU (MUMBLE)
UGHH... ANOTHER NOISY GUY...
HE'S SUPER-SCARY ...!!!
BEER
HE CALLED ME NOISY! COLLEGE STUDENTS ARE SO SCARY!!!
DIDN'T MEAN TO SPEAK OUT LOUD LIKE THAT...
GAKU (TREMBLE) GAKU
NICE MEETIN' YA...
ALL RIGHT, WE'RE GOING TO HEAD OVER THAT WAY.
CONTACT ME IF ANYTHING HAPPENS.
'KAAAY!

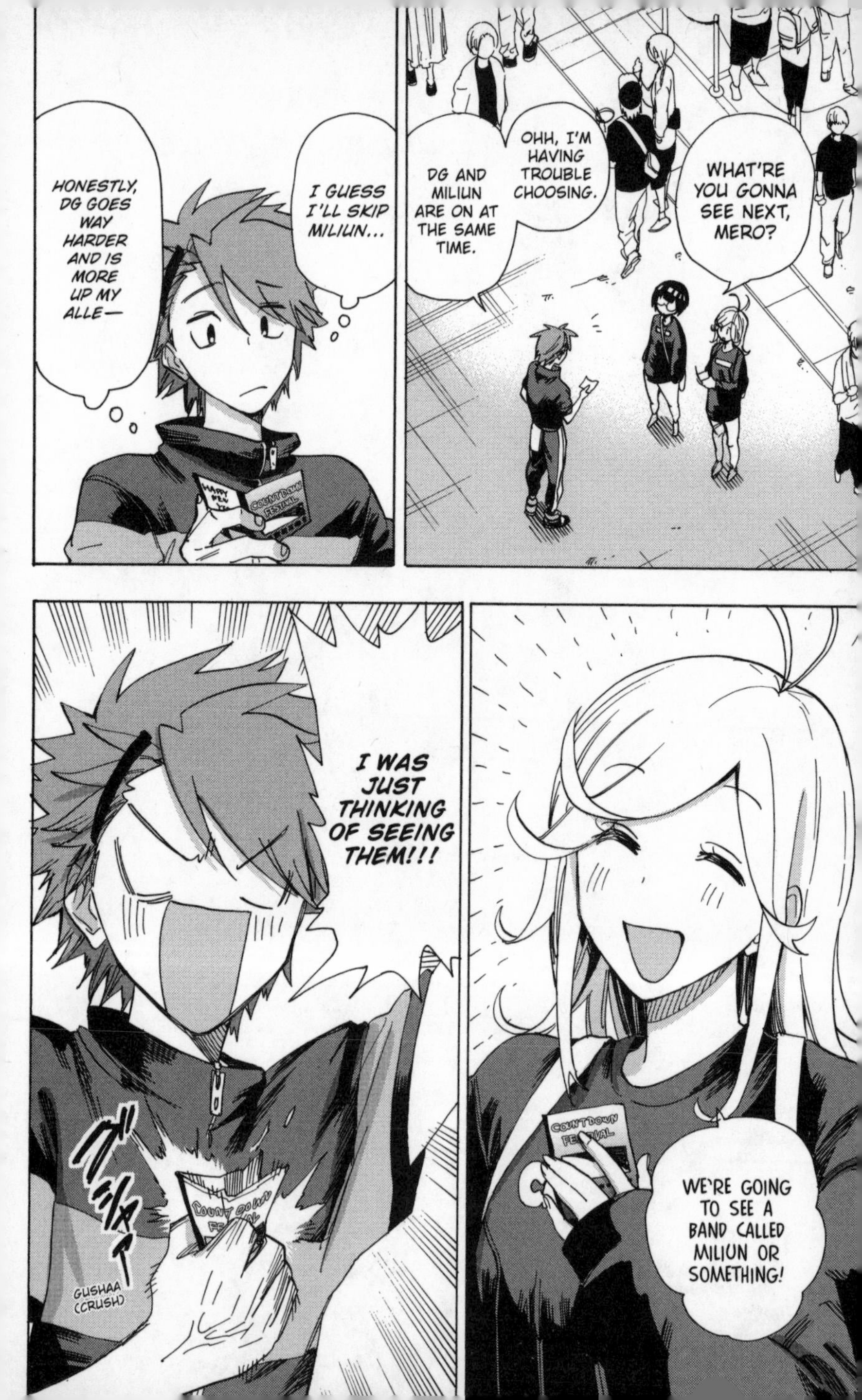
WHAT'RE YOU GONNA SEE NEXT, MERO?
OHH, I'M HAVING TROUBLE CHOOSING.
DG AND MILIUN ARE ON AT THE SAME TIME.
I GUESS I'LL SKIP MILIUN...
HONESTLY, DG GOES WAY HARDER AND IS MORE UP MY ALLE—
COUNTDOWN FESTIVAL
COUNTDOWN FESTIVAL
WE'RE GOING TO SEE A BAND CALLED MILIUN OR SOMETHING!
I WAS JUST THINKING OF SEEING THEM!!!
GUSHAA (CRUSH)

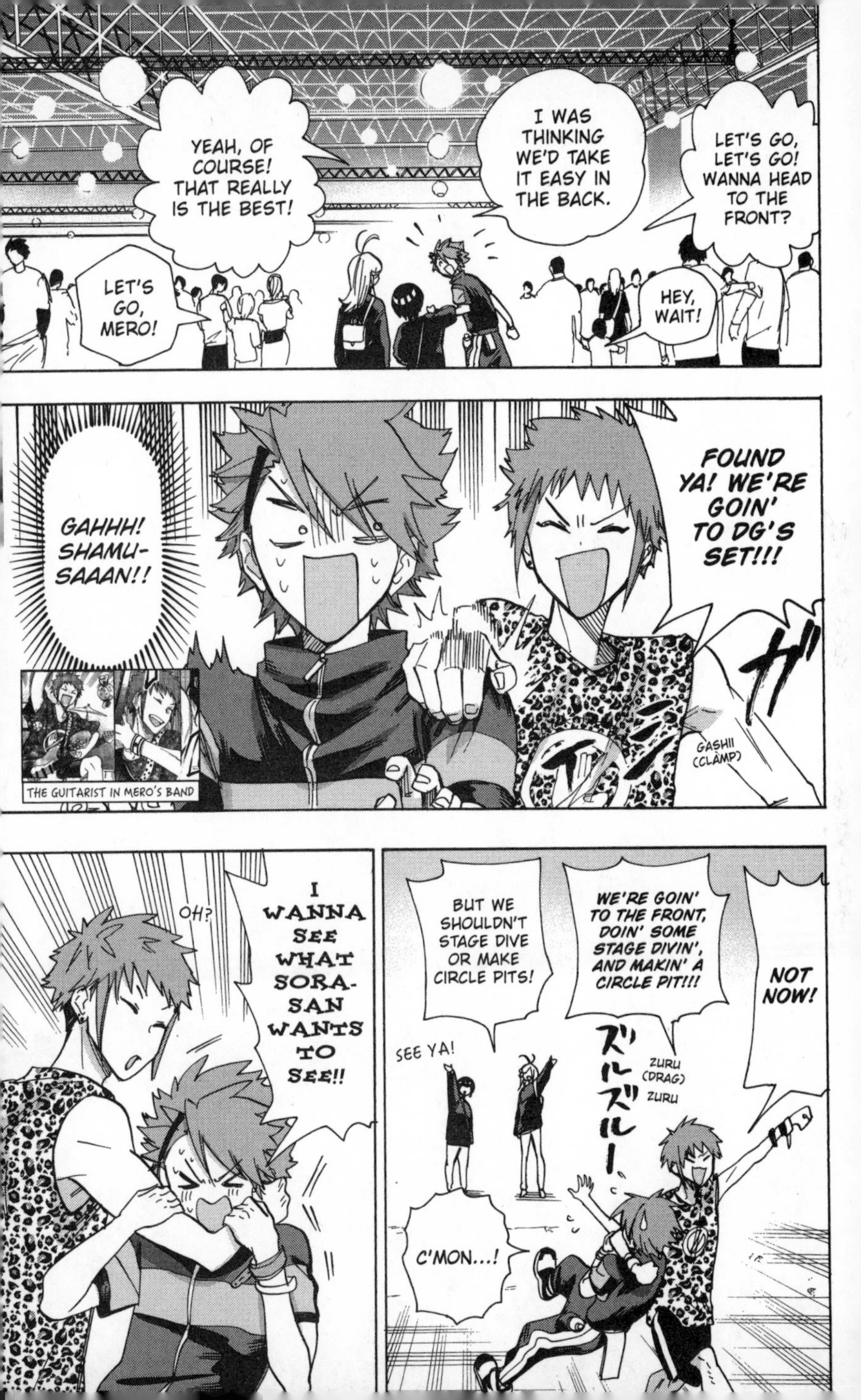
LET'S GO, LET'S GO! WANNA HEAD TO THE FRONT?
HEY, WAIT!
I WAS THINKING WE'D TAKE IT EASY IN THE BACK.
YEAH, OF COURSE! THAT REALLY IS THE BEST!
LET'S GO, MERO!
FOUND YA! WE'RE GOIN' TO DG'S SET!!!
GASHII (CLAMP)
GAHHH! SHAMU-SAAAN!!
THE GUITARIST IN MERO'S BAND
NOT NOW!
WE'RE GOIN' TO THE FRONT, DOIN' SOME STAGE DIVIN', AND MAKIN' A CIRCLE PIT!!!
BUT WE SHOULDN'T STAGE DIVE OR MAKE CIRCLE PITS!
ZURU (DRAG) ZURU
ズルズルー
SEE YA!
C'MON...!
I WANNA SEE WHAT SORA-SAN WANTS TO SEE!!
OH?

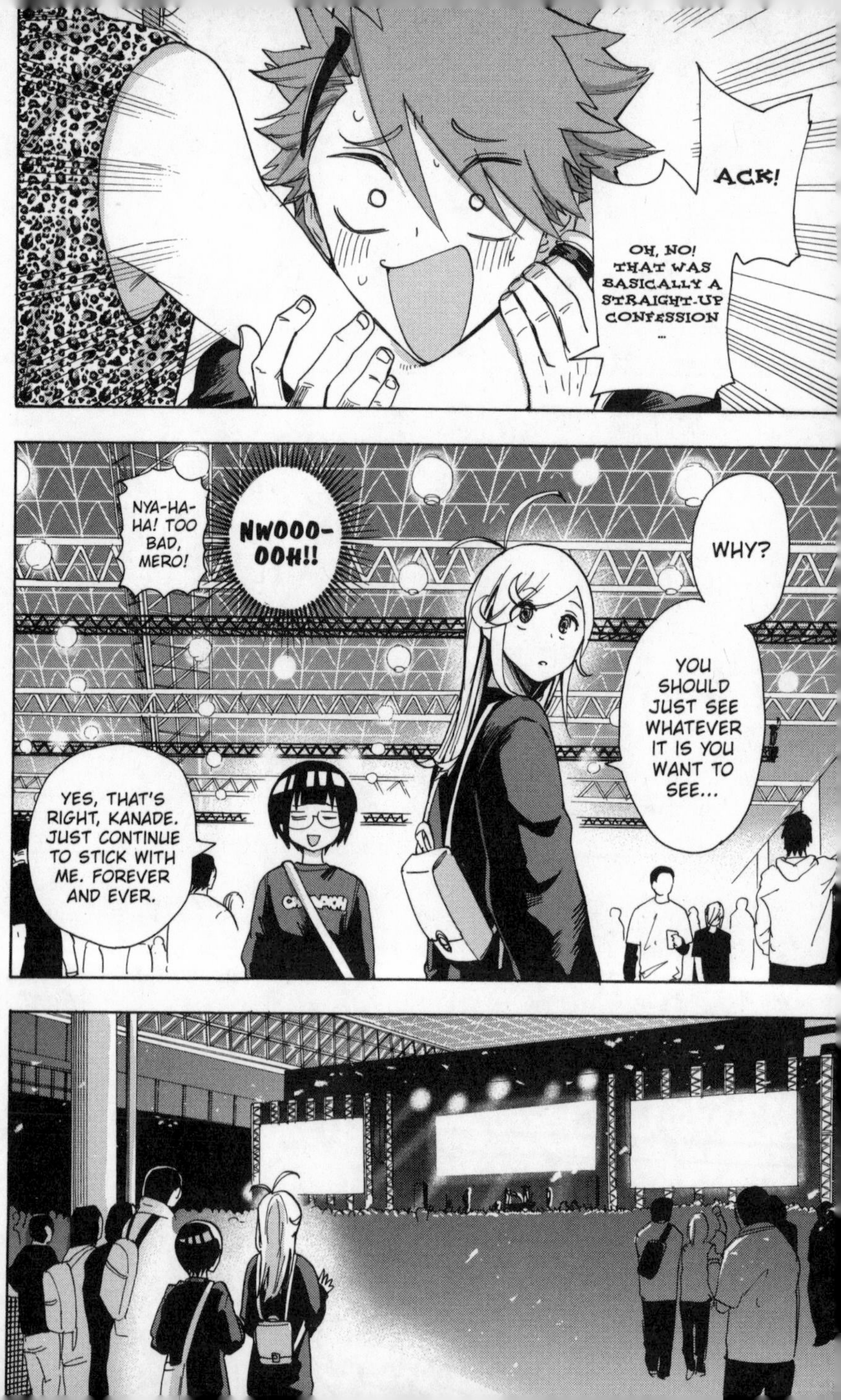
ACK!
OH, NO! THAT WAS BASICALLY A STRAIGHT-UP CONFESSION...
WHY?
YOU SHOULD JUST SEE WHATEVER IT IS YOU WANT TO SEE...
NWOOO-OOH!!
NYA-HA-HA! TOO BAD, MERO!
YES, THAT'S RIGHT, KANADE. JUST CONTINUE TO STICK WITH ME. FOREVER AND EVER.

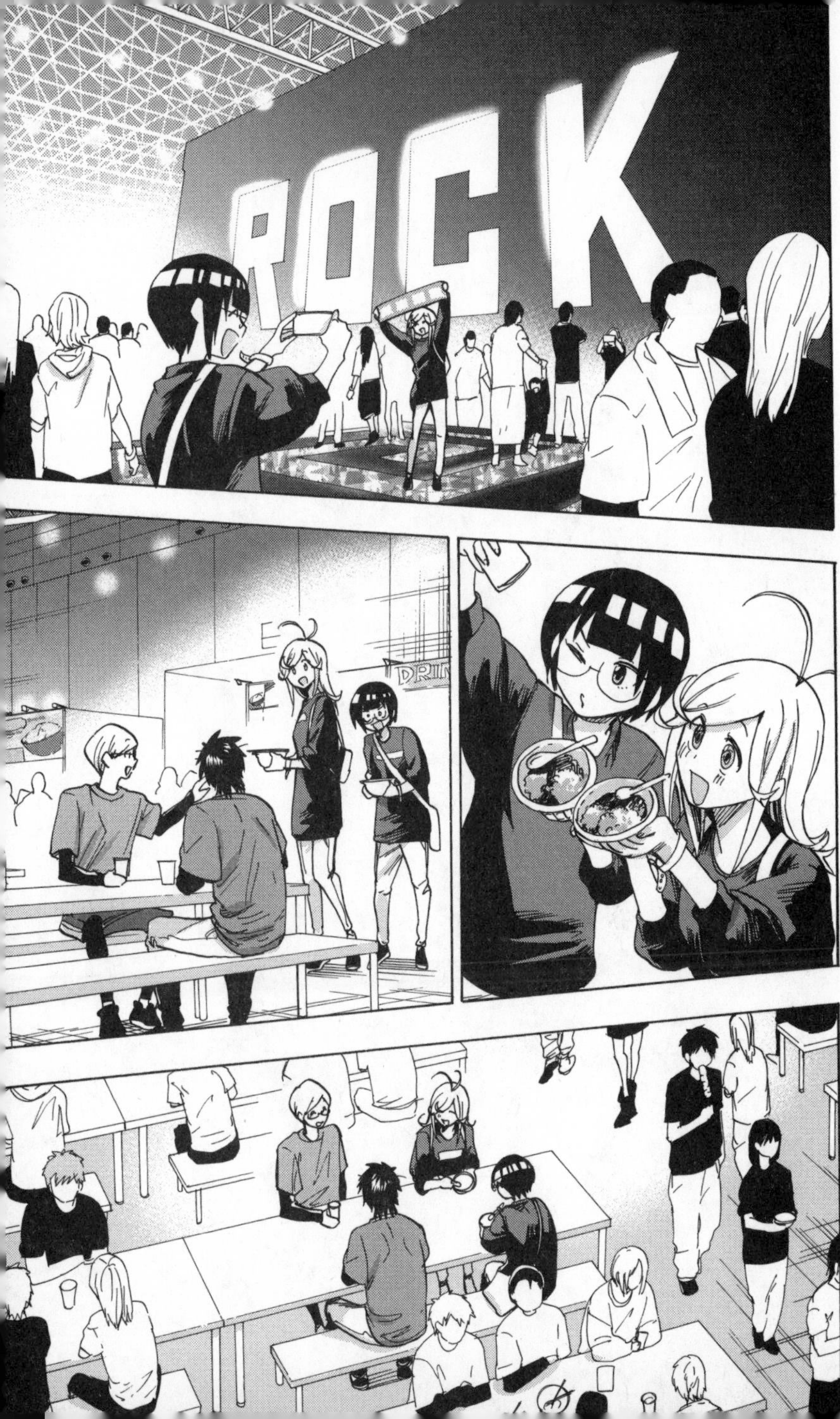
ROCK

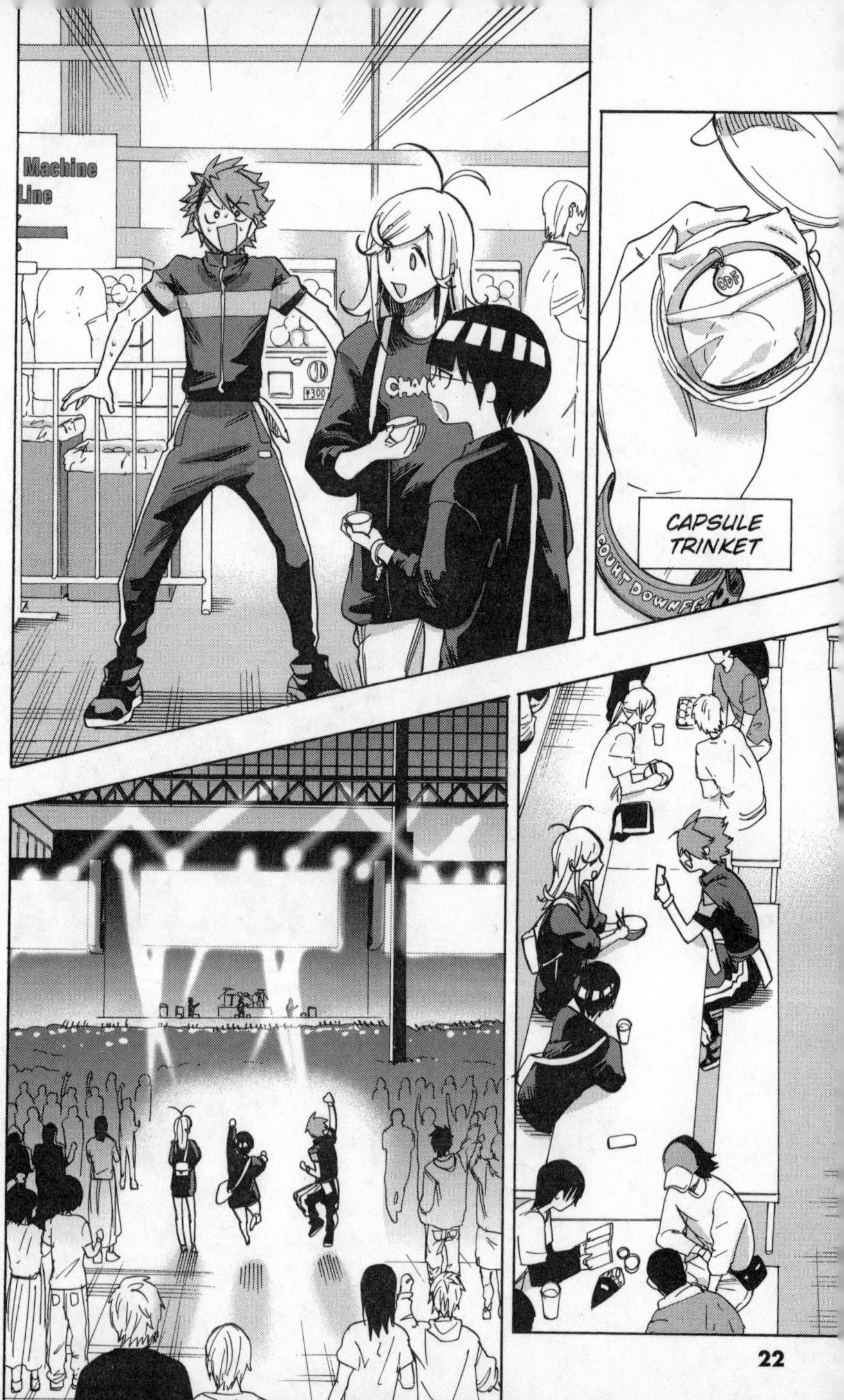
CAPSULE TRINKET
COUNTDOWNFES
CDF
Machine Line
¥300

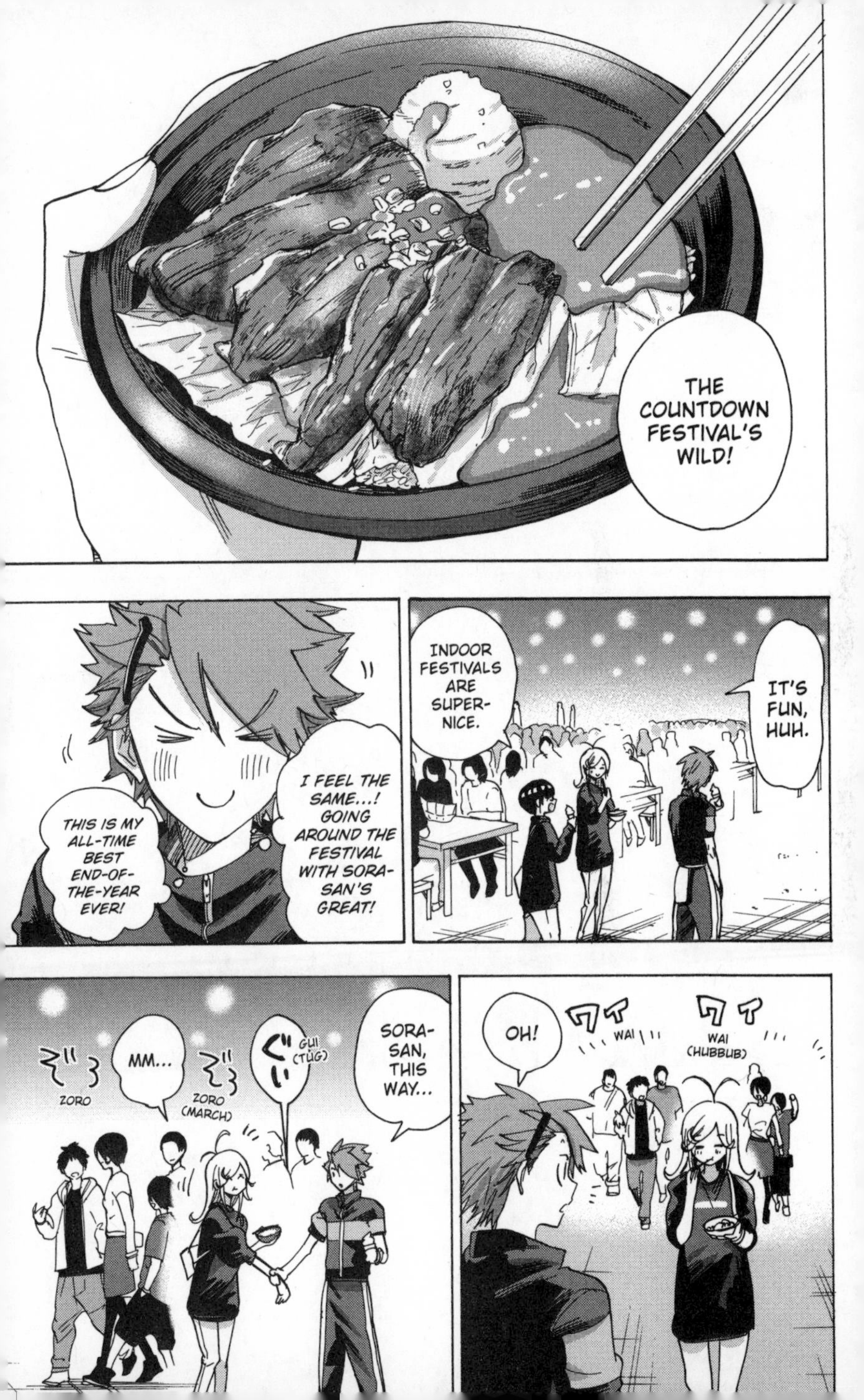
THE COUNTDOWN FESTIVAL'S WILD!
IT'S FUN, HUH.
INDOOR FESTIVALS ARE SUPER-NICE.
I FEEL THE SAME...! GOING AROUND THE FESTIVAL WITH SORA-SAN'S GREAT!
THIS IS MY ALL-TIME BEST END-OF-THE-YEAR EVER!
WAI (HUBBUB)
WAI
OH!
SORA-SAN, THIS WAY...
GUI (TUG)
ZORO (MARCH)
MM...
ZORO

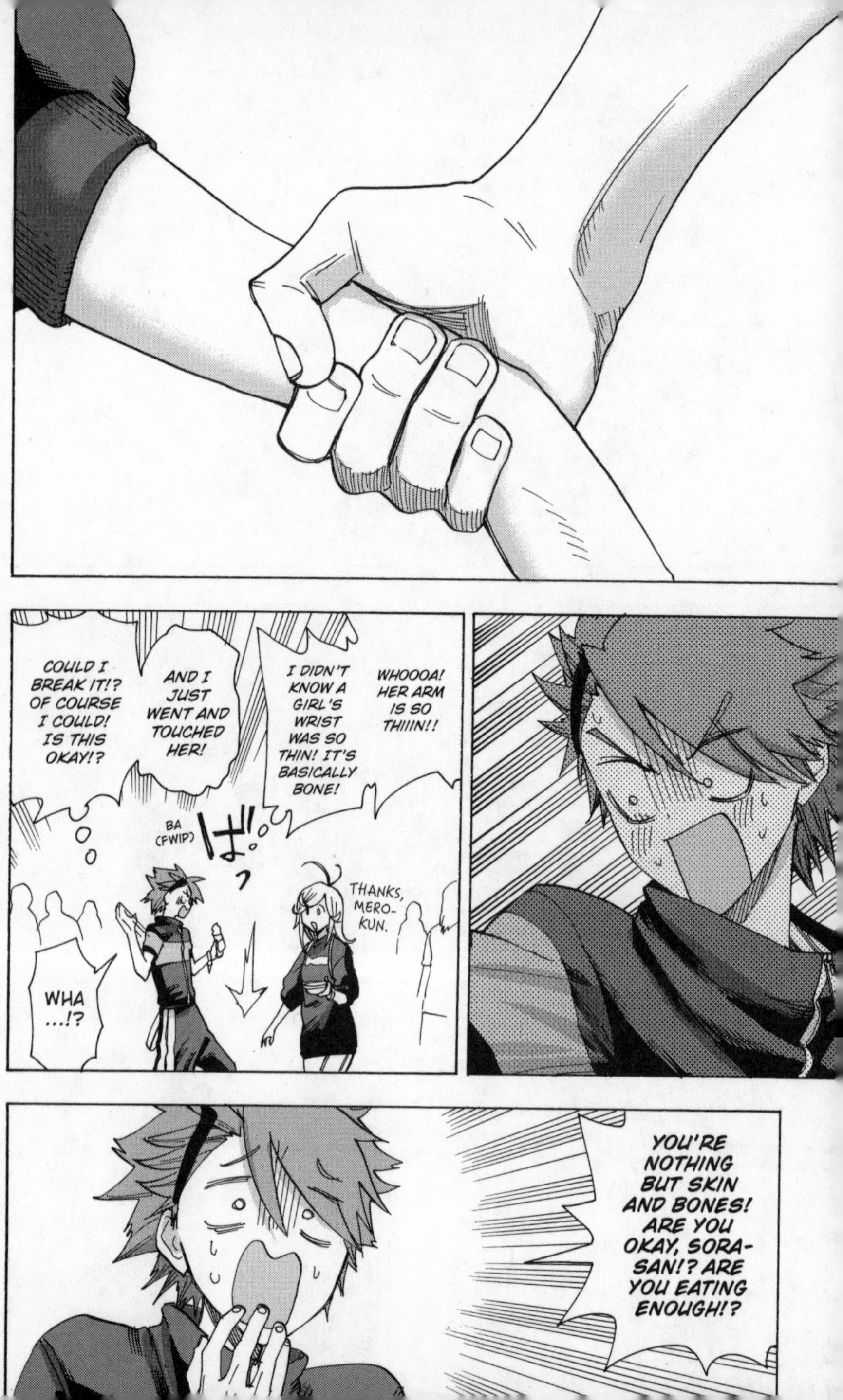
WHOOOA! HER ARM IS SO THIIIN!!
I DIDN'T KNOW A GIRL'S WRIST WAS SO THIN! IT'S BASICALLY BONE!
AND I JUST WENT AND TOUCHED HER!
COULD I BREAK IT!? OF COURSE I COULD! IS THIS OKAY!?
ぱっ
BA (FWIP)
THANKS, MERO-KUN.
WHA ...!?
YOU'RE NOTHING BUT SKIN AND BONES! ARE YOU OKAY, SORA-SAN!? ARE YOU EATING ENOUGH!?

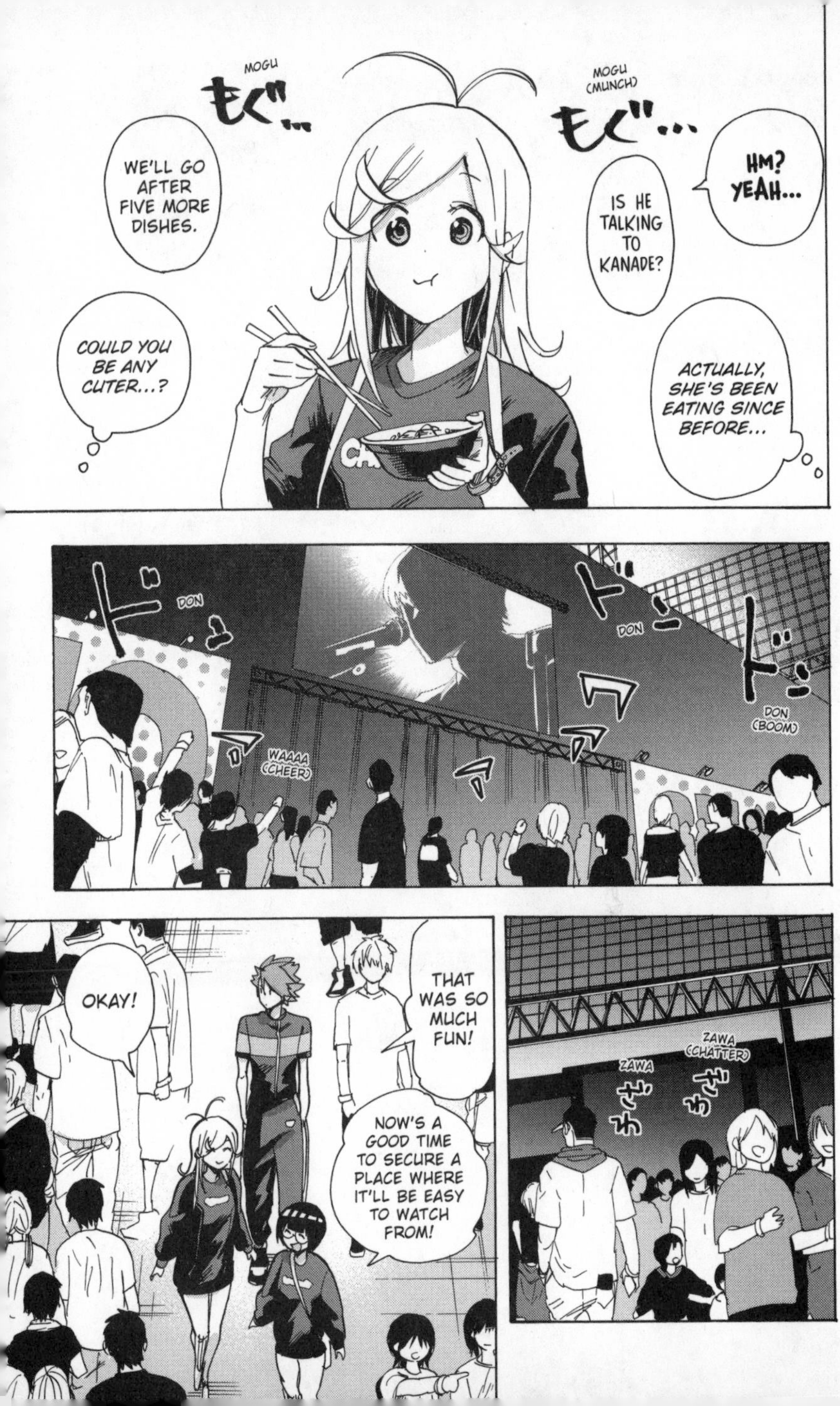
MOGU (MUNCH)
もぐ…
HM? YEAH...
IS HE TALKING TO KANADE?
MOGU
もぐ…
WE'LL GO AFTER FIVE MORE DISHES.
ACTUALLY, SHE'S BEEN EATING SINCE BEFORE...
COULD YOU BE ANY CUTER...?
DON (BOOM)
ドン
DON
ドン
WAAAA (CHEER)
ワァァァ
DON
ドン
ZAWA (CHATTER)
ざわ
ZAWA
ざわ
THAT WAS SO MUCH FUN!
OKAY!
NOW'S A GOOD TIME TO SECURE A PLACE WHERE IT'LL BE EASY TO WATCH FROM!

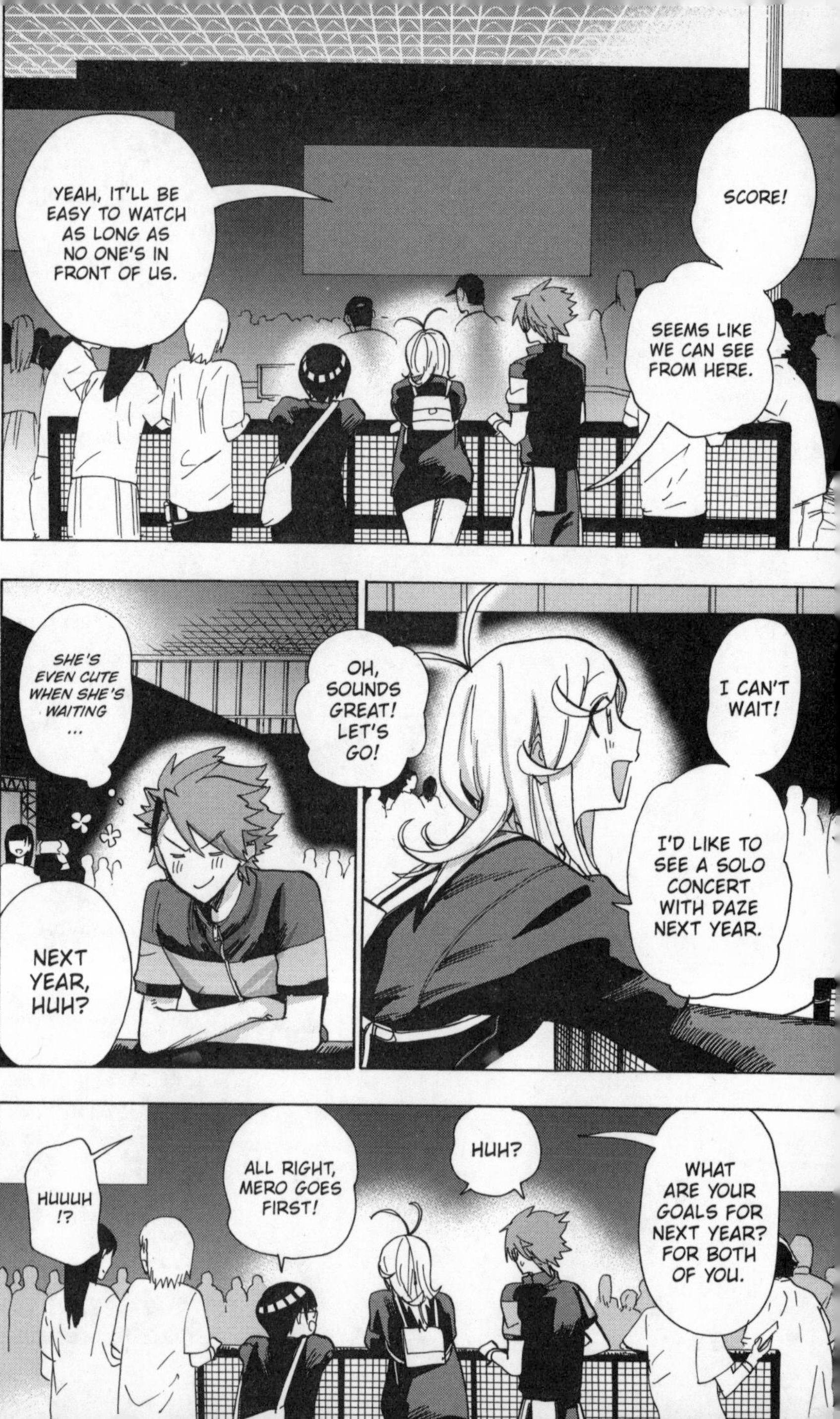
SCORE!
SEEMS LIKE WE CAN SEE FROM HERE.
YEAH, IT'LL BE EASY TO WATCH AS LONG AS NO ONE'S IN FRONT OF US.
I CAN'T WAIT!
I'D LIKE TO SEE A SOLO CONCERT WITH DAZE NEXT YEAR.
OH, SOUNDS GREAT! LET'S GO!
SHE'S EVEN CUTE WHEN SHE'S WAITING ...
NEXT YEAR, HUH?
WHAT ARE YOUR GOALS FOR NEXT YEAR? FOR BOTH OF YOU.
HUH?
ALL RIGHT, MERO GOES FIRST!
HUUUH !?

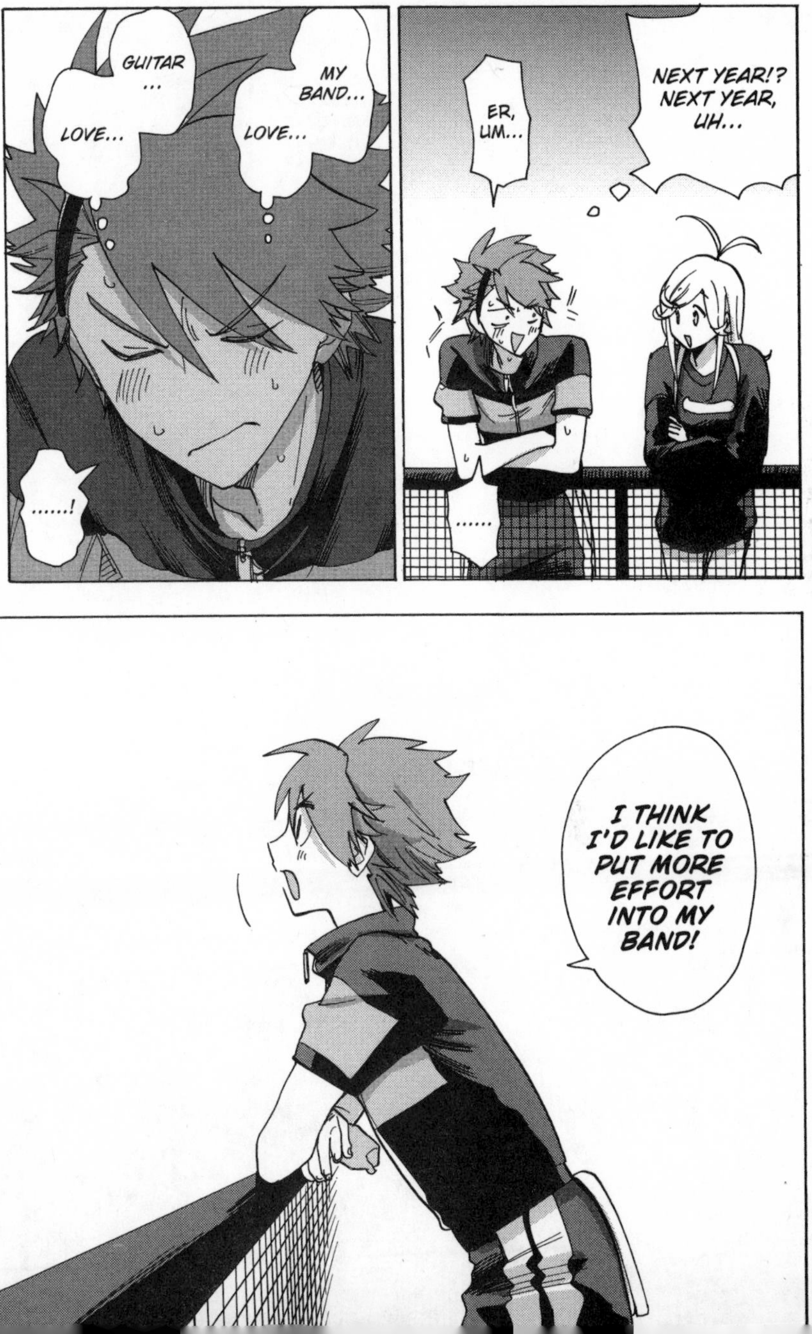
NEXT YEAR!? NEXT YEAR, UH...
ER, UM...
......
MY BAND... LOVE...
GUITAR ... LOVE...
......!
I THINK I'D LIKE TO PUT MORE EFFORT INTO MY BAND!

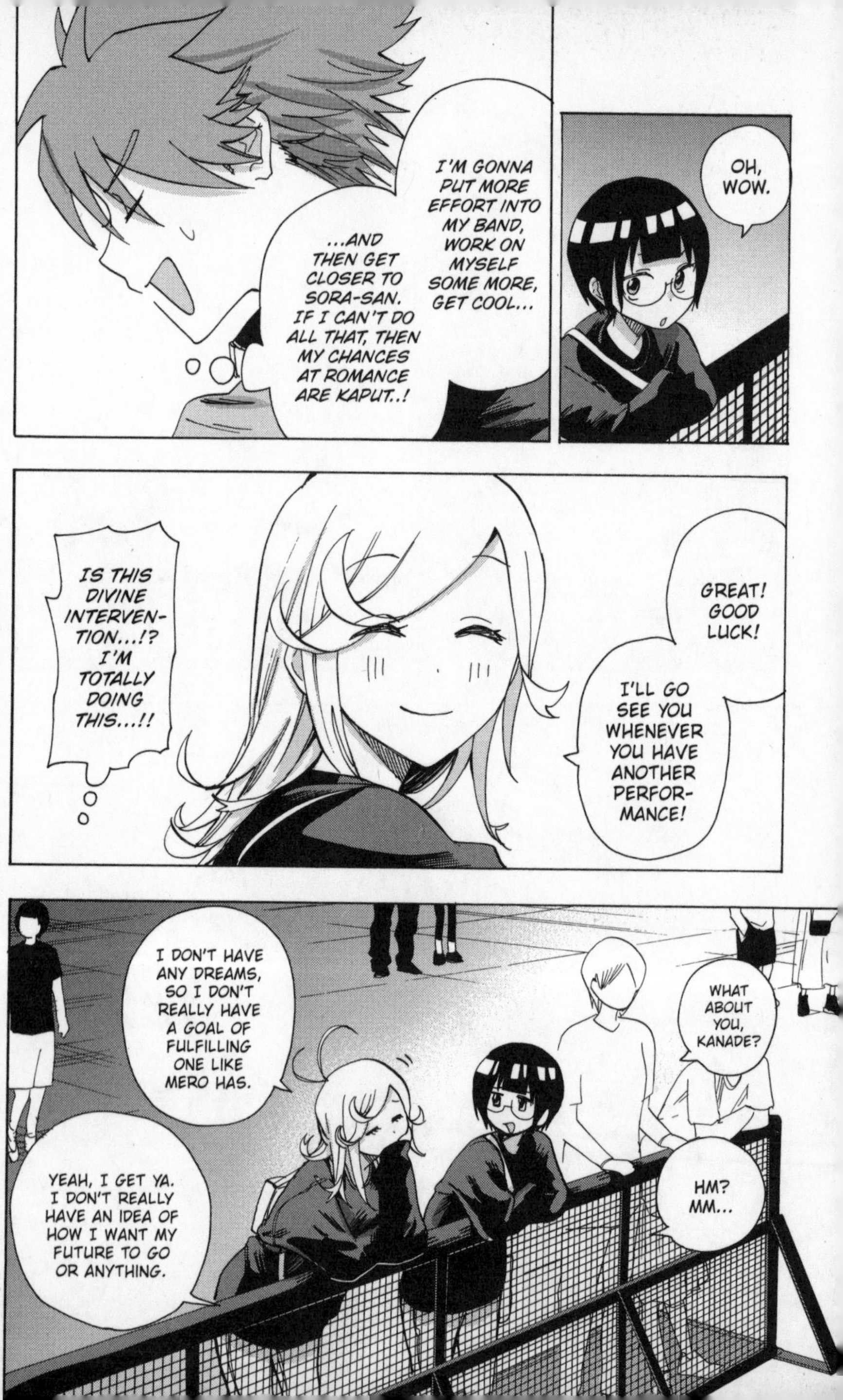
OH, WOW.
I'M GONNA PUT MORE EFFORT INTO MY BAND, WORK ON MYSELF SOME MORE, GET COOL...
...AND THEN GET CLOSER TO SORA-SAN. IF I CAN'T DO ALL THAT, THEN MY CHANCES AT ROMANCE ARE KAPUT..!
GREAT! GOOD LUCK!
I'LL GO SEE YOU WHENEVER YOU HAVE ANOTHER PERFORMANCE!
IS THIS DIVINE INTERVENTION...!? I'M TOTALLY DOING THIS...!!
WHAT ABOUT YOU, KANADE?
HM? MM...
I DON'T HAVE ANY DREAMS, SO I DON'T REALLY HAVE A GOAL OF FULFILLING ONE LIKE MERO HAS.
YEAH, I GET YA. I DON'T REALLY HAVE AN IDEA OF HOW I WANT MY FUTURE TO GO OR ANYTHING.

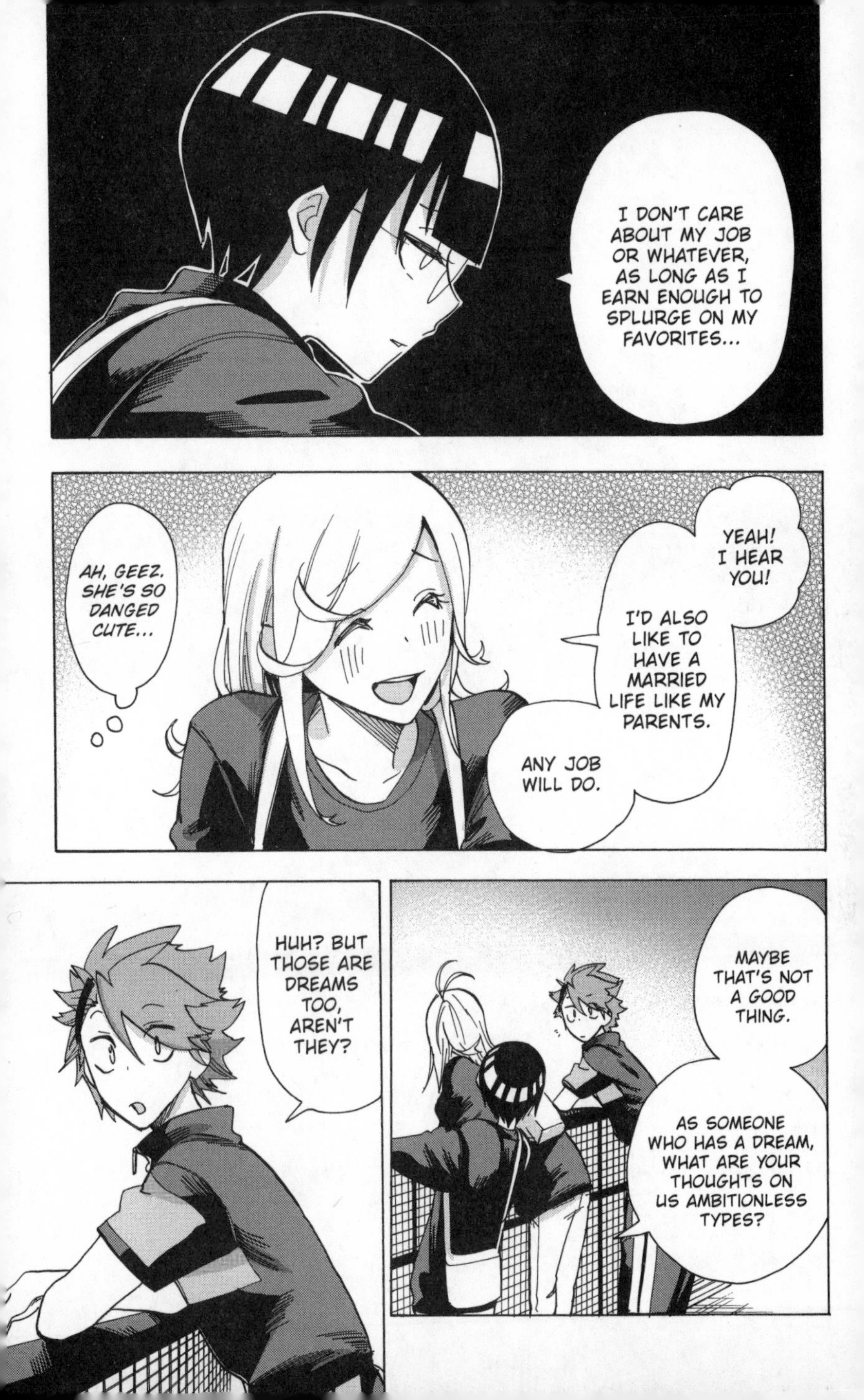
I DON'T CARE ABOUT MY JOB OR WHATEVER, AS LONG AS I EARN ENOUGH TO SPLURGE ON MY FAVORITES...
YEAH! I HEAR YOU!
I'D ALSO LIKE TO HAVE A MARRIED LIFE LIKE MY PARENTS.
ANY JOB WILL DO.
AH, GEEZ. SHE'S SO DANGED CUTE...
MAYBE THAT'S NOT A GOOD THING.
AS SOMEONE WHO HAS A DREAM, WHAT ARE YOUR THOUGHTS ON US AMBITIONLESS TYPES?
HUH? BUT THOSE ARE DREAMS TOO, AREN'T THEY?

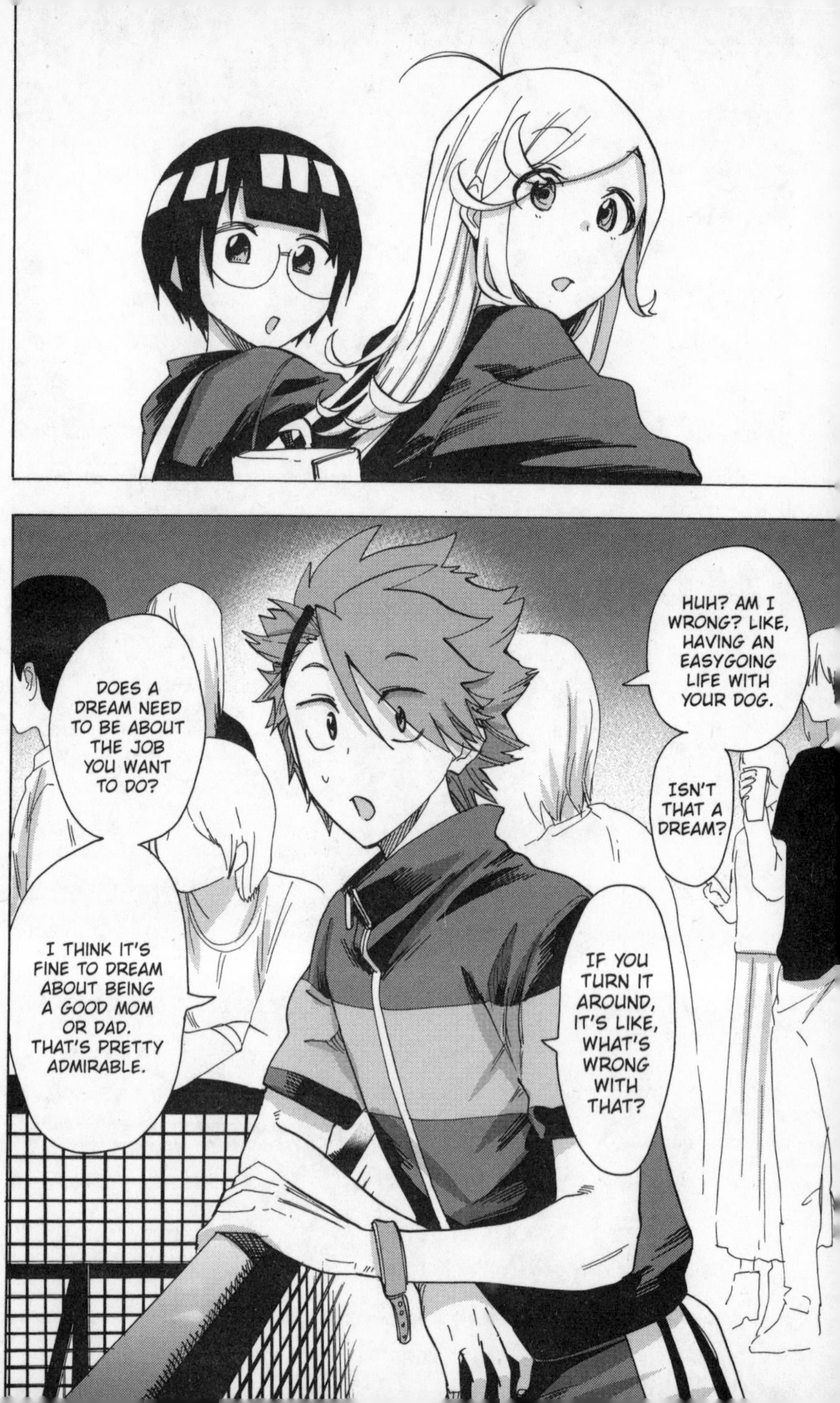
HUH? AM I WRONG? LIKE, HAVING AN EASYGOING LIFE WITH YOUR DOG.
ISN'T THAT A DREAM?
DOES A DREAM NEED TO BE ABOUT THE JOB YOU WANT TO DO?
IF YOU TURN IT AROUND, IT'S LIKE, WHAT'S WRONG WITH THAT?
I THINK IT'S FINE TO DREAM ABOUT BEING A GOOD MOM OR DAD. THAT'S PRETTY ADMIRABLE.

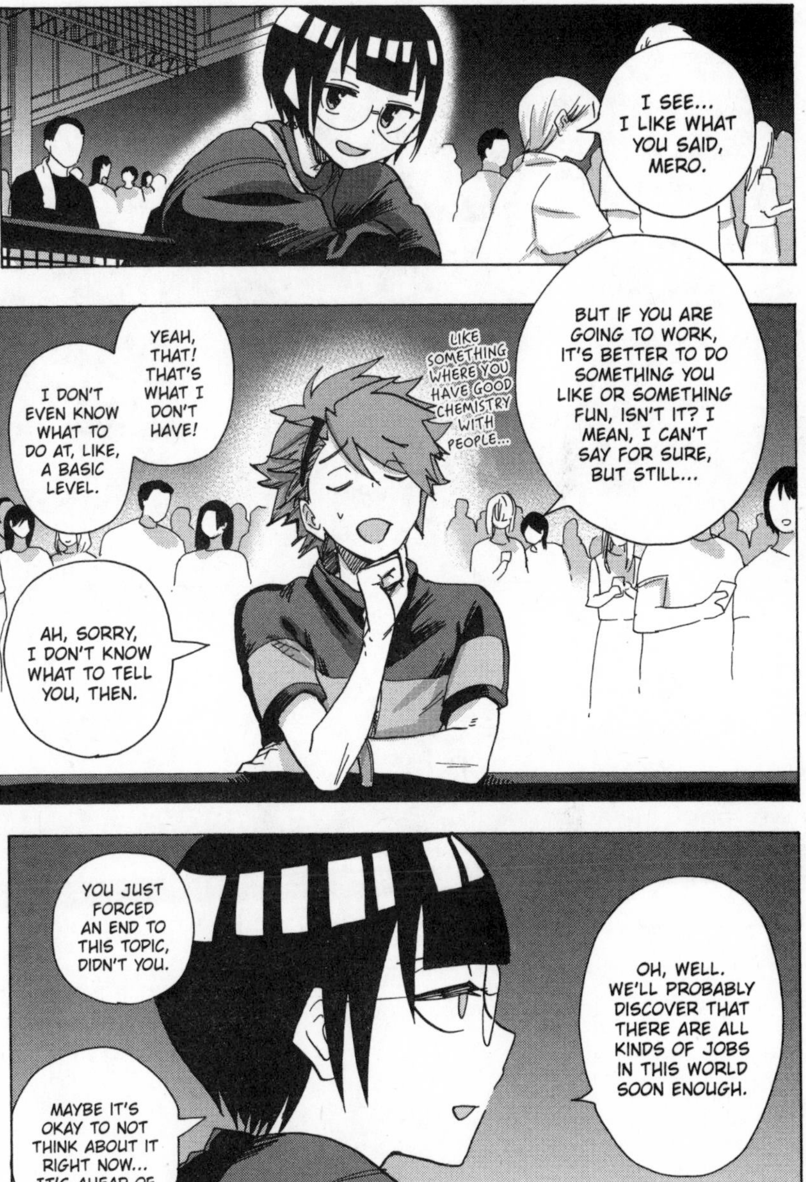
I SEE... I LIKE WHAT YOU SAID, MERO.
BUT IF YOU ARE GOING TO WORK, IT'S BETTER TO DO SOMETHING YOU LIKE OR SOMETHING FUN, ISN'T IT? I MEAN, I CAN'T SAY FOR SURE, BUT STILL...
LIKE SOMETHING WHERE YOU HAVE GOOD CHEMISTRY WITH PEOPLE...
YEAH, THAT! THAT'S WHAT I DON'T HAVE!
I DON'T EVEN KNOW WHAT TO DO AT, LIKE, A BASIC LEVEL.
AH, SORRY, I DON'T KNOW WHAT TO TELL YOU, THEN.
YOU JUST FORCED AN END TO THIS TOPIC, DIDN'T YOU.
OH, WELL. WE'LL PROBABLY DISCOVER THAT THERE ARE ALL KINDS OF JOBS IN THIS WORLD SOON ENOUGH.
MAYBE IT'S OKAY TO NOT THINK ABOUT IT RIGHT NOW... IT'S AHEAD OF US ANYWAY.

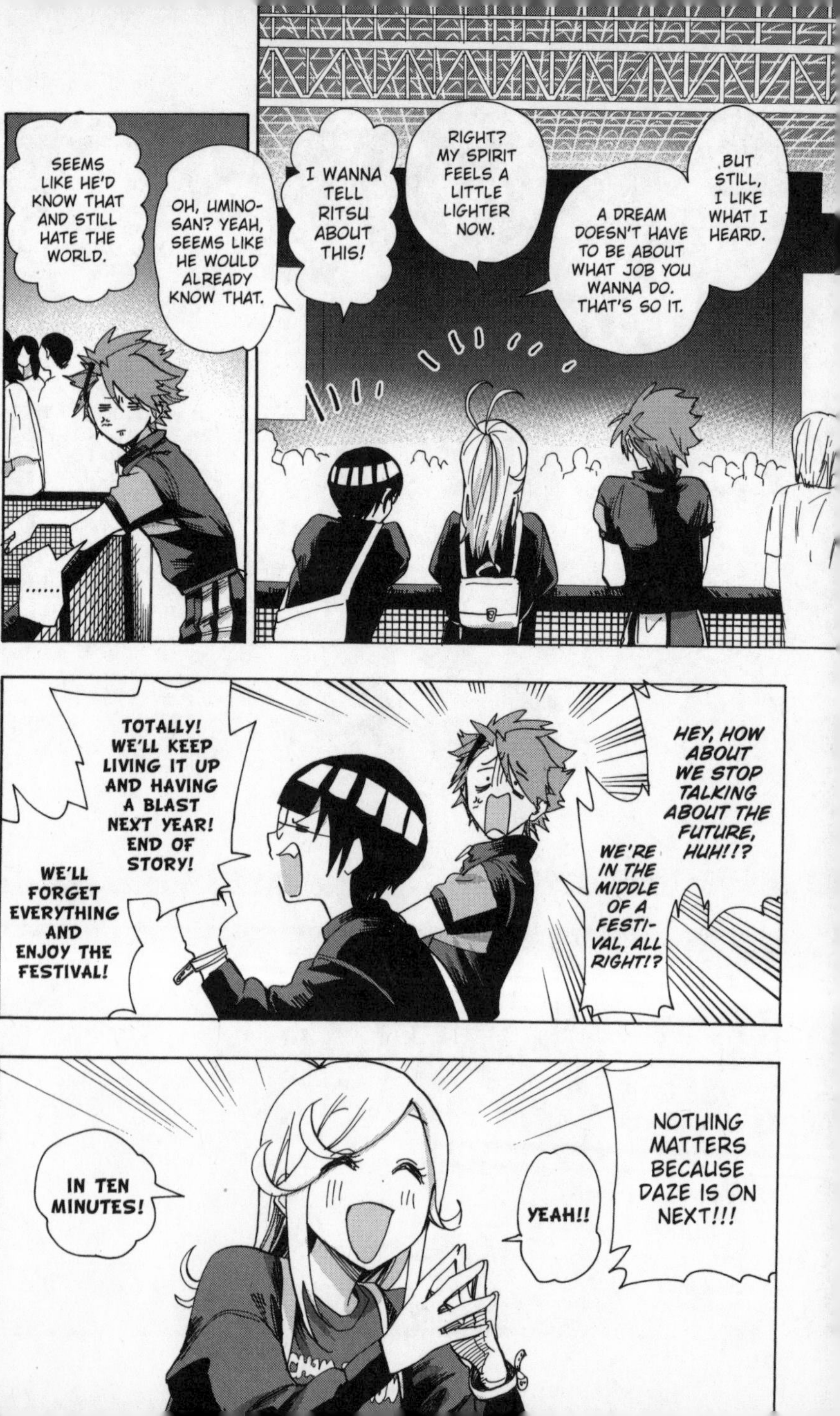
BUT STILL, I LIKE WHAT I HEARD.
A DREAM DOESN'T HAVE TO BE ABOUT WHAT JOB YOU WANNA DO. THAT'S SO IT.
RIGHT? MY SPIRIT FEELS A LITTLE LIGHTER NOW.
I WANNA TELL RITSU ABOUT THIS!
OH, UMINO-SAN? YEAH, SEEMS LIKE HE WOULD ALREADY KNOW THAT.
SEEMS LIKE HE'D KNOW THAT AND STILL HATE THE WORLD.
......
HEY, HOW ABOUT WE STOP TALKING ABOUT THE FUTURE, HUH!!?
WE'RE IN THE MIDDLE OF A FESTIVAL, ALL RIGHT!?
TOTALLY! WE'LL KEEP LIVING IT UP AND HAVING A BLAST NEXT YEAR! END OF STORY!
WE'LL FORGET EVERYTHING AND ENJOY THE FESTIVAL!
NOTHING MATTERS BECAUSE DAZE IS ON NEXT!!!
YEAH!!
IN TEN MINUTES!

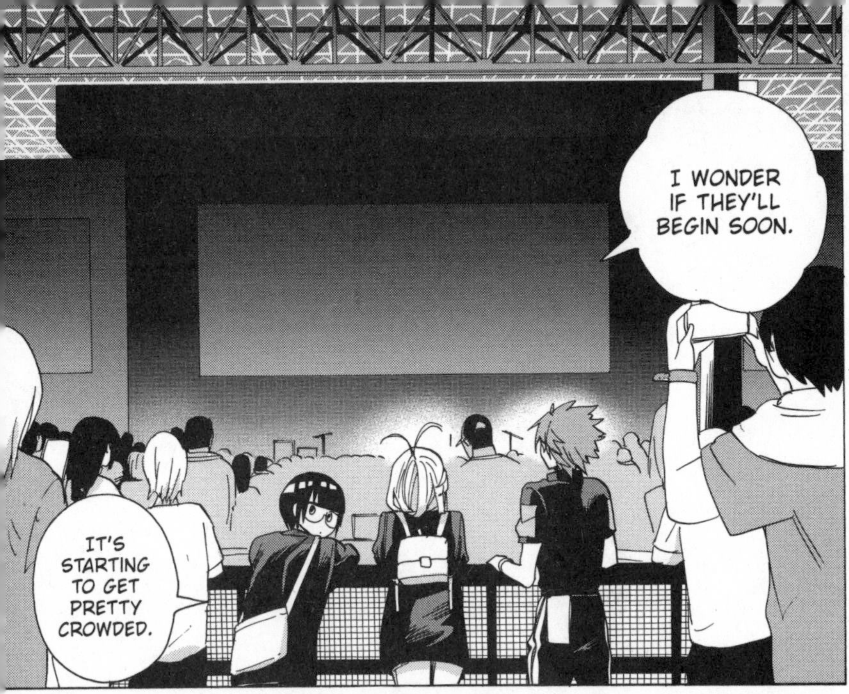
I WONDER IF THEY'LL BEGIN SOON.
IT'S STARTING TO GET PRETTY CROWDED.

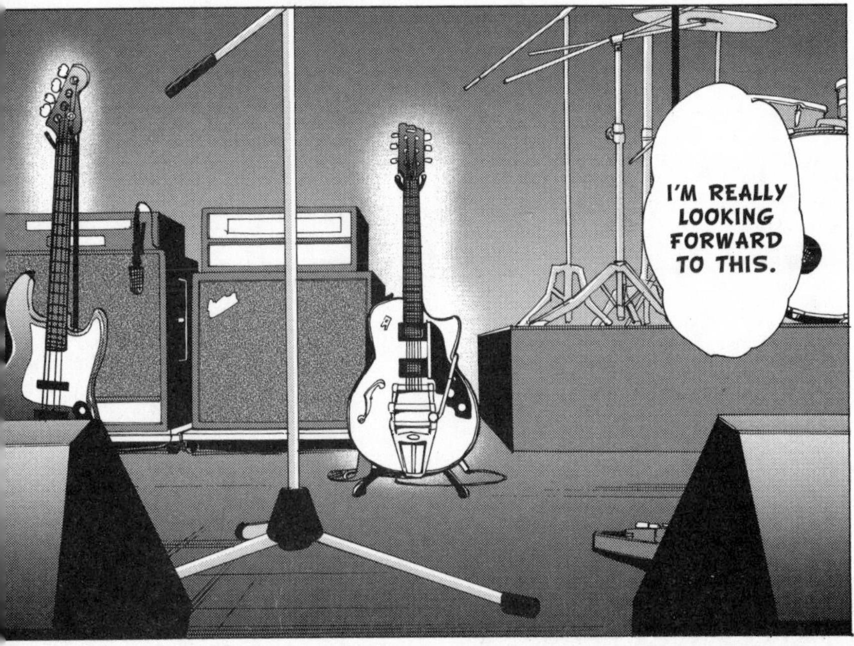
I'M REALLY LOOKING FORWARD TO THIS.

Days on Fes

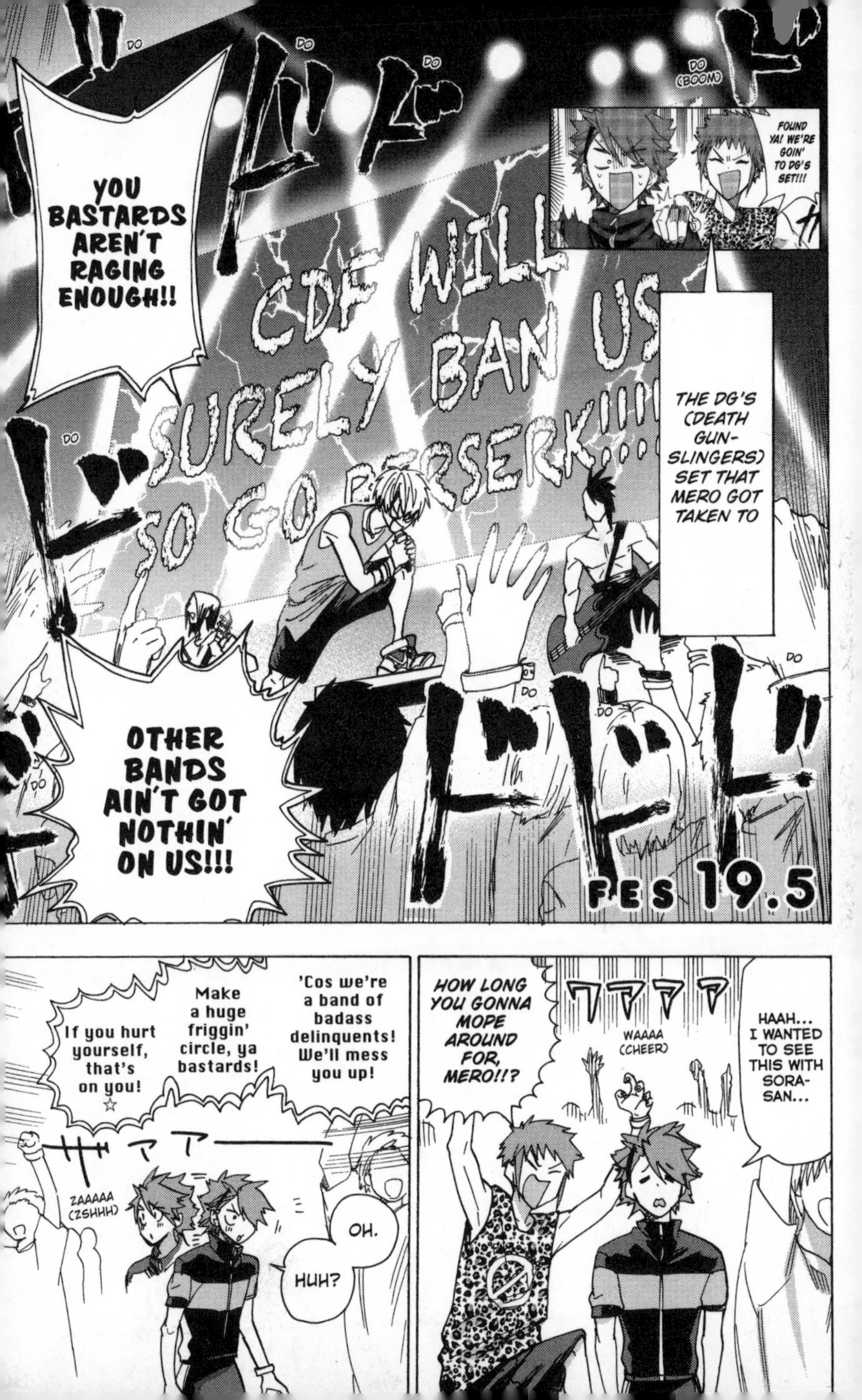
DO (BOOM)
FOUND YA! WE'RE GOIN' TO DG'S SET!!!
THE DG'S (DEATH GUN-SLINGERS) SET THAT MERO GOT TAKEN TO
DO
DO
DO
YOU BASTARDS AREN'T RAGING ENOUGH!!
CDF WILL SURELY BAN US SO GO BERSERK!!!!
DO
DO
DO
DO
OTHER BANDS AIN'T GOT NOTHIN' ON US!!!
FES 19.5
HAAH... I WANTED TO SEE THIS WITH SORA-SAN...
WAAAA (CHEER)
HOW LONG YOU GONNA MOPE AROUND FOR, MERO!!?
'Cos we're a band of badass delinquents! We'll mess you up!
Make a huge friggin' circle, ya bastards!
If you hurt yourself, that's on you! ☆
ZAAAAA (ZSHHH)
OH.
HUH?

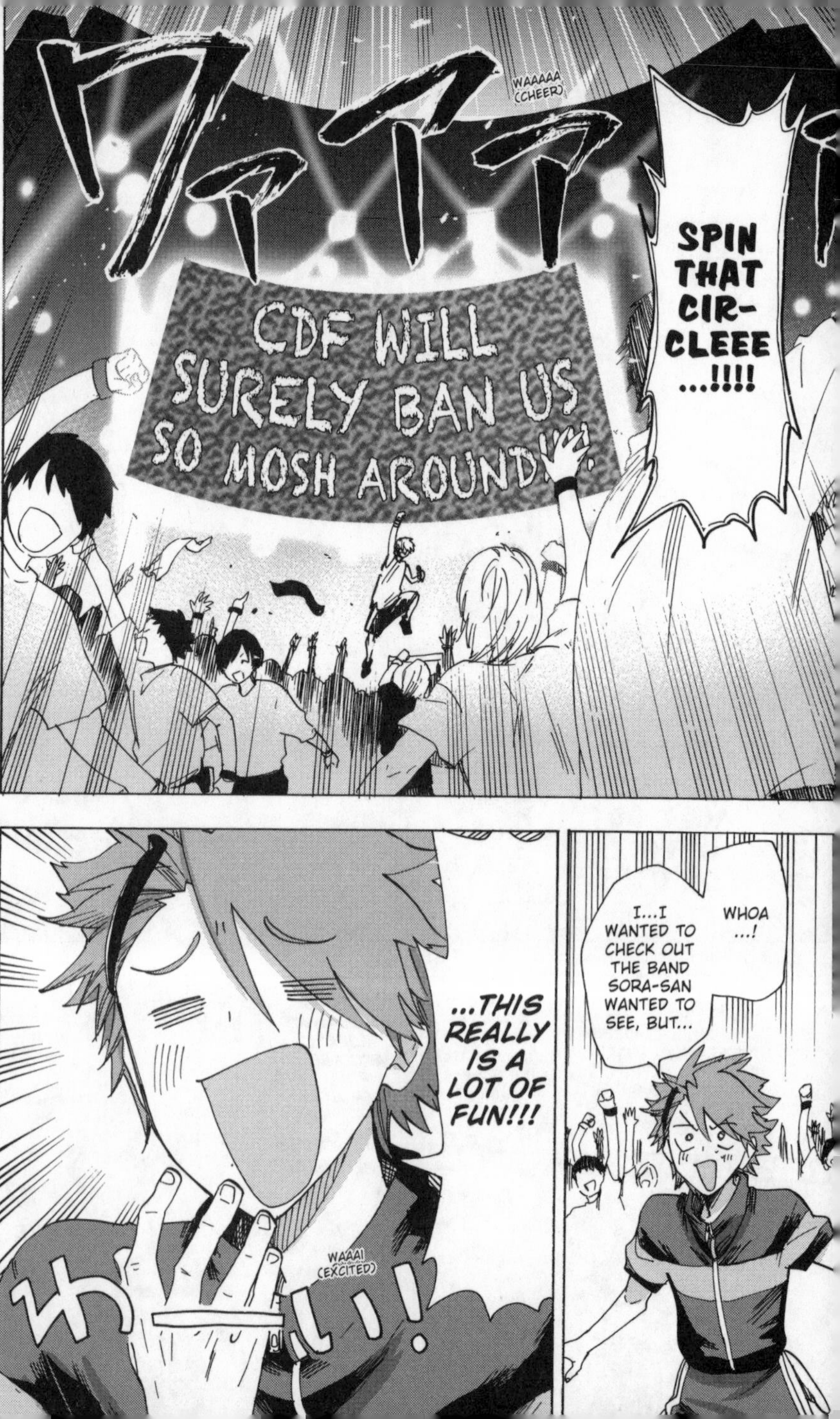
SPIN THAT CIR-CLEEE...!!!!!
WAAAAA (CHEER)
CDF WILL SURELY BAN US SO MOSH AROUND!!
WHOA...!
I...I WANTED TO CHECK OUT THE BAND SORA-SAN WANTED TO SEE, BUT...
...THIS REALLY IS A LOT OF FUN!!!
WAAAI (EXCITED)

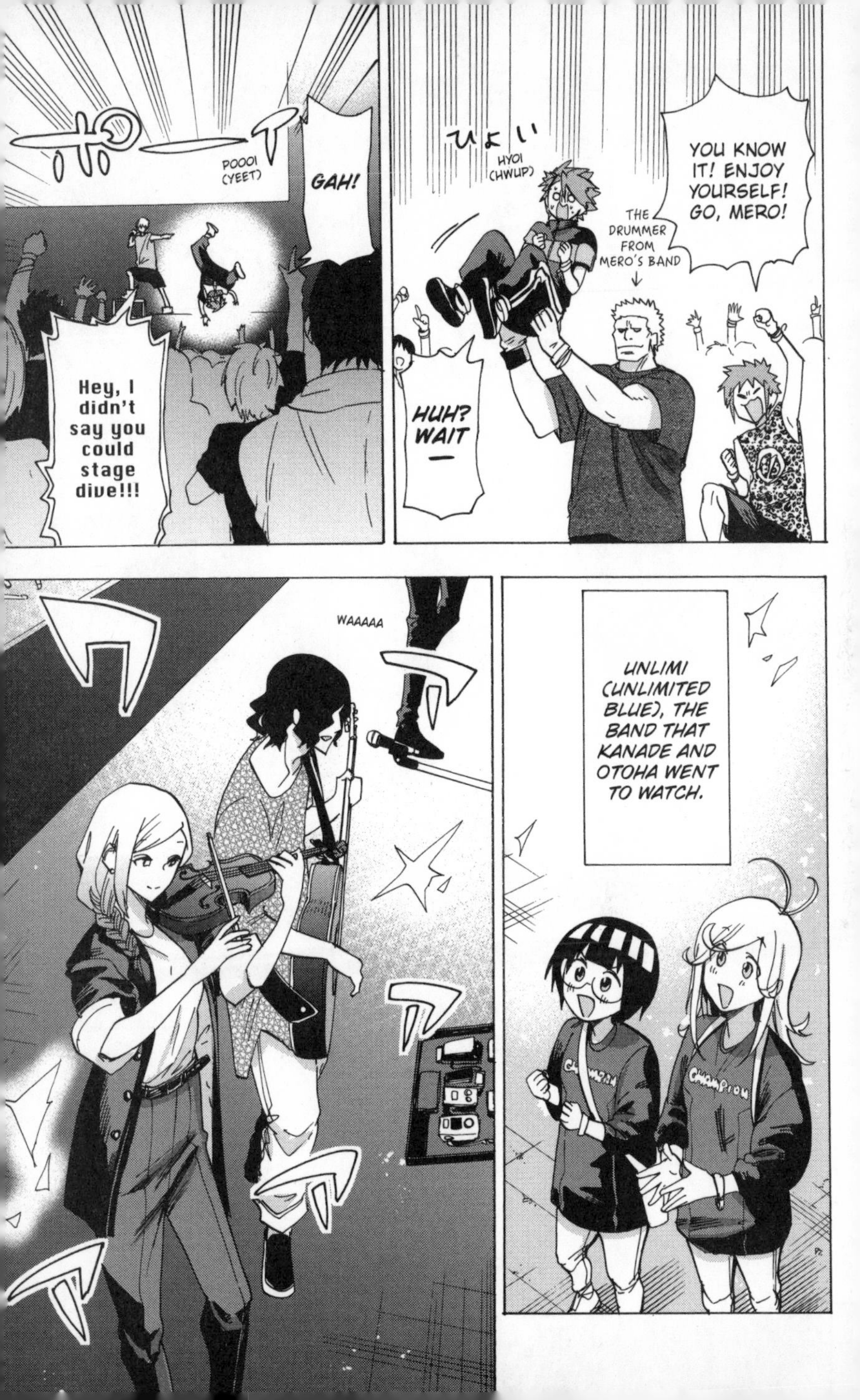
YOU KNOW IT! ENJOY YOURSELF! GO, MERO!
ひょい
HYOI (HWUP)
THE DRUMMER FROM MERO'S BAND
HUH? WAIT—
GAH!
ポーーイ
POOOI (YEET)
Hey, I didn't say you could stage dive!!!
UNLIMI (UNLIMITED BLUE), THE BAND THAT KANADE AND OTOHA WENT TO WATCH.
WAAAAA

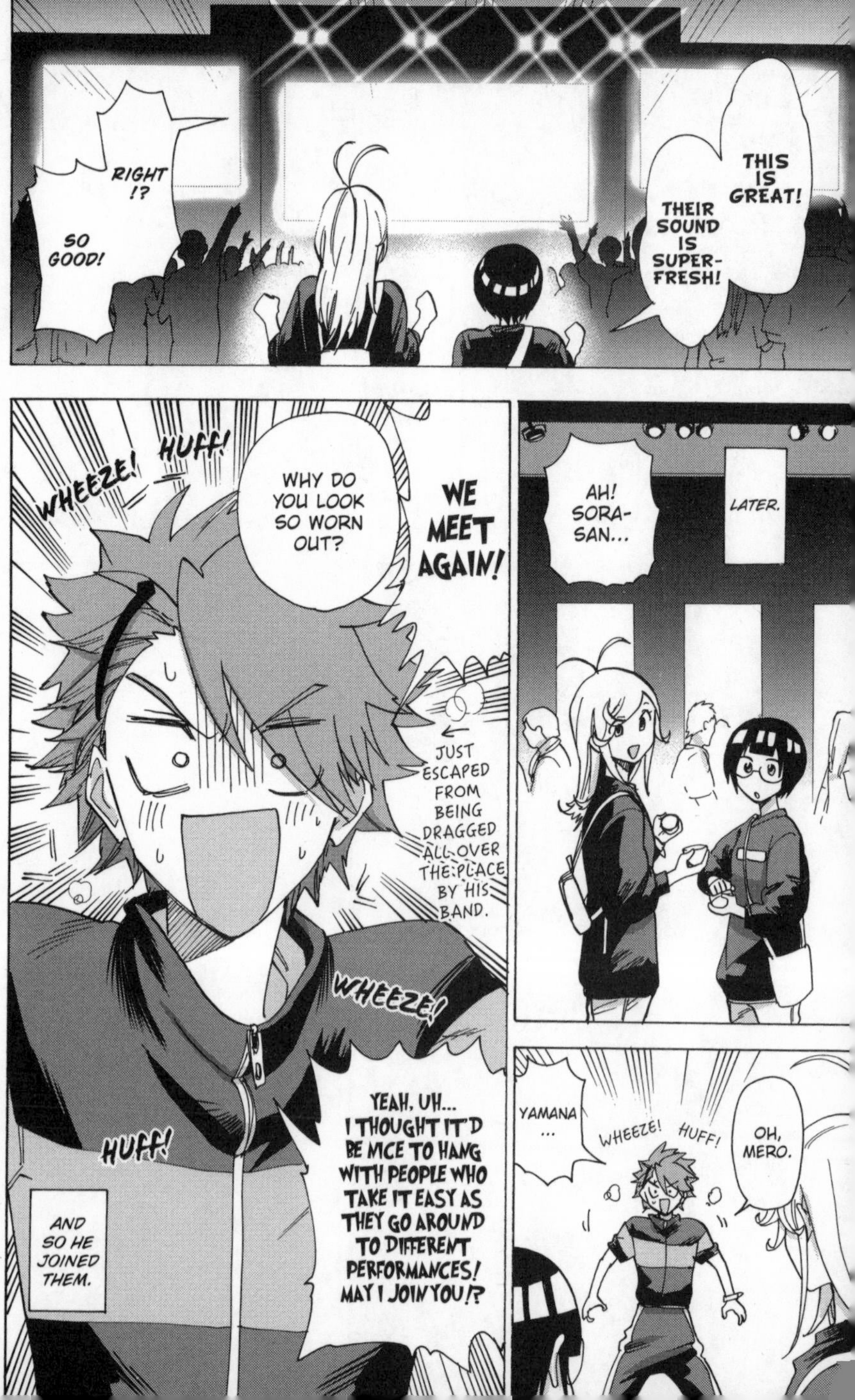

THIS IS GREAT!
THEIR SOUND IS SUPER-FRESH!
RIGHT!?
SO GOOD!
LATER.
AH! SORA-SAN...
OH, MERO.
HUFF!
WHEEZE!
YAMANA ...
WE MEET AGAIN!
WHY DO YOU LOOK SO WORN OUT?
HUFF!
WHEEZE!
JUST ESCAPED FROM BEING DRAGGED ALL OVER THE PLACE BY HIS BAND.
WHEEZE!
YEAH, UH... I THOUGHT IT'D BE NICE TO HANG WITH PEOPLE WHO TAKE IT EASY AS THEY GO AROUND TO DIFFERENT PERFORMANCES! MAY I JOIN YOU!?
HUFF!
AND SO HE JOINED THEM.

Days on Fes

Days on Fes

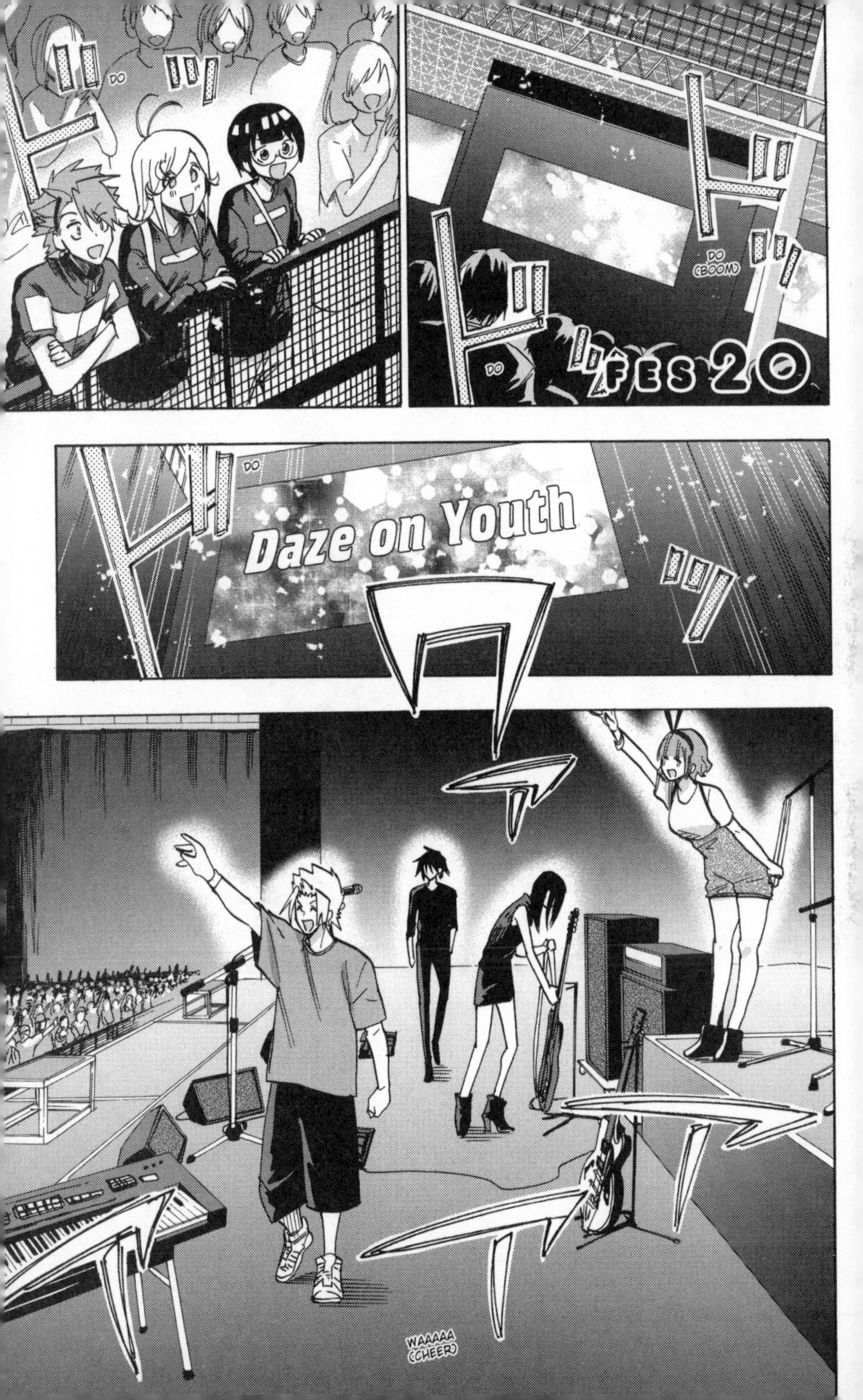
DO
(BOOM)
DO
FES 20
DO
DO
Daze on Youth
WAAAAA
(CHEER)

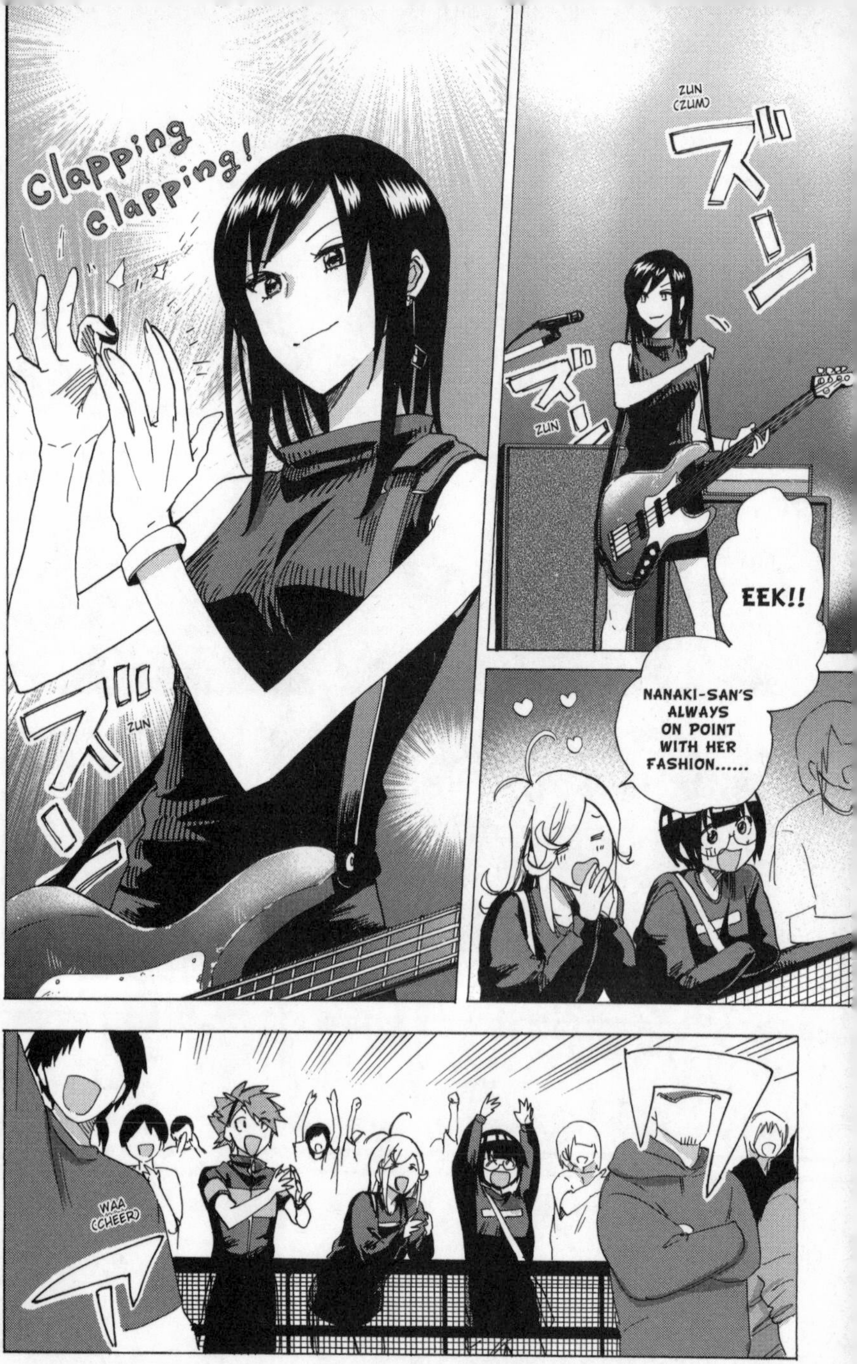
ZUN (ZUM)
ZUN
EEK!!
NANAKI-SAN'S ALWAYS ON POINT WITH HER FASHION......
Clapping clapping!
ZUN
WAA (CHEER)

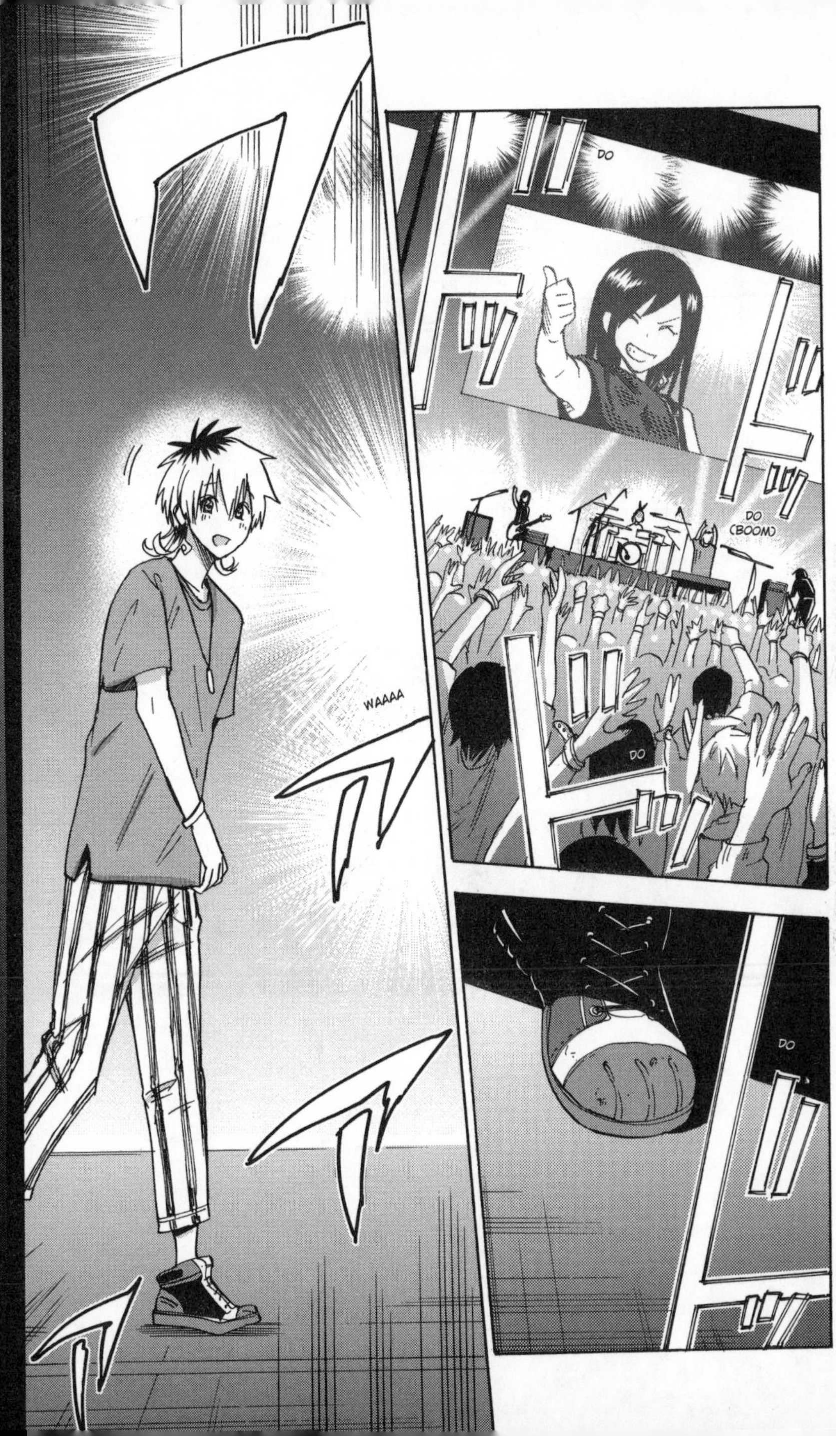
DO
DO
(BOOM)
DO
DO
WAAAA

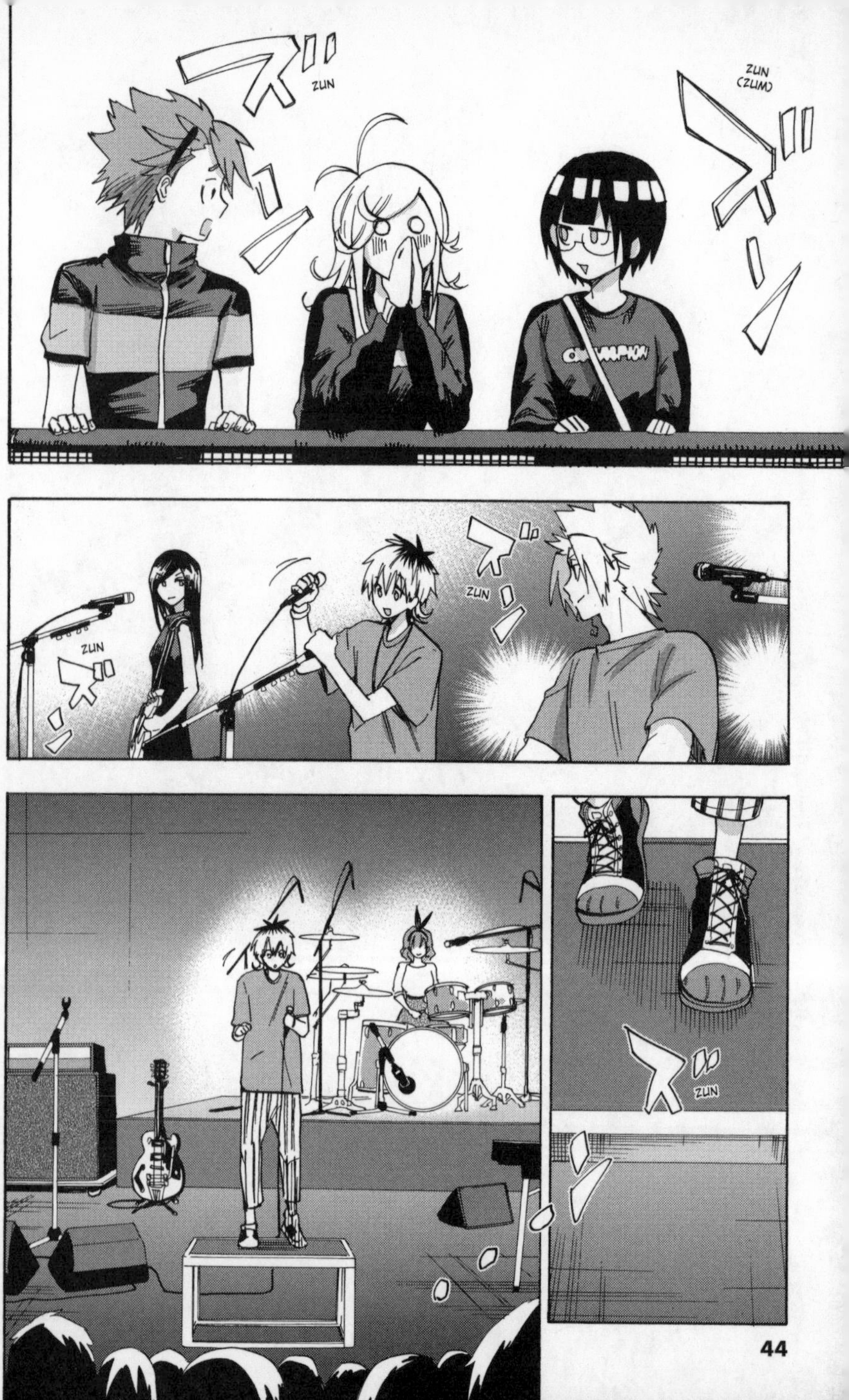
ズン
ZUN (ZUM)
ズン
ZUN
ズン
ZUN
ズン
ZUN
ズン
ZUN

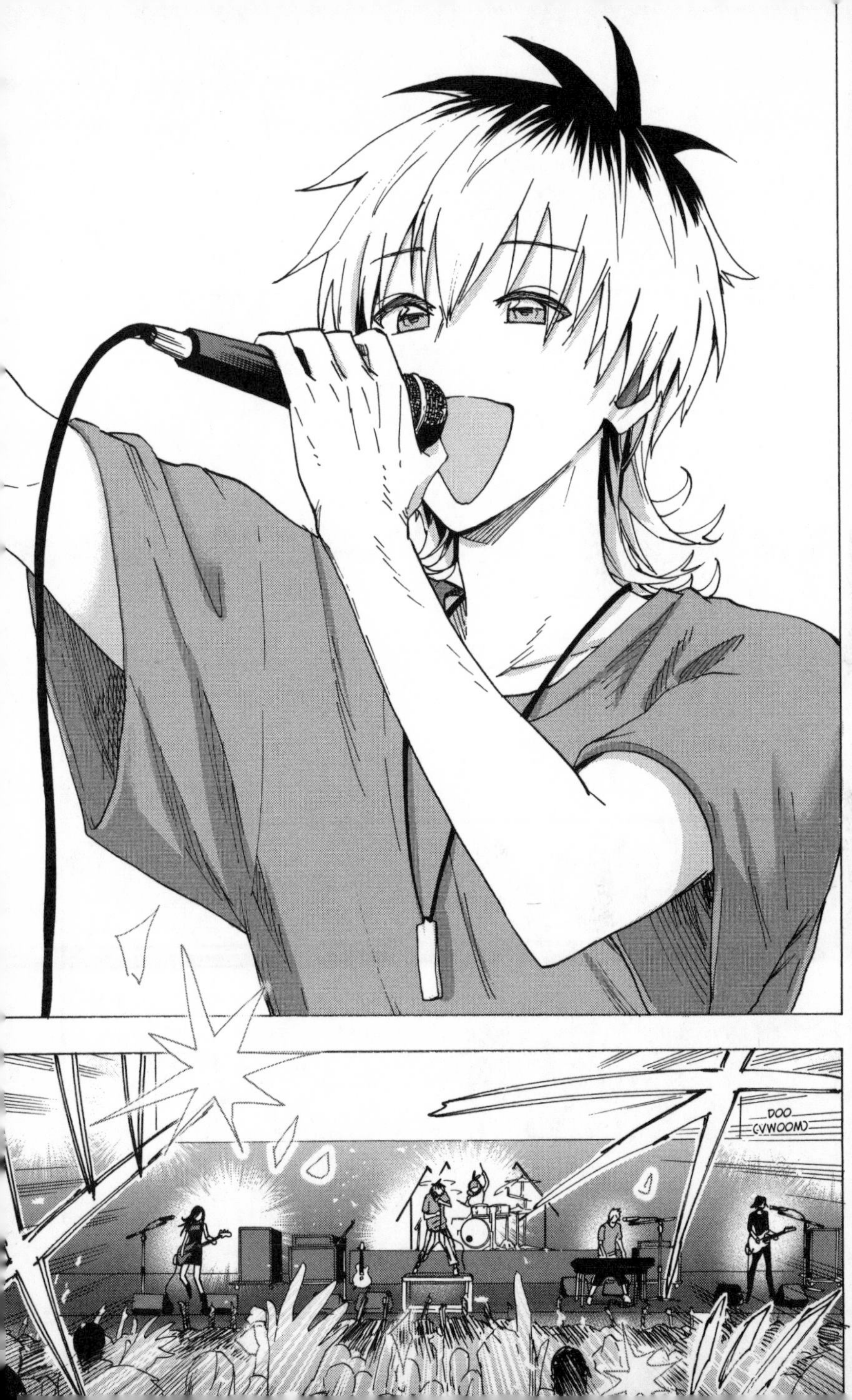
DOO
(VWOOM)

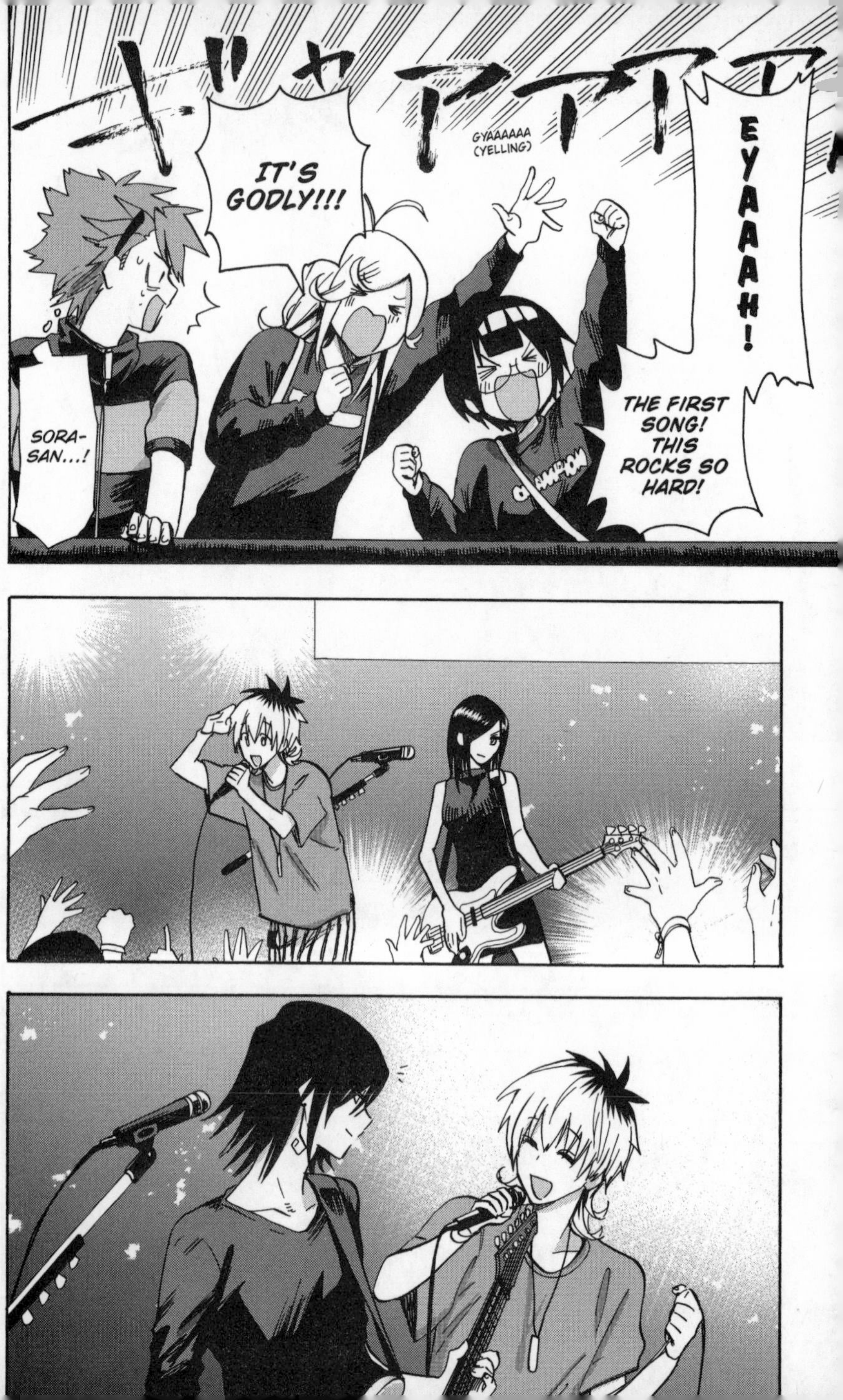
EYAAAAH!
GYAAAAAA (YELLING)
IT'S GODLY!!!
THE FIRST SONG! THIS ROCKS SO HARD!
SORA-SAN...!

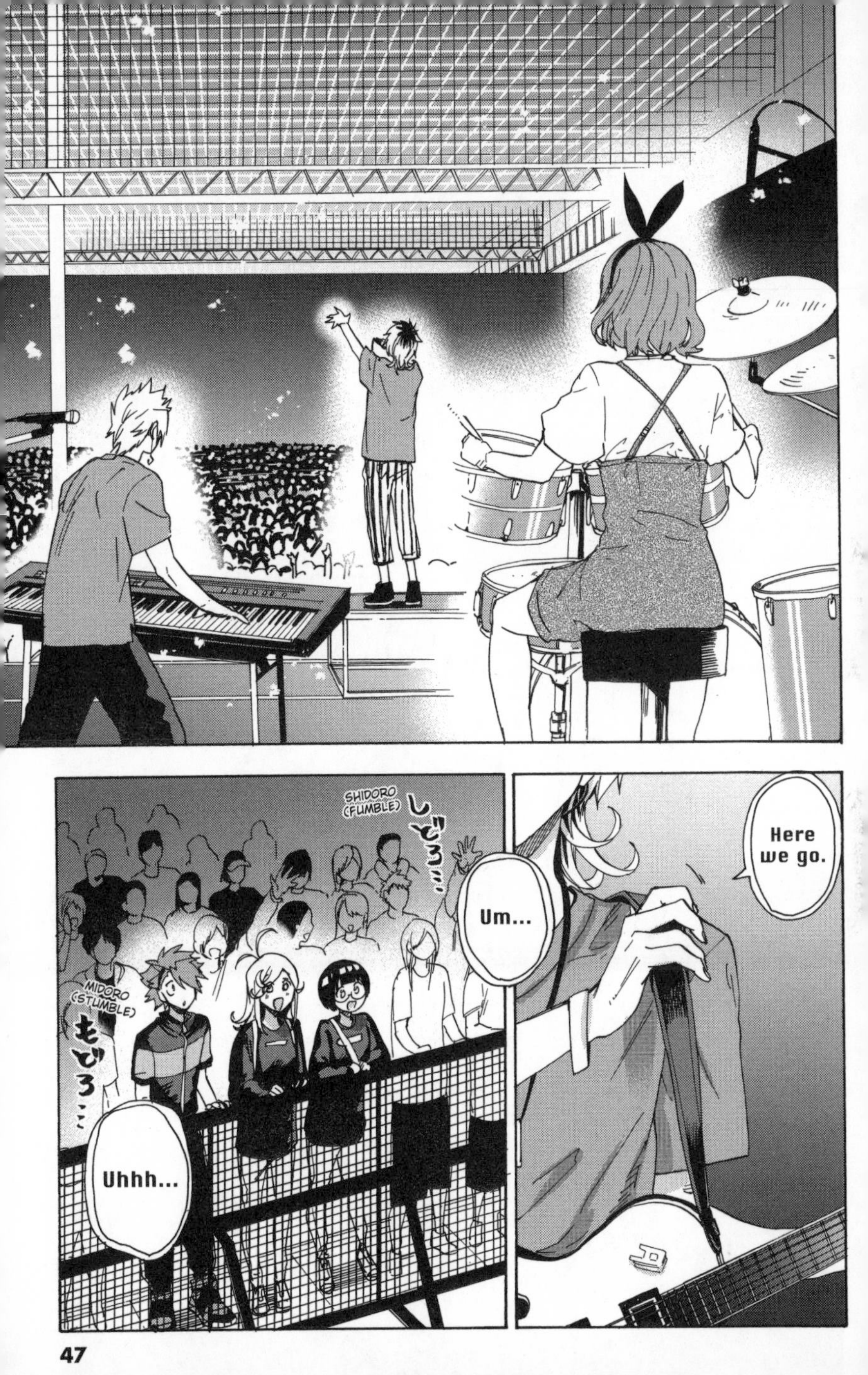
Here we go.
Um...
SHIDORO (FUMBLE)
しどろ
MIDORO (STUMBLE)
もどろ
Uhhh...

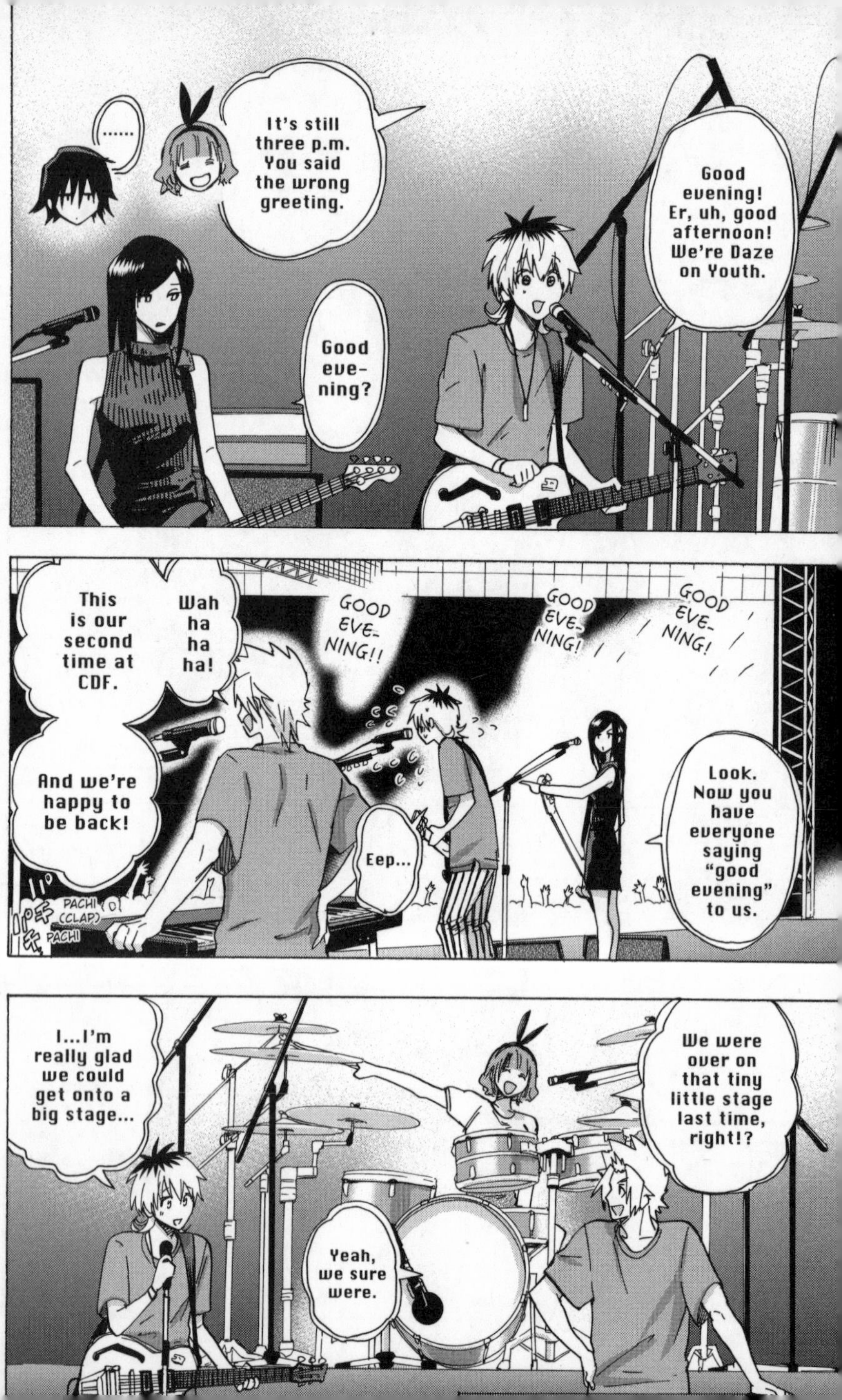
Good evening! Er, uh, good afternoon! We're Daze on Youth.
Good eve-ning?
It's still three p.m. You said the wrong greeting.
......
GOOD EVE-NING!
GOOD EVE-NING!
GOOD EVE-NING!!
Look. Now you have everyone saying "good evening" to us.
Eep...
Wah ha ha ha!
This is our second time at CDF.
And we're happy to be back!
PACHI (CLAP) PACHI
We were over on that tiny little stage last time, right!?
Yeah, we sure were.
I...I'm really glad we could get onto a big stage...

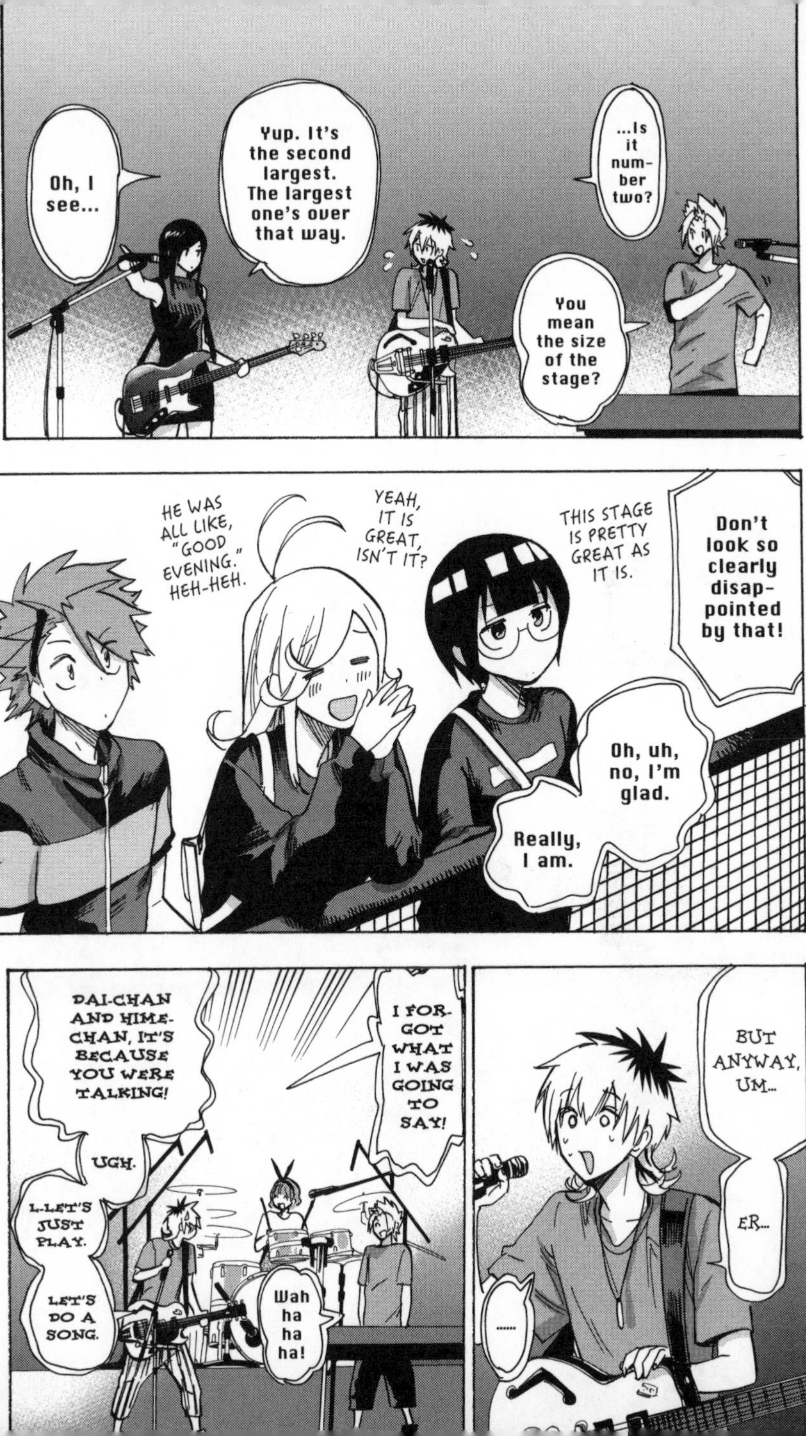
...Is it number two?
You mean the size of the stage?
Yup. It's the second largest. The largest one's over that way.
Oh, I see...
Don't look so clearly disappointed by that!
THIS STAGE IS PRETTY GREAT AS IT IS.
Oh, uh, no, I'm glad.
Really, I am.
YEAH, IT IS GREAT, ISN'T IT?
HE WAS ALL LIKE, "GOOD EVENING." HEH-HEH.
BUT ANYWAY, UM...
ER...
......
I FORGOT WHAT I WAS GOING TO SAY!
DAI-CHAN AND HIME-CHAN, IT'S BECAUSE YOU WERE TALKING!
UGH.
Wah ha ha ha!
L-LET'S JUST PLAY.
LET'S DO A SONG.

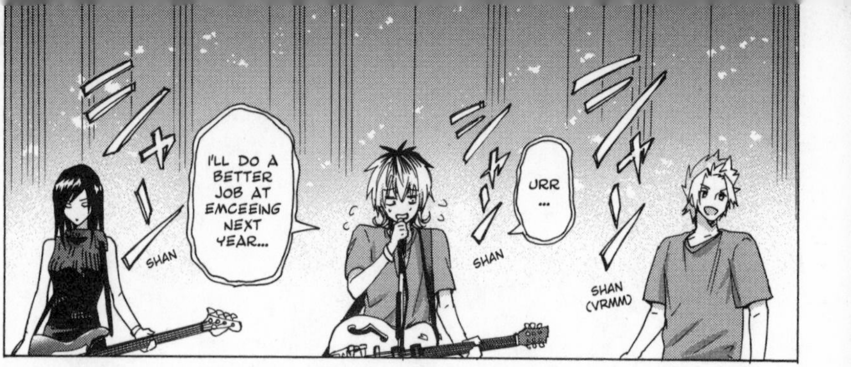
SHAN (VRMM)
URR ...
SHAN
I'LL DO A BETTER JOB AT EMCEEING NEXT YEAR...
SHAN
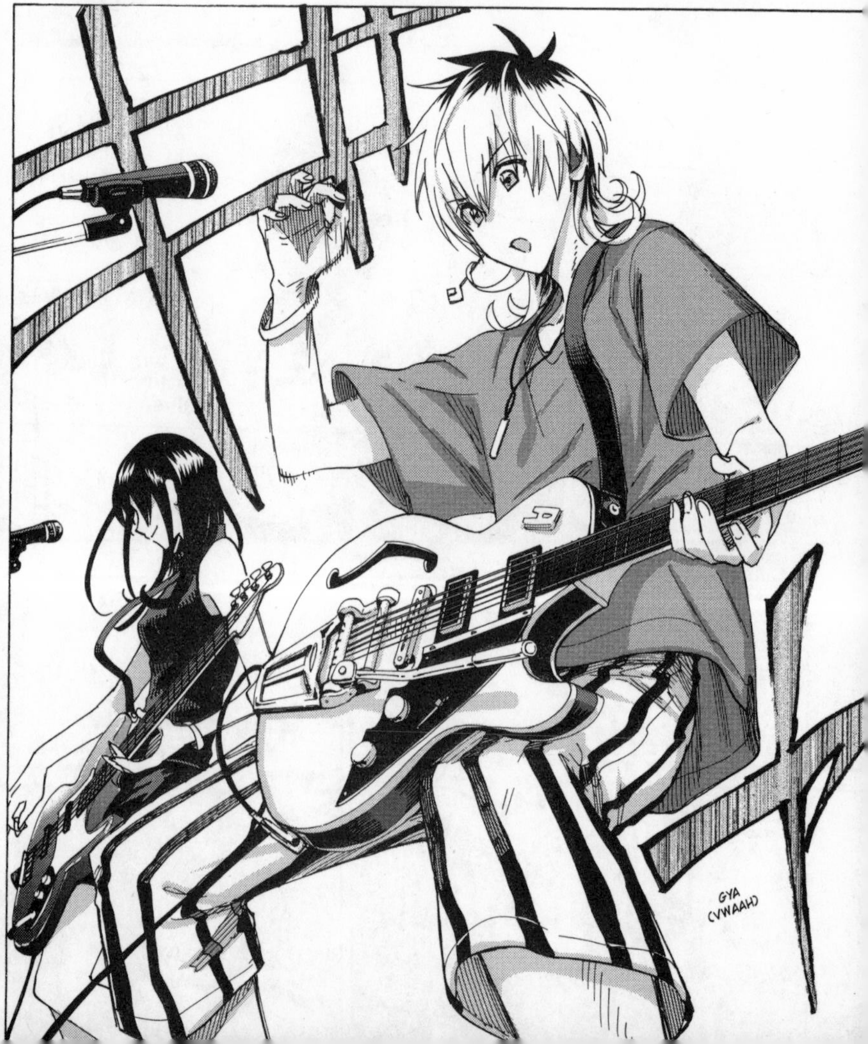
GYA (VWAAH)

DO
(BOOM)

DO

DO

DO

DO

DO

CHAMPION

CA

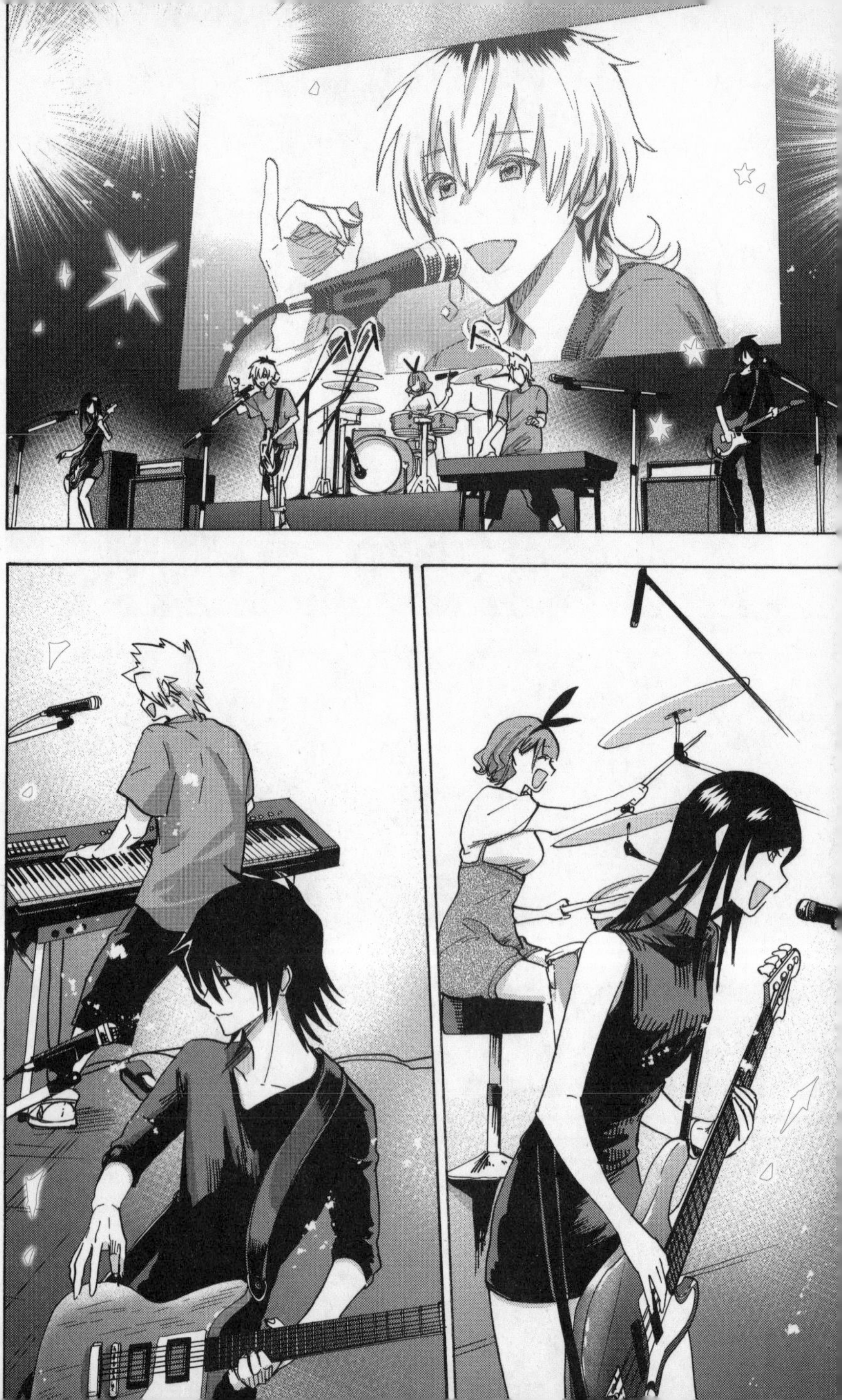

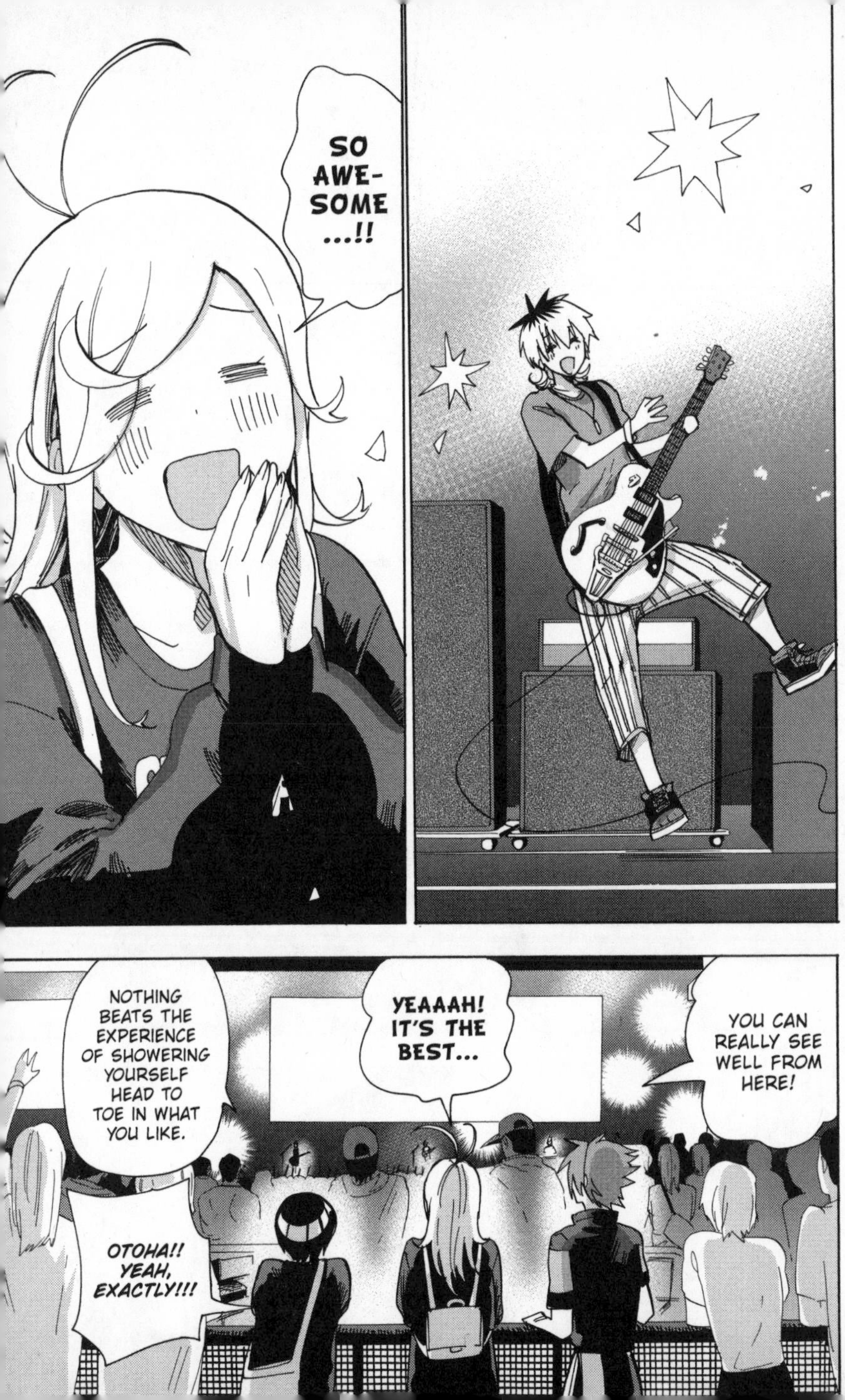
SO AWE-SOME ...!!
YOU CAN REALLY SEE WELL FROM HERE!
YEAAAH! IT'S THE BEST...
NOTHING BEATS THE EXPERIENCE OF SHOWERING YOURSELF HEAD TO TOE IN WHAT YOU LIKE.
OTOHA!! YEAH, EXACTLY!!!

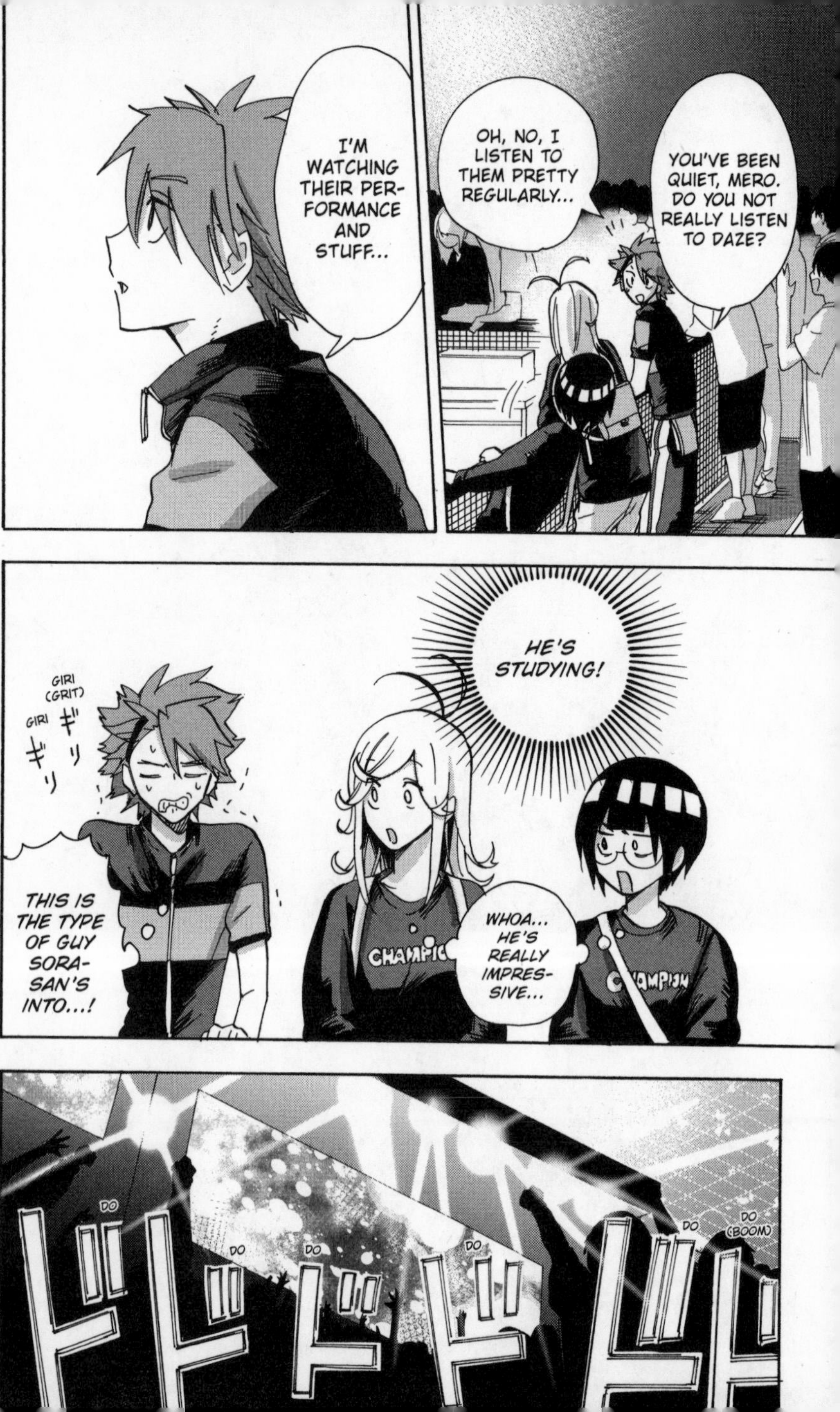
YOU'VE BEEN QUIET, MERO. DO YOU NOT REALLY LISTEN TO DAZE?
OH, NO, I LISTEN TO THEM PRETTY REGULARLY...
I'M WATCHING THEIR PERFORMANCE AND STUFF...
HE'S STUDYING!
WHOA... HE'S REALLY IMPRESSIVE...
GIRI (GRIT) GIRI
ギリ ギリ
THIS IS THE TYPE OF GUY SORA-SAN'S INTO...!
CHAMPION
DO (BOOM) DO DO DO DO DO
ドドドドドド

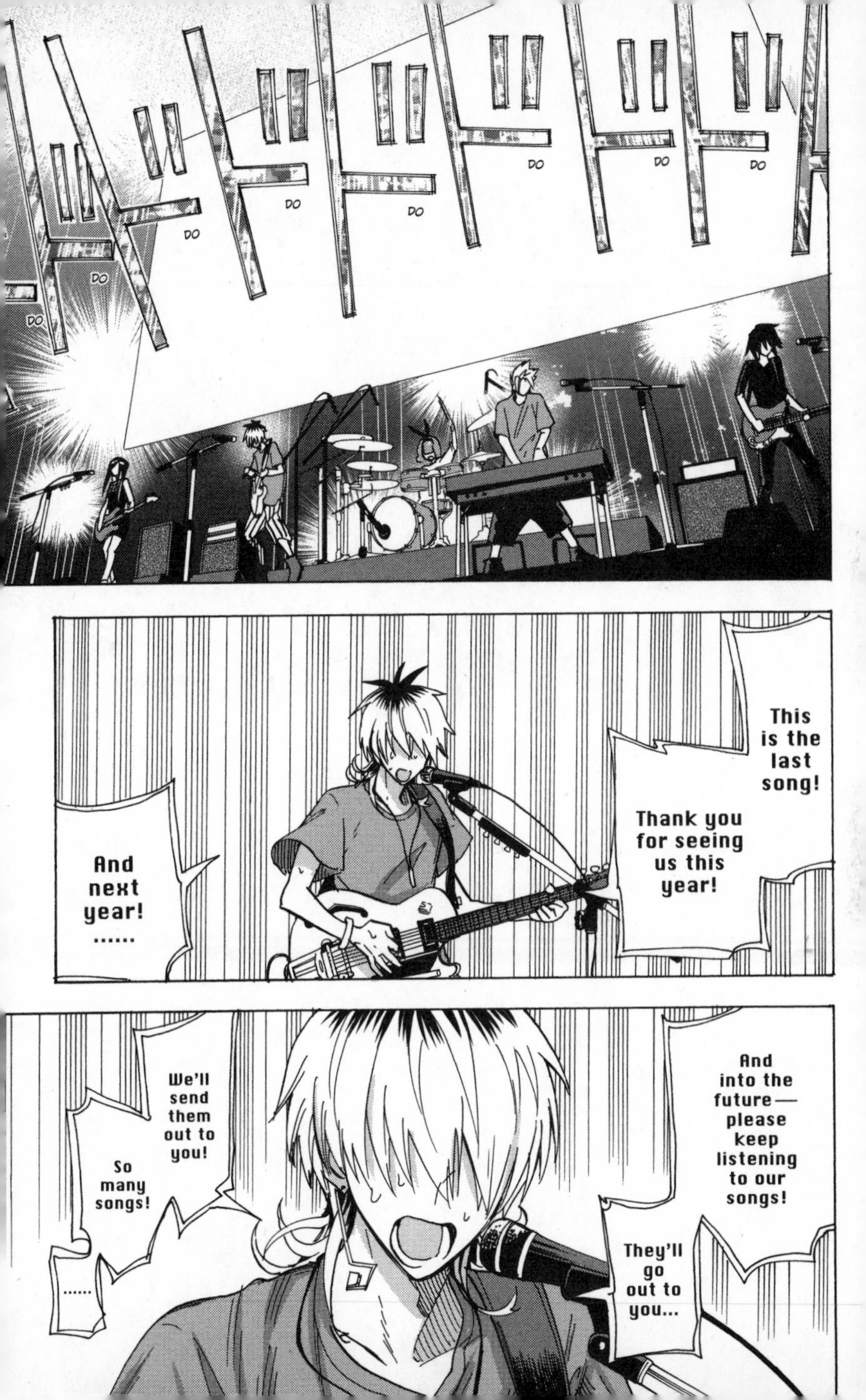
DO DO DO DO DO DO DO DO
This is the last song!
Thank you for seeing us this year!
And next year! ......
And into the future—please keep listening to our songs!
They'll go out to you...
We'll send them out to you!
So many songs!
......

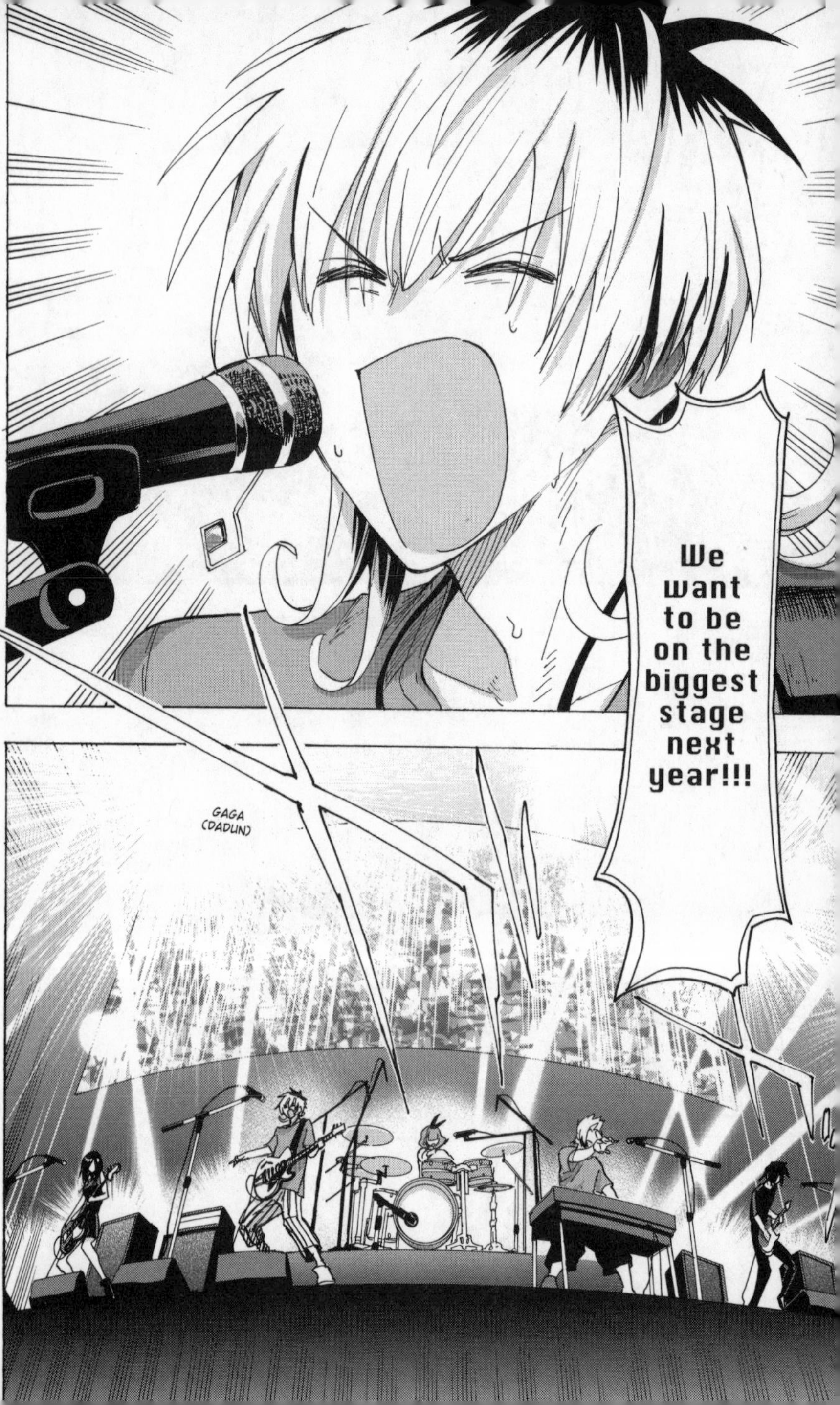
We want to be on the biggest stage next year!!!
GAGA (DADUN)

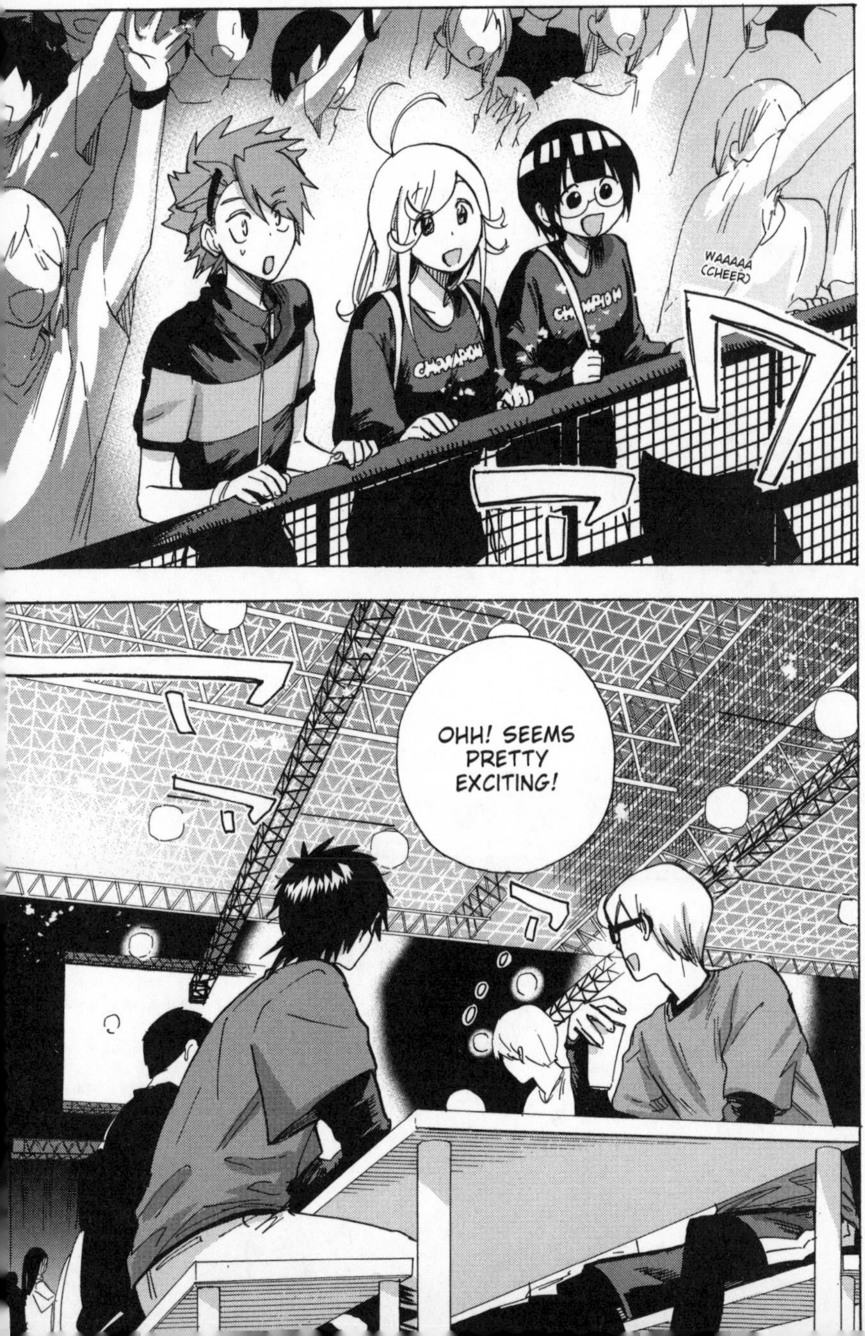
WAAAAA
(CHEER)
CHAMPION
CHAMPION
OHH! SEEMS PRETTY EXCITING!

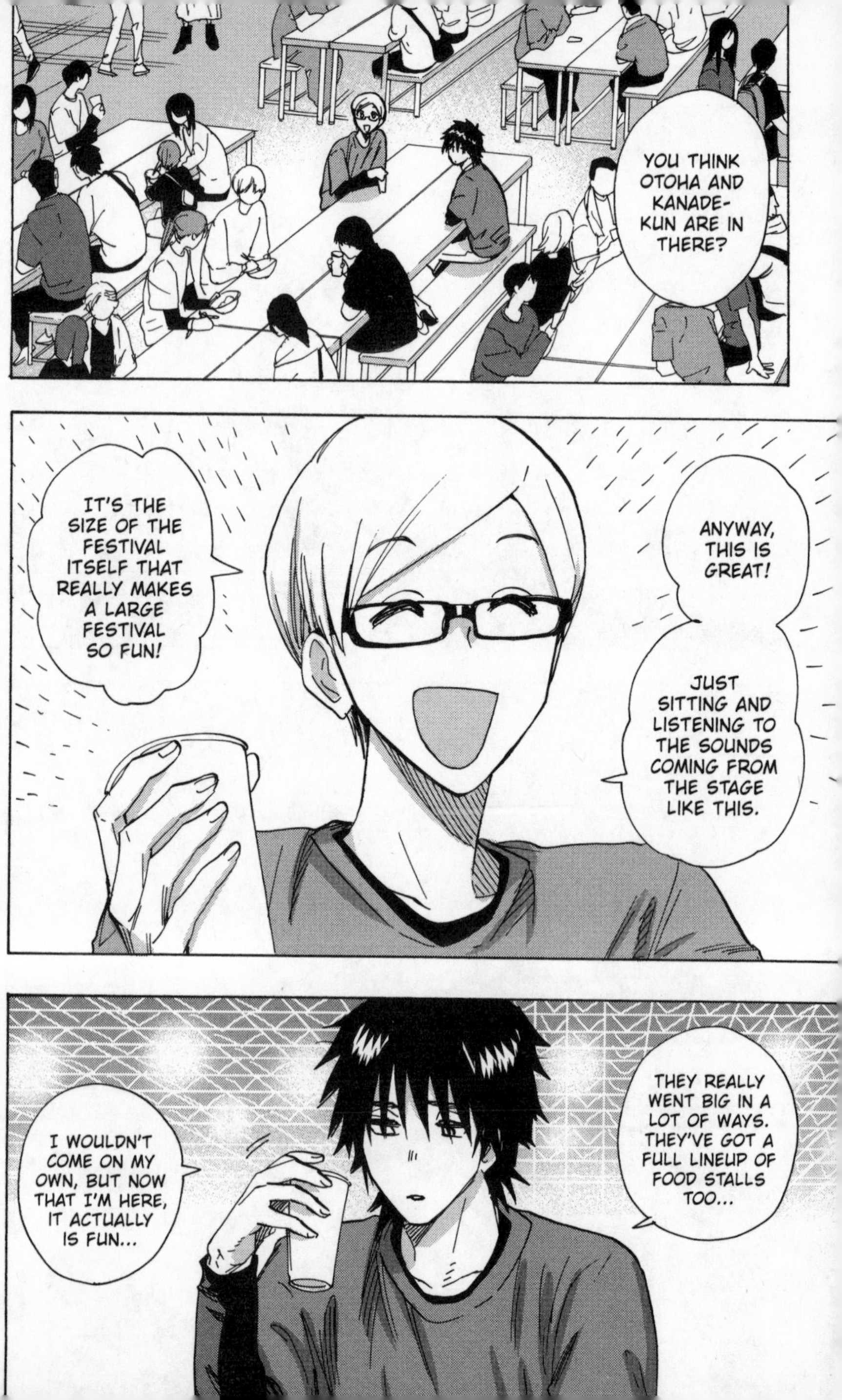
YOU THINK OTOHA AND KANADE-KUN ARE IN THERE?
ANYWAY, THIS IS GREAT!
JUST SITTING AND LISTENING TO THE SOUNDS COMING FROM THE STAGE LIKE THIS.
IT'S THE SIZE OF THE FESTIVAL ITSELF THAT REALLY MAKES A LARGE FESTIVAL SO FUN!
THEY REALLY WENT BIG IN A LOT OF WAYS. THEY'VE GOT A FULL LINEUP OF FOOD STALLS TOO...
I WOULDN'T COME ON MY OWN, BUT NOW THAT I'M HERE, IT ACTUALLY IS FUN...

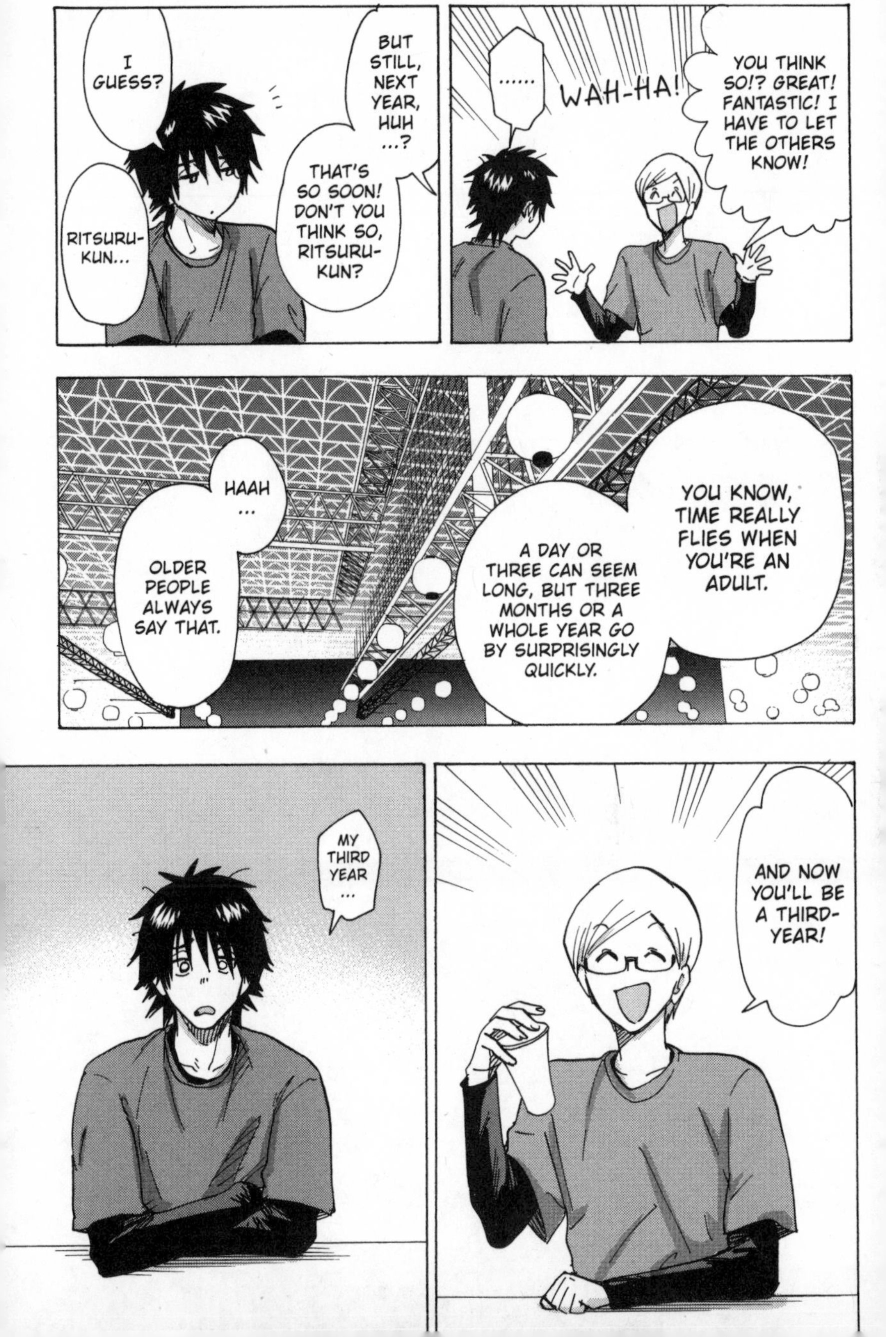
BUT STILL, NEXT YEAR, HUH ...?
THAT'S SO SOON! DON'T YOU THINK SO, RITSURU-KUN?
I GUESS?
RITSURU-KUN...
YOU THINK SO!? GREAT! FANTASTIC! I HAVE TO LET THE OTHERS KNOW!
WAH-HA!
......
YOU KNOW, TIME REALLY FLIES WHEN YOU'RE AN ADULT.
A DAY OR THREE CAN SEEM LONG, BUT THREE MONTHS OR A WHOLE YEAR GO BY SURPRISINGLY QUICKLY.
HAAH ...
OLDER PEOPLE ALWAYS SAY THAT.
AND NOW YOU'LL BE A THIRD-YEAR!
MY THIRD YEAR ...

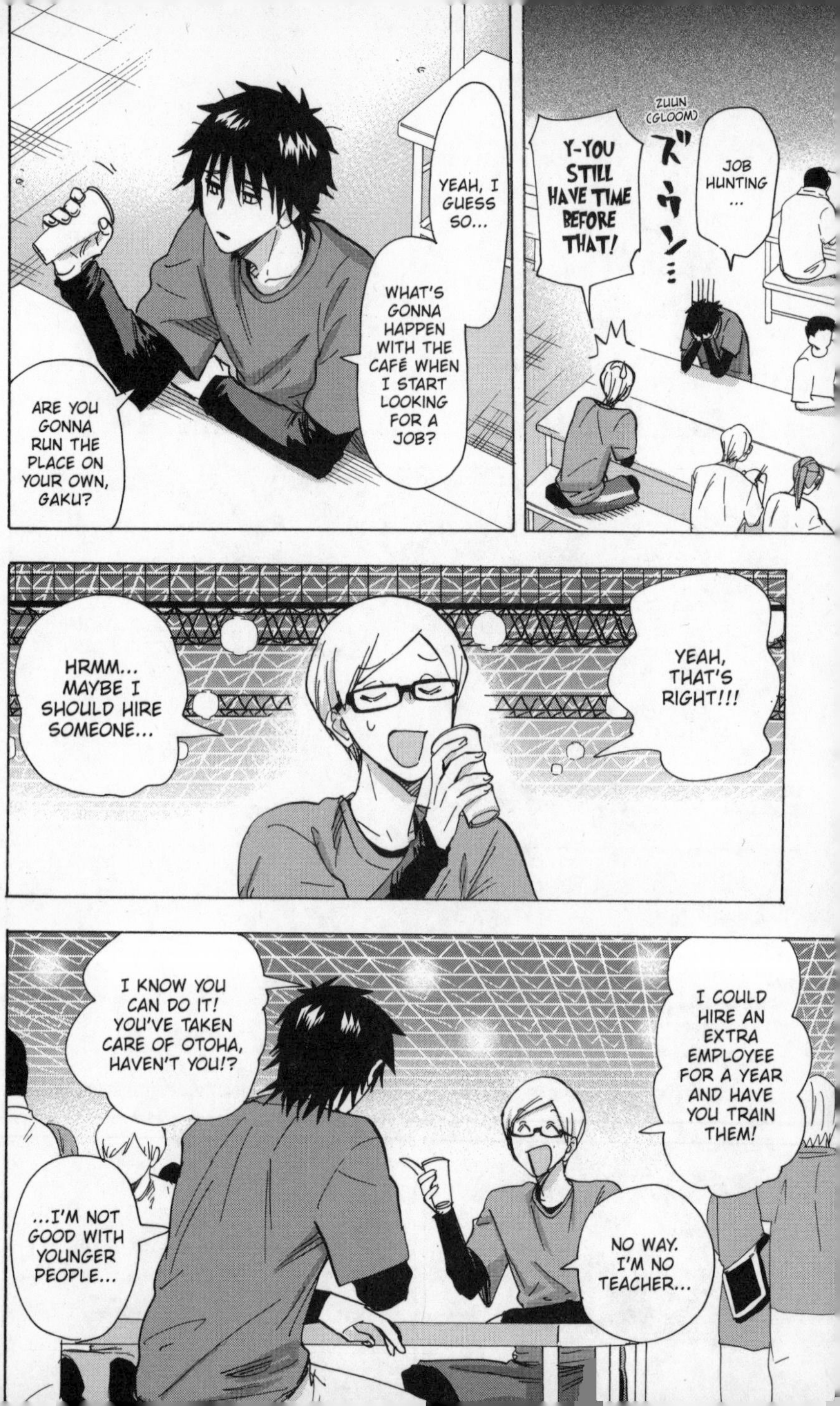
JOB HUNTING ...
ZUUN (GLOOM)
ズゥン
Y-YOU STILL HAVE TIME BEFORE THAT!
YEAH, I GUESS SO...
WHAT'S GONNA HAPPEN WITH THE CAFÉ WHEN I START LOOKING FOR A JOB?
ARE YOU GONNA RUN THE PLACE ON YOUR OWN, GAKU?
YEAH, THAT'S RIGHT!!!
HRMM... MAYBE I SHOULD HIRE SOMEONE...
I COULD HIRE AN EXTRA EMPLOYEE FOR A YEAR AND HAVE YOU TRAIN THEM!
I KNOW YOU CAN DO IT! YOU'VE TAKEN CARE OF OTOHA, HAVEN'T YOU!?
NO WAY. I'M NO TEACHER...
...I'M NOT GOOD WITH YOUNGER PEOPLE...

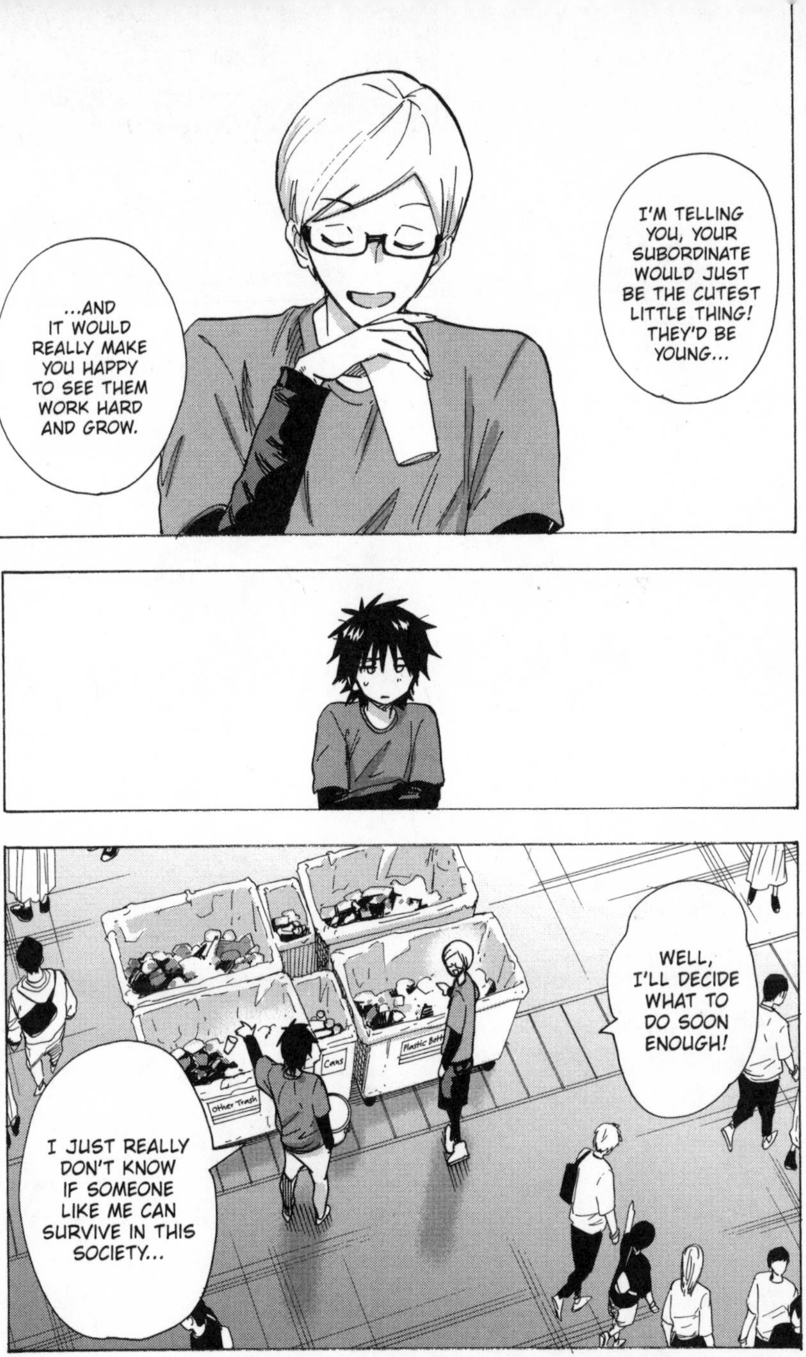
I'M TELLING YOU, YOUR SUBORDINATE WOULD JUST BE THE CUTEST LITTLE THING! THEY'D BE YOUNG...
...AND IT WOULD REALLY MAKE YOU HAPPY TO SEE THEM WORK HARD AND GROW.
WELL, I'LL DECIDE WHAT TO DO SOON ENOUGH!
Cans
Other Trash
I JUST REALLY DON'T KNOW IF SOMEONE LIKE ME CAN SURVIVE IN THIS SOCIETY...

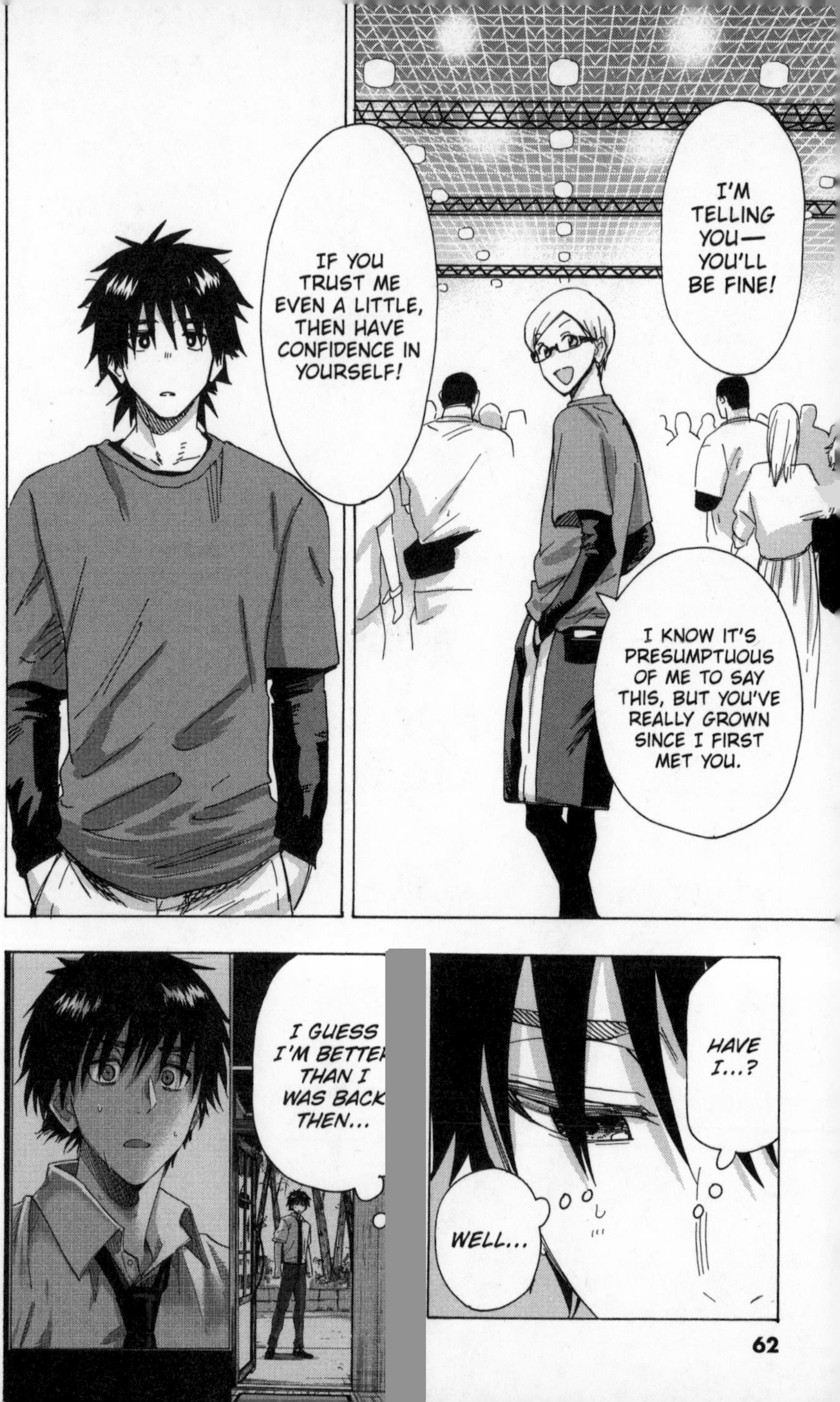
I'M TELLING YOU— YOU'LL BE FINE!
IF YOU TRUST ME EVEN A LITTLE, THEN HAVE CONFIDENCE IN YOURSELF!
I KNOW IT'S PRESUMPTUOUS OF ME TO SAY THIS, BUT YOU'VE REALLY GROWN SINCE I FIRST MET YOU.
HAVE I...?
WELL...
I GUESS I'M BETTEF THAN I WAS BACK THEN...

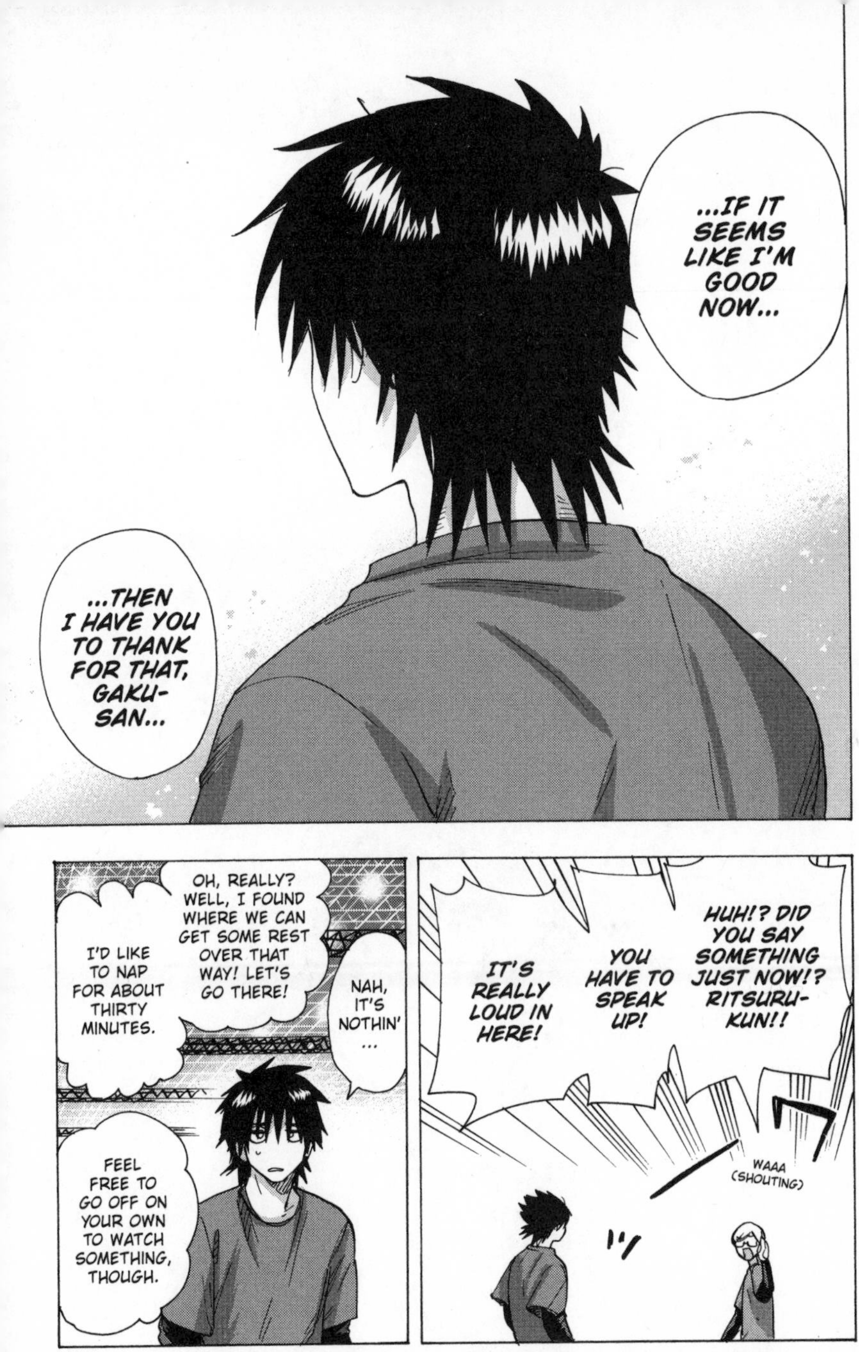
...IF IT SEEMS LIKE I'M GOOD NOW...
...THEN I HAVE YOU TO THANK FOR THAT, GAKU-SAN...
HUH!? DID YOU SAY SOMETHING JUST NOW!? RITSURU-KUN!!
YOU HAVE TO SPEAK UP!
IT'S REALLY LOUD IN HERE!
WAAA (SHOUTING)
NAH, IT'S NOTHIN' ...
OH, REALLY? WELL, I FOUND WHERE WE CAN GET SOME REST OVER THAT WAY! LET'S GO THERE!
I'D LIKE TO NAP FOR ABOUT THIRTY MINUTES.
FEEL FREE TO GO OFF ON YOUR OWN TO WATCH SOMETHING, THOUGH.

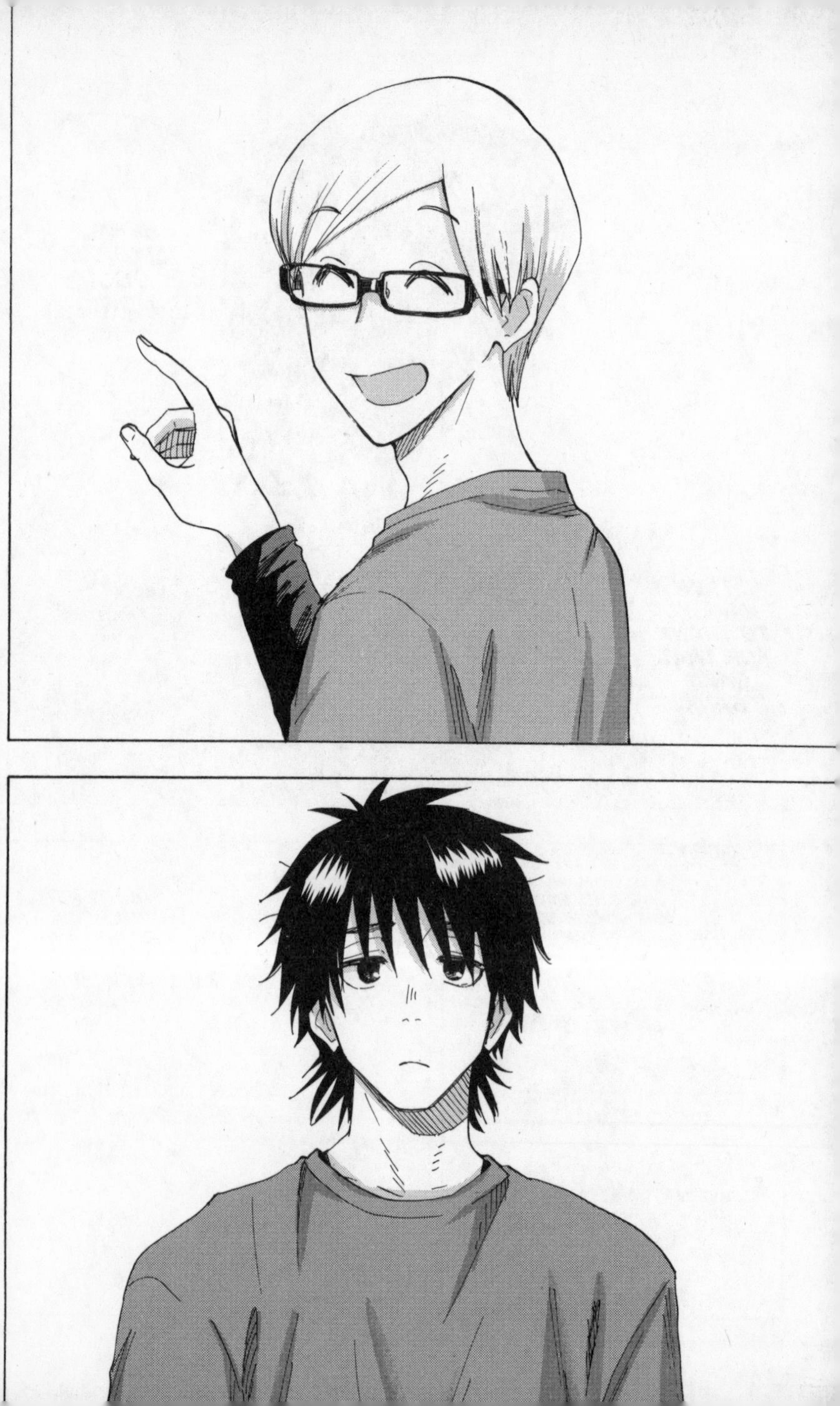

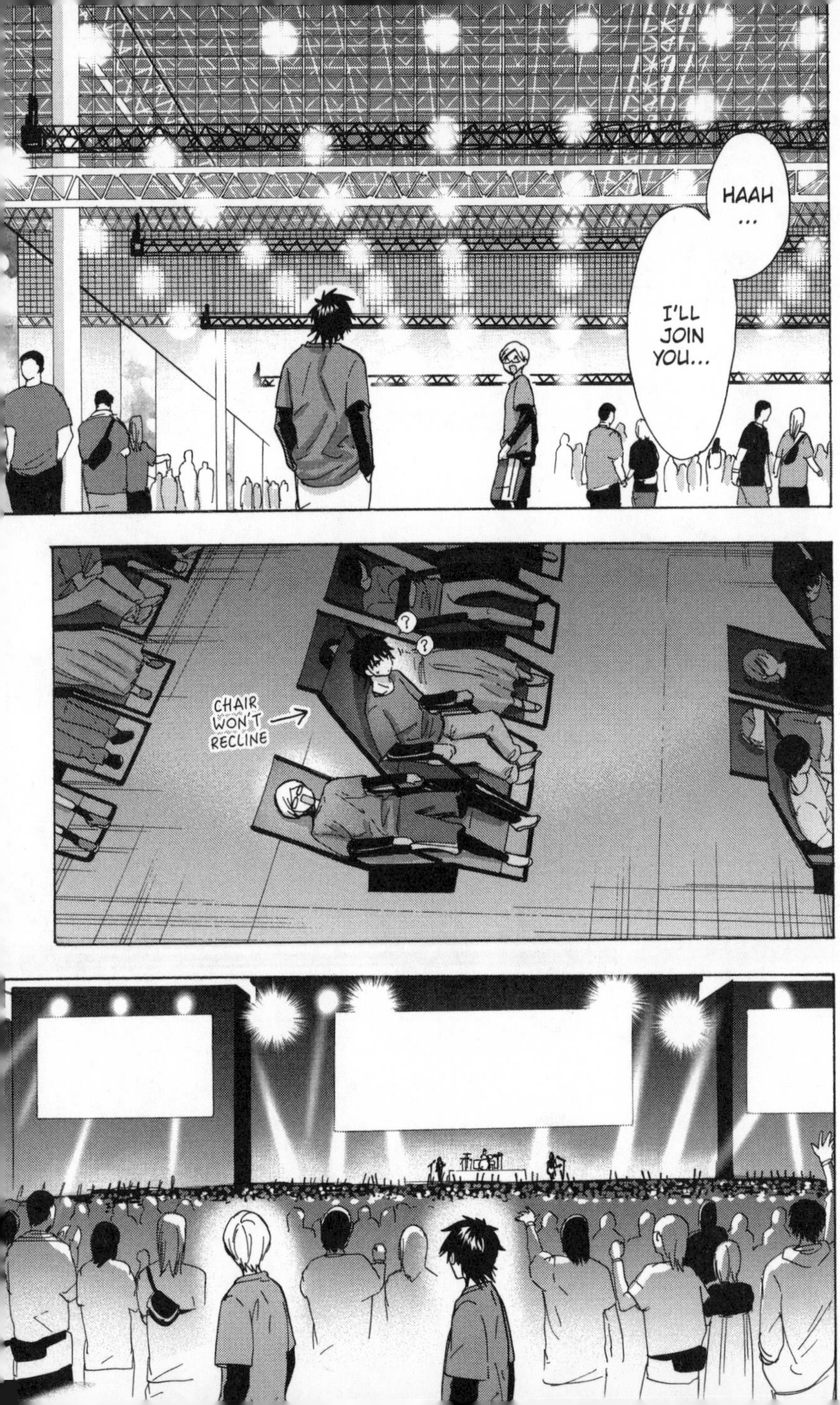
HAAH ...
I'LL JOIN YOU...
?
?
CHAIR WON'T RECLINE

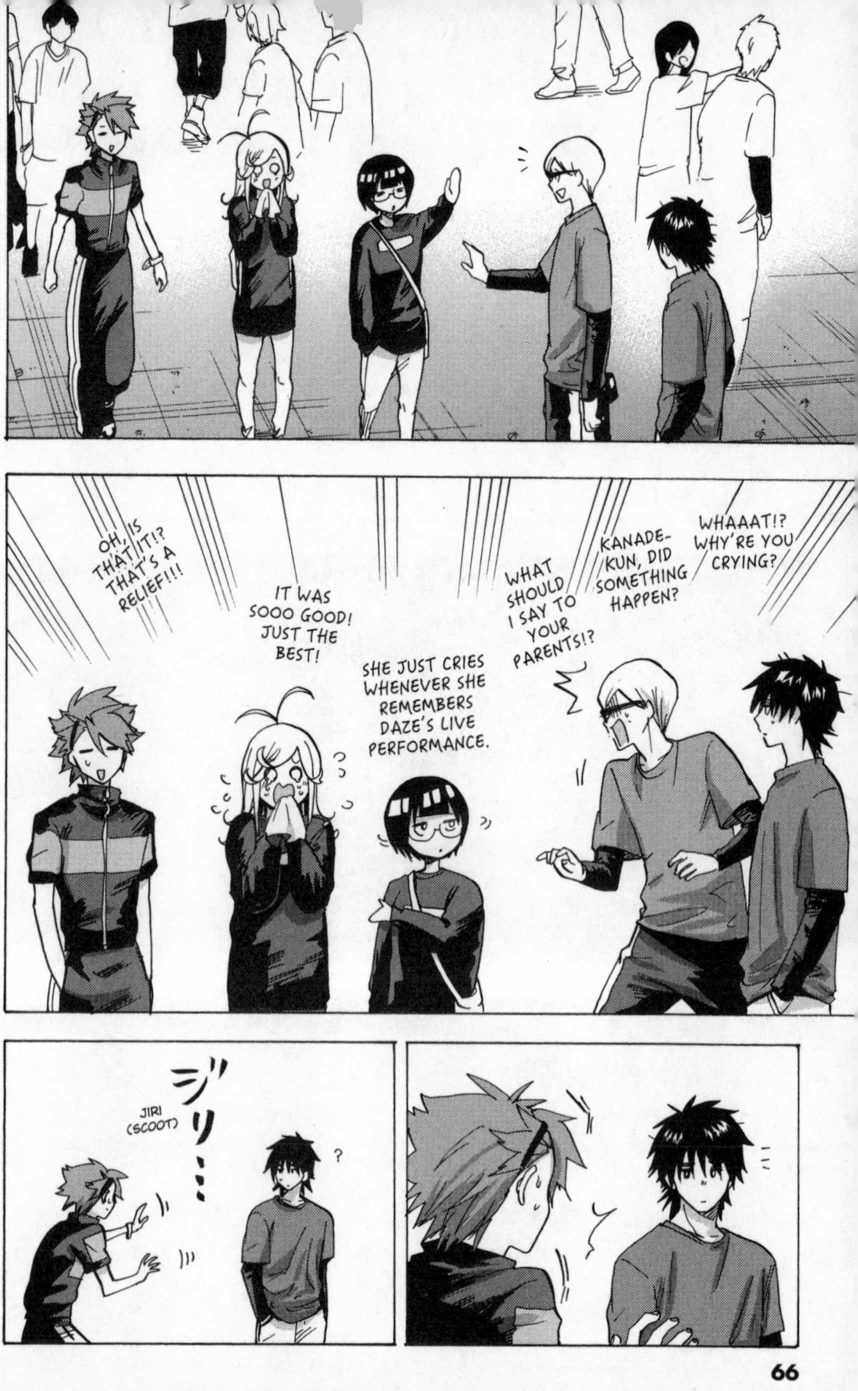
WHAAAT!? WHY'RE YOU CRYING?
KANADE-KUN, DID SOMETHING HAPPEN?
WHAT SHOULD I SAY TO YOUR PARENTS!?
SHE JUST CRIES WHENEVER SHE REMEMBERS DAZE'S LIVE PERFORMANCE.
IT WAS SOOO GOOD! JUST THE BEST!
OH, IS THAT IT!? THAT'S A RELIEF!!!
ジリ…
JIRI (SCOOT)

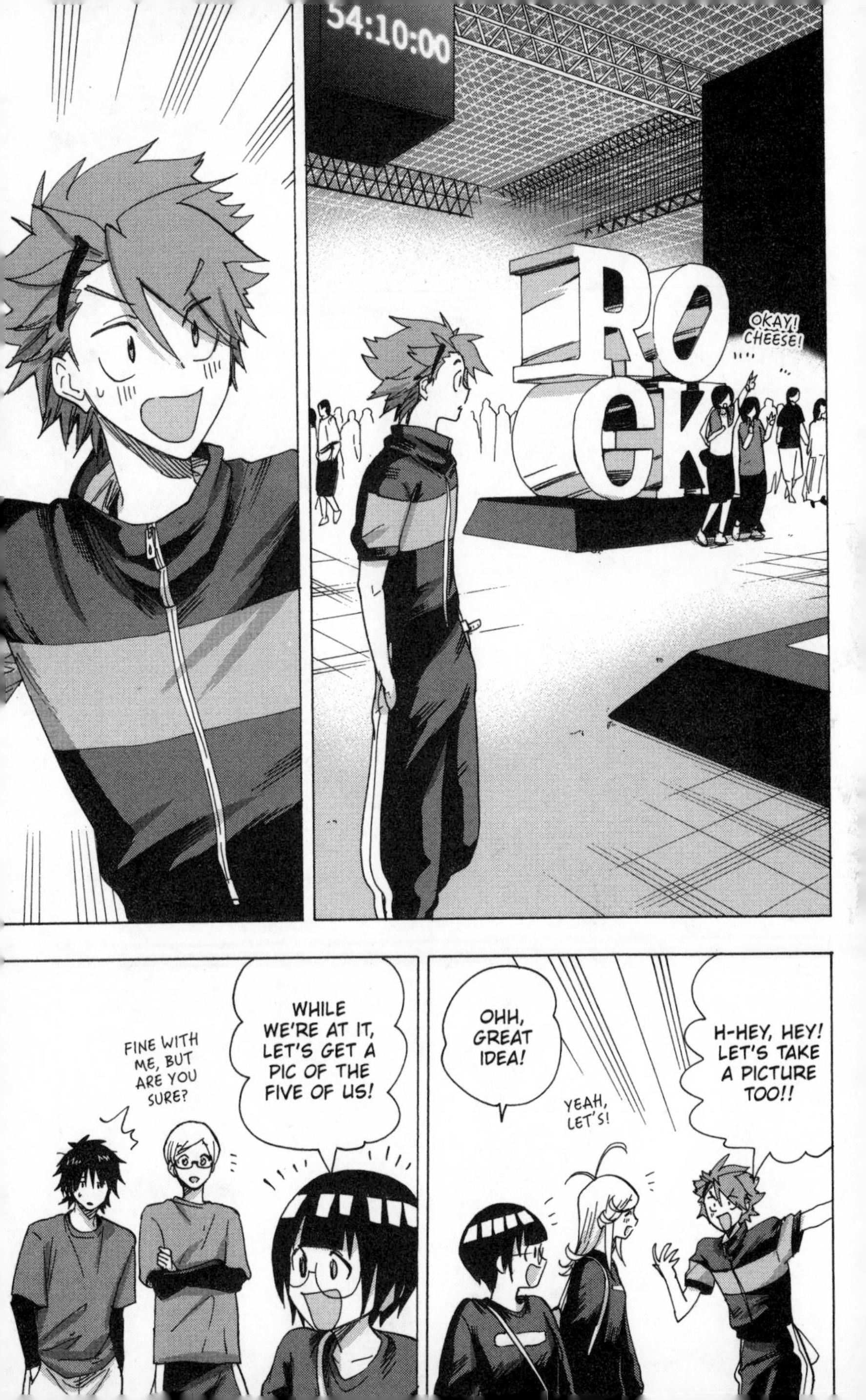

54:10:00
ROCK
OKAY! CHEESE!
H-HEY, HEY! LET'S TAKE A PICTURE TOO!!
OHH, GREAT IDEA!
YEAH, LET'S!
WHILE WE'RE AT IT, LET'S GET A PIC OF THE FIVE OF US!
FINE WITH ME, BUT ARE YOU SURE?

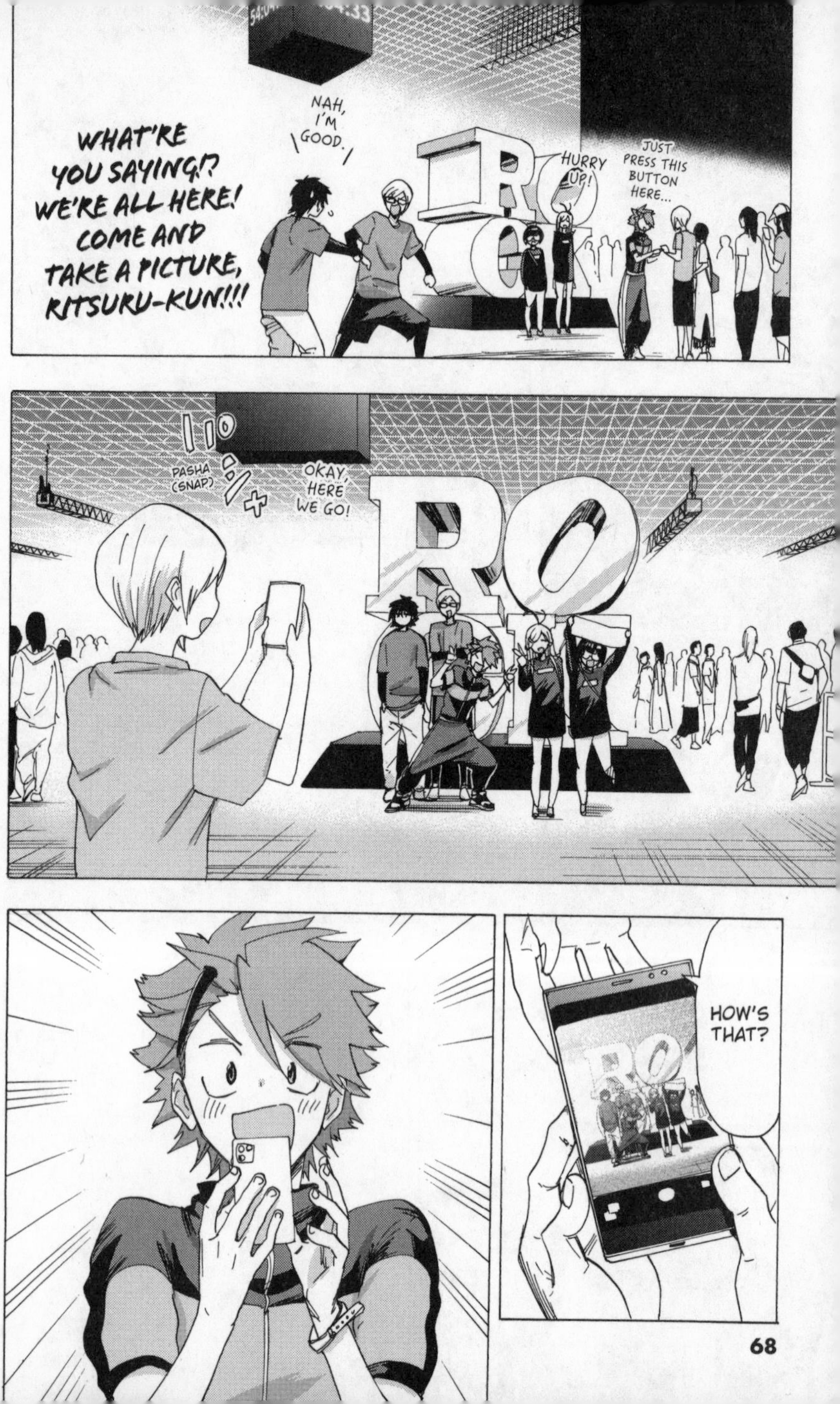
JUST PRESS THIS BUTTON HERE...
HURRY UP!
NAH, I'M GOOD.
WHAT'RE YOU SAYING!? WE'RE ALL HERE! COME AND TAKE A PICTURE, RITSURU-KUN!!!
OKAY, HERE WE GO!
PASHA (SNAP)
HOW'S THAT?

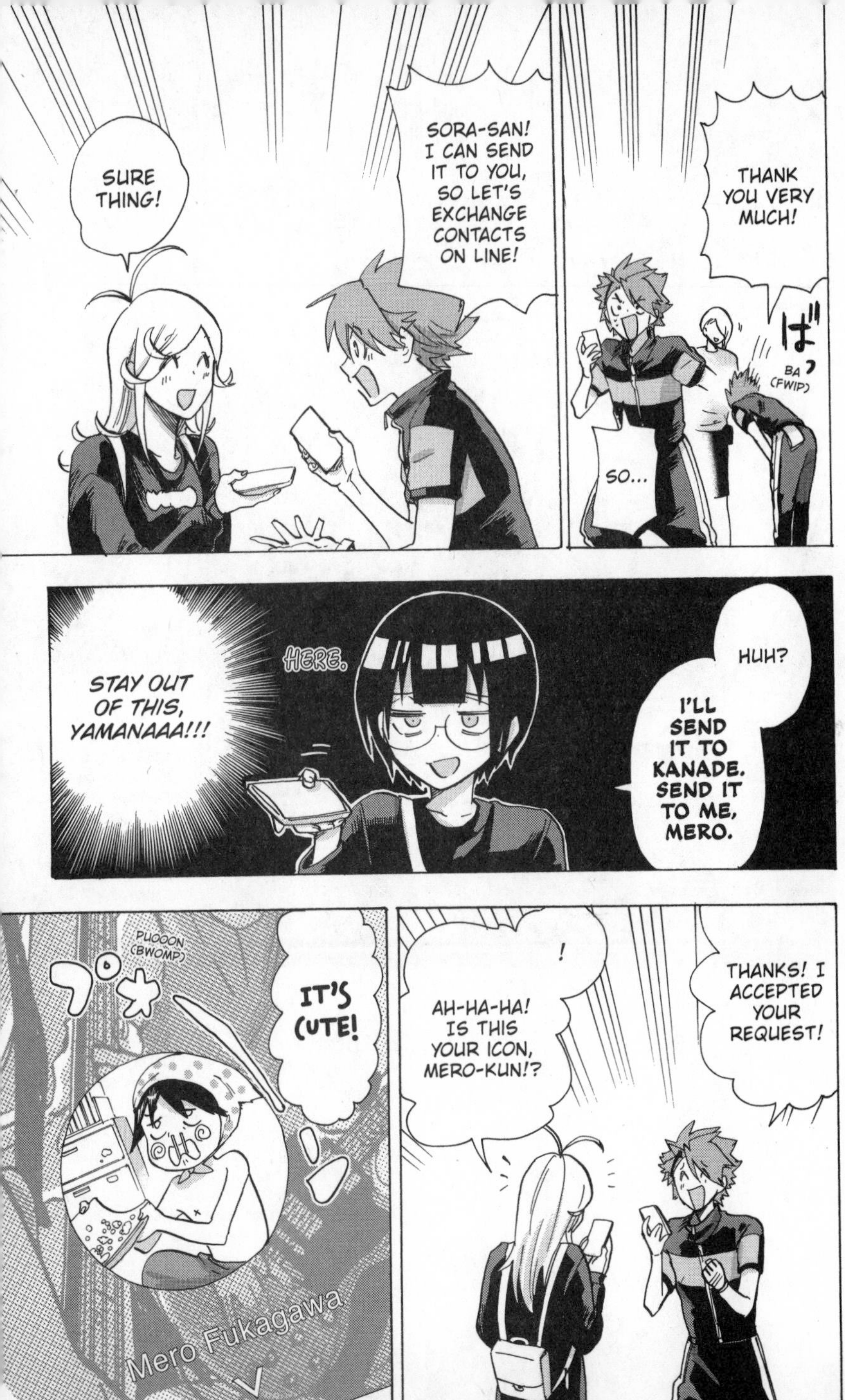
THANK YOU VERY MUCH!
ば
BA (FWIP)
SO...
SORA-SAN! I CAN SEND IT TO YOU, SO LET'S EXCHANGE CONTACTS ON LINE!
SURE THING!
HUH?
I'LL SEND IT TO KANADE. SEND IT TO ME, MERO.
HERE.
STAY OUT OF THIS, YAMANAAA!!!
THANKS! I ACCEPTED YOUR REQUEST!
!
AH-HA-HA! IS THIS YOUR ICON, MERO-KUN!?
IT'S CUTE!
PUOOON (BWOMP)
Mero Fukagawa

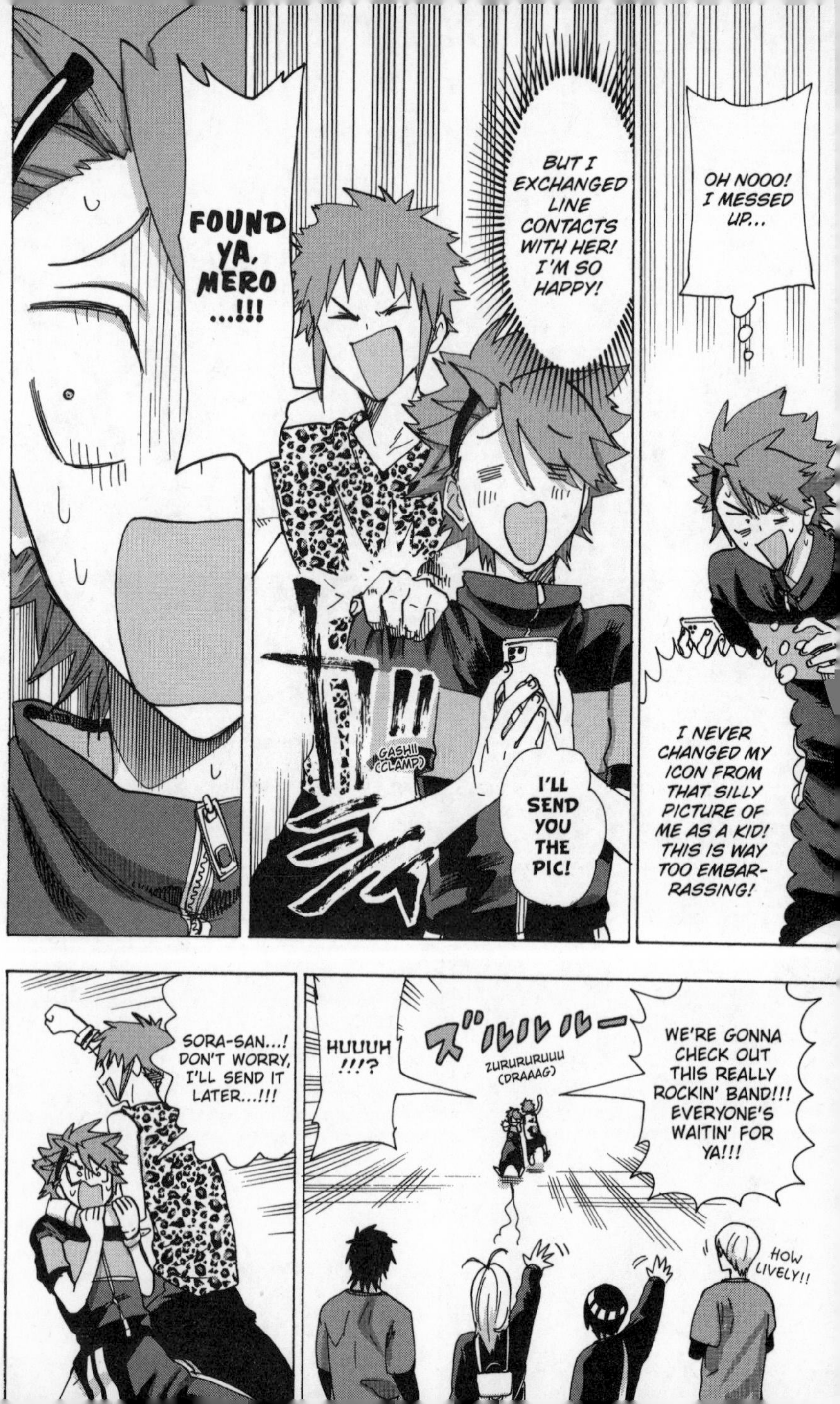

OH NOOO! I MESSED UP...
I NEVER CHANGED MY ICON FROM THAT SILLY PICTURE OF ME AS A KID! THIS IS WAY TOO EMBAR-RASSING!
BUT I EXCHANGED LINE CONTACTS WITH HER! I'M SO HAPPY!
I'LL SEND YOU THE PIC!
GASHI (CLAMP)
FOUND YA, MERO ...!!!
WE'RE GONNA CHECK OUT THIS REALLY ROCKIN' BAND!!! EVERYONE'S WAITIN' FOR YA!!!
ズルルルルー
ZURURURUUU (DRAAAG)
HUUUH !!!?
HOW LIVELY!!
SORA-SAN...! DON'T WORRY, I'LL SEND IT LATER...!!!

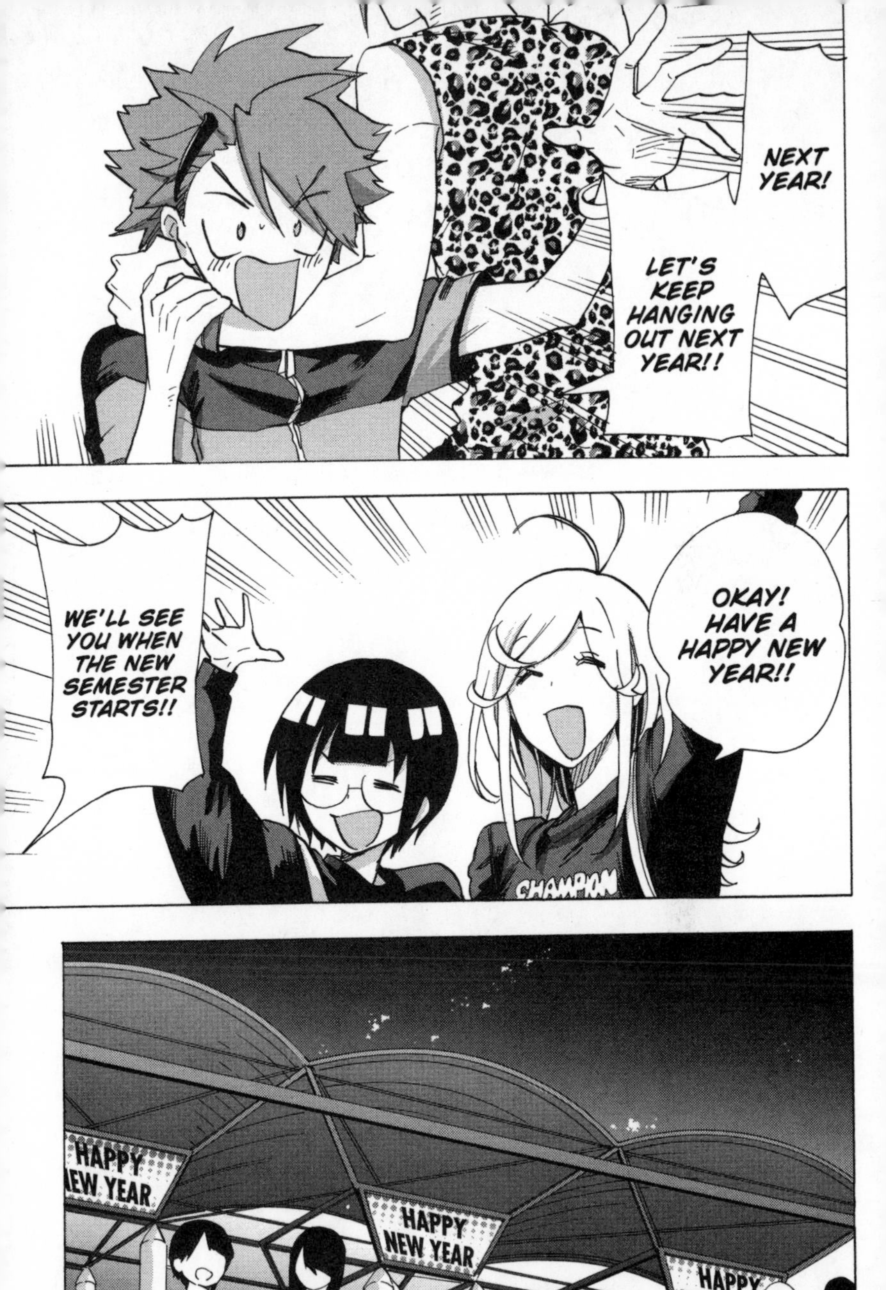
NEXT YEAR!
LET'S KEEP HANGING OUT NEXT YEAR!!
OKAY! HAVE A HAPPY NEW YEAR!!
WE'LL SEE YOU WHEN THE NEW SEMESTER STARTS!!
CHAMPION
HAPPY NEW YEAR
HAPPY NEW YEAR
HAPPY NEW YEAR

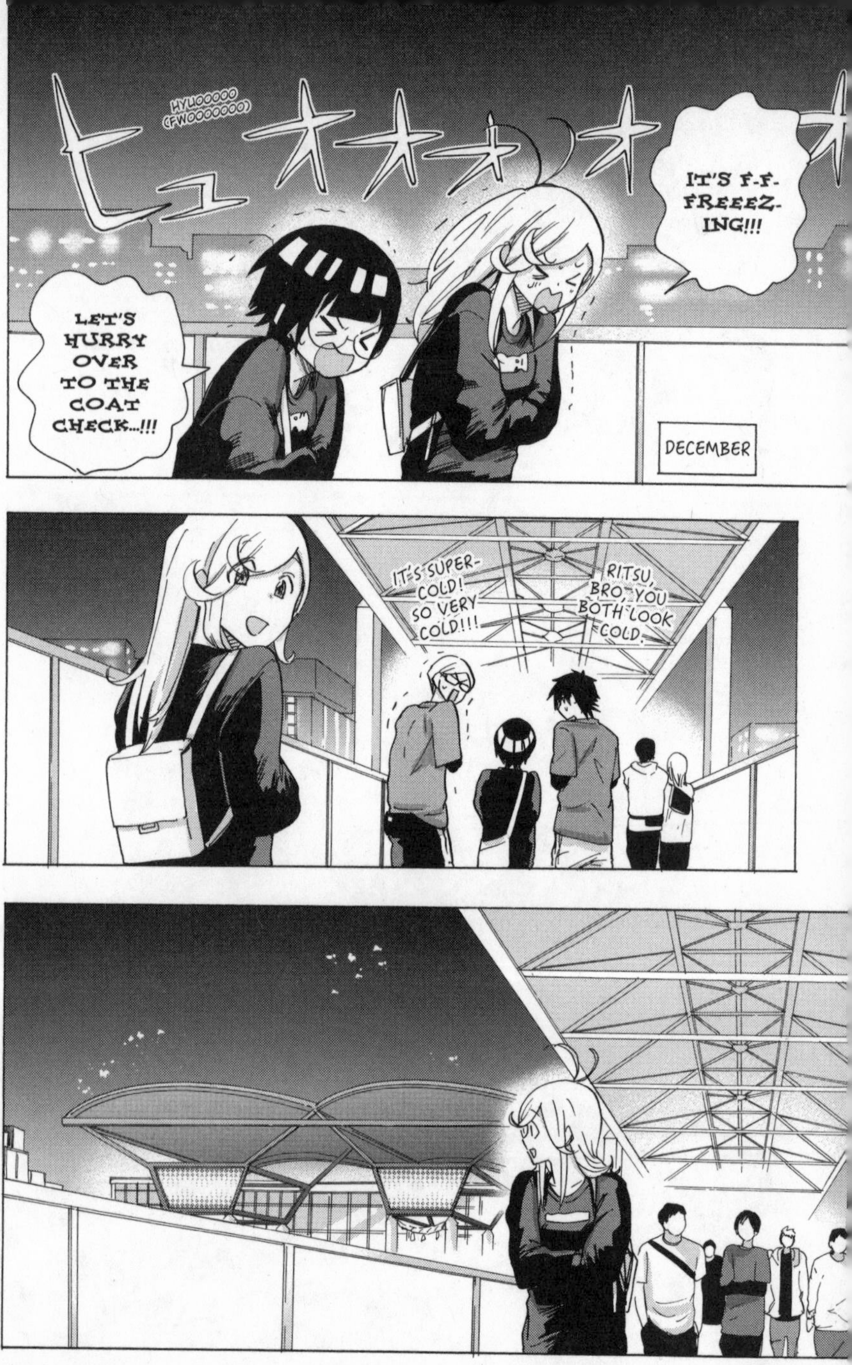
HYUOOOOO (FWOOOOOOOO)
IT'S F-F-FREEEZ-ING!!!
LET'S HURRY OVER TO THE COAT CHECK...!!!
DECEMBER
RITSU, BRO, YOU BOTH LOOK COLD.
IT'S SUPER-COLD! SO VERY COLD!!!

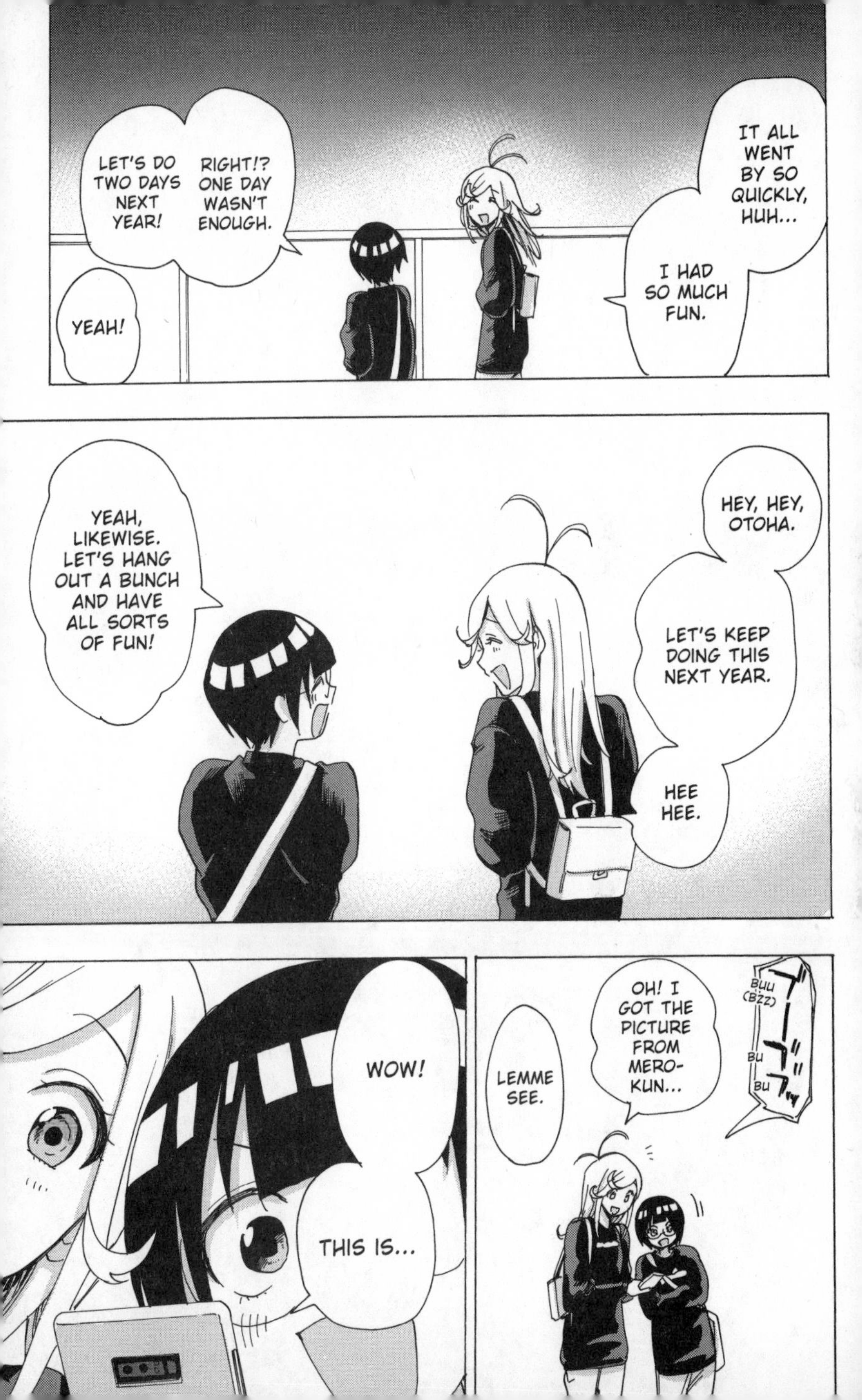
IT ALL WENT BY SO QUICKLY, HUH...
I HAD SO MUCH FUN.
RIGHT!? ONE DAY WASN'T ENOUGH.
LET'S DO TWO DAYS NEXT YEAR!
YEAH!
HEY, HEY, OTOHA.
LET'S KEEP DOING THIS NEXT YEAR.
HEE HEE.
YEAH, LIKEWISE. LET'S HANG OUT A BUNCH AND HAVE ALL SORTS OF FUN!
Buu (BZZ) Bu Bu
OH! I GOT THE PICTURE FROM MERO-KUN...
LEMME SEE.
WOW!
THIS IS...

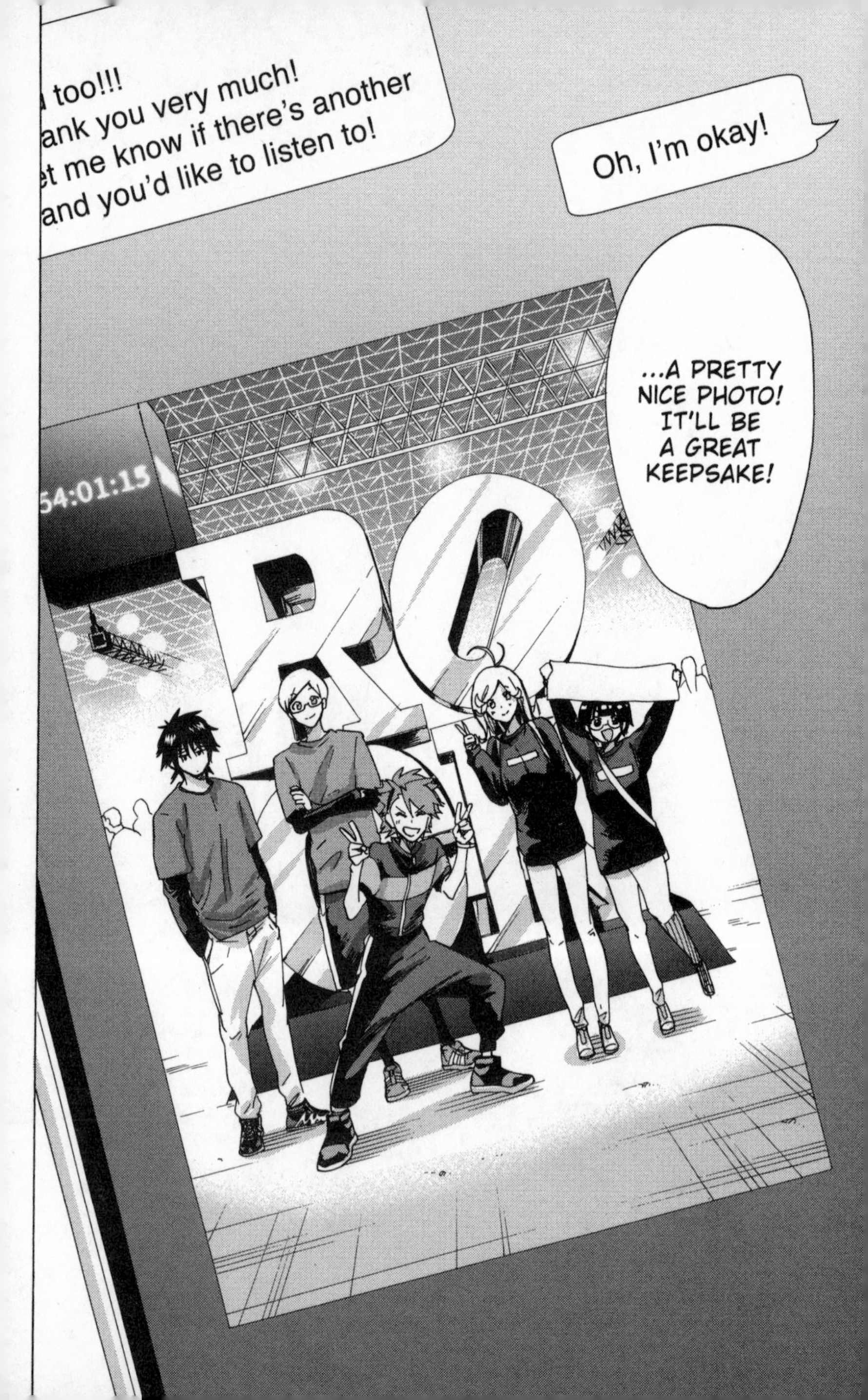
too!!!
ank you very much!
et me know if there's another
and you'd like to listen to!
Oh, I'm okay!
54:01:15
...A PRETTY NICE PHOTO! IT'LL BE A GREAT KEEPSAKE!

Days on Fes

Days on Fes

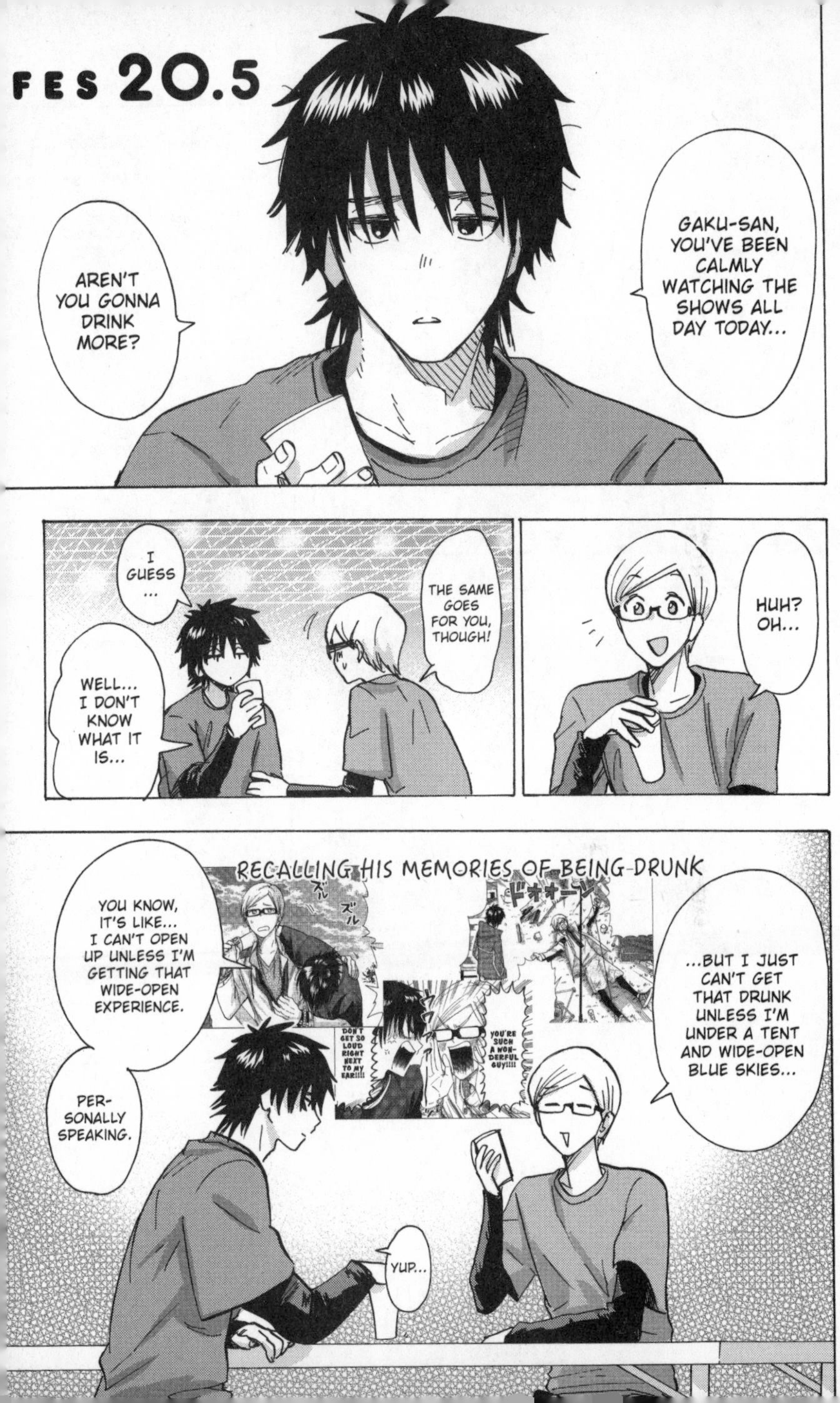
FES 20.5
GAKU-SAN, YOU'VE BEEN CALMLY WATCHING THE SHOWS ALL DAY TODAY...
AREN'T YOU GONNA DRINK MORE?
HUH? OH...
THE SAME GOES FOR YOU, THOUGH!
I GUESS...
WELL... I DON'T KNOW WHAT IT IS...
RECALLING HIS MEMORIES OF BEING DRUNK
...BUT I JUST CAN'T GET THAT DRUNK UNLESS I'M UNDER A TENT AND WIDE-OPEN BLUE SKIES...
ズル
ズル
YOU'RE SUCH A WONDERFUL GUY!!!!
DON'T GET SO LOUD RIGHT NEXT TO MY EAR!!!!
YOU KNOW, IT'S LIKE... I CAN'T OPEN UP UNLESS I'M GETTING THAT WIDE-OPEN EXPERIENCE.
PERSONALLY SPEAKING.
YUP...

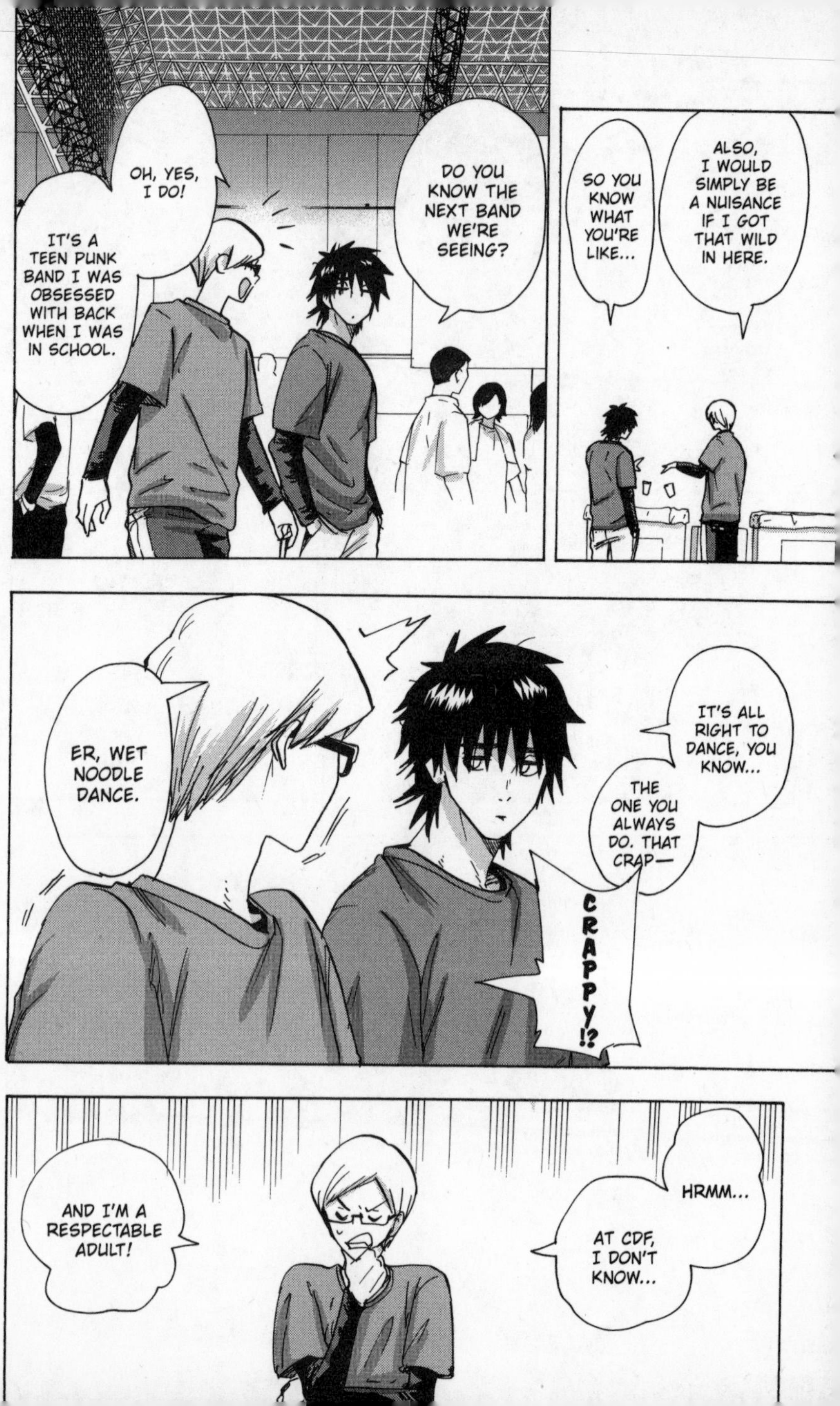
DO YOU KNOW THE NEXT BAND WE'RE SEEING?
OH, YES, I DO!
IT'S A TEEN PUNK BAND I WAS OBSESSED WITH BACK WHEN I WAS IN SCHOOL.
ALSO, I WOULD SIMPLY BE A NUISANCE IF I GOT THAT WILD IN HERE.
SO YOU KNOW WHAT YOU'RE LIKE...
IT'S ALL RIGHT TO DANCE, YOU KNOW...
THE ONE YOU ALWAYS DO. THAT CRAP—
CRAPPY!?
ER, WET NOODLE DANCE.
HRMM...
AT CDF, I DON'T KNOW...
AND I'M A RESPECTABLE ADULT!

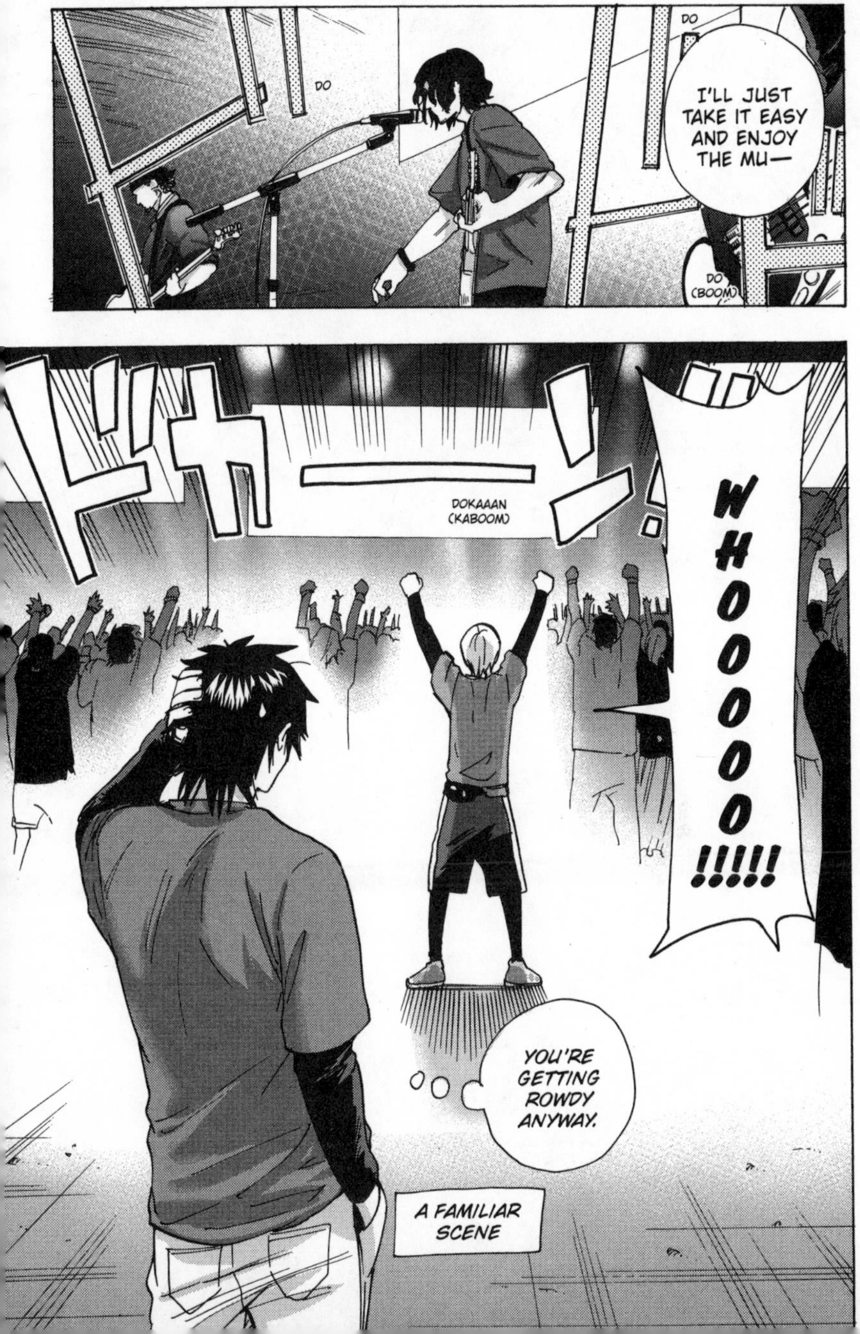
DO
I'LL JUST TAKE IT EASY AND ENJOY THE MU—
DO
DO (BOOM)
WHOOOOOO!!!!!
DOKAAAN (KABOOM)
YOU'RE GETTING ROWDY ANYWAY.
A FAMILIAR SCENE

Days on Fes

FES 21

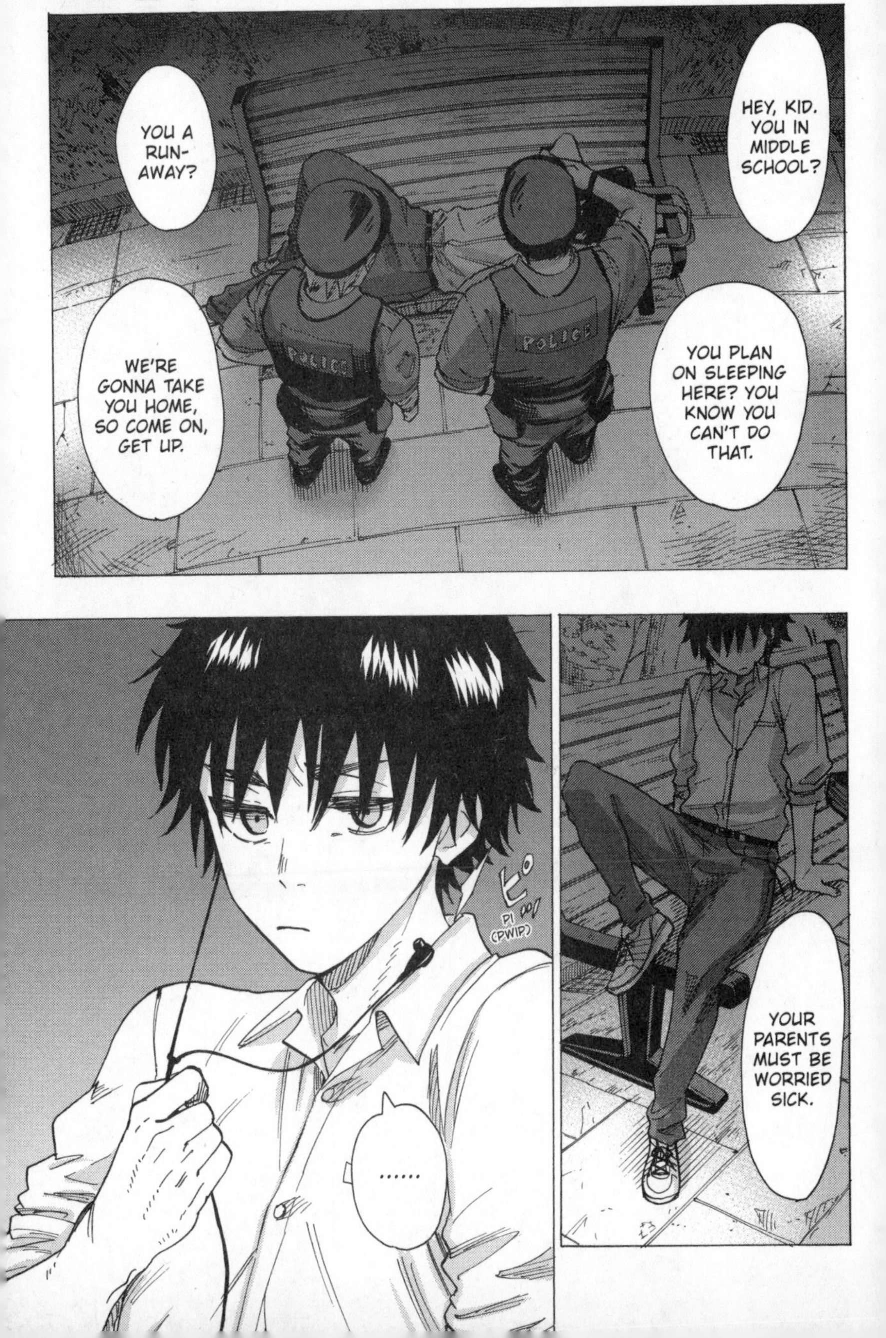
HEY, KID. YOU IN MIDDLE SCHOOL?
YOU A RUN-AWAY?
YOU PLAN ON SLEEPING HERE? YOU KNOW YOU CAN'T DO THAT.
WE'RE GONNA TAKE YOU HOME, SO COME ON, GET UP.
YOUR PARENTS MUST BE WORRIED SICK.
ピ
PI (PWIP)
......

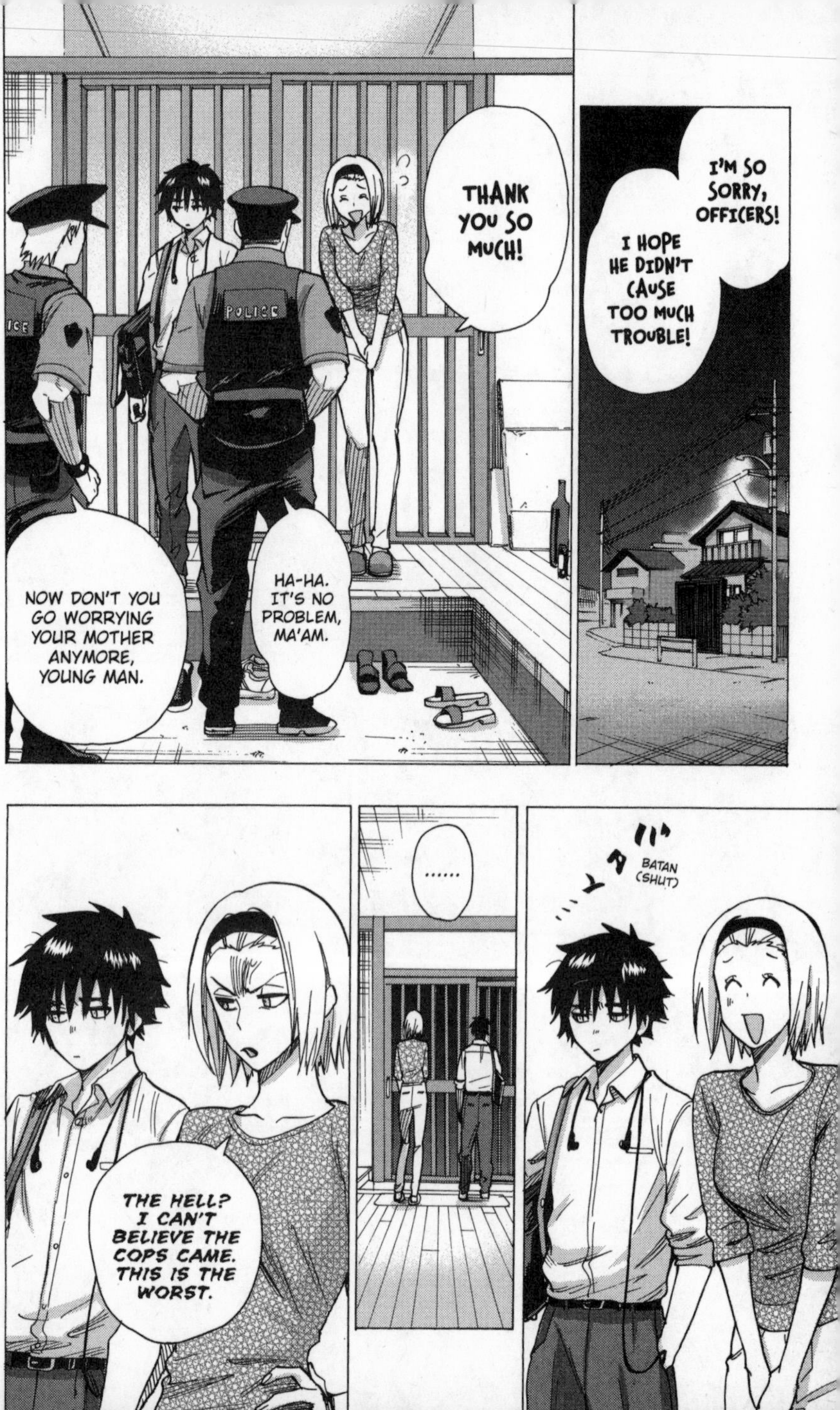
I'M SO SORRY, OFFICERS!
I HOPE HE DIDN'T CAUSE TOO MUCH TROUBLE!
THANK YOU SO MUCH!
HA-HA. IT'S NO PROBLEM, MA'AM.
NOW DON'T YOU GO WORRYING YOUR MOTHER ANYMORE, YOUNG MAN.
BATAN (SHUT)
......
THE HELL? I CAN'T BELIEVE THE COPS CAME. THIS IS THE WORST.

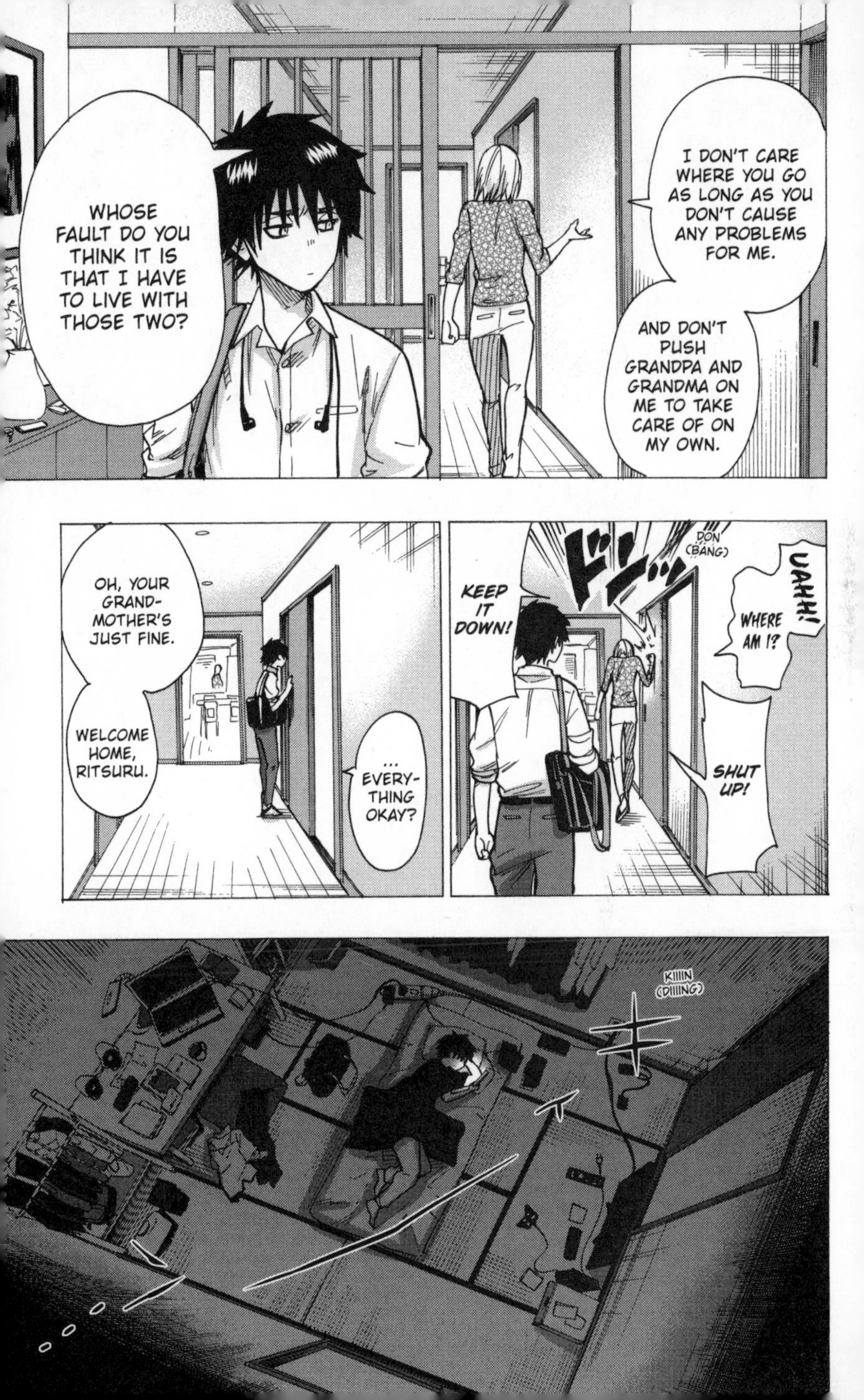
I DON'T CARE WHERE YOU GO AS LONG AS YOU DON'T CAUSE ANY PROBLEMS FOR ME.
AND DON'T PUSH GRANDPA AND GRANDMA ON ME TO TAKE CARE OF ON MY OWN.
WHOSE FAULT DO YOU THINK IT IS THAT I HAVE TO LIVE WITH THOSE TWO?
UAHH!
WHERE AM I!?
DON (BANG)
KEEP IT DOWN!
SHUT UP!
... EVERY-THING OKAY?
OH, YOUR GRAND-MOTHER'S JUST FINE.
WELCOME HOME, RITSURU.
KIIIN (DIIIING)

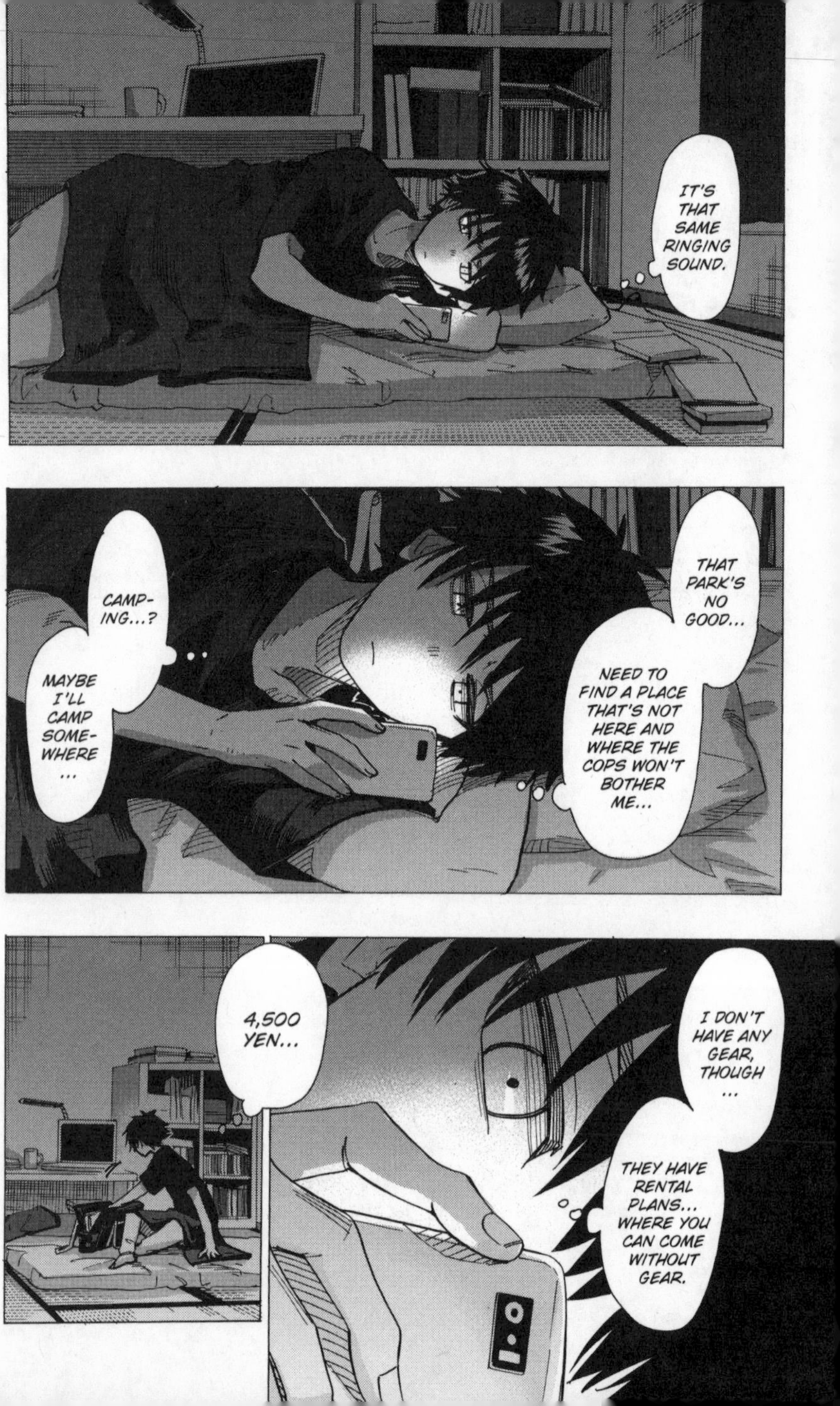
IT'S THAT SAME RINGING SOUND.
THAT PARK'S NO GOOD...
NEED TO FIND A PLACE THAT'S NOT HERE AND WHERE THE COPS WON'T BOTHER ME...
CAMPING...?
MAYBE I'LL CAMP SOMEWHERE...
I DON'T HAVE ANY GEAR, THOUGH...
THEY HAVE RENTAL PLANS... WHERE YOU CAN COME WITHOUT GEAR.
4,500 YEN...

6-05	Card		★100		★10,136★
6-05	Fee		★100		
6-10	Transfer	Keiji Umino	★15,000		★25,136★
6-18	Card		★5,000	Convenience store ATM	

......

6-18	Fee		★100		★20,036★
6-20	Phone		★8,617		★11,399★
7-01	Card		★3,000	Convenience store ATM	
7-01	Fee		★100		★8,299★
	Transfer	Keiji Umino	★15,000		★23,299★

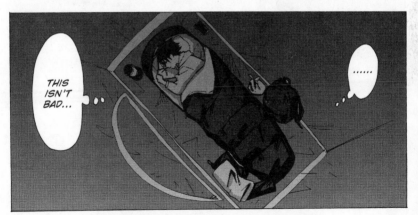

THIS ISN'T BAD...

......

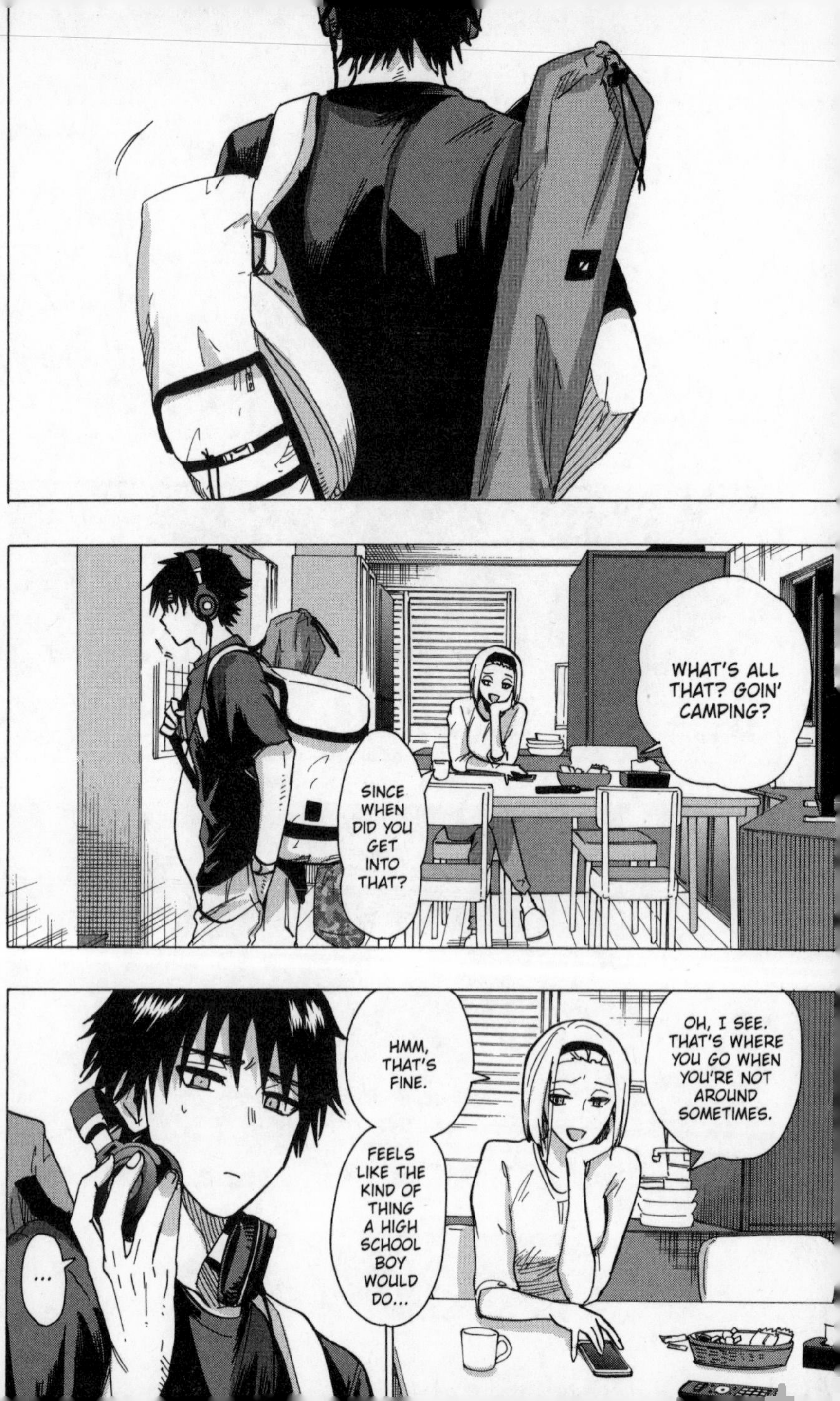
WHAT'S ALL THAT? GOIN' CAMPING?
SINCE WHEN DID YOU GET INTO THAT?
OH, I SEE. THAT'S WHERE YOU GO WHEN YOU'RE NOT AROUND SOMETIMES.
HMM, THAT'S FINE.
FEELS LIKE THE KIND OF THING A HIGH SCHOOL BOY WOULD DO...
...

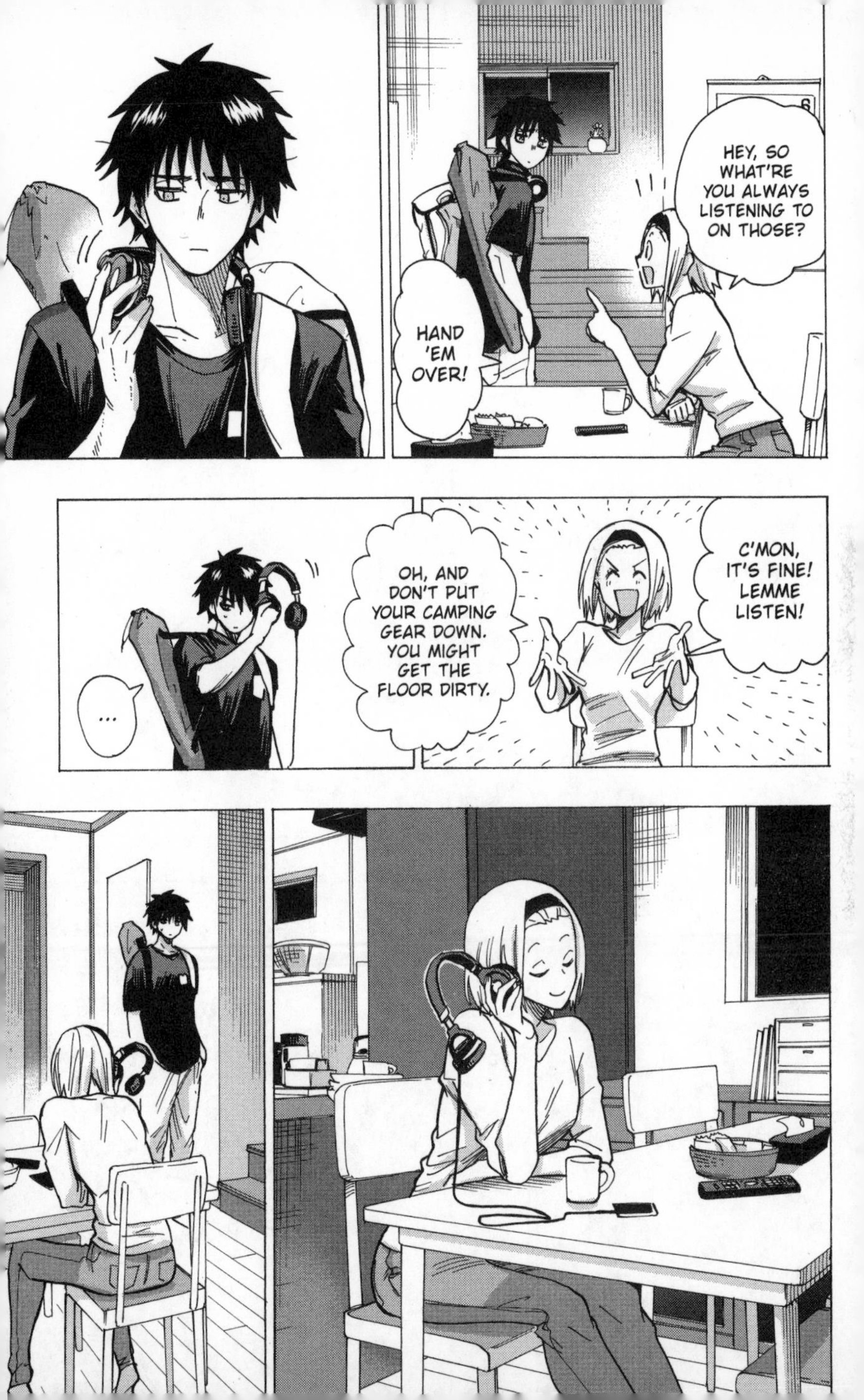
HEY, SO WHAT'RE YOU ALWAYS LISTENING TO ON THOSE?
HAND 'EM OVER!
C'MON, IT'S FINE! LEMME LISTEN!
OH, AND DON'T PUT YOUR CAMPING GEAR DOWN. YOU MIGHT GET THE FLOOR DIRTY.
...

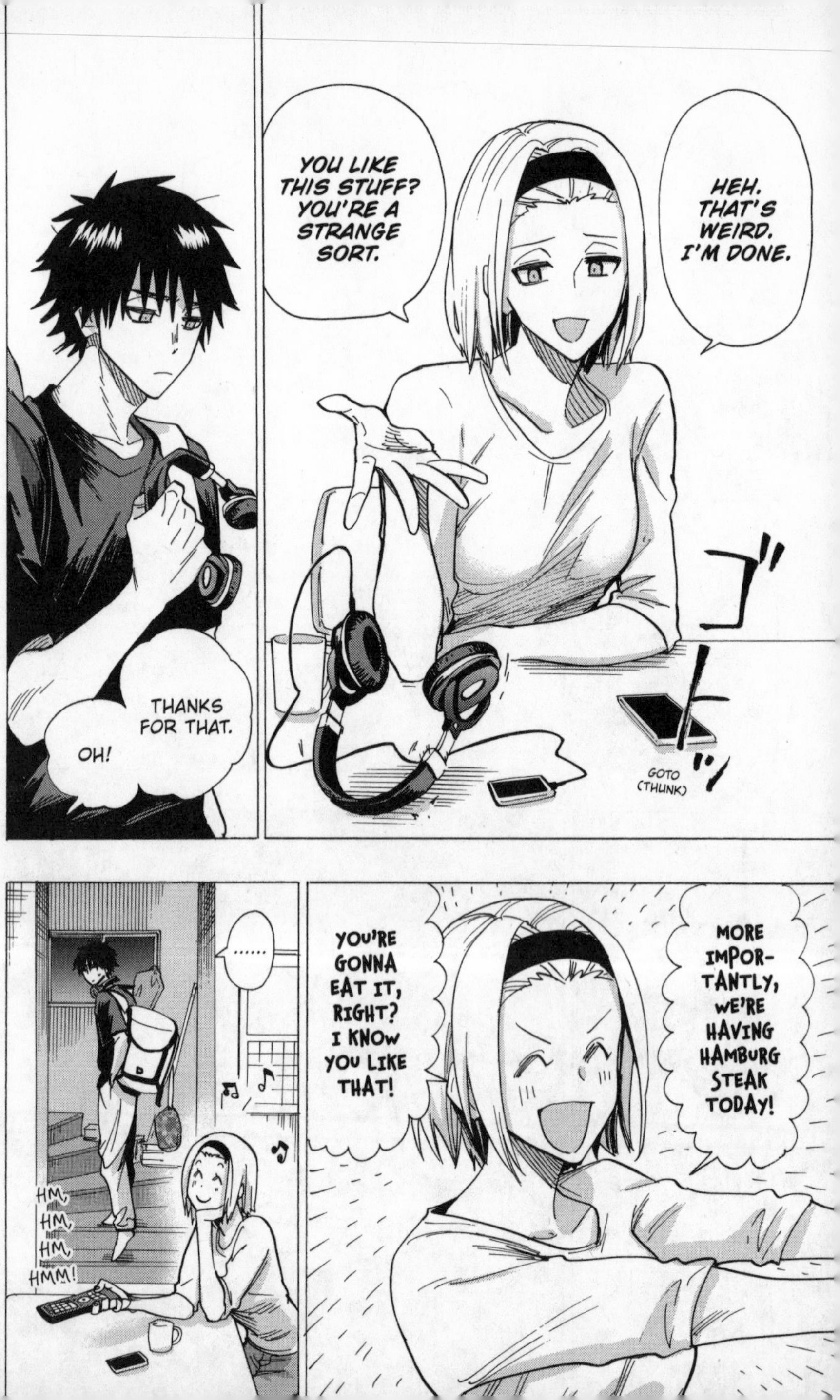
HEH. THAT'S WEIRD. I'M DONE.
YOU LIKE THIS STUFF? YOU'RE A STRANGE SORT.
GOTO (THUNK)
OH! THANKS FOR THAT.
MORE IMPOR-TANTLY, WE'RE HAVING HAMBURG STEAK TODAY!
YOU'RE GONNA EAT IT, RIGHT? I KNOW YOU LIKE THAT!
......
HM, HM, HM, HMM!

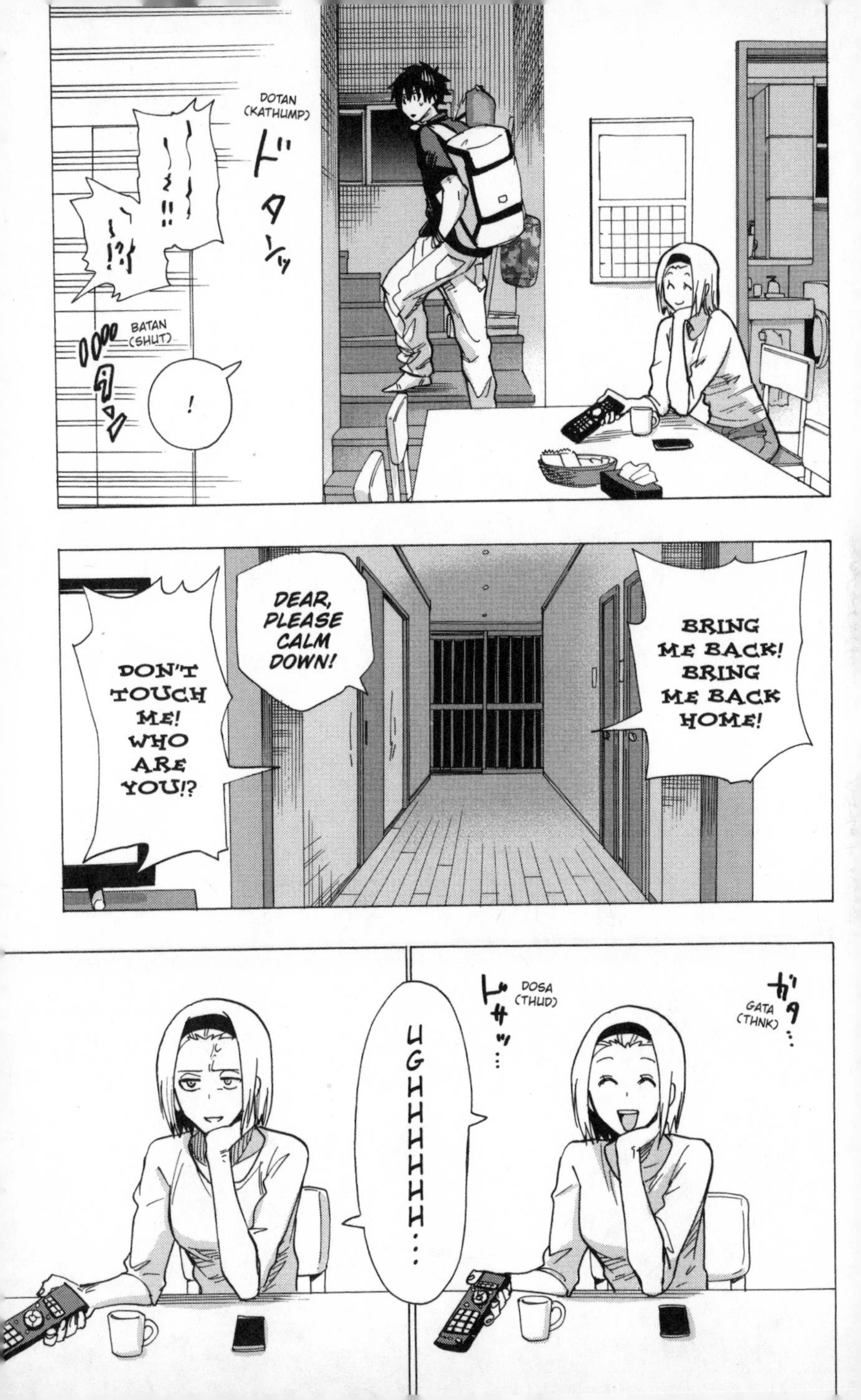
DOTAN (KATHUMP)
ドタンッ
!
BATAN (SHUT)
BRING ME BACK! BRING ME BACK HOME!
DEAR, PLEASE CALM DOWN!
DON'T TOUCH ME! WHO ARE YOU!?
GATA (THNK)
DOSA (THUD)
UGHHHHHH...

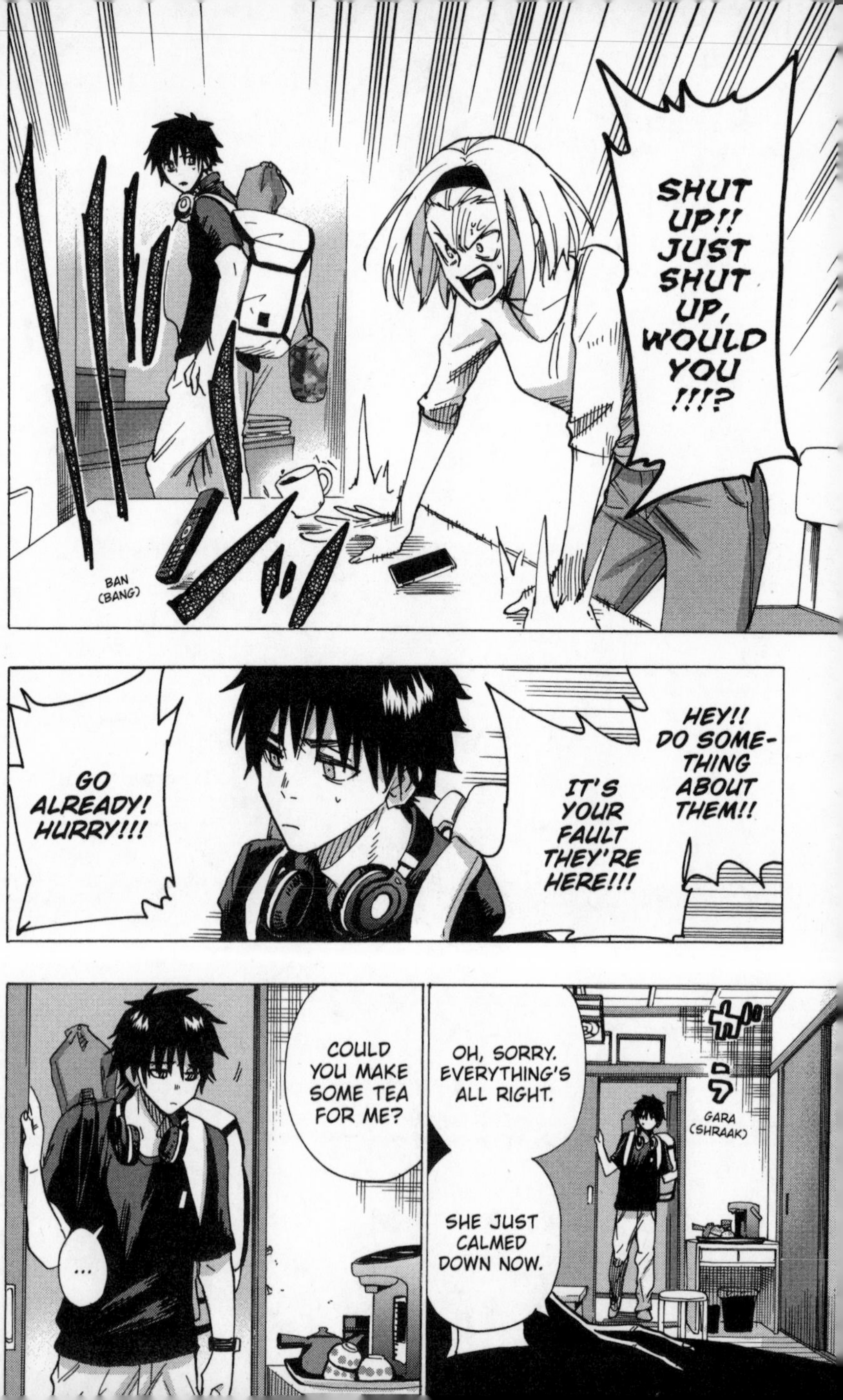
SHUT UP!! JUST SHUT UP, WOULD YOU!!!?
BAN (BANG)
HEY!! DO SOME-THING ABOUT THEM!!
IT'S YOUR FAULT THEY'RE HERE!!!
GO ALREADY! HURRY!!!
GARA (SHRAAK)
OH, SORRY. EVERYTHING'S ALL RIGHT.
SHE JUST CALMED DOWN NOW.
COULD YOU MAKE SOME TEA FOR ME?
...

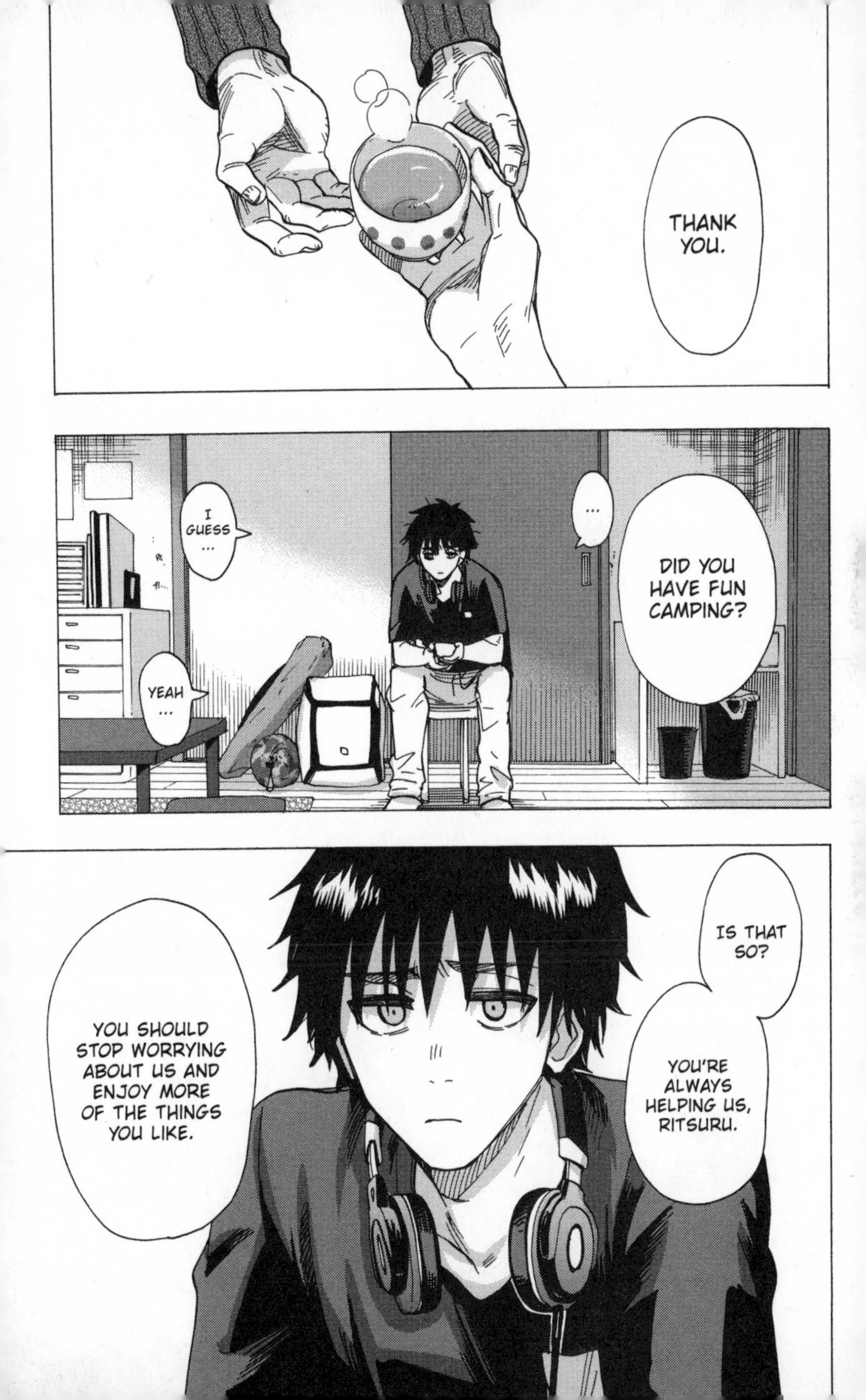
THANK YOU.
...
DID YOU HAVE FUN CAMPING?
I GUESS...
YEAH...
IS THAT SO?
YOU'RE ALWAYS HELPING US, RITSURU.
YOU SHOULD STOP WORRYING ABOUT US AND ENJOY MORE OF THE THINGS YOU LIKE.

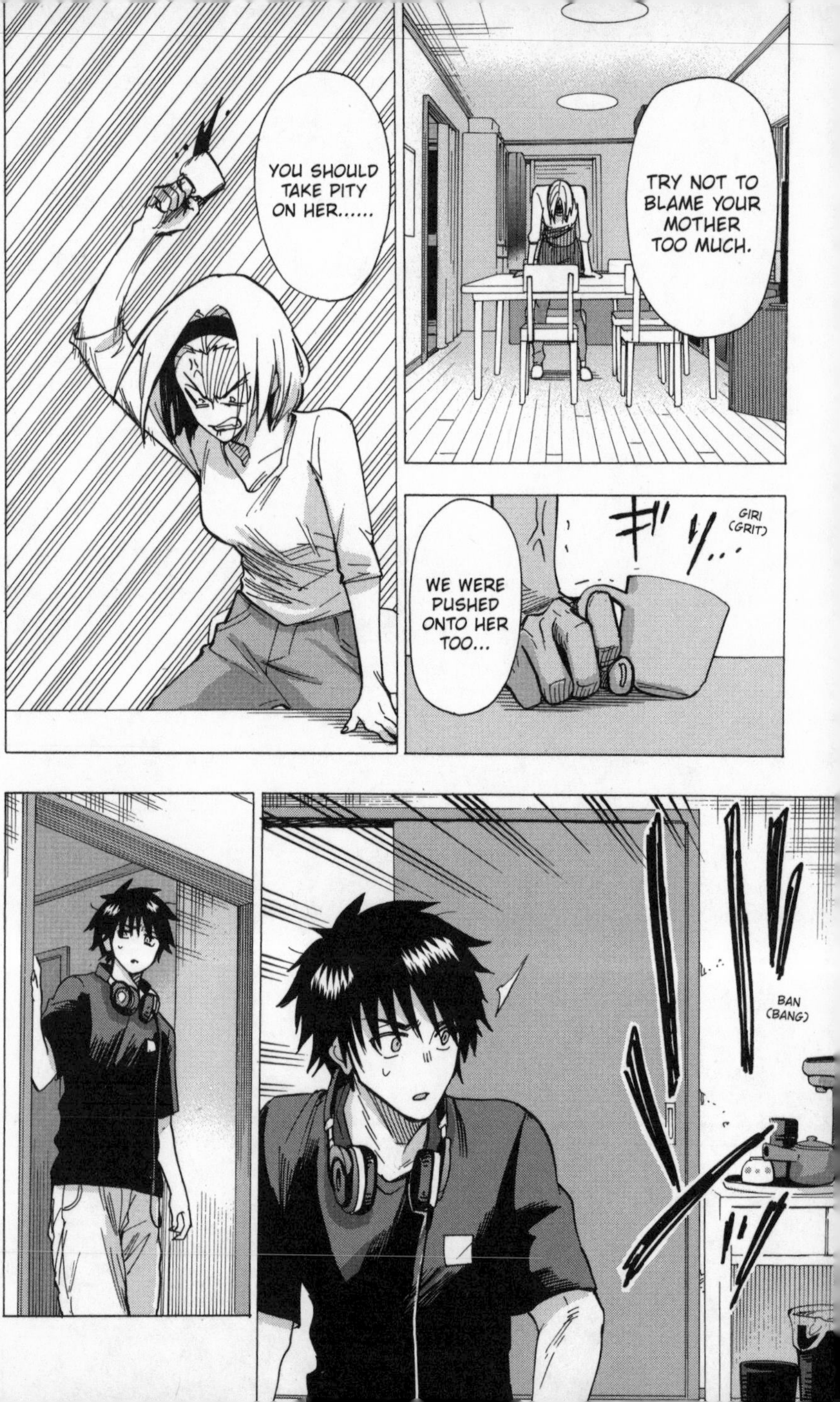
TRY NOT TO BLAME YOUR MOTHER TOO MUCH.
WE WERE PUSHED ONTO HER TOO...
GIRI (GRIT)
YOU SHOULD TAKE PITY ON HER......
BAN (BANG)

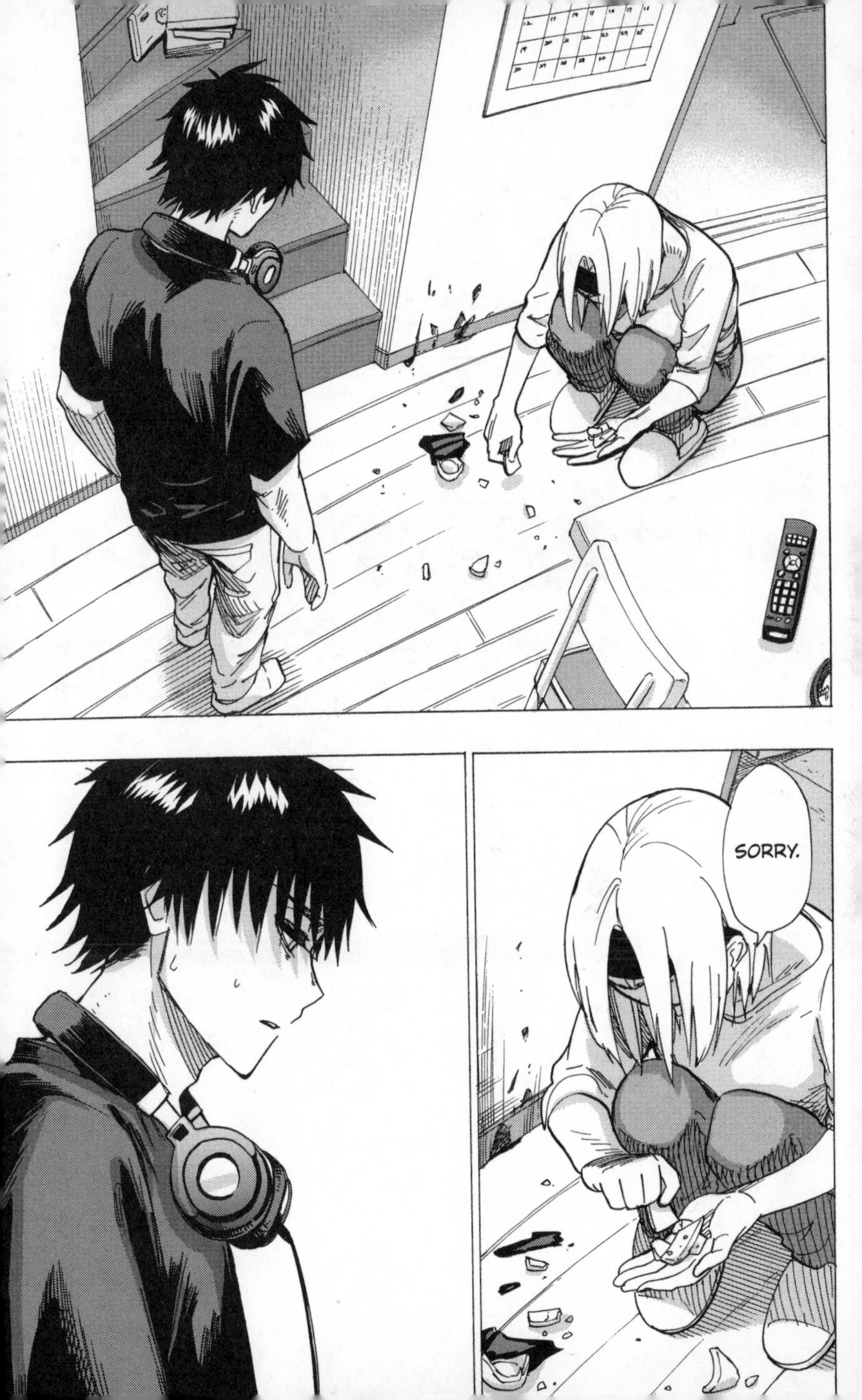
SORRY.

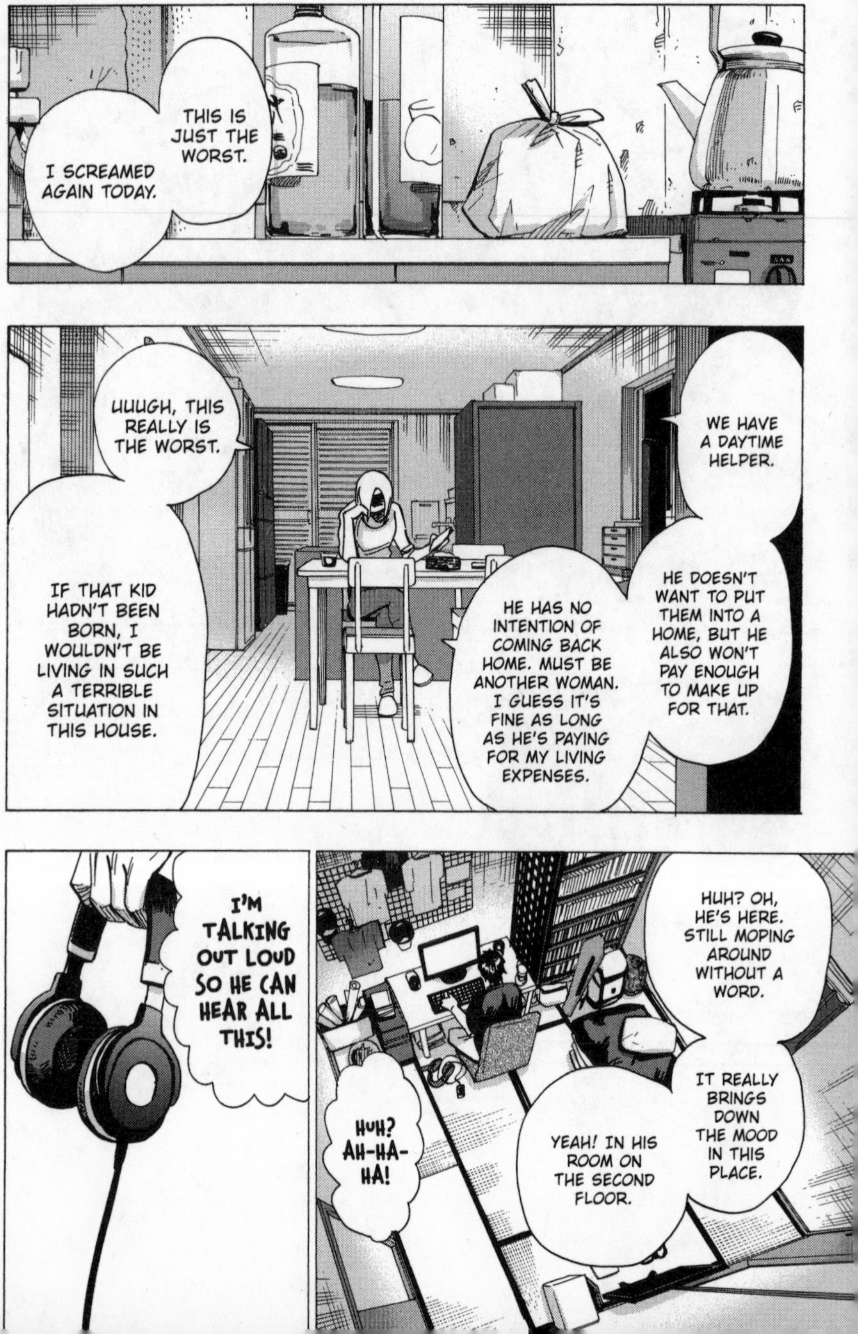
THIS IS JUST THE WORST.
I SCREAMED AGAIN TODAY.
WE HAVE A DAYTIME HELPER.
HE DOESN'T WANT TO PUT THEM INTO A HOME, BUT HE ALSO WON'T PAY ENOUGH TO MAKE UP FOR THAT.
HE HAS NO INTENTION OF COMING BACK HOME. MUST BE ANOTHER WOMAN. I GUESS IT'S FINE AS LONG AS HE'S PAYING FOR MY LIVING EXPENSES.
UUUGH, THIS REALLY IS THE WORST.
IF THAT KID HADN'T BEEN BORN, I WOULDN'T BE LIVING IN SUCH A TERRIBLE SITUATION IN THIS HOUSE.
HUH? OH, HE'S HERE. STILL MOPING AROUND WITHOUT A WORD.
IT REALLY BRINGS DOWN THE MOOD IN THIS PLACE.
YEAH! IN HIS ROOM ON THE SECOND FLOOR.
HUH? AH-HA-HA!
I'M TALKING OUT LOUD SO HE CAN HEAR ALL THIS!

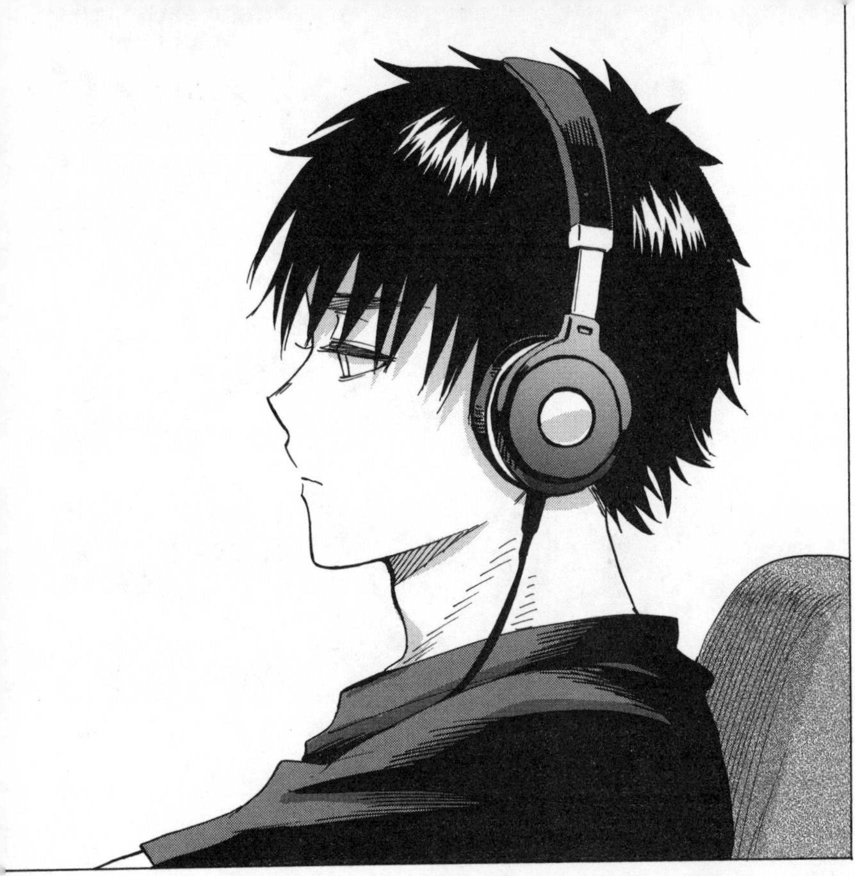

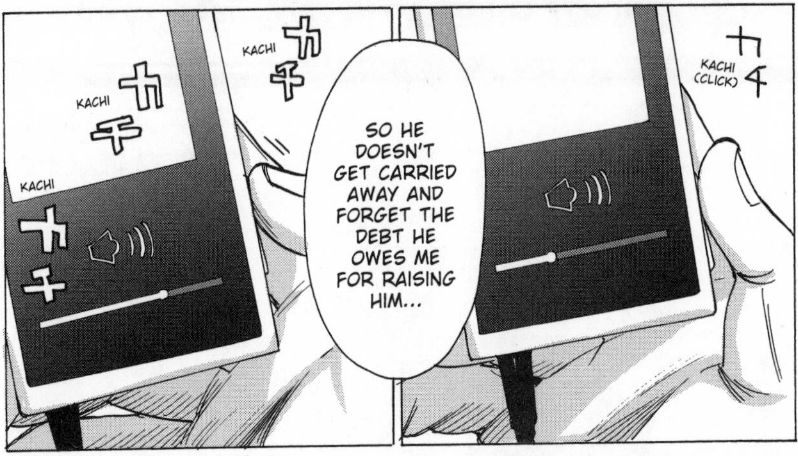
KACHI (CLICK)
SO HE DOESN'T GET CARRIED AWAY AND FORGET THE DEBT HE OWES ME FOR RAISING HIM...
KACHI
KACHI
KACHI

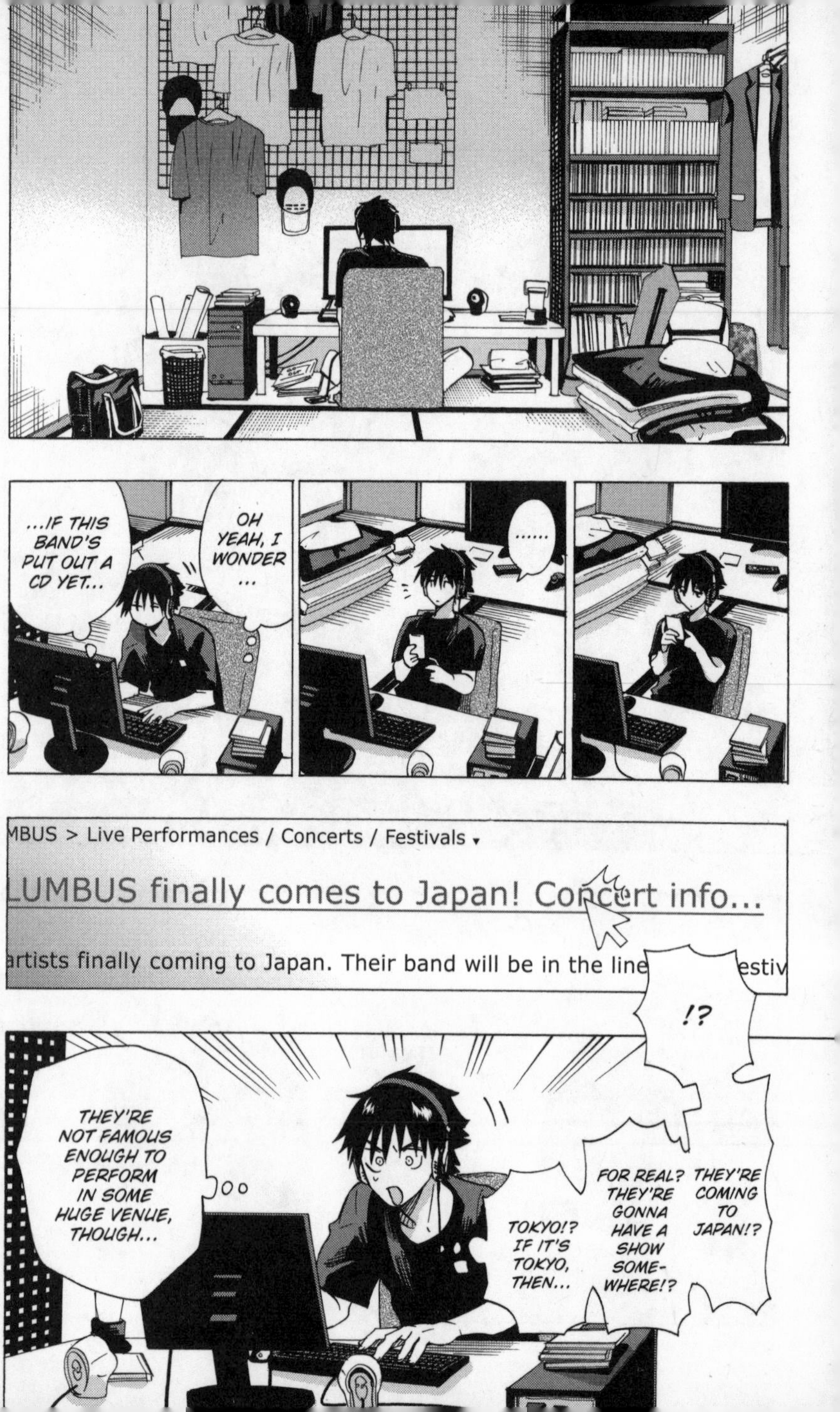
......
OH YEAH, I WONDER ...
...IF THIS BAND'S PUT OUT A CD YET...
MBUS > Live Performances / Concerts / Festivals
LUMBUS finally comes to Japan! Concert info...
artists finally coming to Japan. Their band will be in the line
!?
THEY'RE COMING TO JAPAN!?
FOR REAL? THEY'RE GONNA HAVE A SHOW SOME-WHERE!?
TOKYO!? IF IT'S TOKYO, THEN...
THEY'RE NOT FAMOUS ENOUGH TO PERFORM IN SOME HUGE VENUE, THOUGH...

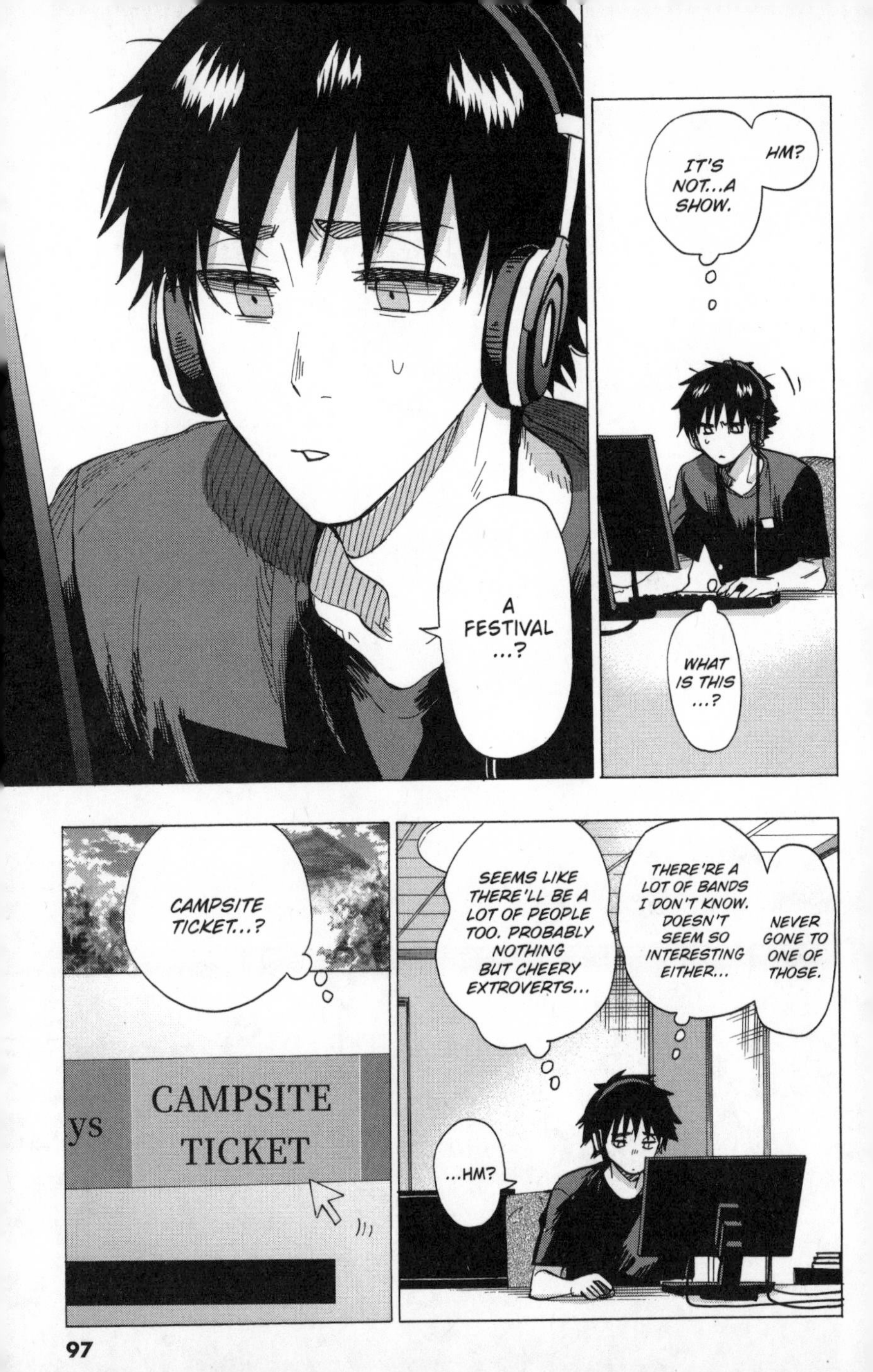
HM?
IT'S NOT...A SHOW.
WHAT IS THIS ...?
A FESTIVAL ...?
NEVER GONE TO ONE OF THOSE.
THERE'RE A LOT OF BANDS I DON'T KNOW. DOESN'T SEEM SO INTERESTING EITHER...
SEEMS LIKE THERE'LL BE A LOT OF PEOPLE TOO. PROBABLY NOTHING BUT CHEERY EXTROVERTS...
...HM?
CAMPSITE TICKET...?
ys
CAMPSITE TICKET

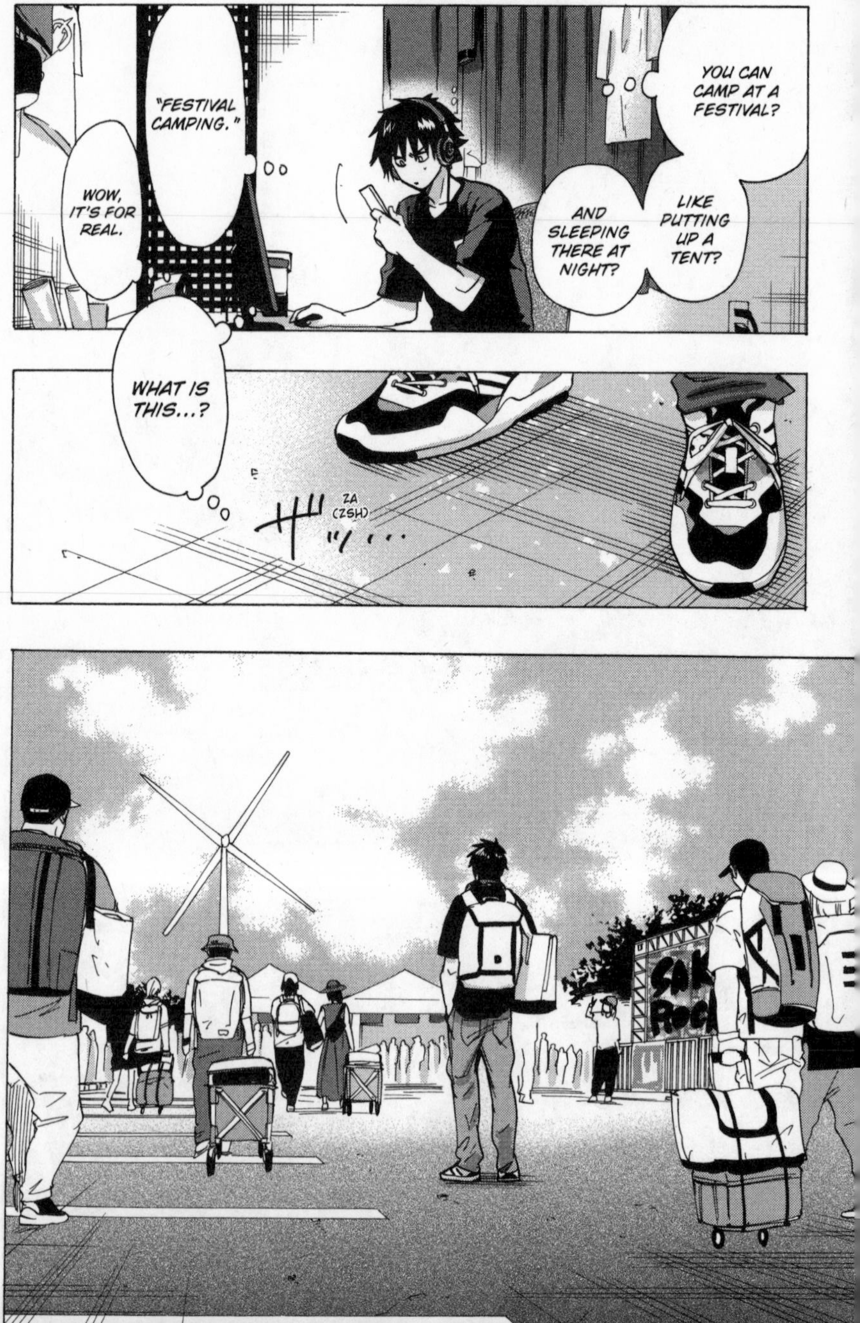
YOU CAN CAMP AT A FESTIVAL?
LIKE PUTTING UP A TENT?
AND SLEEPING THERE AT NIGHT?
"FESTIVAL CAMPING."
WOW, IT'S FOR REAL.
WHAT IS THIS...?
ZA (ZSH)

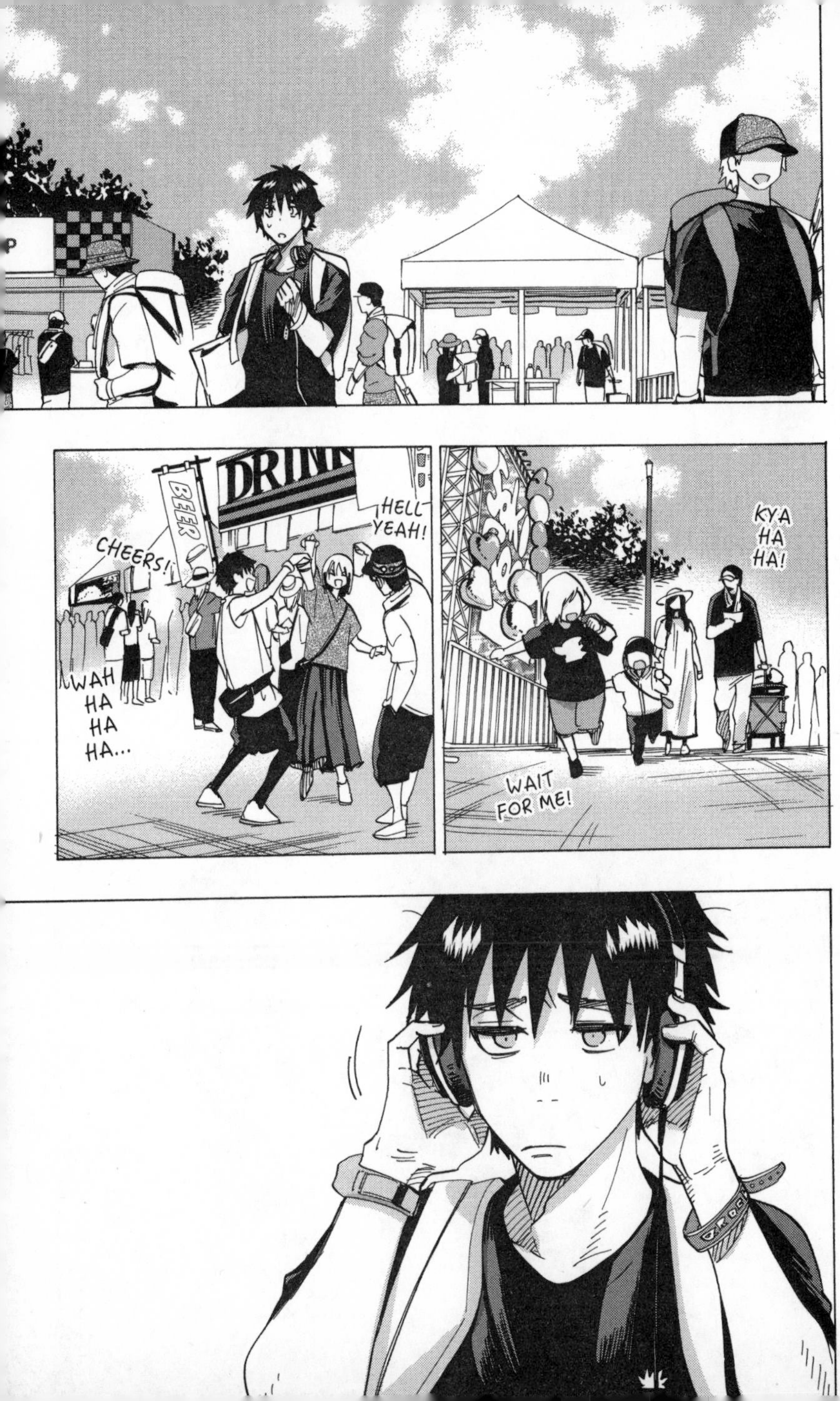
KYA HA HA!
WAIT FOR ME!
DRINK
BEER
HELL YEAH!
CHEERS!
WAH HA HA HA...

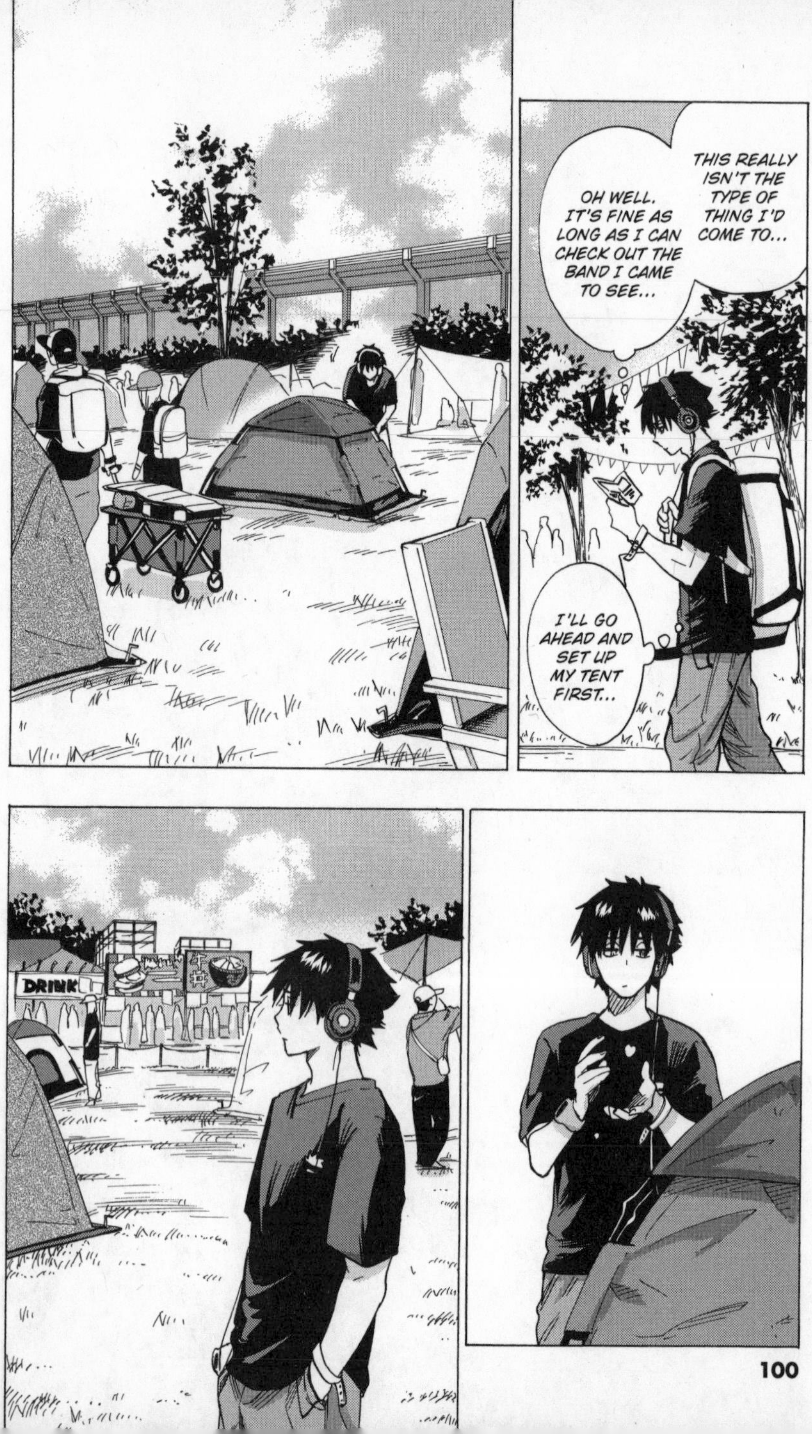
THIS REALLY ISN'T THE TYPE OF THING I'D COME TO...
OH WELL. IT'S FINE AS LONG AS I CAN CHECK OUT THE BAND I CAME TO SEE...
I'LL GO AHEAD AND SET UP MY TENT FIRST...
DRINK

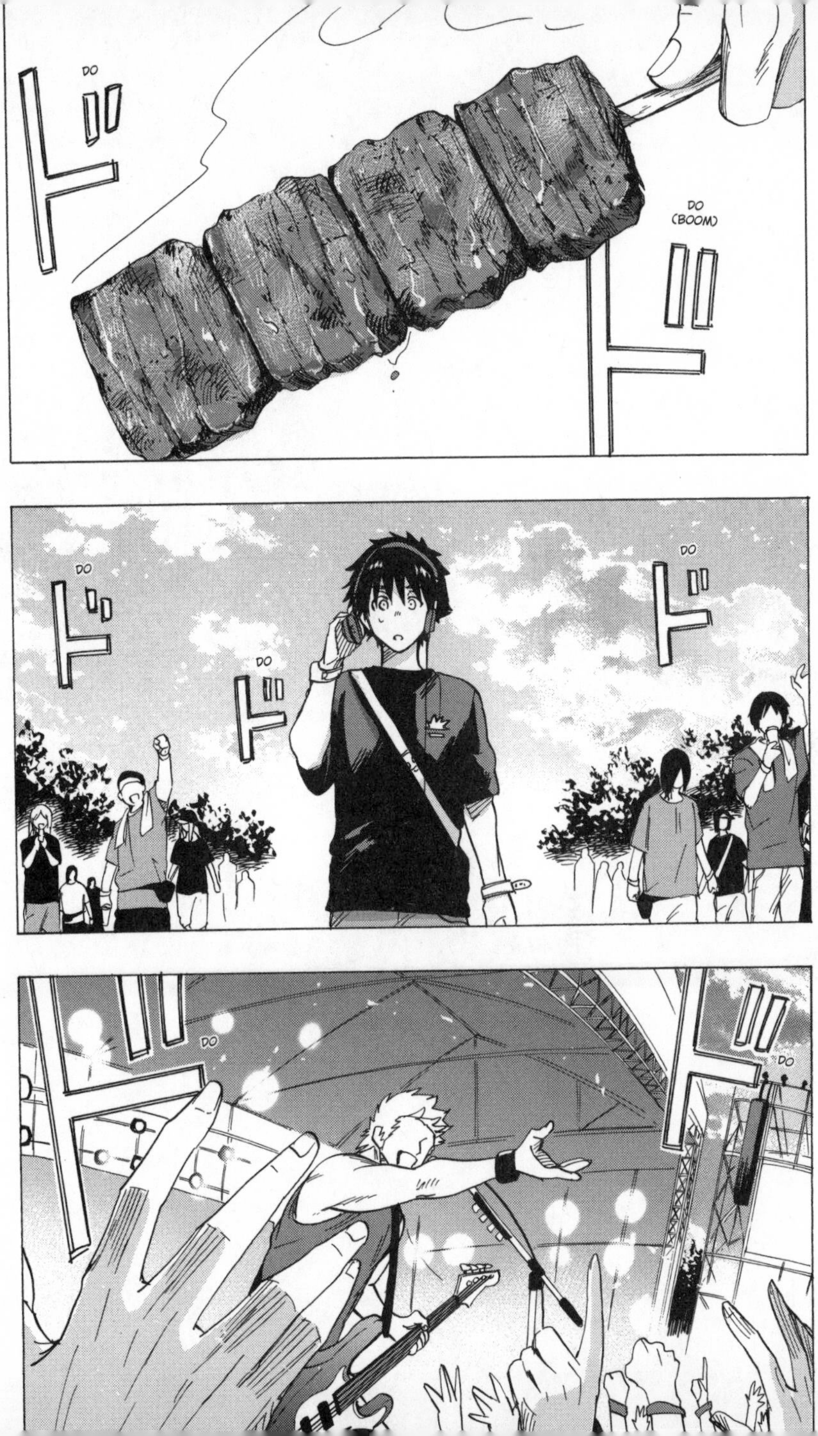
DO (BOOM)
DO
DO
DO
DO
DO
DO

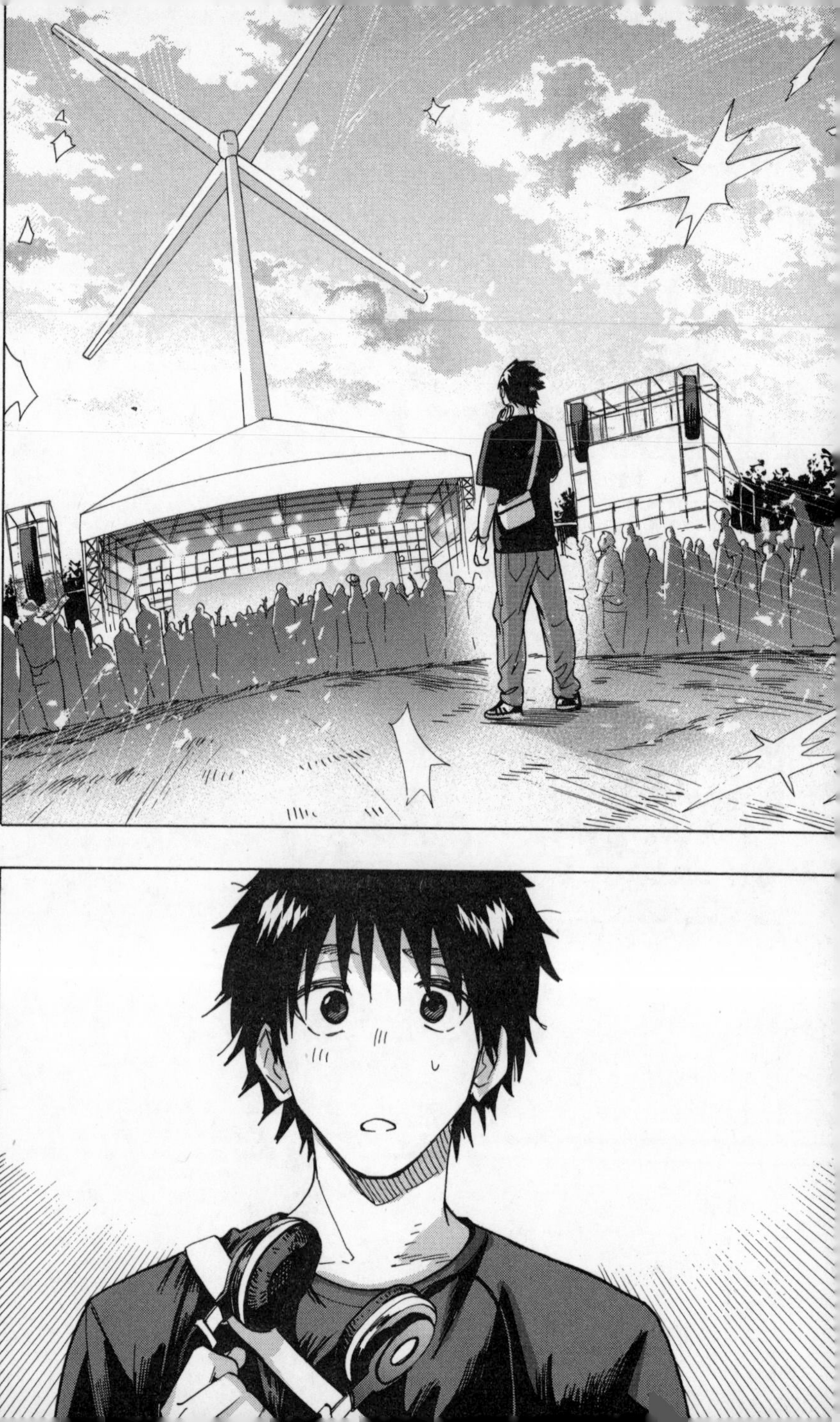

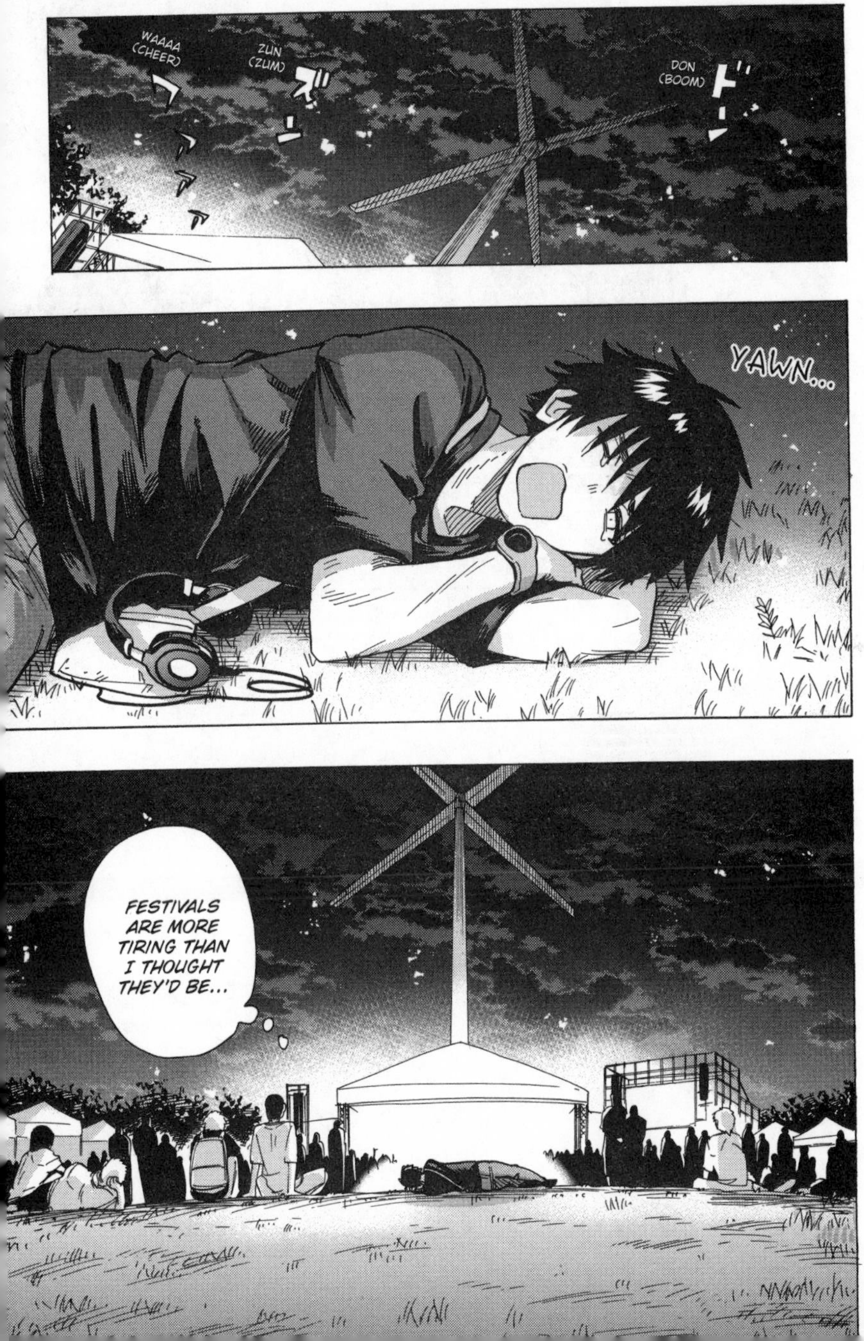
DON (BOOM)
ZUN (ZUM)
WAAAA (CHEER)
YAWN...
FESTIVALS ARE MORE TIRING THAN I THOUGHT THEY'D BE...

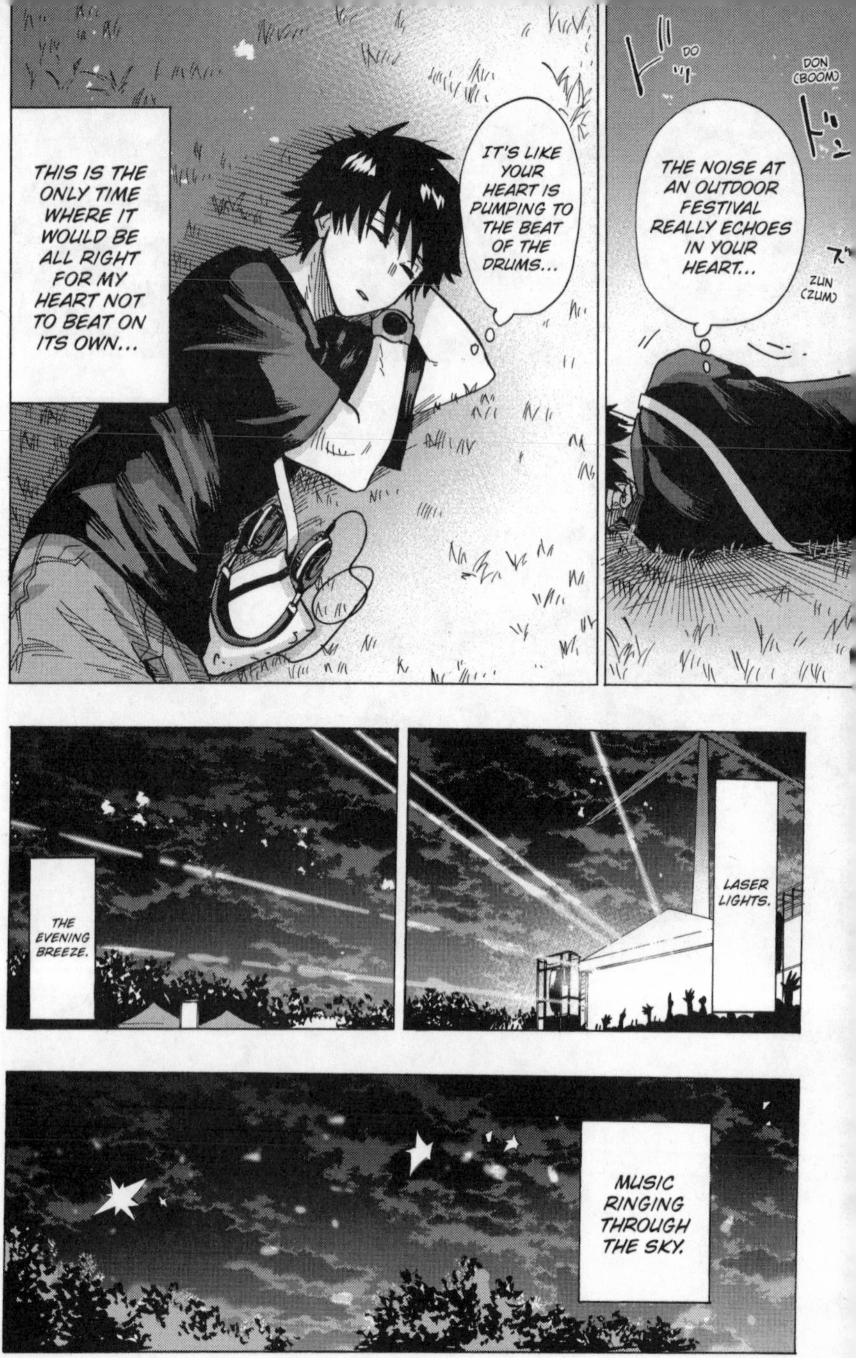
DON (BOOM)
DO
THE NOISE AT AN OUTDOOR FESTIVAL REALLY ECHOES IN YOUR HEART...
ZUN (ZUM)
IT'S LIKE YOUR HEART IS PUMPING TO THE BEAT OF THE DRUMS...
THIS IS THE ONLY TIME WHERE IT WOULD BE ALL RIGHT FOR MY HEART NOT TO BEAT ON ITS OWN...
LASER LIGHTS.
THE EVENING BREEZE.
MUSIC RINGING THROUGH THE SKY.

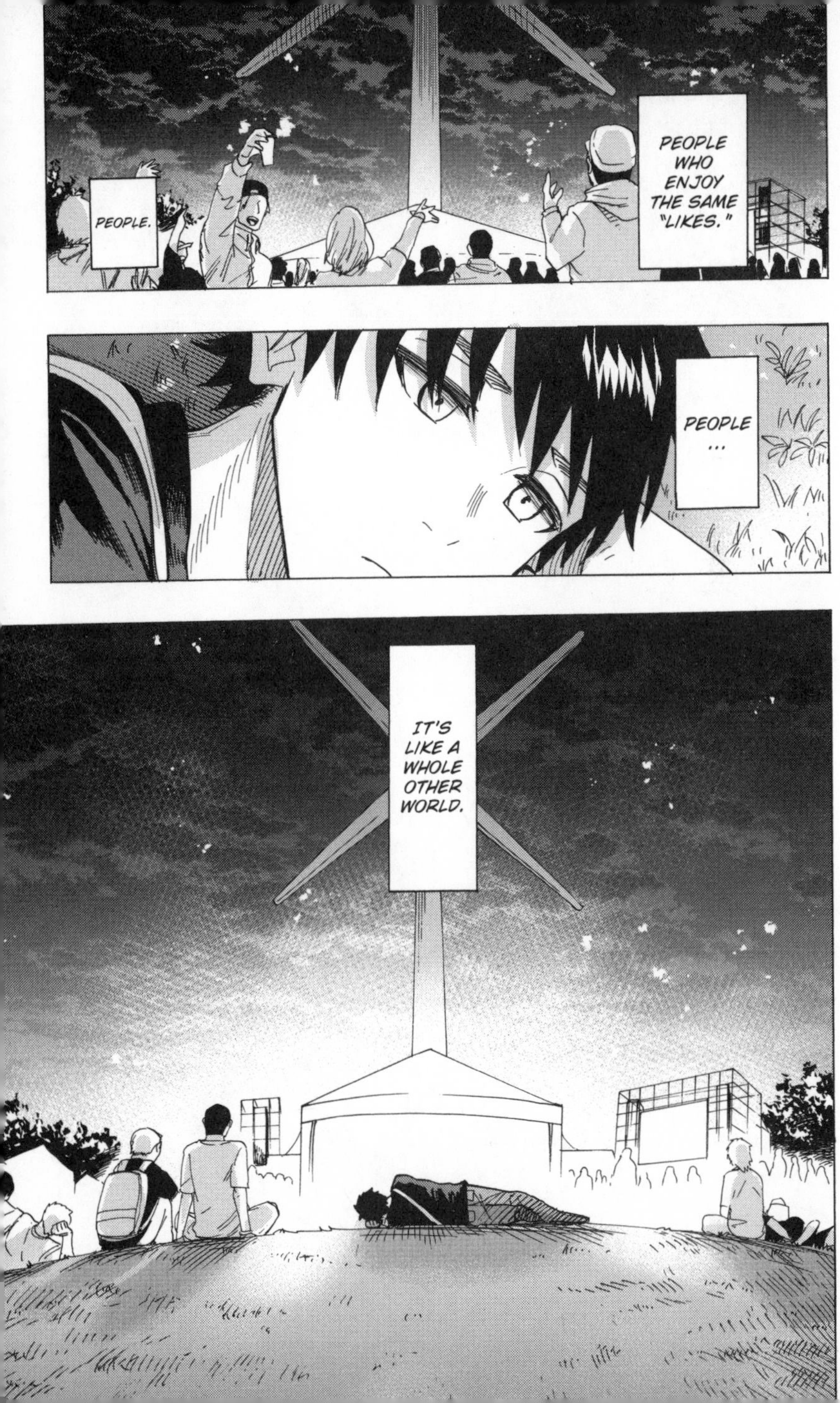
PEOPLE WHO ENJOY THE SAME "LIKES."
PEOPLE.
PEOPLE ...
IT'S LIKE A WHOLE OTHER WORLD.

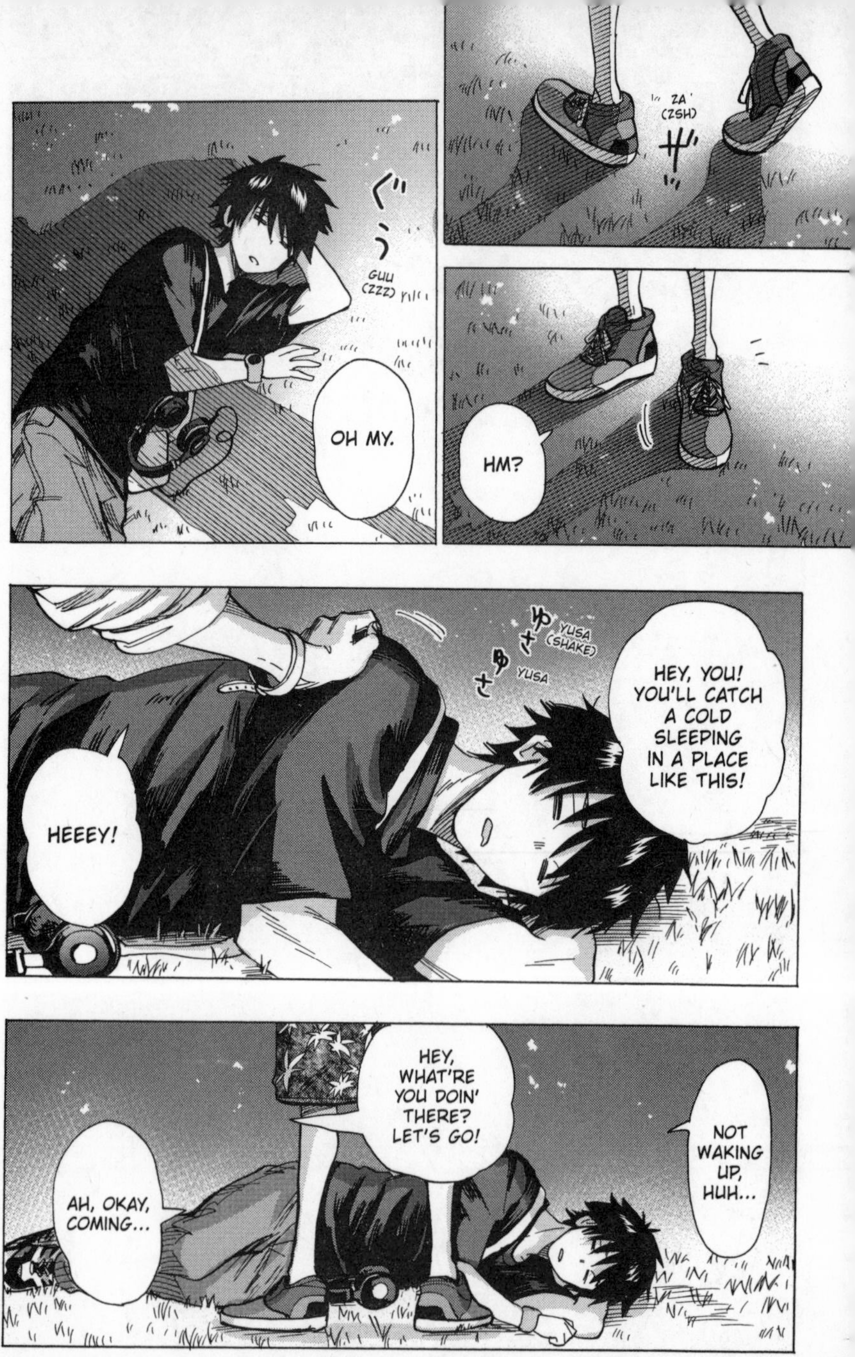
ザッ
ZA (ZSH)
HM?
ぐう
GUU (ZZZ)
OH MY.
ゆさ ゆさ
YUSA (SHAKE)
YUSA
HEY, YOU! YOU'LL CATCH A COLD SLEEPING IN A PLACE LIKE THIS!
HEEEY!
NOT WAKING UP, HUH...
HEY, WHAT'RE YOU DOIN' THERE? LET'S GO!
AH, OKAY, COMING...

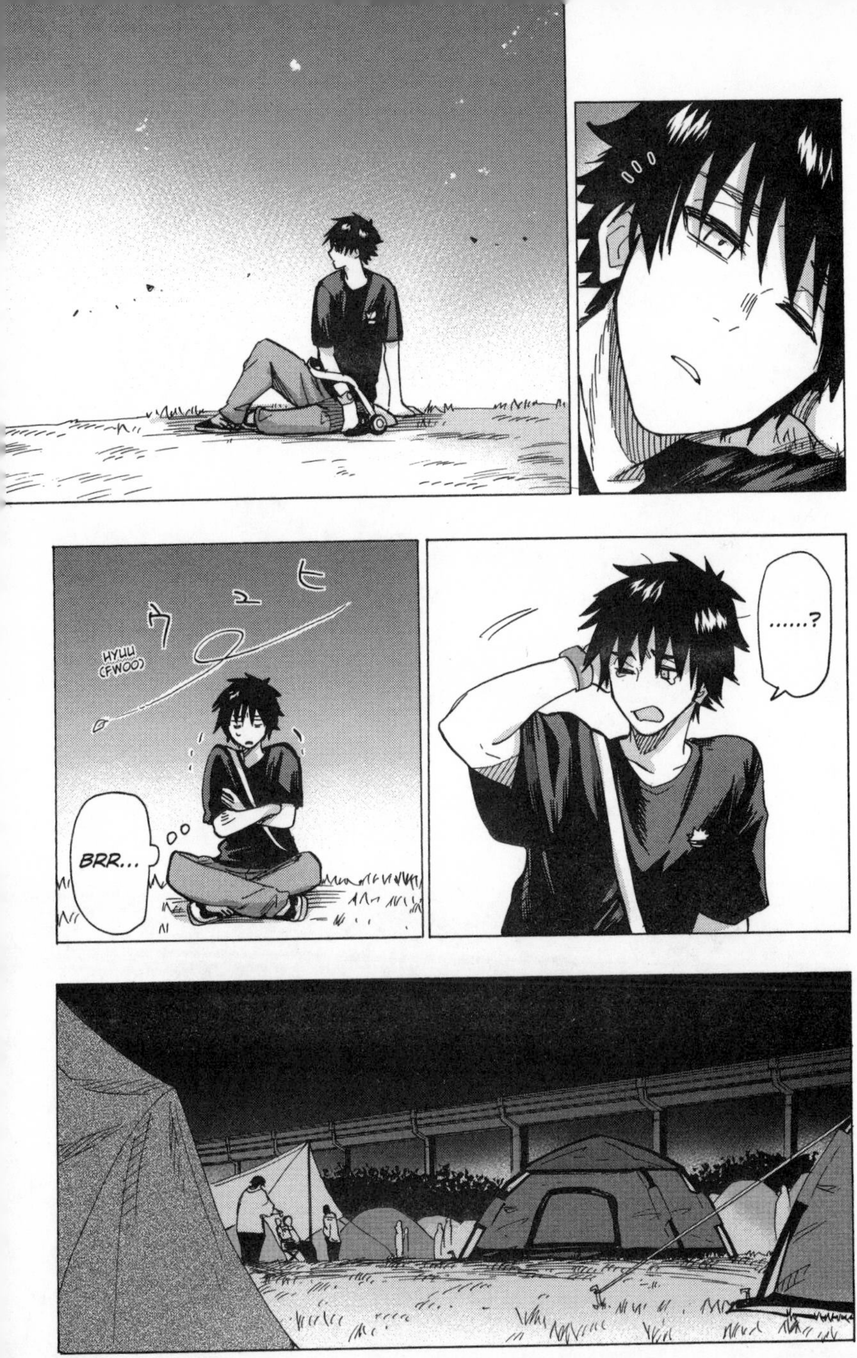
......?
ヒュウ
HYUU (FWOO)
BRR...

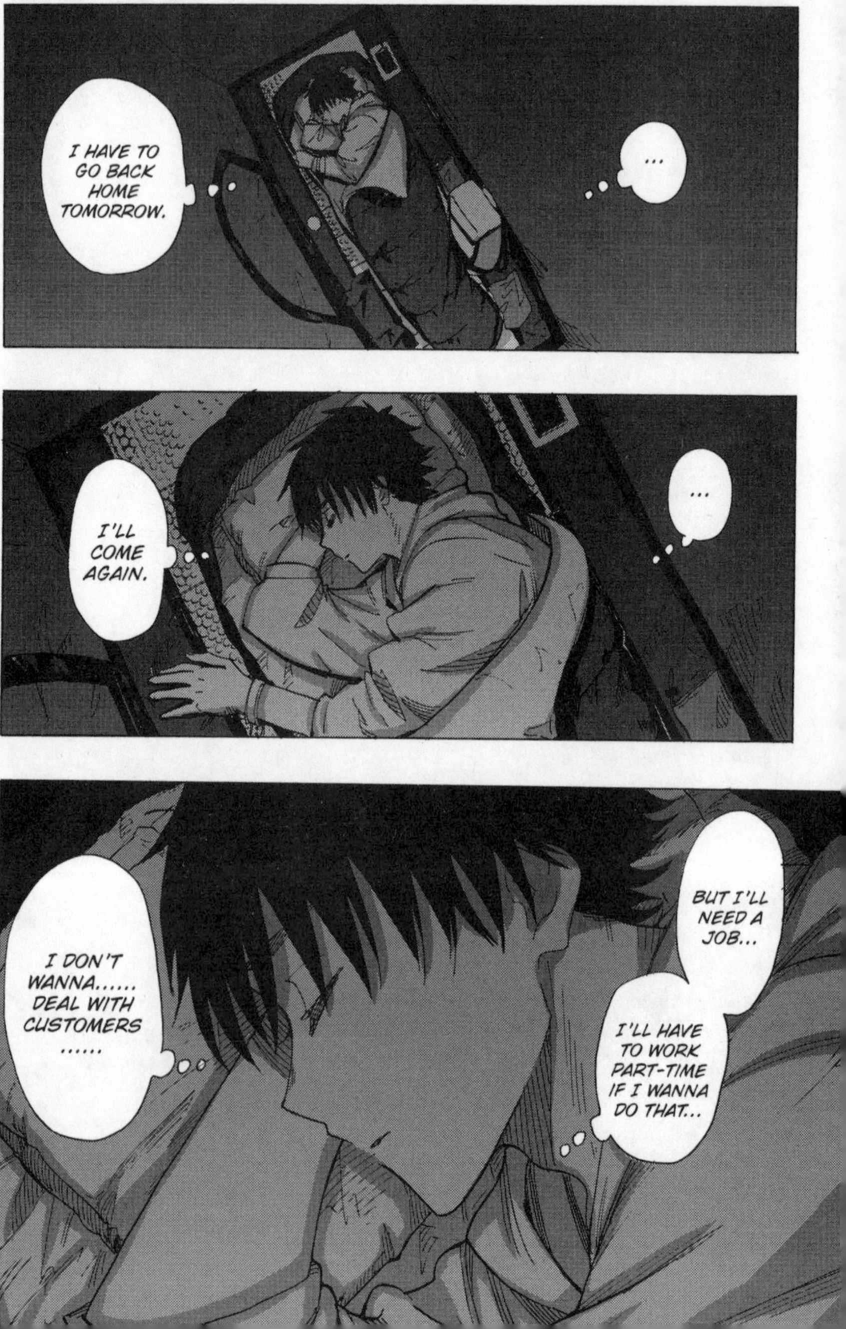
...
I HAVE TO GO BACK HOME TOMORROW.
...
I'LL COME AGAIN.
BUT I'LL NEED A JOB...
I'LL HAVE TO WORK PART-TIME IF I WANNA DO THAT...
I DON'T WANNA...... DEAL WITH CUSTOMERS ......

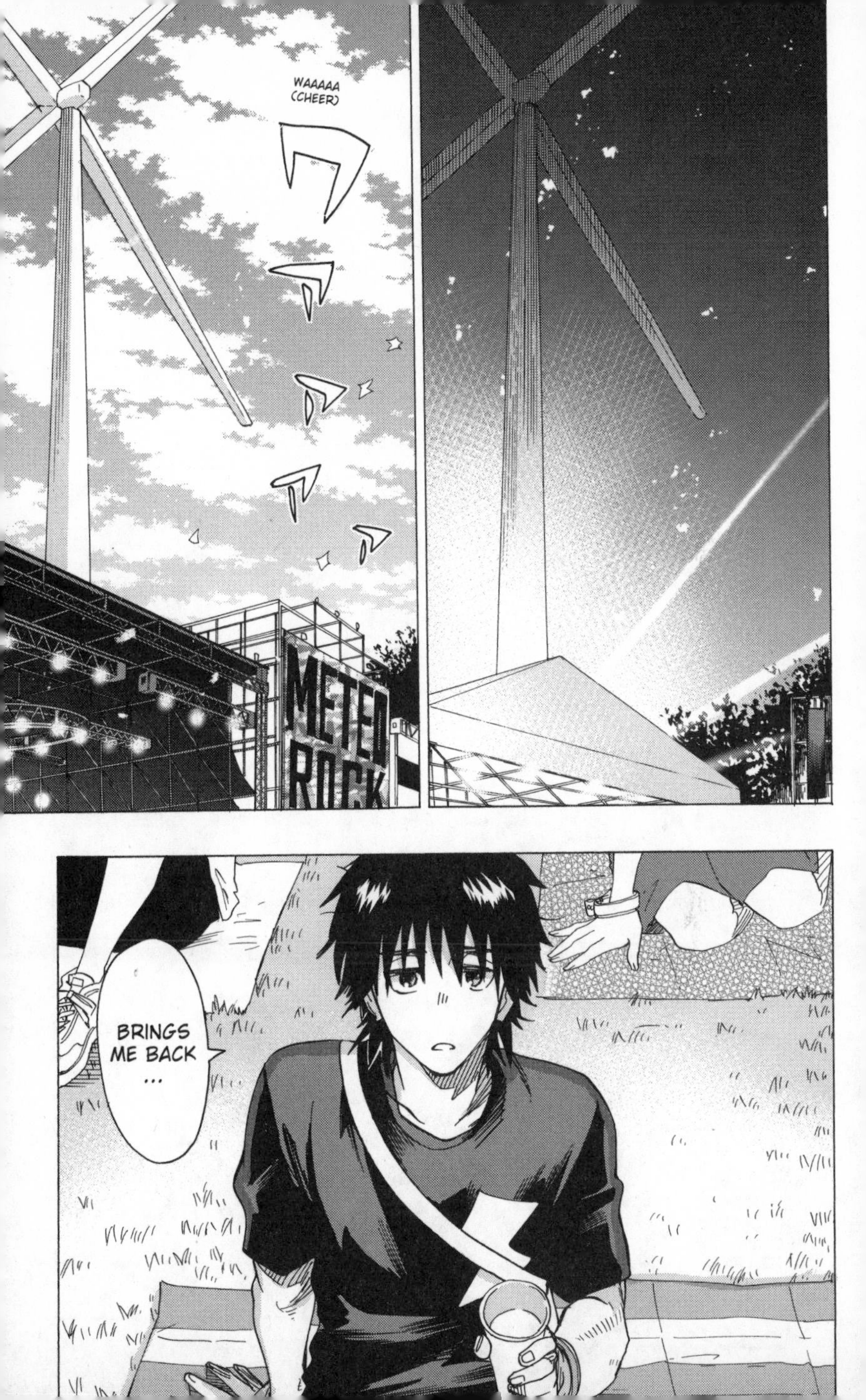
WAAAAA (CHEER)
ワァァァァ
METEO ROCK
BRINGS ME BACK ...

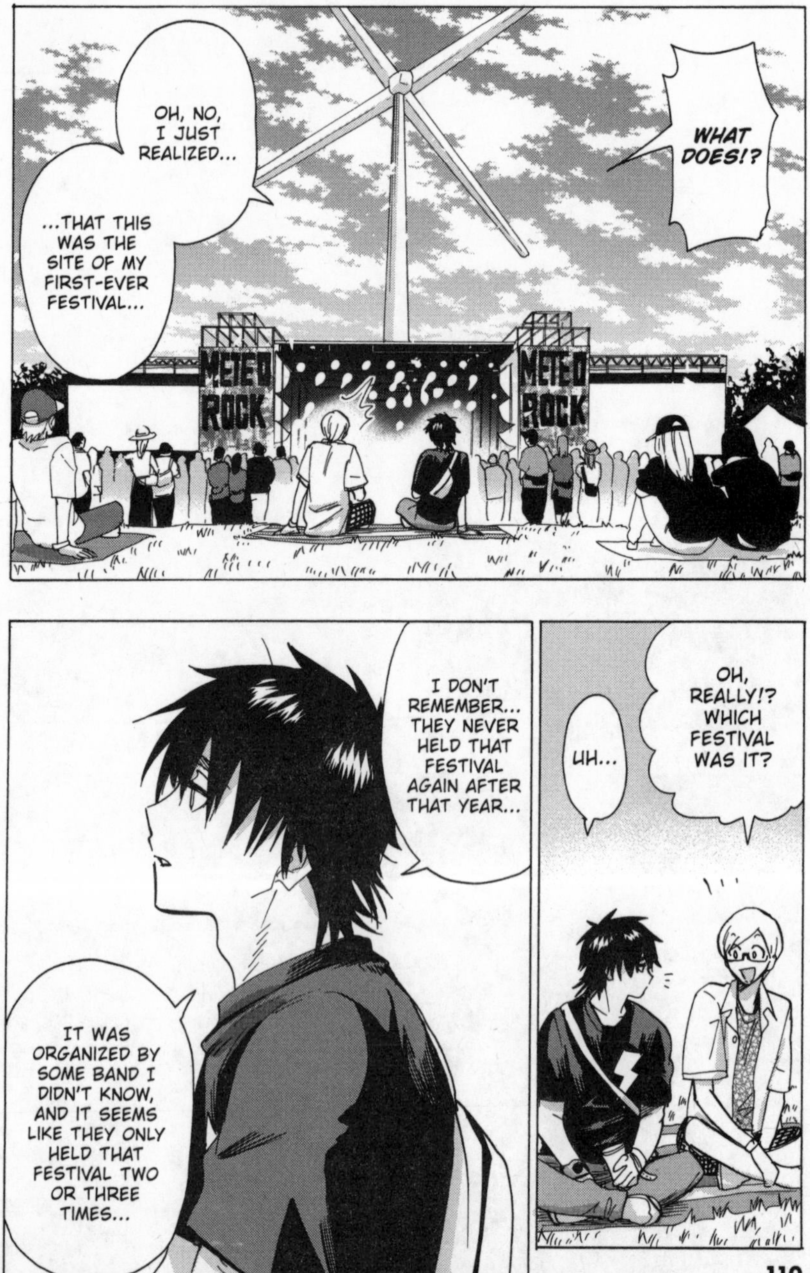
WHAT DOES!?
OH, NO, I JUST REALIZED...
...THAT THIS WAS THE SITE OF MY FIRST-EVER FESTIVAL...
METEO ROCK
METEO ROCK
OH, REALLY!? WHICH FESTIVAL WAS IT?
UH...
I DON'T REMEMBER... THEY NEVER HELD THAT FESTIVAL AGAIN AFTER THAT YEAR...
IT WAS ORGANIZED BY SOME BAND I DIDN'T KNOW, AND IT SEEMS LIKE THEY ONLY HELD THAT FESTIVAL TWO OR THREE TIMES...

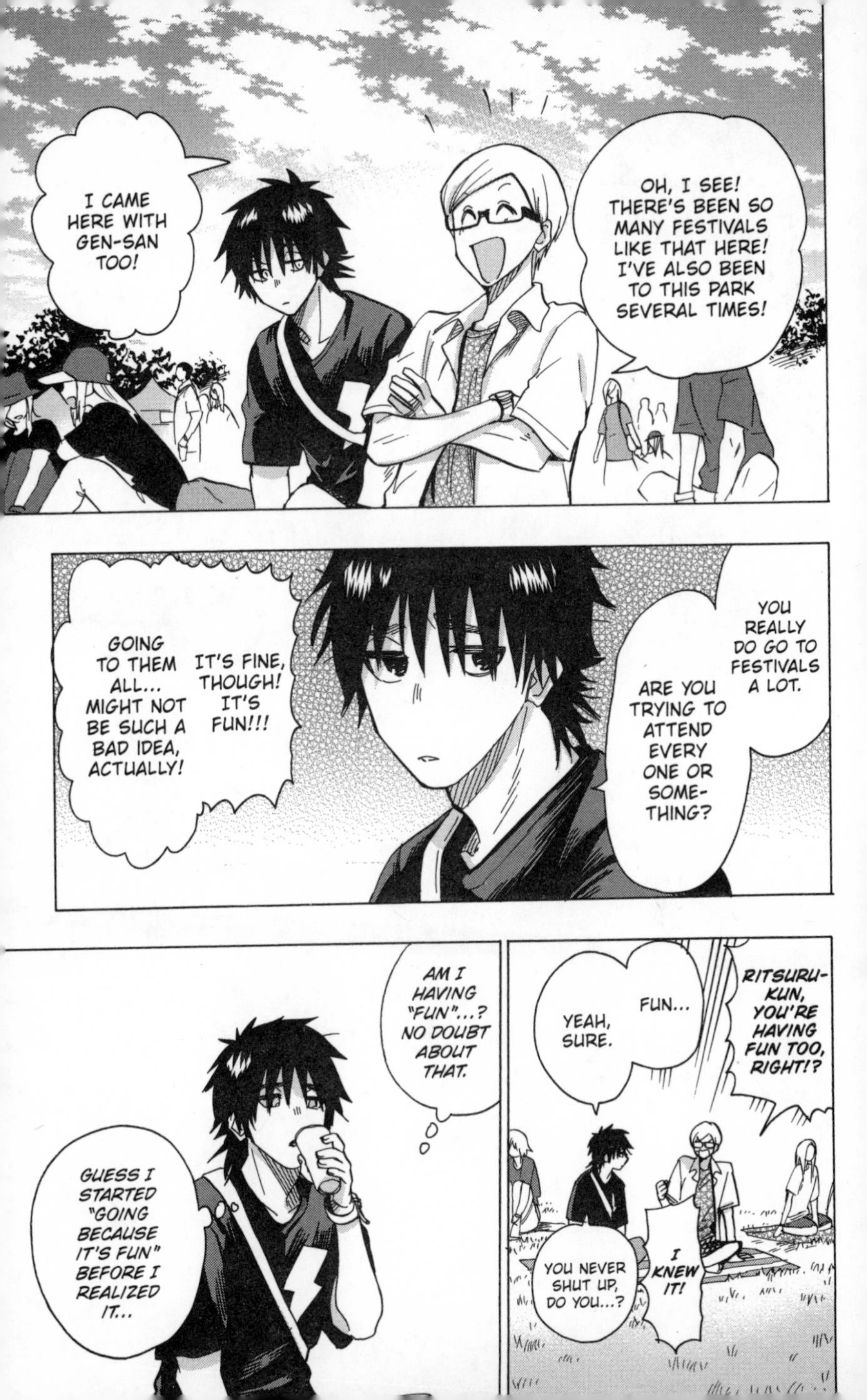
OH, I SEE! THERE'S BEEN SO MANY FESTIVALS LIKE THAT HERE! I'VE ALSO BEEN TO THIS PARK SEVERAL TIMES!
I CAME HERE WITH GEN-SAN TOO!
YOU REALLY DO GO TO FESTIVALS A LOT.
ARE YOU TRYING TO ATTEND EVERY ONE OR SOME-THING?
IT'S FINE, THOUGH! IT'S FUN!!!
GOING TO THEM ALL... MIGHT NOT BE SUCH A BAD IDEA, ACTUALLY!
RITSURU-KUN, YOU'RE HAVING FUN TOO, RIGHT!?
FUN...
YEAH, SURE.
I KNEW IT!
YOU NEVER SHUT UP, DO YOU...?
AM I HAVING "FUN"...? NO DOUBT ABOUT THAT.
GUESS I STARTED "GOING BECAUSE IT'S FUN" BEFORE I REALIZED IT...

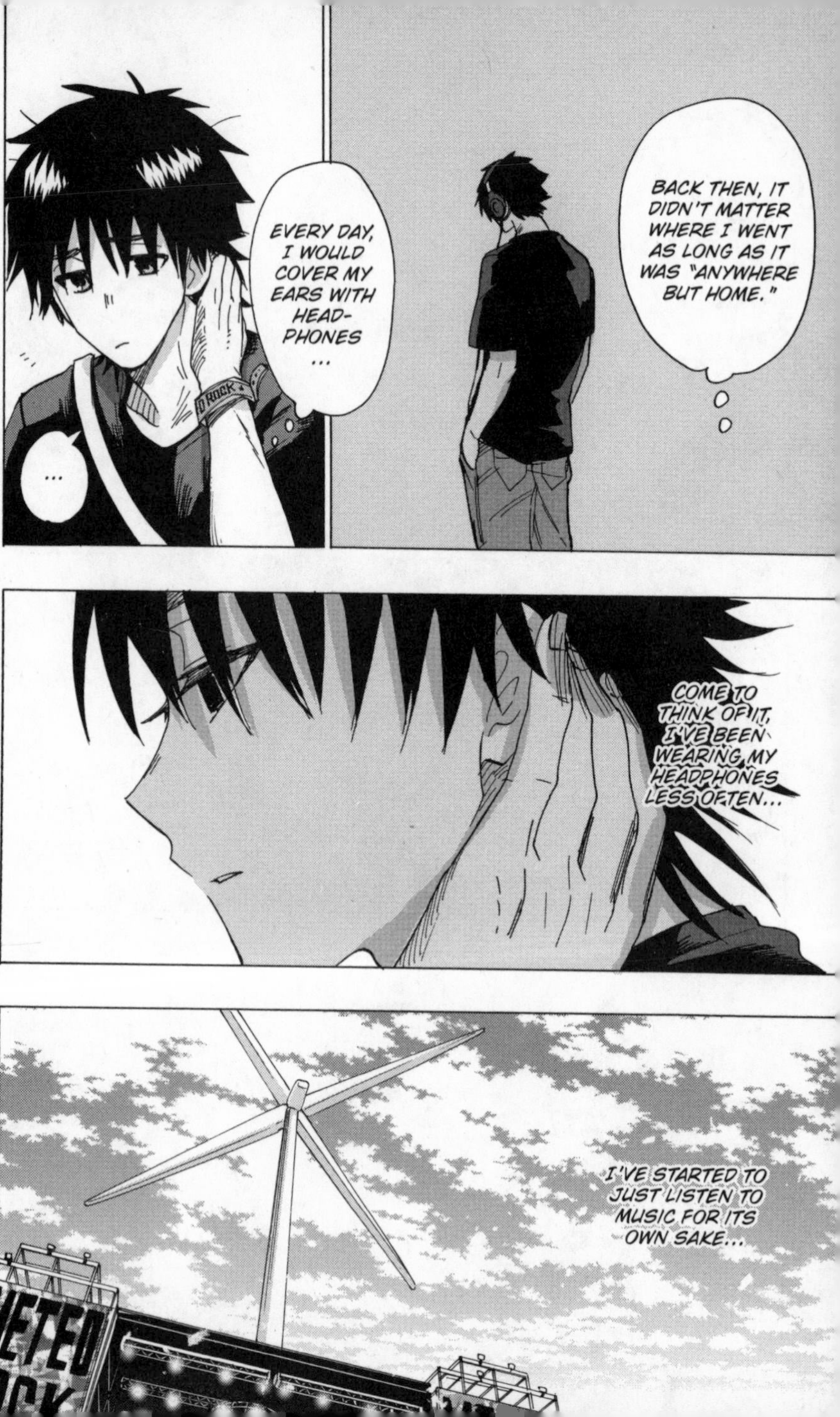
BACK THEN, IT DIDN'T MATTER WHERE I WENT AS LONG AS IT WAS "ANYWHERE BUT HOME."
EVERY DAY, I WOULD COVER MY EARS WITH HEAD-PHONES ...
...
COME TO THINK OF IT, I'VE BEEN WEARING MY HEADPHONES LESS OFTEN...
I'VE STARTED TO JUST LISTEN TO MUSIC FOR ITS OWN SAKE...

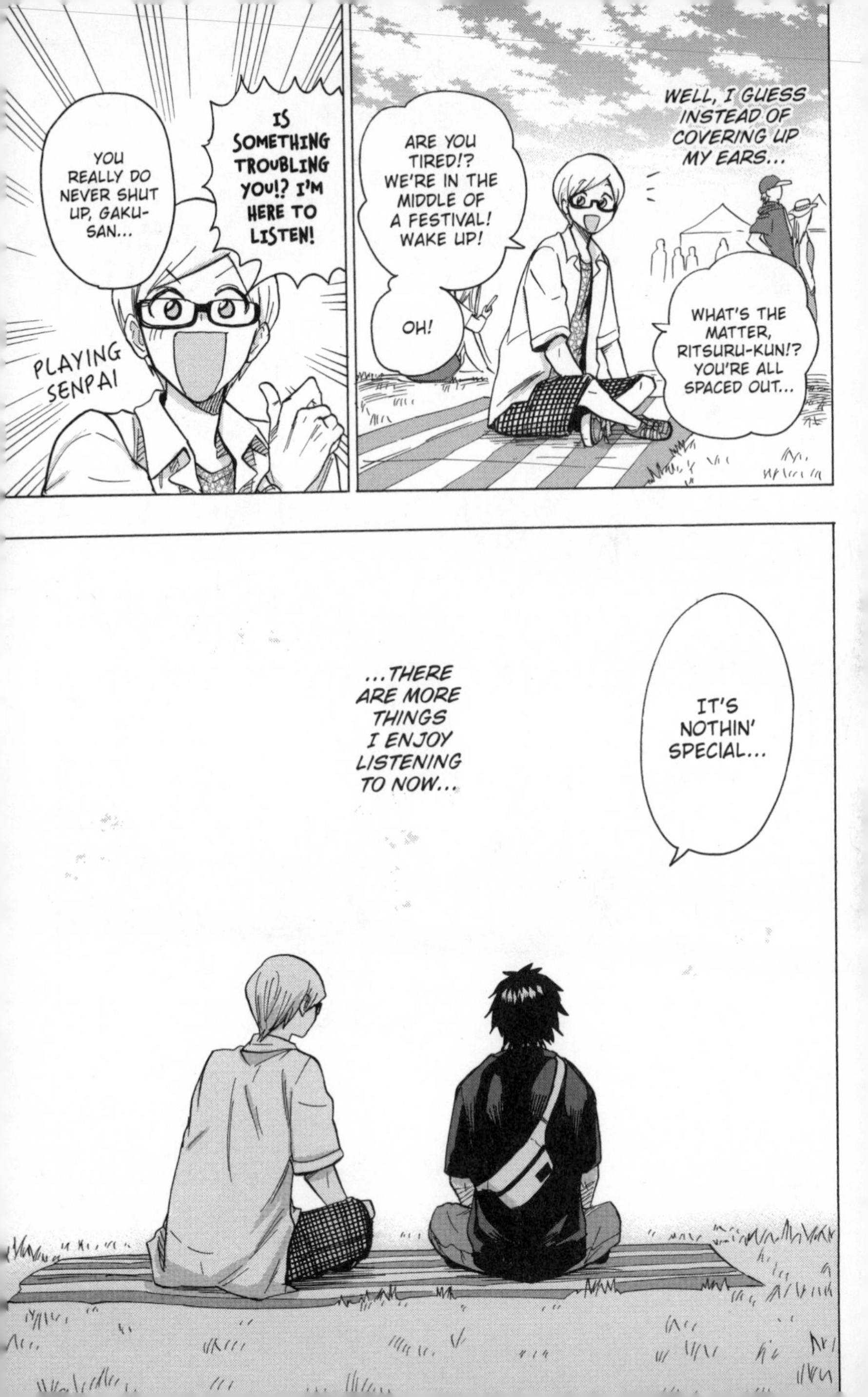
WELL, I GUESS INSTEAD OF COVERING UP MY EARS...
ARE YOU TIRED!? WE'RE IN THE MIDDLE OF A FESTIVAL! WAKE UP!
WHAT'S THE MATTER, RITSURU-KUN!? YOU'RE ALL SPACED OUT...
OH!
IS SOMETHING TROUBLING YOU!? I'M HERE TO LISTEN!
YOU REALLY DO NEVER SHUT UP, GAKU-SAN...
PLAYING SENPAI
IT'S NOTHIN' SPECIAL...
...THERE ARE MORE THINGS I ENJOY LISTENING TO NOW...

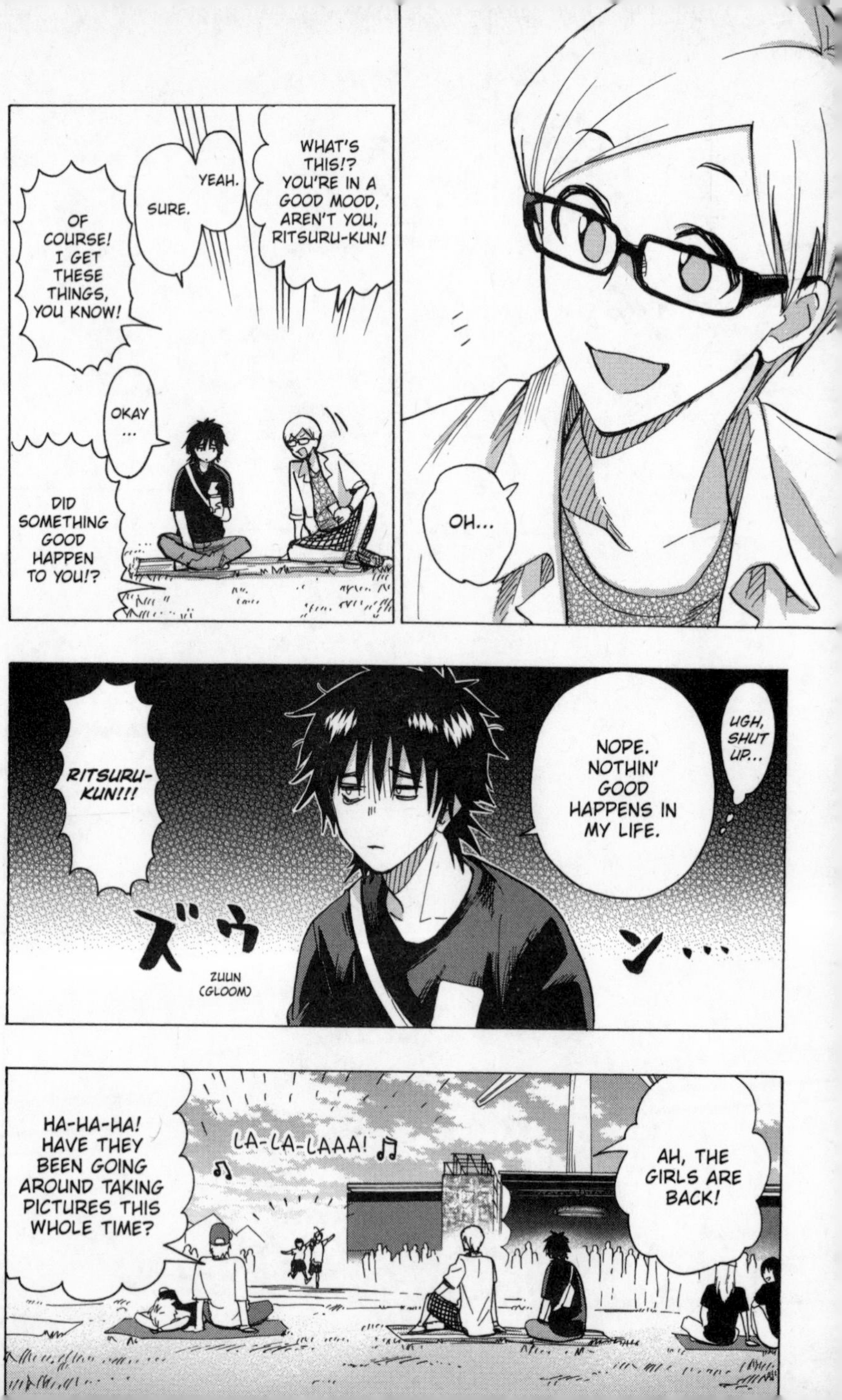
OH...
WHAT'S THIS!? YOU'RE IN A GOOD MOOD, AREN'T YOU, RITSURU-KUN!
YEAH.
SURE.
OF COURSE! I GET THESE THINGS, YOU KNOW!
OKAY ...
DID SOMETHING GOOD HAPPEN TO YOU!?
UGH, SHUT UP...
NOPE. NOTHIN' GOOD HAPPENS IN MY LIFE.
RITSURU-KUN!!!
ズウン…
ZUUN (GLOOM)
AH, THE GIRLS ARE BACK!
LA-LA-LAAA! ♫
HA-HA-HA! HAVE THEY BEEN GOING AROUND TAKING PICTURES THIS WHOLE TIME?

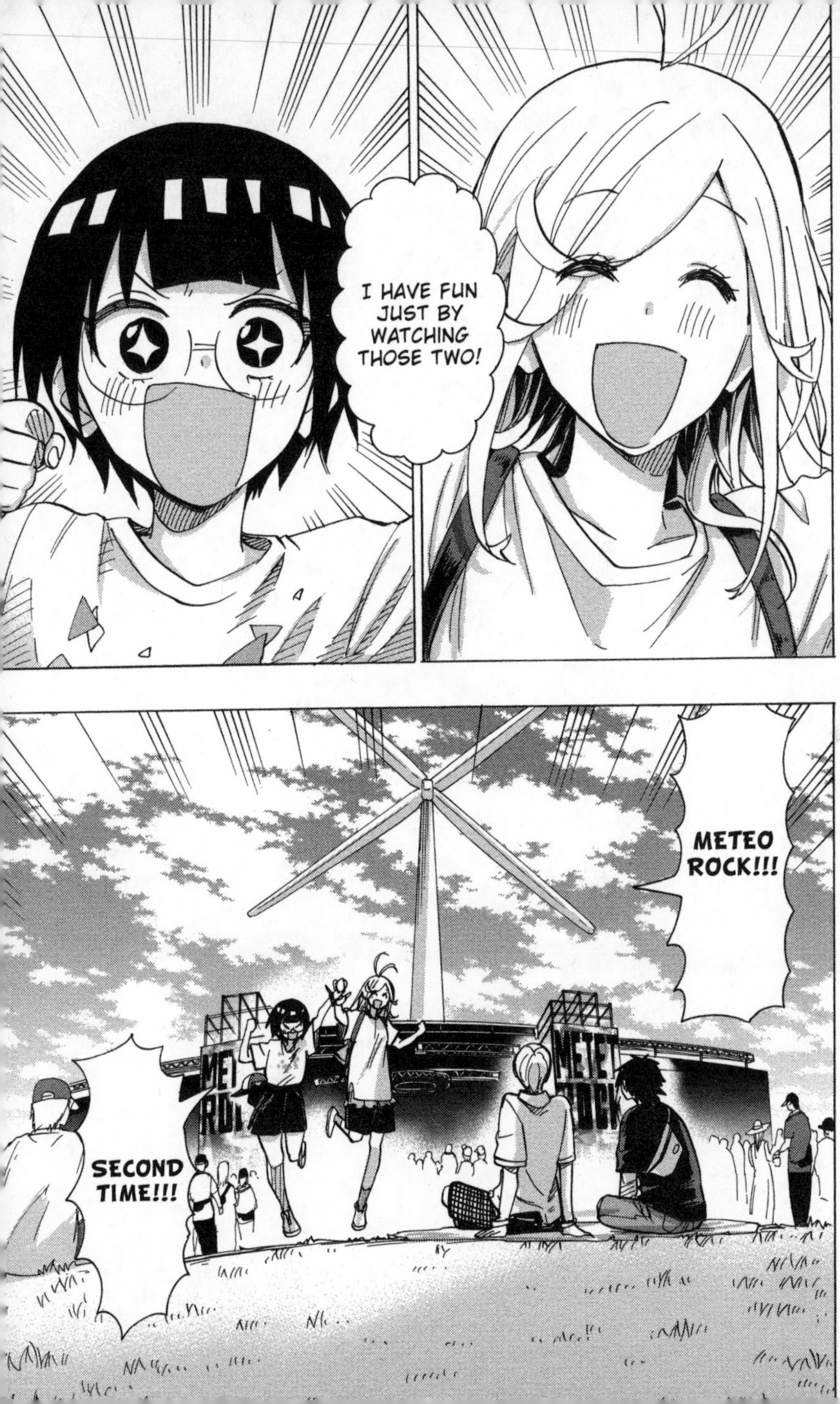
I HAVE FUN JUST BY WATCHING THOSE TWO!
METEO ROCK!!!
SECOND TIME!!!

Days on Fes

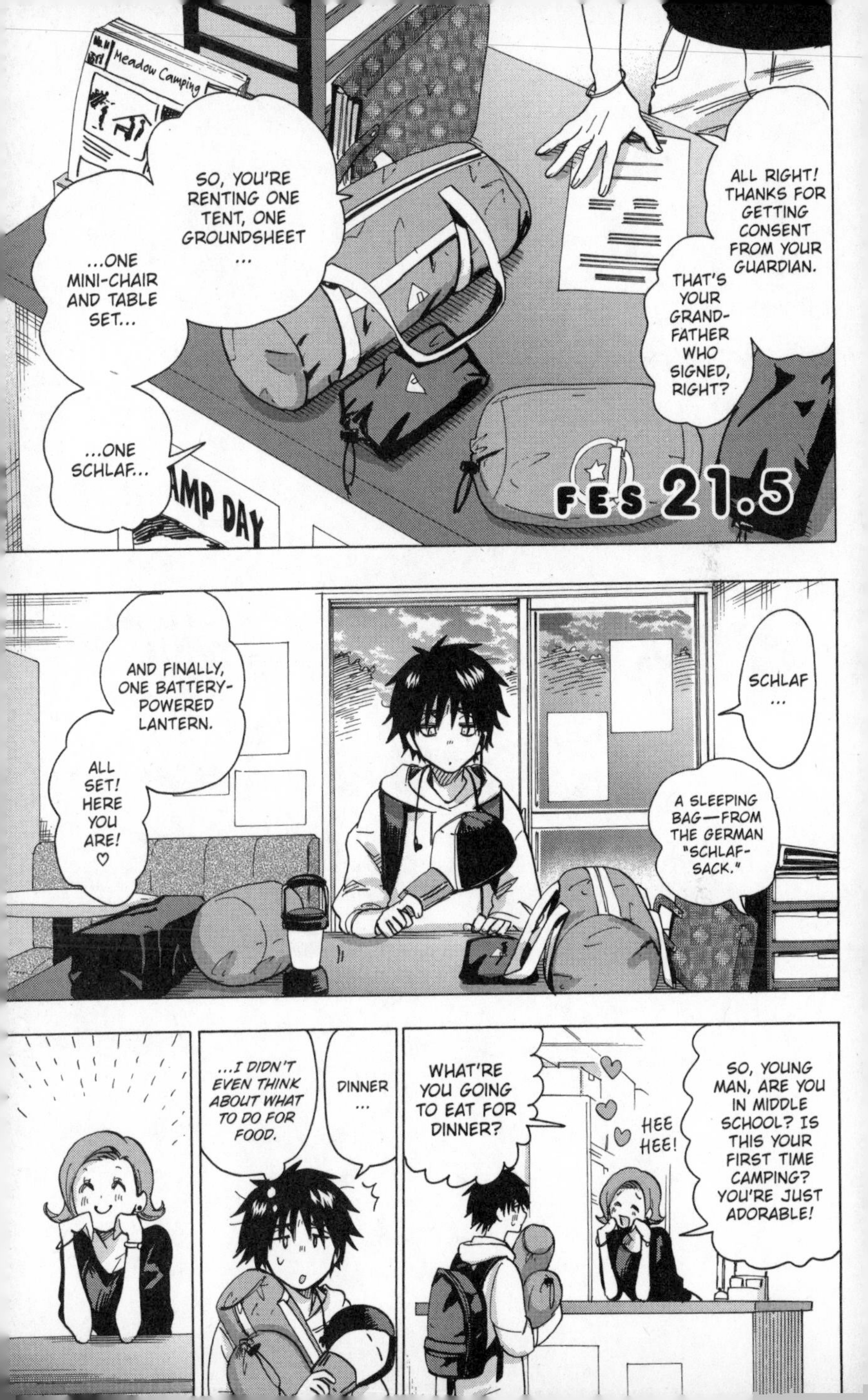
FES 21.5
Meadow Camping
AMP DAY
ALL RIGHT! THANKS FOR GETTING CONSENT FROM YOUR GUARDIAN.
THAT'S YOUR GRANDFATHER WHO SIGNED, RIGHT?
SO, YOU'RE RENTING ONE TENT, ONE GROUNDSHEET ...
...ONE MINI-CHAIR AND TABLE SET...
...ONE SCHLAF...
SCHLAF ...
A SLEEPING BAG—FROM THE GERMAN "SCHLAF-SACK."
AND FINALLY, ONE BATTERY-POWERED LANTERN.
ALL SET! HERE YOU ARE! ♡
SO, YOUNG MAN, ARE YOU IN MIDDLE SCHOOL? IS THIS YOUR FIRST TIME CAMPING? YOU'RE JUST ADORABLE!
HEE HEE!
WHAT'RE YOU GOING TO EAT FOR DINNER?
DINNER ...
...I DIDN'T EVEN THINK ABOUT WHAT TO DO FOR FOOD.

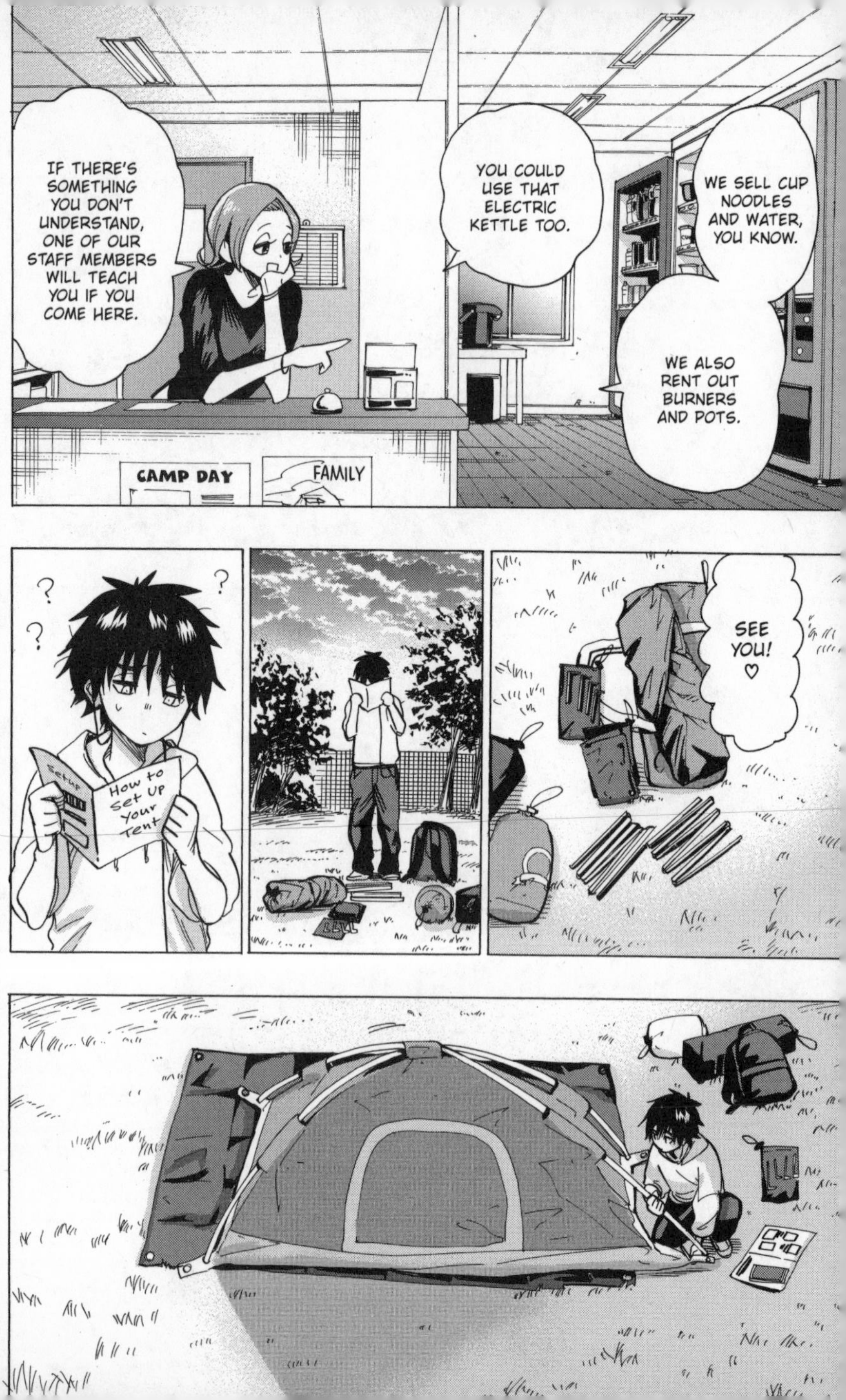
WE SELL CUP NOODLES AND WATER, YOU KNOW.
WE ALSO RENT OUT BURNERS AND POTS.
YOU COULD USE THAT ELECTRIC KETTLE TOO.
IF THERE'S SOMETHING YOU DON'T UNDERSTAND, ONE OF OUR STAFF MEMBERS WILL TEACH YOU IF YOU COME HERE.
FAMILY
CAMP DAY
SEE YOU! ♥
How to Set Up Your Tent
Setup

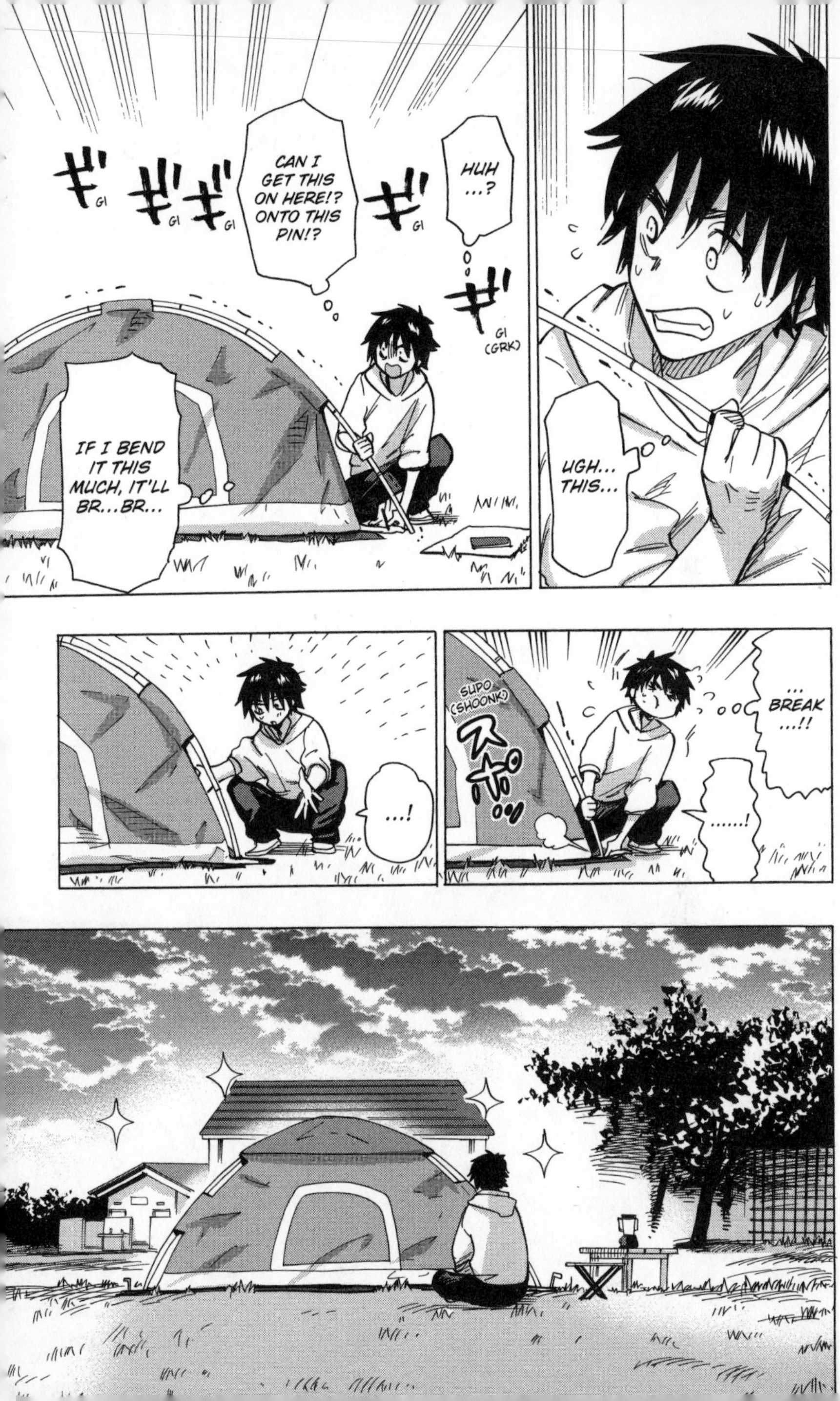

UGH... THIS...
HUH ...?
ギ GI
CAN I GET THIS ON HERE!? ONTO THIS PIN!?
ギ GI
ギ GI
ギ GI
ギ GI (GRK)
IF I BEND IT THIS MUCH, IT'LL BR...BR...
... BREAK ...!!
......!
SUPO (SHOONK)
スポッ
...!

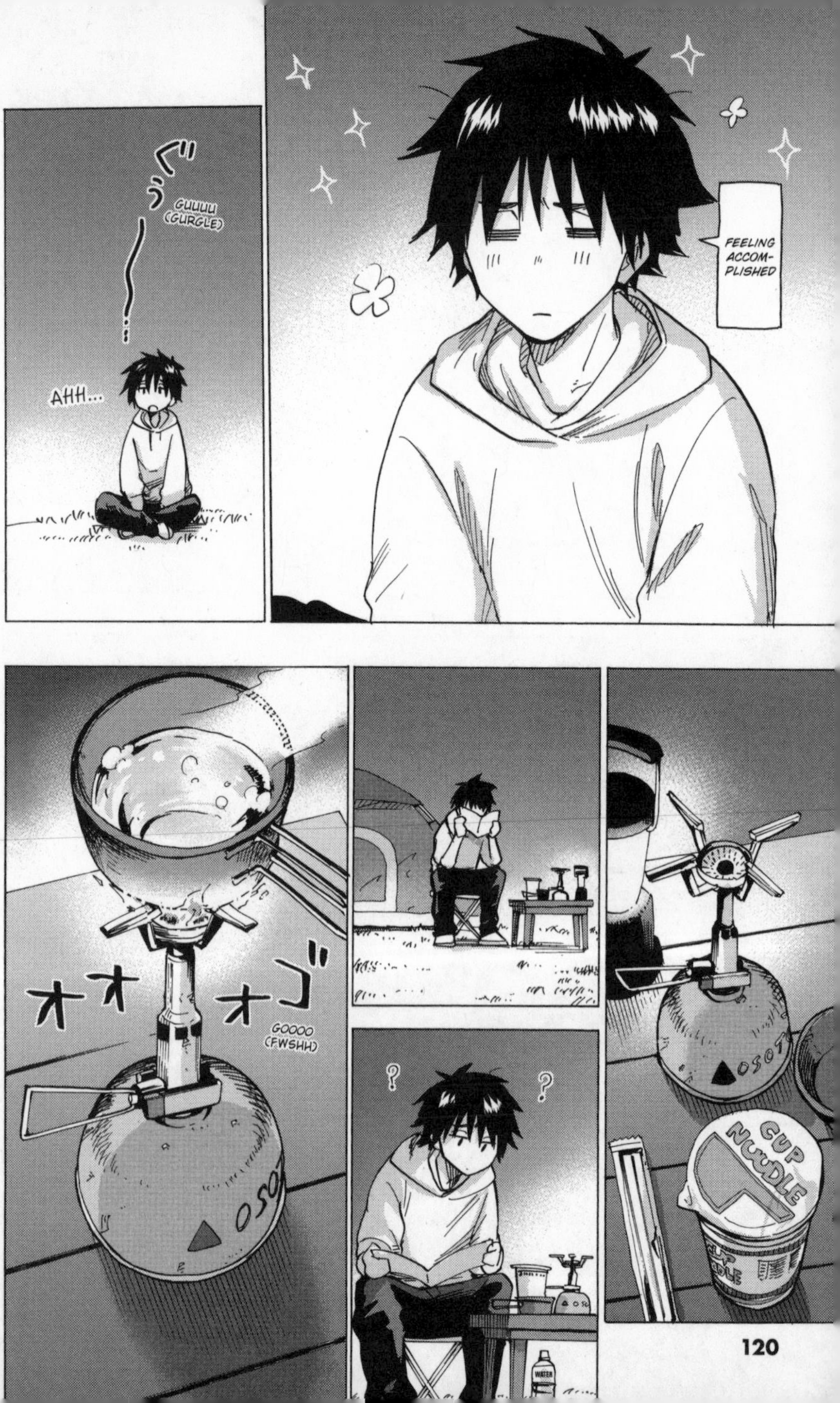
FEELING ACCOMPLISHED
ぐぅ~~~!?
GUUUU (GURGLE)
AHH...
CUP NOODLE
? ?
WATER
ゴオオオ
GOOOO (FWSHH)

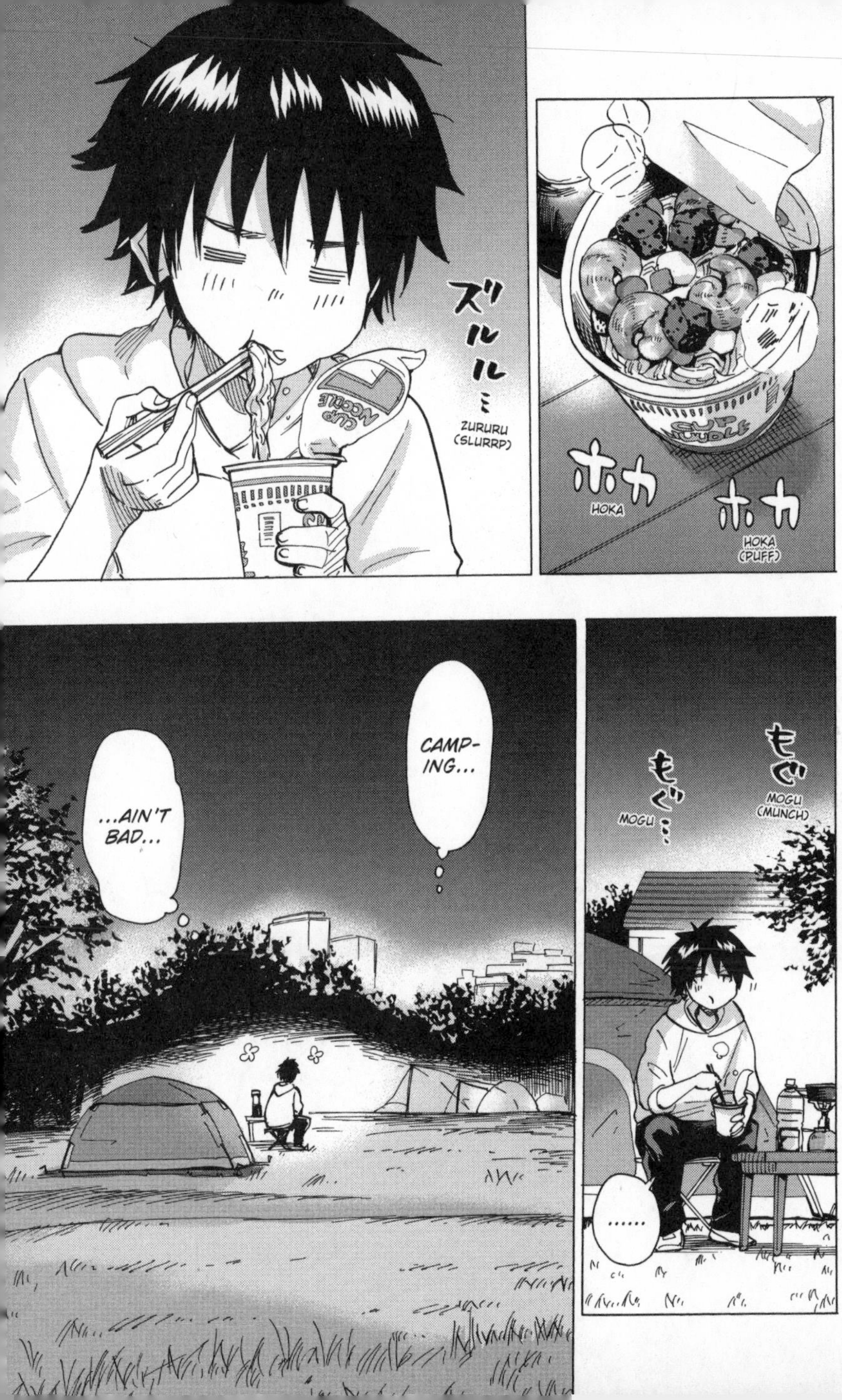
ホカ
HOKA
(PUFF)
ホカ
HOKA
ズルルミ
ZURURU
(SLURRP)
もぐ
MOGU
(MUNCH)
もぐ…
MOGU
......
CAMP-
ING...
...AIN'T
BAD...

Days on Fes

FES 22

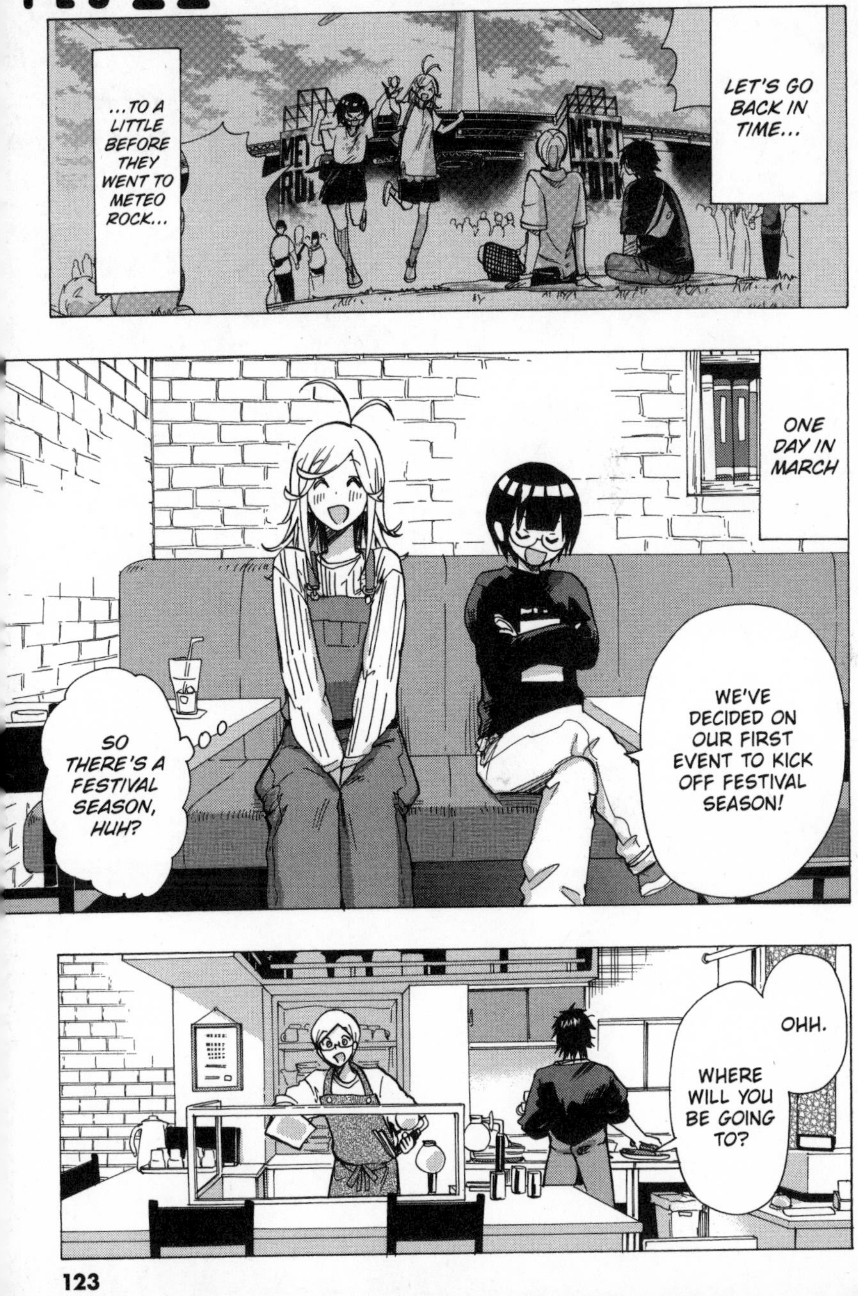
LET'S GO BACK IN TIME...
...TO A LITTLE BEFORE THEY WENT TO METEO ROCK...
ONE DAY IN MARCH
WE'VE DECIDED ON OUR FIRST EVENT TO KICK OFF FESTIVAL SEASON!
SO THERE'S A FESTIVAL SEASON, HUH?
OHH.
WHERE WILL YOU BE GOING TO?

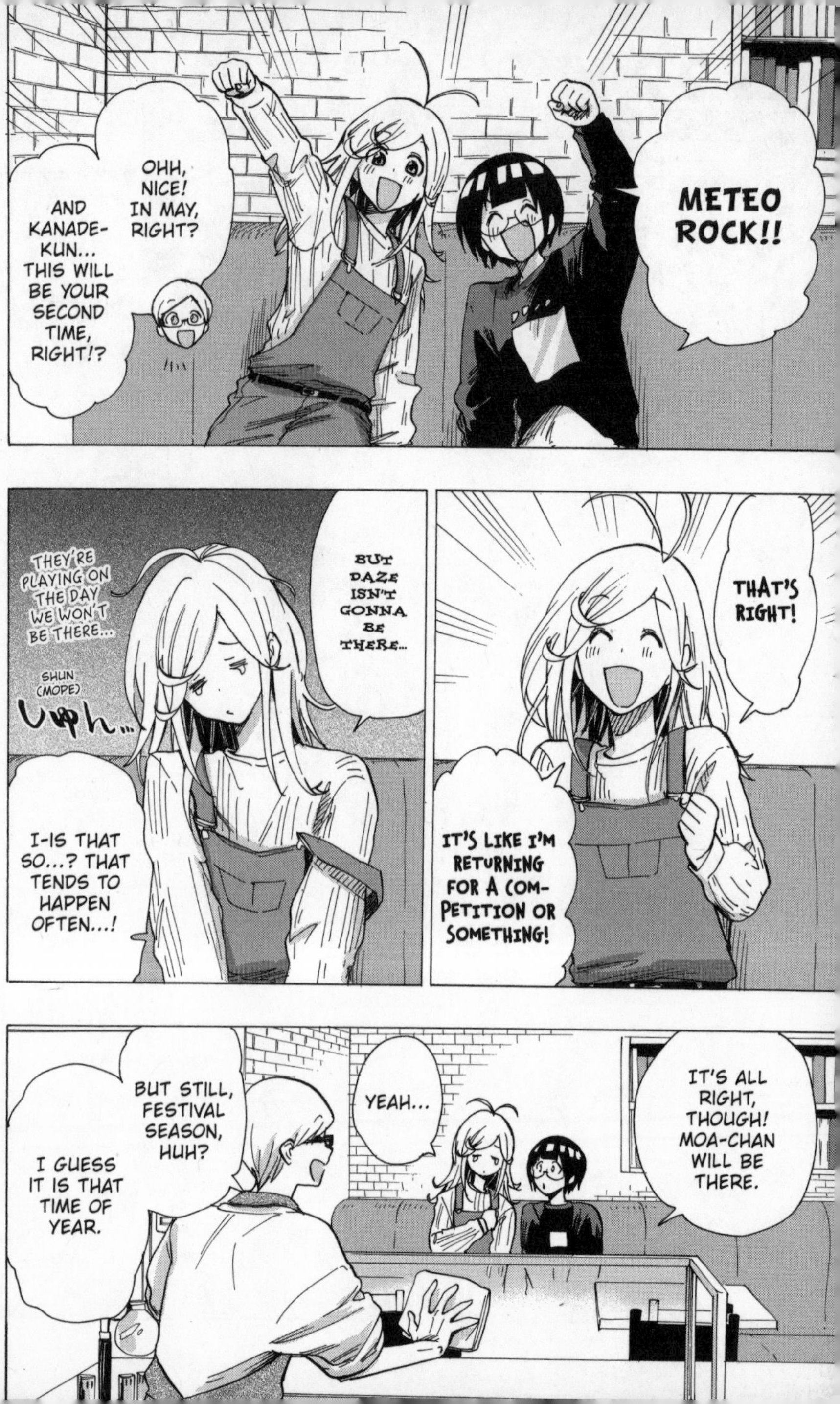
METEO ROCK!!
OHH, NICE! IN MAY, RIGHT?
AND KANADE-KUN... THIS WILL BE YOUR SECOND TIME, RIGHT!?
THAT'S RIGHT!
IT'S LIKE I'M RETURNING FOR A COMPETITION OR SOMETHING!
BUT DAZE ISN'T GONNA BE THERE...
THEY'RE PLAYING ON THE DAY WE WON'T BE THERE...
SHUN (MOPE)
しゅん…
I-IS THAT SO...? THAT TENDS TO HAPPEN OFTEN...!
IT'S ALL RIGHT, THOUGH! MOA-CHAN WILL BE THERE.
YEAH...
BUT STILL, FESTIVAL SEASON, HUH?
I GUESS IT IS THAT TIME OF YEAR.

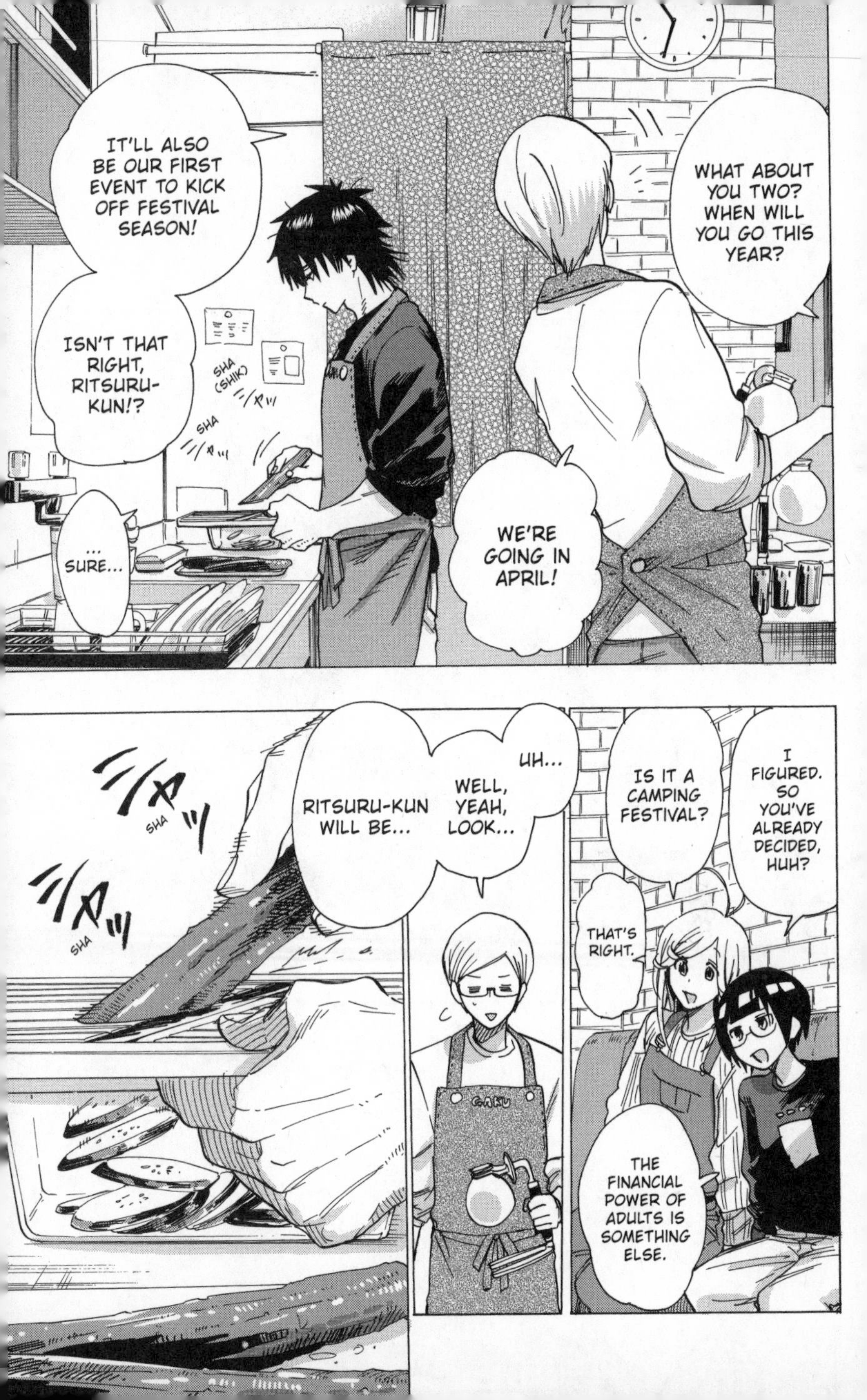
WHAT ABOUT YOU TWO? WHEN WILL YOU GO THIS YEAR?
WE'RE GOING IN APRIL!
IT'LL ALSO BE OUR FIRST EVENT TO KICK OFF FESTIVAL SEASON!
ISN'T THAT RIGHT, RITSURU-KUN!?
SHA (SHIK)
SHA
... SURE...
I FIGURED. SO YOU'VE ALREADY DECIDED, HUH?
IS IT A CAMPING FESTIVAL?
THAT'S RIGHT.
THE FINANCIAL POWER OF ADULTS IS SOMETHING ELSE.
UH...
WELL, YEAH, LOOK...
RITSURU-KUN WILL BE...
SHA
SHA

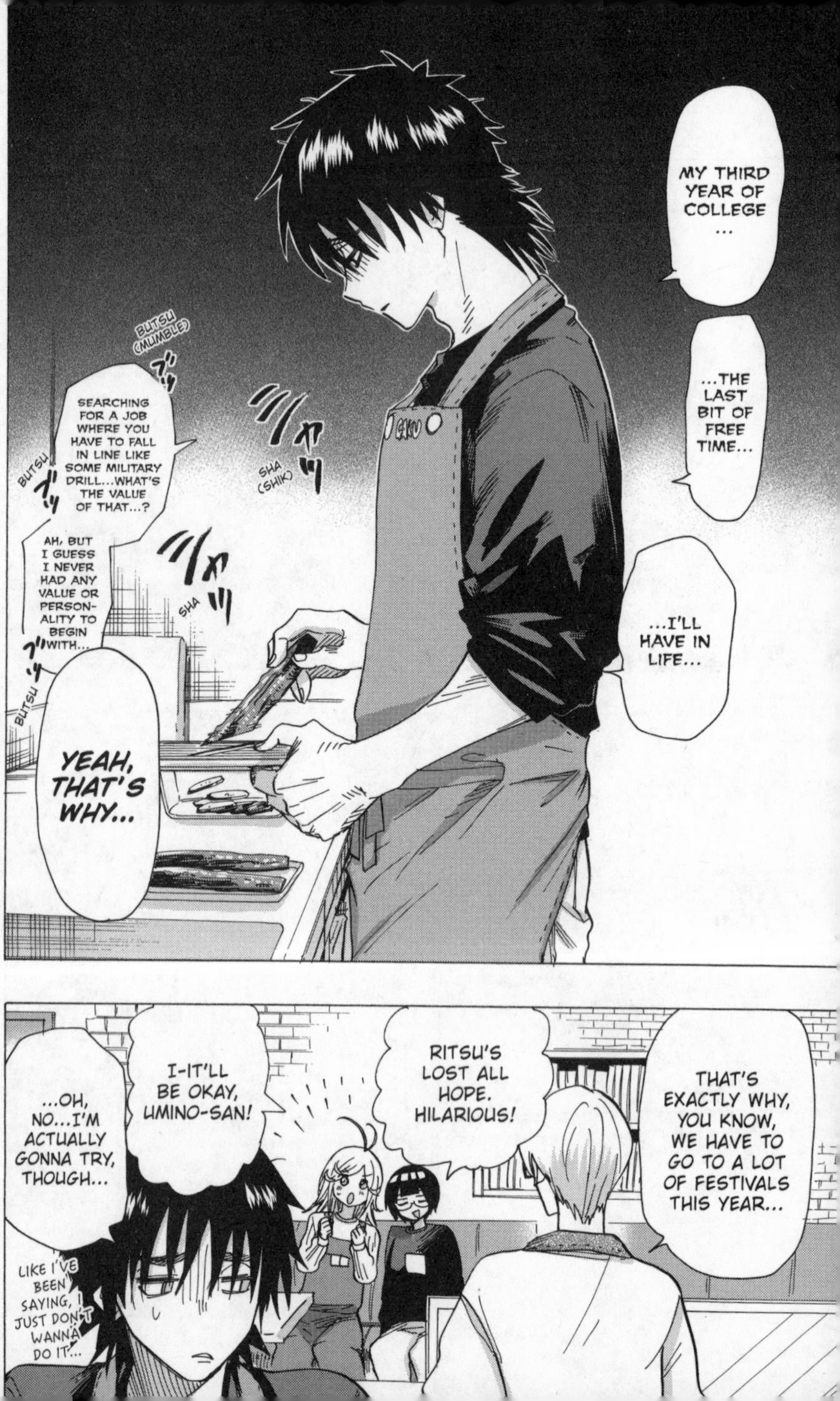
MY THIRD YEAR OF COLLEGE ...
...THE LAST BIT OF FREE TIME...
...I'LL HAVE IN LIFE...
SHA (SHIK)
SHA
BUTSU (MUMBLE)
SEARCHING FOR A JOB WHERE YOU HAVE TO FALL IN LINE LIKE SOME MILITARY DRILL...WHAT'S THE VALUE OF THAT...?
BUTSU
AH, BUT I GUESS I NEVER HAD ANY VALUE OR PERSON-ALITY TO BEGIN WITH...
BUTSU
YEAH, THAT'S WHY...
THAT'S EXACTLY WHY, YOU KNOW, WE HAVE TO GO TO A LOT OF FESTIVALS THIS YEAR...
RITSU'S LOST ALL HOPE. HILARIOUS!
I-IT'LL BE OKAY, UMINO-SAN!
...OH, NO...I'M ACTUALLY GONNA TRY, THOUGH...
LIKE I'VE BEEN SAYING, I JUST DON'T WANNA DO IT...

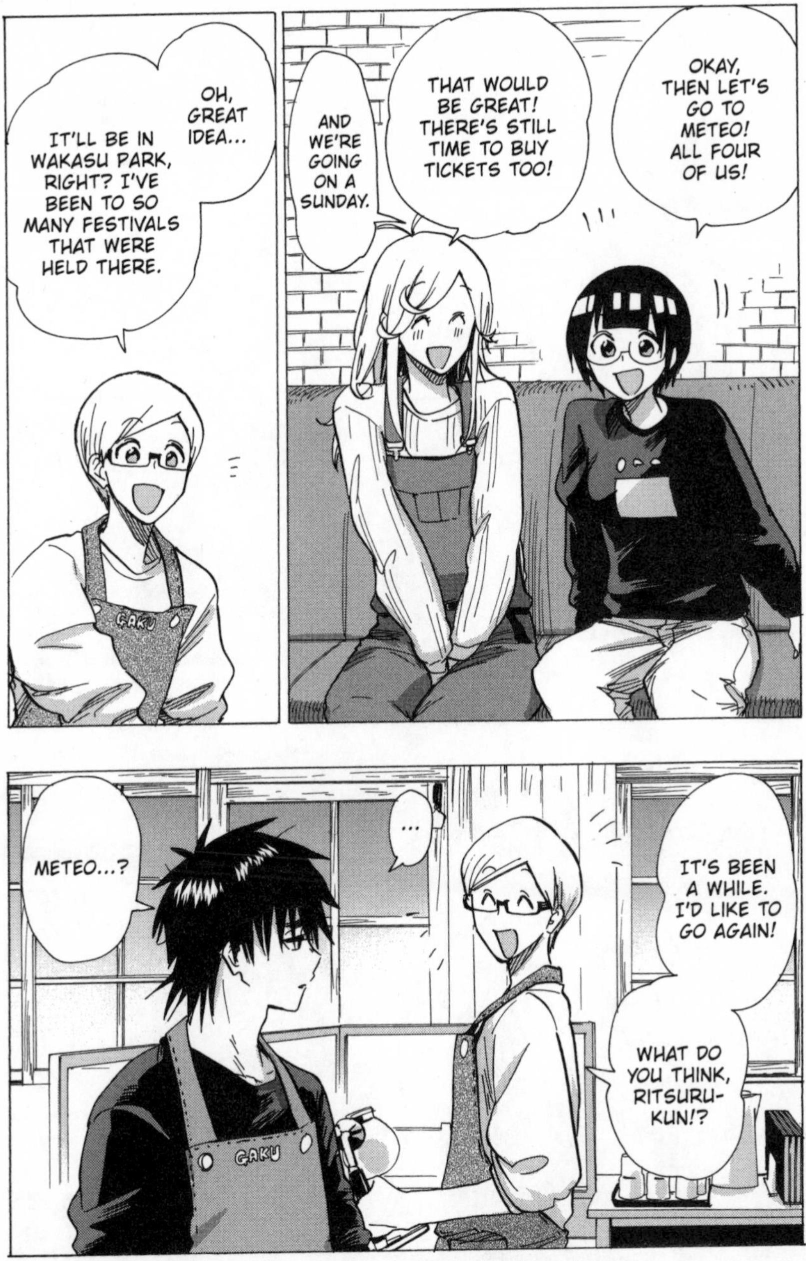
OKAY, THEN LET'S GO TO METEO! ALL FOUR OF US!
THAT WOULD BE GREAT! THERE'S STILL TIME TO BUY TICKETS TOO!
AND WE'RE GOING ON A SUNDAY.
OH, GREAT IDEA...
IT'LL BE IN WAKASU PARK, RIGHT? I'VE BEEN TO SO MANY FESTIVALS THAT WERE HELD THERE.
IT'S BEEN A WHILE. I'D LIKE TO GO AGAIN!
WHAT DO YOU THINK, RITSURU-KUN!?
...
METEO...?

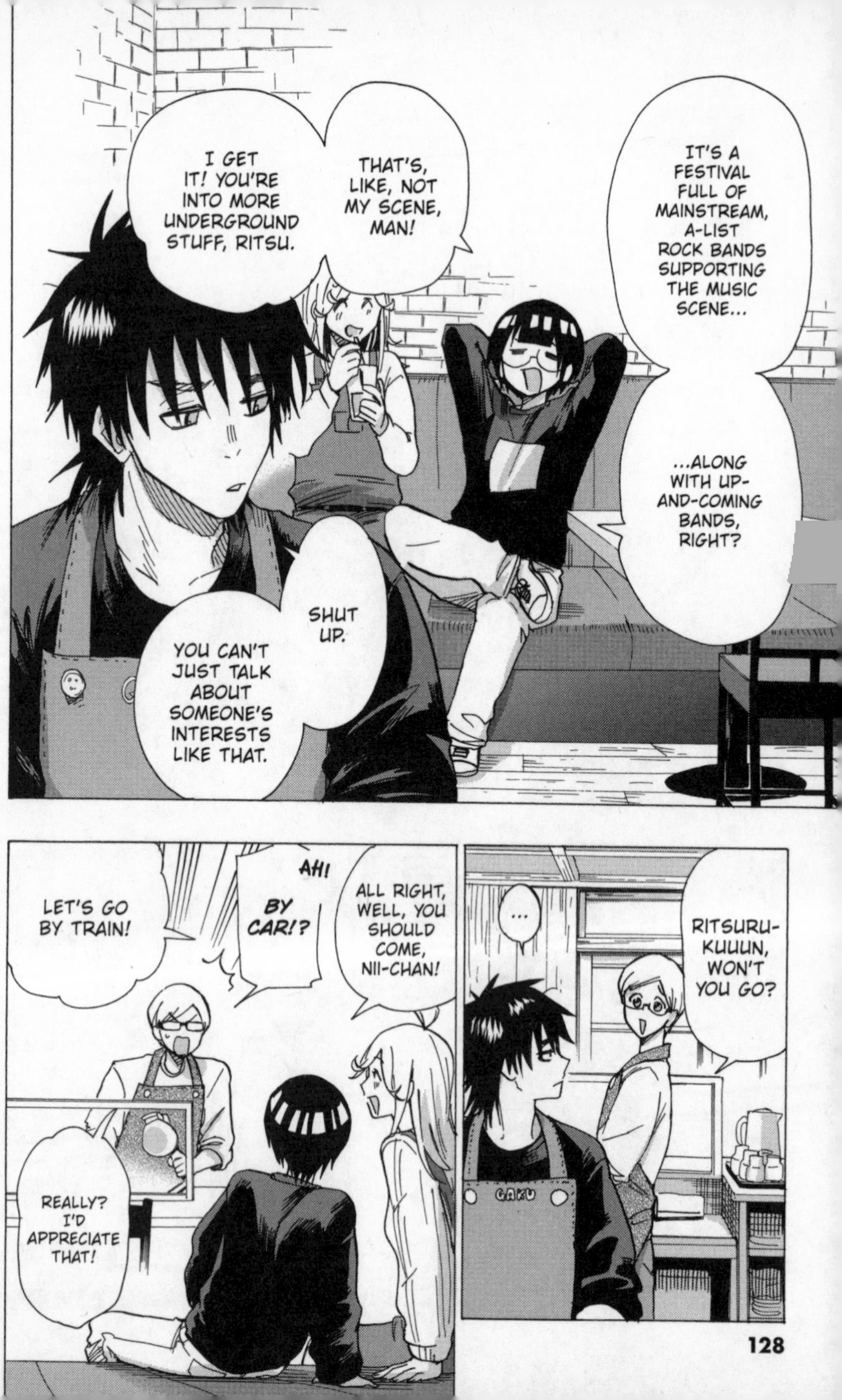
IT'S A FESTIVAL FULL OF MAINSTREAM, A-LIST ROCK BANDS SUPPORTING THE MUSIC SCENE...
...ALONG WITH UP-AND-COMING BANDS, RIGHT?
THAT'S, LIKE, NOT MY SCENE, MAN!
I GET IT! YOU'RE INTO MORE UNDERGROUND STUFF, RITSU.
SHUT UP.
YOU CAN'T JUST TALK ABOUT SOMEONE'S INTERESTS LIKE THAT.
RITSURU-KUUUN, WON'T YOU GO?
...
ALL RIGHT, WELL, YOU SHOULD COME, NII-CHAN!
AH!
BY CAR!?
LET'S GO BY TRAIN!
REALLY? I'D APPRECIATE THAT!
GAKU

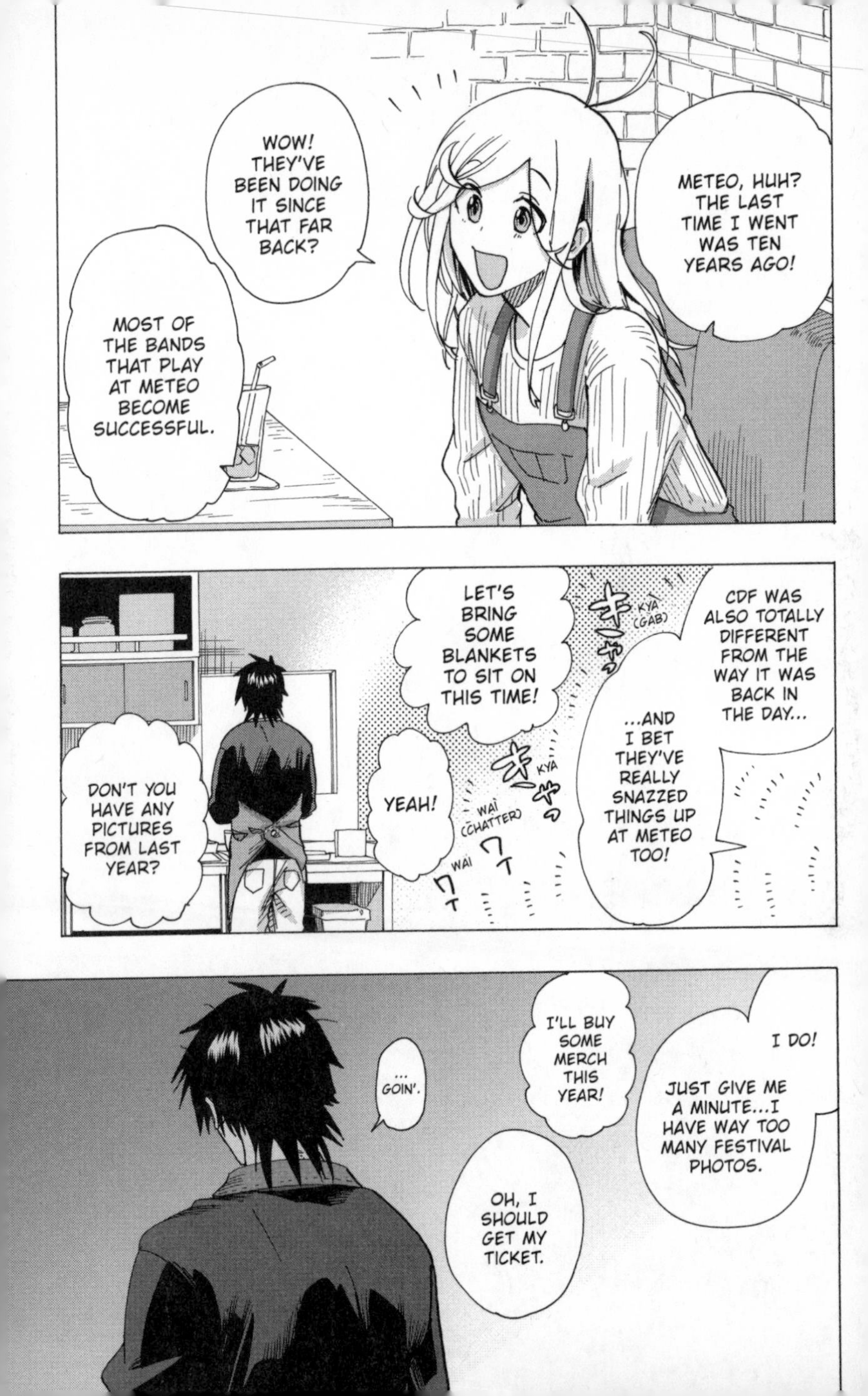
METEO, HUH? THE LAST TIME I WENT WAS TEN YEARS AGO!
WOW! THEY'VE BEEN DOING IT SINCE THAT FAR BACK?
MOST OF THE BANDS THAT PLAY AT METEO BECOME SUCCESSFUL.
CDF WAS ALSO TOTALLY DIFFERENT FROM THE WAY IT WAS BACK IN THE DAY...
...AND I BET THEY'VE REALLY SNAZZED THINGS UP AT METEO TOO!
KYA (GAB)
LET'S BRING SOME BLANKETS TO SIT ON THIS TIME!
KYA
YEAH!
WAI (CHATTER)
WAI
DON'T YOU HAVE ANY PICTURES FROM LAST YEAR?
I DO!
JUST GIVE ME A MINUTE...I HAVE WAY TOO MANY FESTIVAL PHOTOS.
I'LL BUY SOME MERCH THIS YEAR!
OH, I SHOULD GET MY TICKET.
...GOIN'.

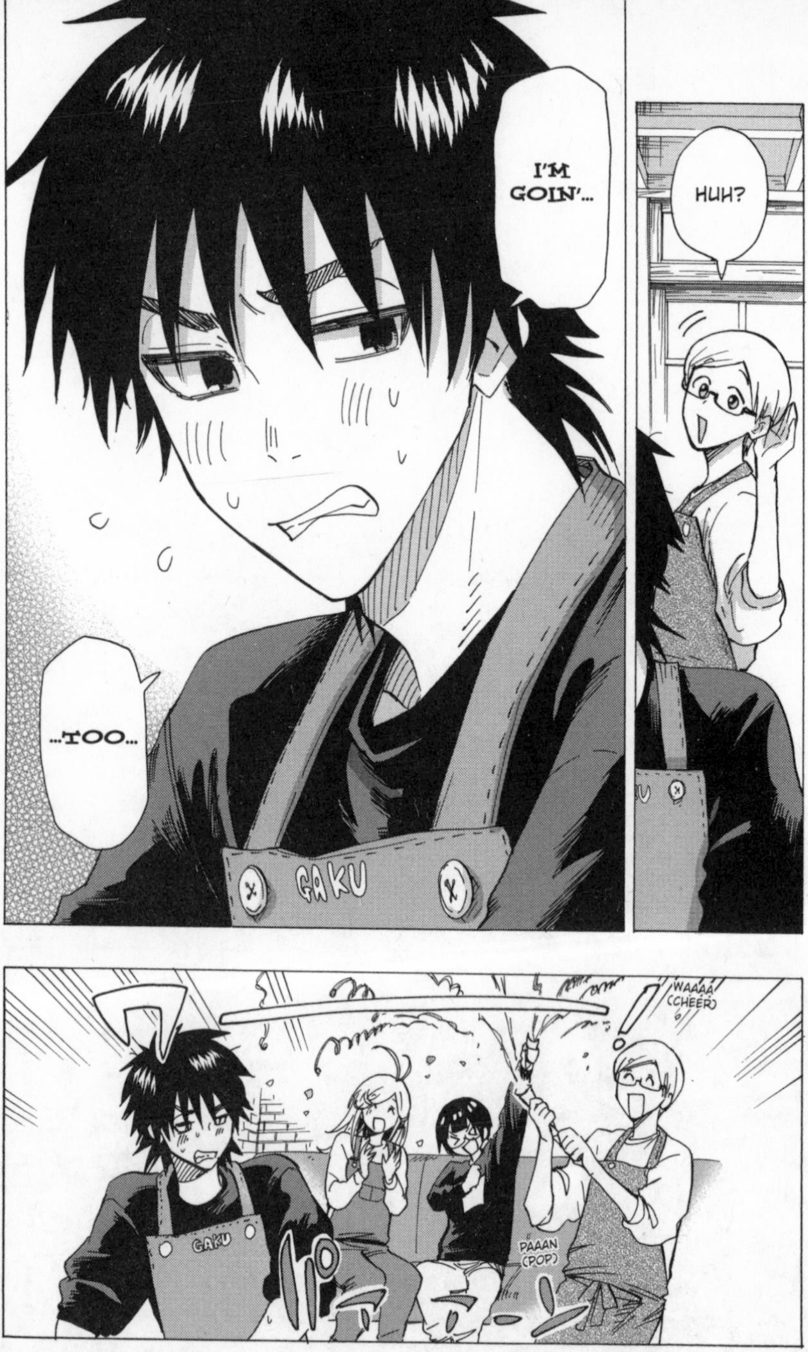
HUH?
I'M GOIN'...
...TOO...
WAAAA (CHEER)
PAAAN (POP)

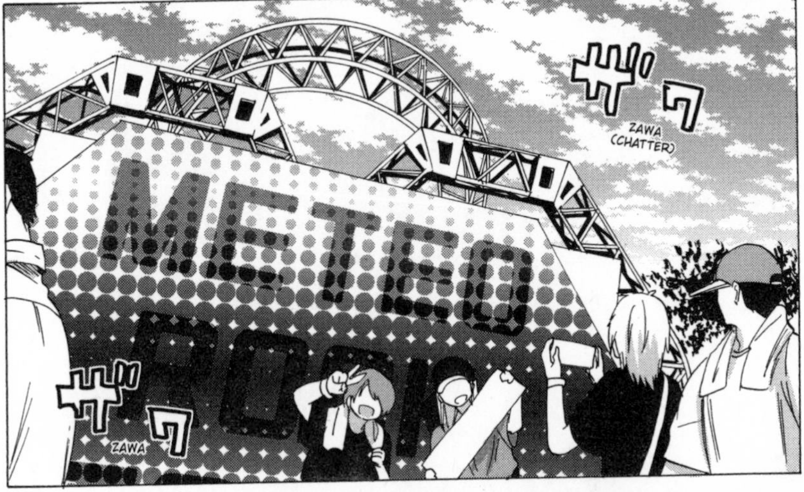
ザワ
ZAWA (CHATTER)
METEO
ザワ
ZAWA

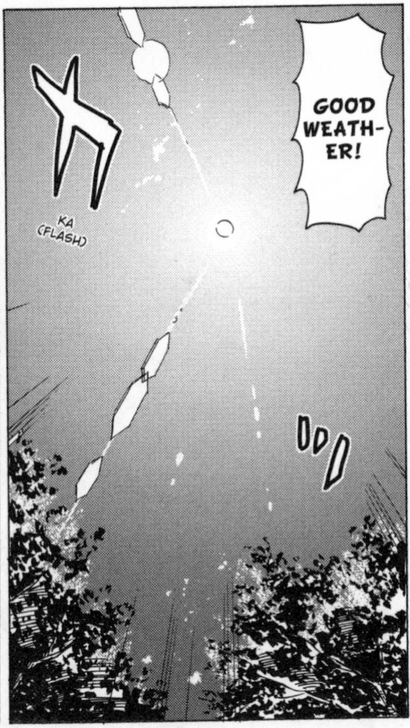
GOOD WEATHER!
カッ
KA (FLASH)

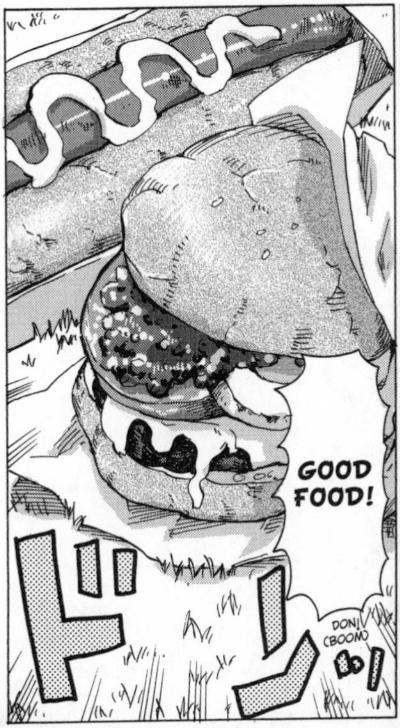
GOOD FOOD!
ドン
DON (BOOM)

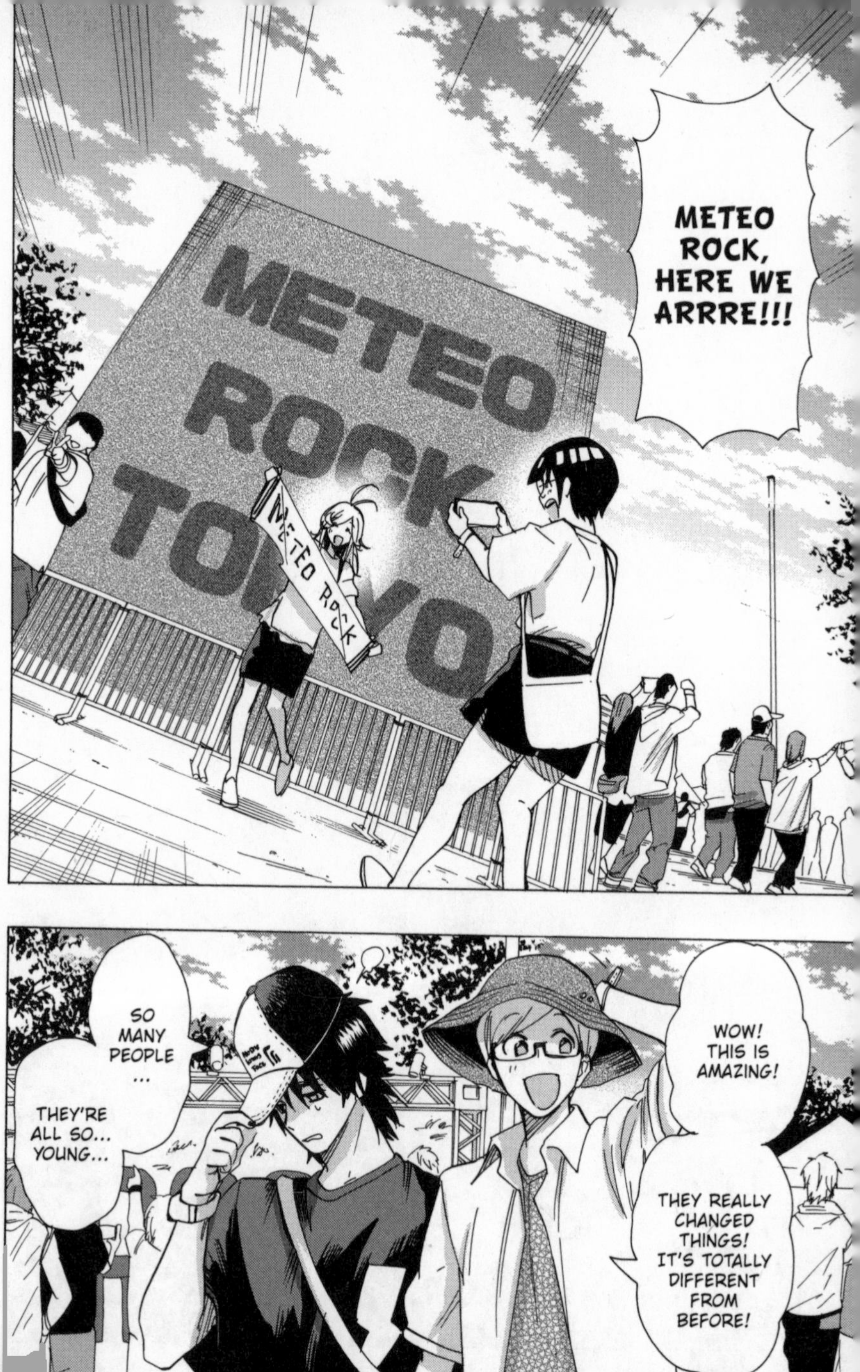
METEO ROCK, HERE WE ARRRE!!!
METEO ROCK
WOW! THIS IS AMAZING!
THEY REALLY CHANGED THINGS! IT'S TOTALLY DIFFERENT FROM BEFORE!
SO MANY PEOPLE ...
THEY'RE ALL SO... YOUNG...

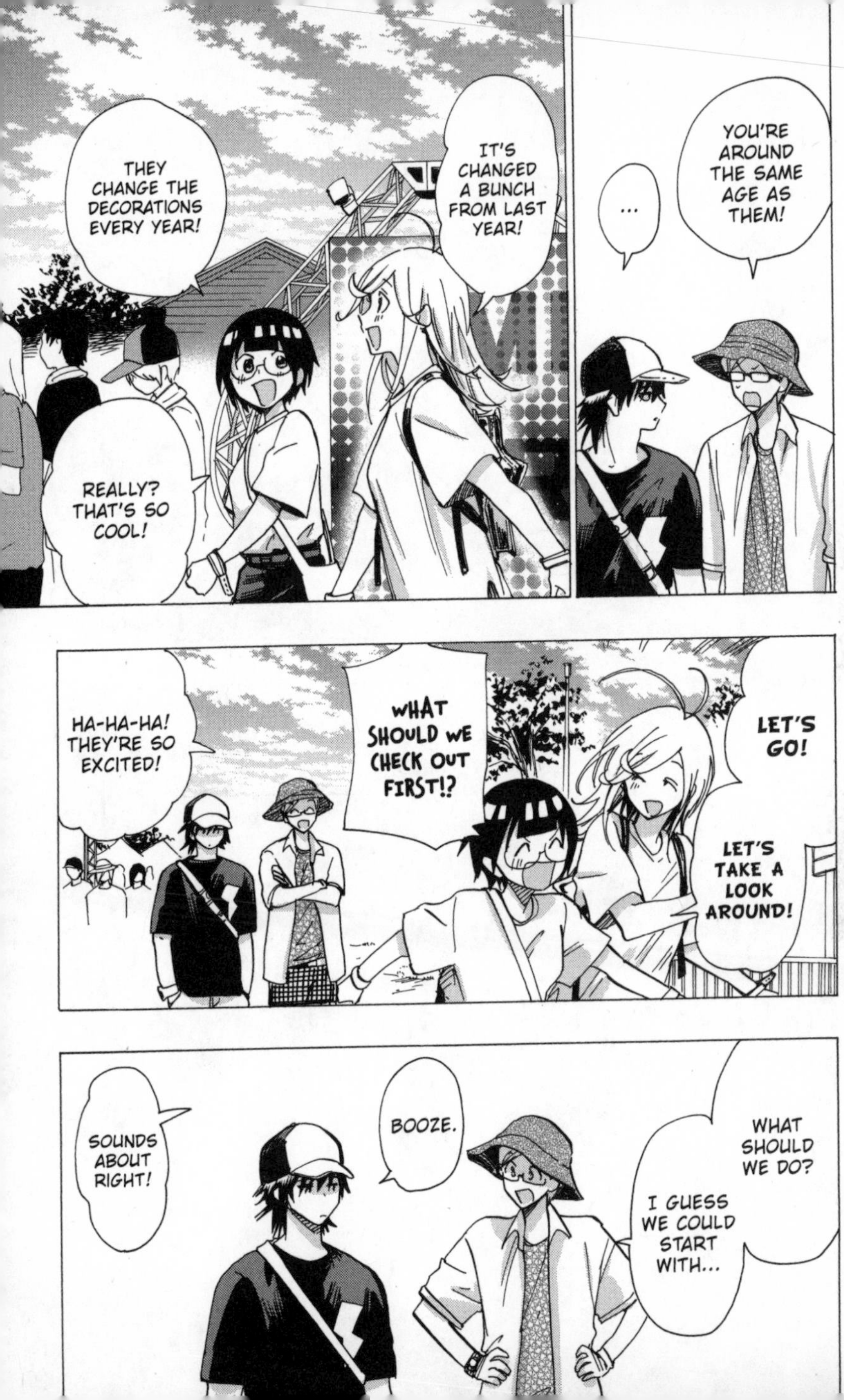
YOU'RE AROUND THE SAME AGE AS THEM!
...
IT'S CHANGED A BUNCH FROM LAST YEAR!
THEY CHANGE THE DECORATIONS EVERY YEAR!
REALLY? THAT'S SO COOL!
LET'S GO!
LET'S TAKE A LOOK AROUND!
WHAT SHOULD WE CHECK OUT FIRST!?
HA-HA-HA! THEY'RE SO EXCITED!
WHAT SHOULD WE DO?
I GUESS WE COULD START WITH...
BOOZE.
SOUNDS ABOUT RIGHT!

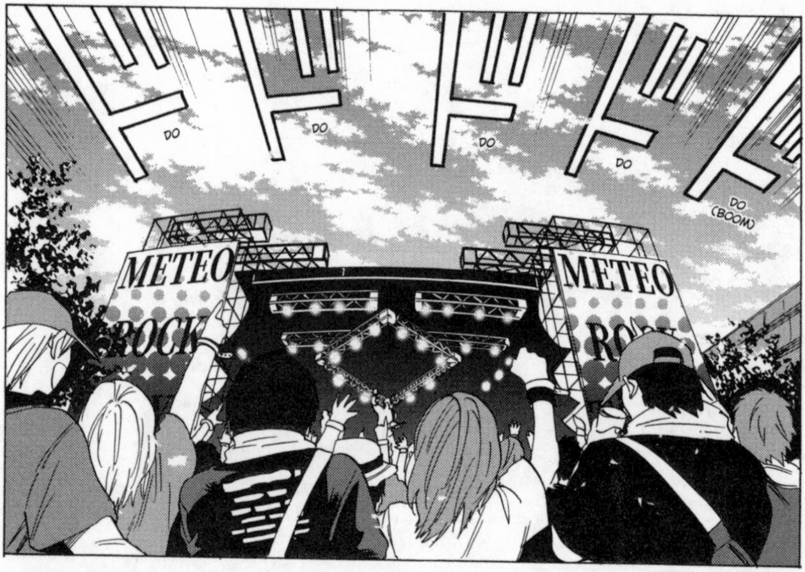
DO
DO
DO
DO
DO
(BOOM)
METEO
ROCK
METEO
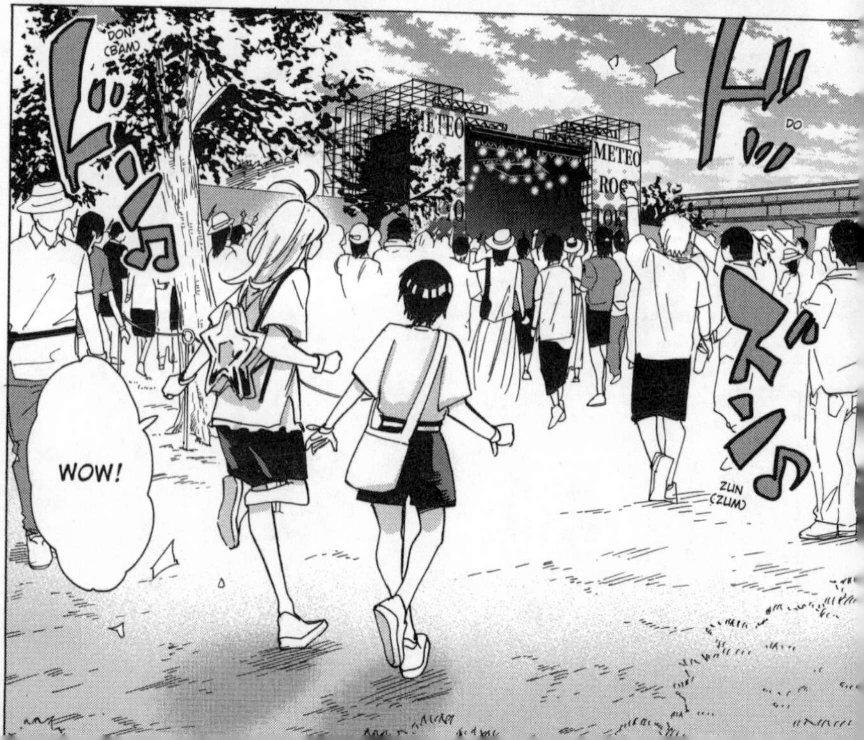
DO
DON
(BAM)
METEO
METEO
ROCK
WOW!
ZUN
(ZUM)

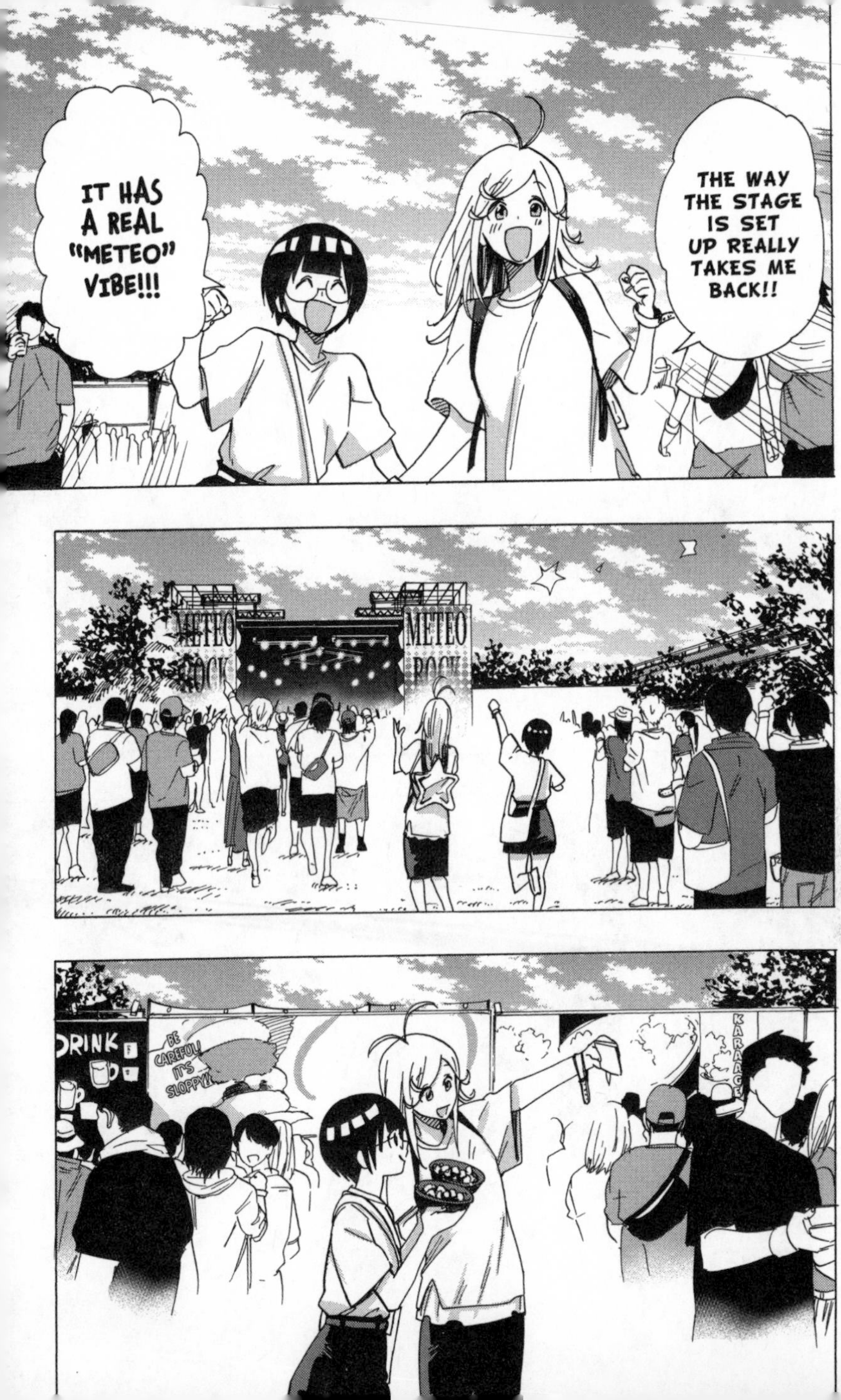
THE WAY THE STAGE IS SET UP REALLY TAKES ME BACK!!
IT HAS A REAL "METEO" VIBE!!!
METEO ROCK
METEO ROCK
KARAAGE
DRINK
BE CAREFUL! IT'S SLOPPY!

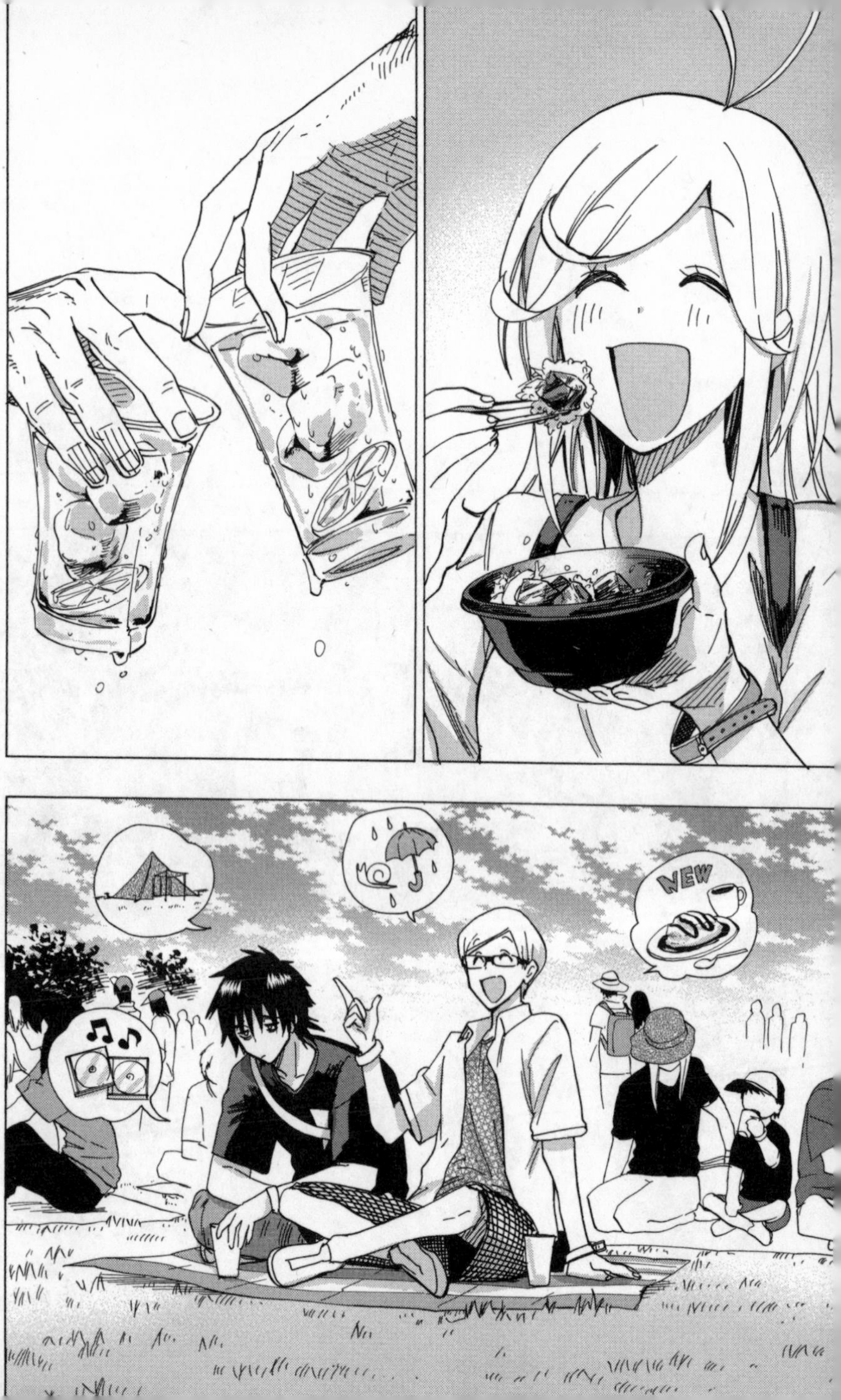
NEW

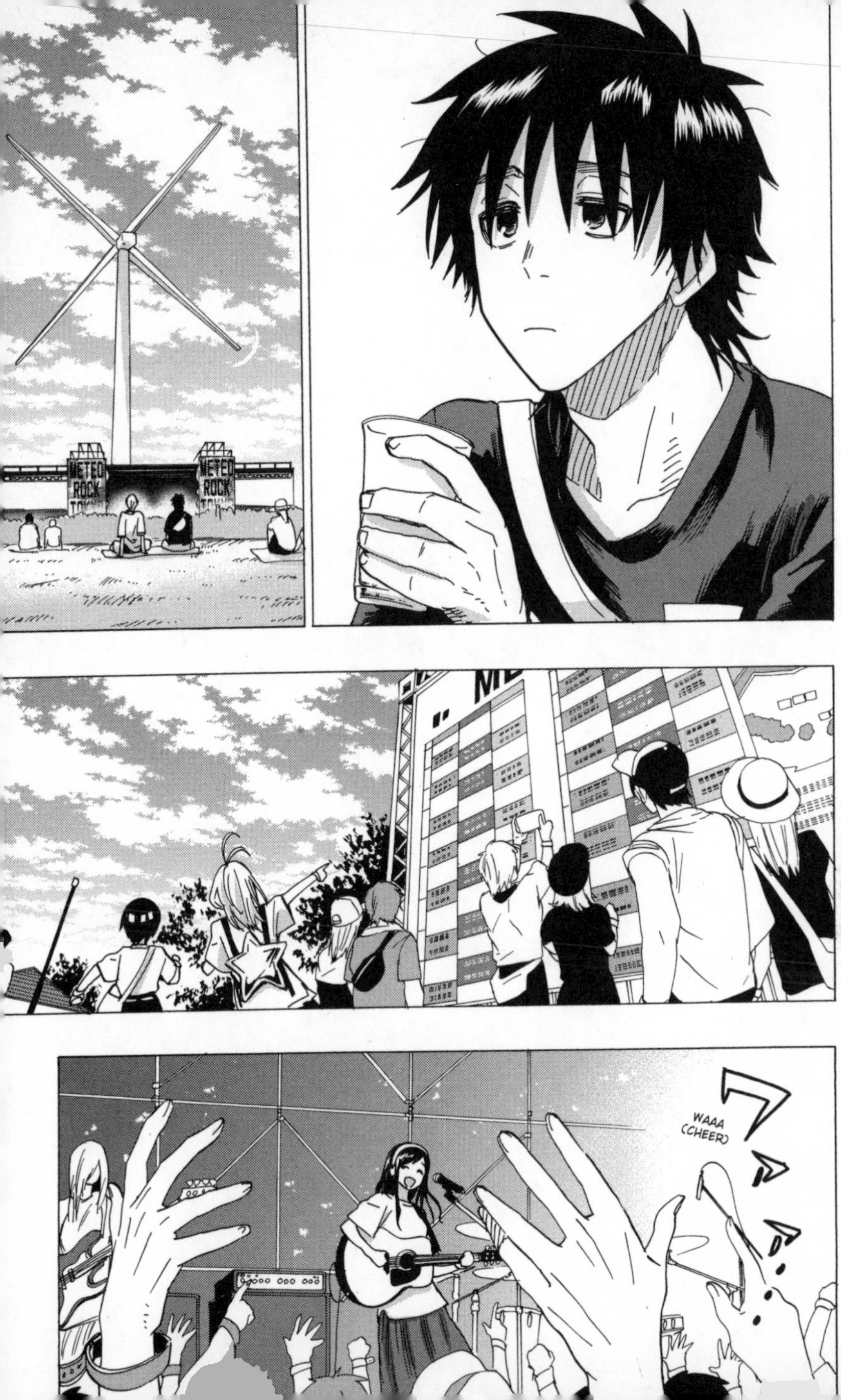
METEO
ROCK
WAAA
(CHEER)

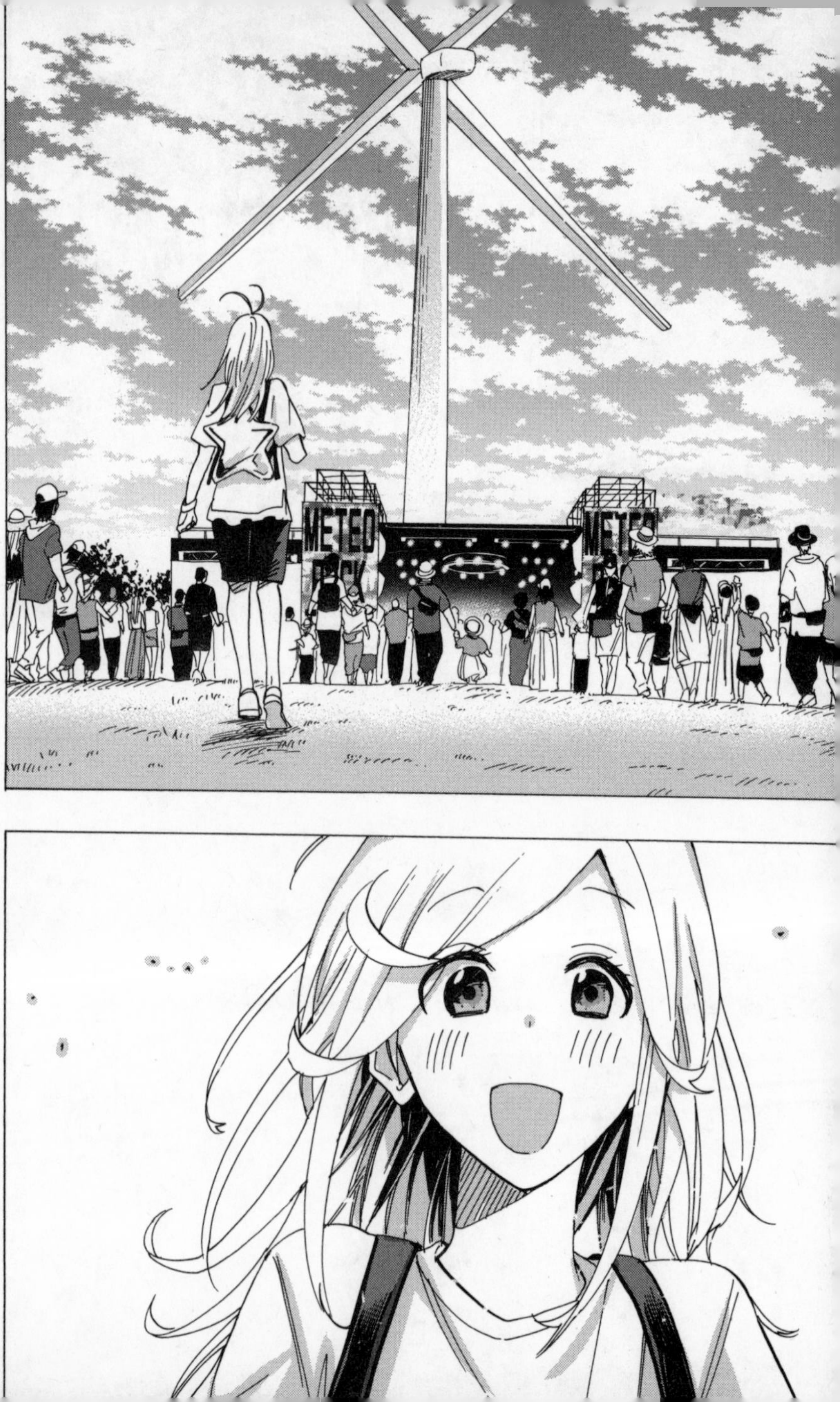
METEO

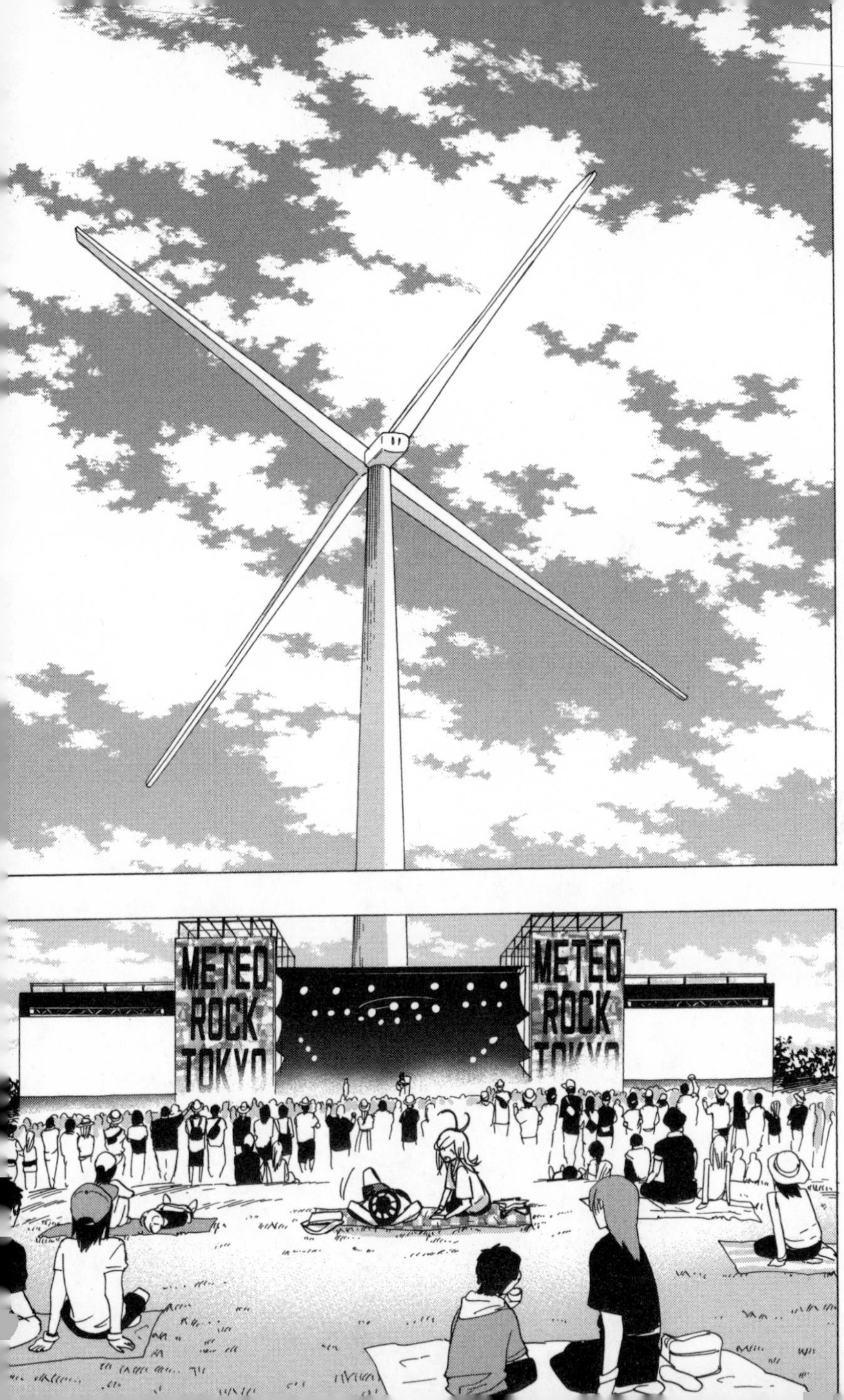
METEO
ROCK
TOKYO
METEO
ROCK

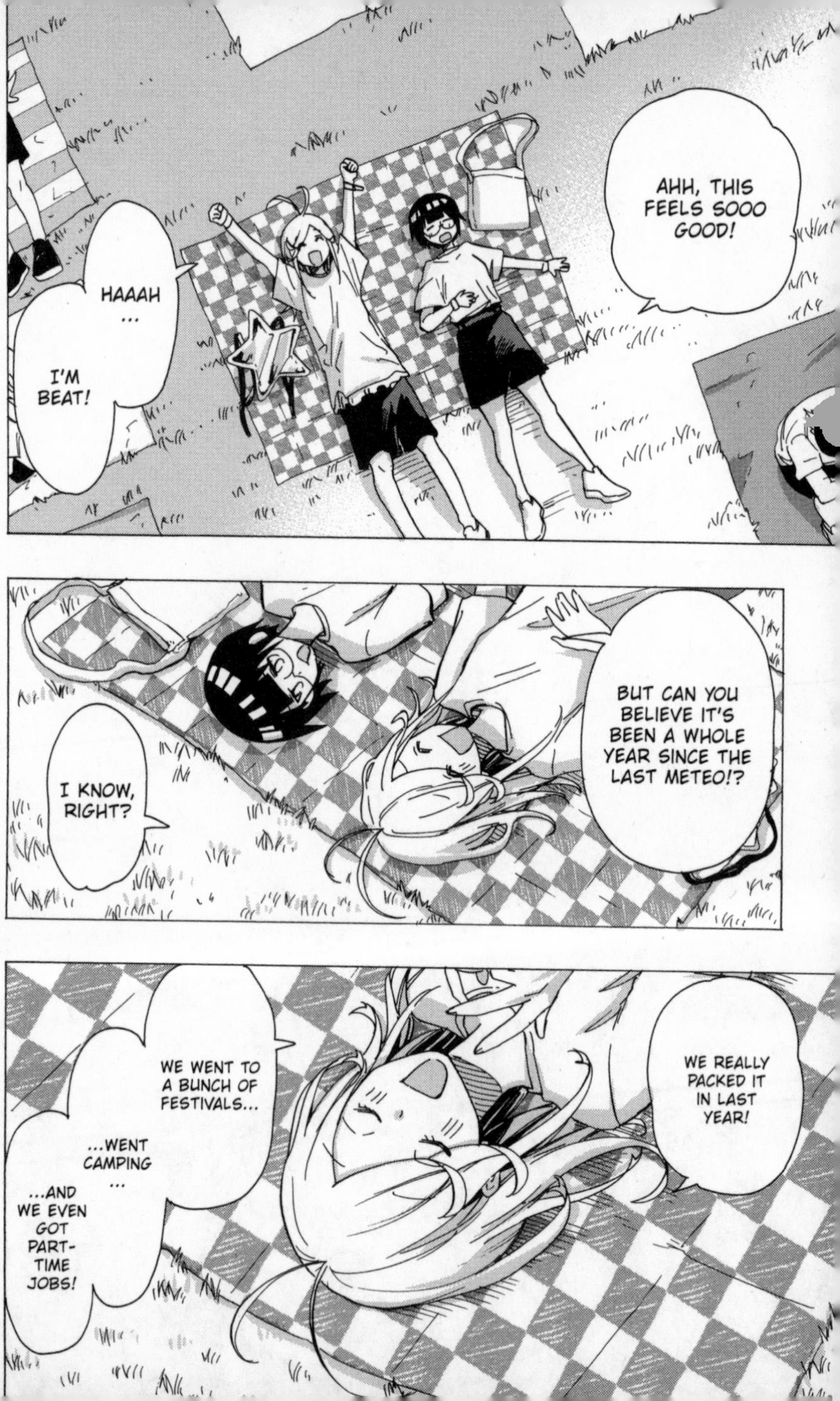
AHH, THIS FEELS SOOO GOOD!
HAAAH ... I'M BEAT!
BUT CAN YOU BELIEVE IT'S BEEN A WHOLE YEAR SINCE THE LAST METEO!?
I KNOW, RIGHT?
WE REALLY PACKED IT IN LAST YEAR!
WE WENT TO A BUNCH OF FESTIVALS...
...WENT CAMPING ...
...AND WE EVEN GOT PART-TIME JOBS!

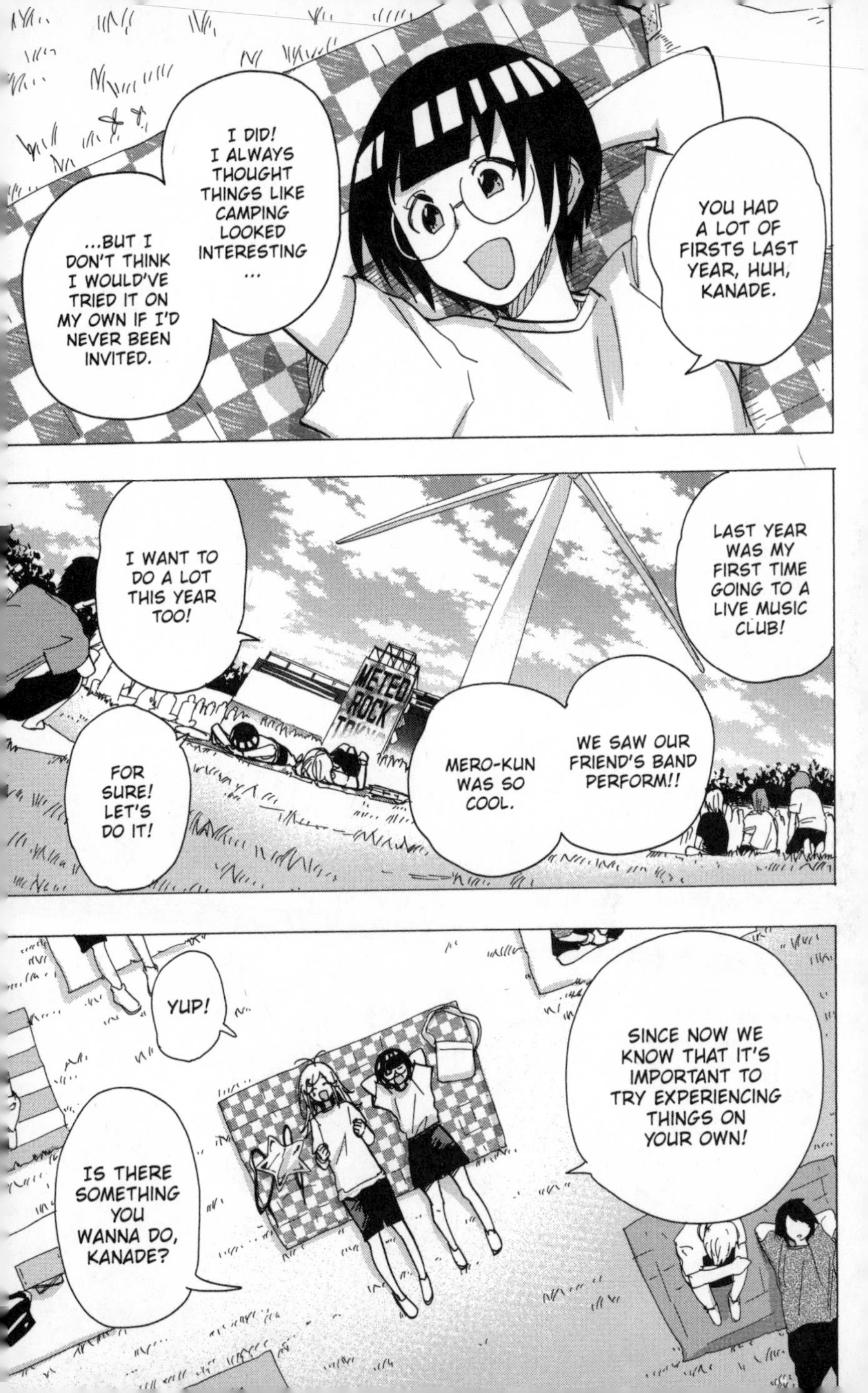
YOU HAD A LOT OF FIRSTS LAST YEAR, HUH, KANADE.
I DID! I ALWAYS THOUGHT THINGS LIKE CAMPING LOOKED INTERESTING ...
...BUT I DON'T THINK I WOULD'VE TRIED IT ON MY OWN IF I'D NEVER BEEN INVITED.
LAST YEAR WAS MY FIRST TIME GOING TO A LIVE MUSIC CLUB!
WE SAW OUR FRIEND'S BAND PERFORM!!
MERO-KUN WAS SO COOL.
I WANT TO DO A LOT THIS YEAR TOO!
METEO ROCK
FOR SURE! LET'S DO IT!
SINCE NOW WE KNOW THAT IT'S IMPORTANT TO TRY EXPERIENCING THINGS ON YOUR OWN!
YUP!
IS THERE SOMETHING YOU WANNA DO, KANADE?

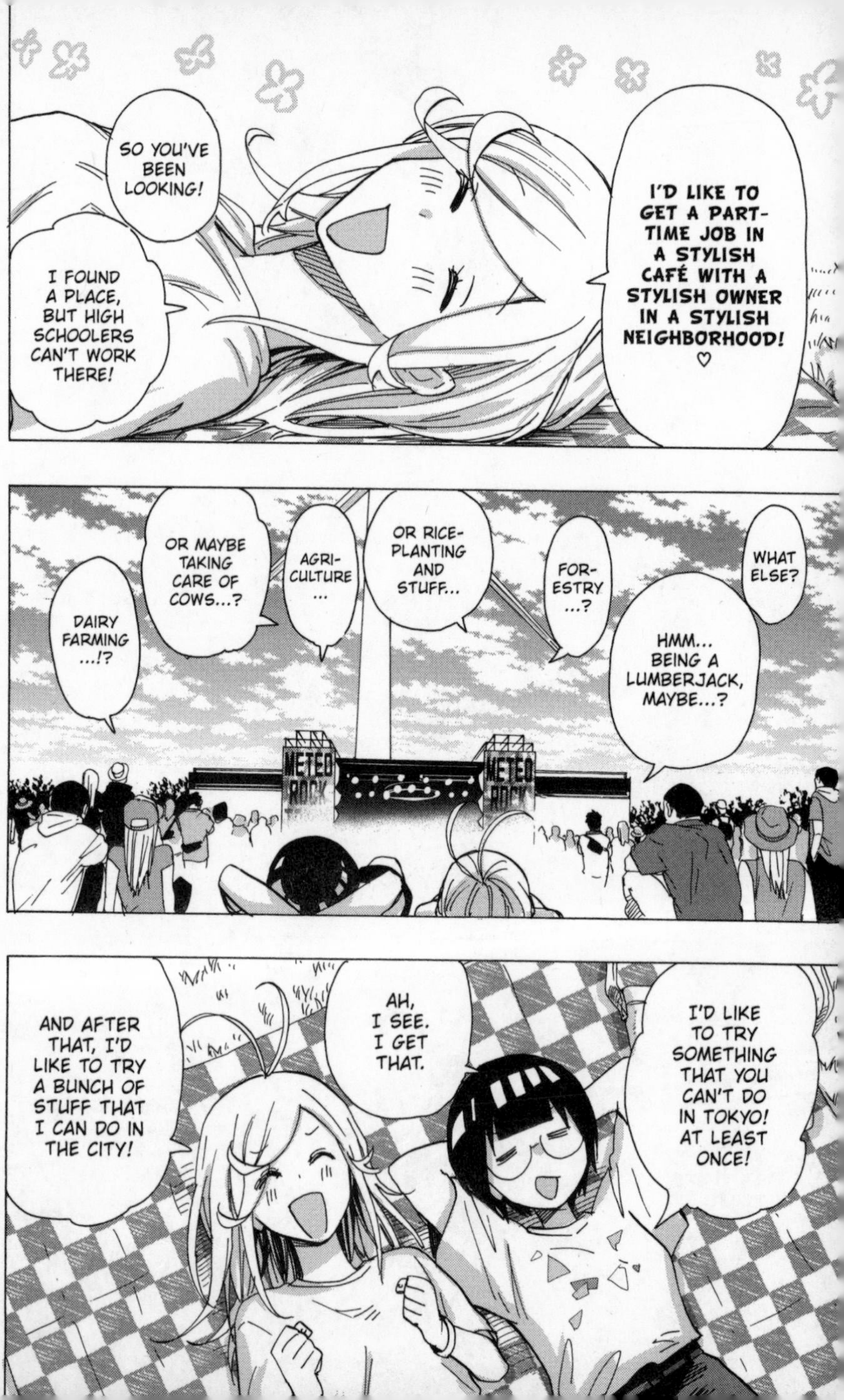
I'D LIKE TO GET A PART-TIME JOB IN A STYLISH CAFÉ WITH A STYLISH OWNER IN A STYLISH NEIGHBORHOOD! ♡
SO YOU'VE BEEN LOOKING!
I FOUND A PLACE, BUT HIGH SCHOOLERS CAN'T WORK THERE!
WHAT ELSE?
HMM... BEING A LUMBERJACK, MAYBE...?
FOR-ESTRY ...?
OR RICE-PLANTING AND STUFF...
AGRI-CULTURE ...
OR MAYBE TAKING CARE OF COWS...?
DAIRY FARMING ...!?
METEO ROCK
METEO ROCK
I'D LIKE TO TRY SOMETHING THAT YOU CAN'T DO IN TOKYO! AT LEAST ONCE!
AH, I SEE. I GET THAT.
AND AFTER THAT, I'D LIKE TO TRY A BUNCH OF STUFF THAT I CAN DO IN THE CITY!

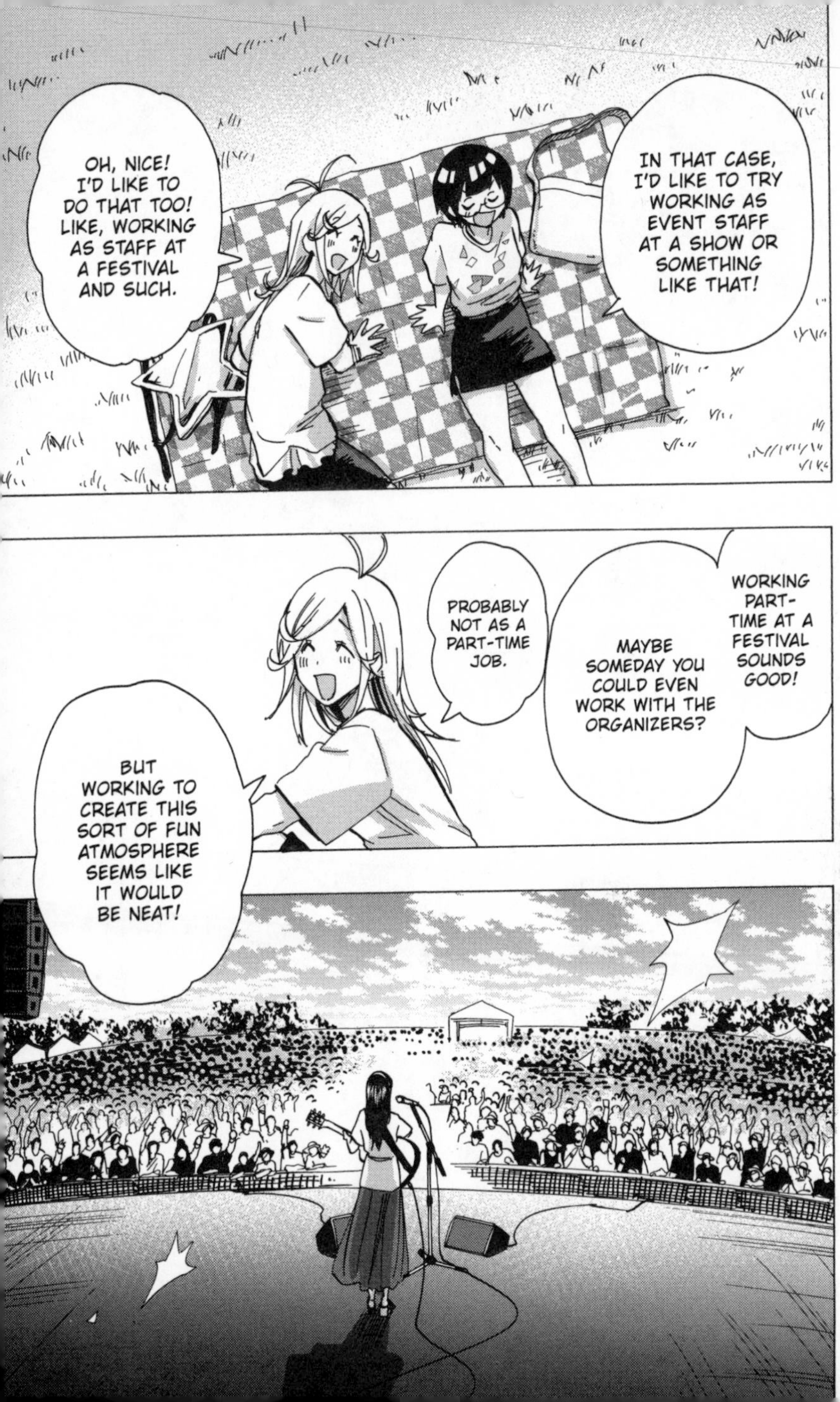
IN THAT CASE, I'D LIKE TO TRY WORKING AS EVENT STAFF AT A SHOW OR SOMETHING LIKE THAT!
OH, NICE! I'D LIKE TO DO THAT TOO! LIKE, WORKING AS STAFF AT A FESTIVAL AND SUCH.
WORKING PART-TIME AT A FESTIVAL SOUNDS GOOD!
MAYBE SOMEDAY YOU COULD EVEN WORK WITH THE ORGANIZERS?
PROBABLY NOT AS A PART-TIME JOB.
BUT WORKING TO CREATE THIS SORT OF FUN ATMOSPHERE SEEMS LIKE IT WOULD BE NEAT!

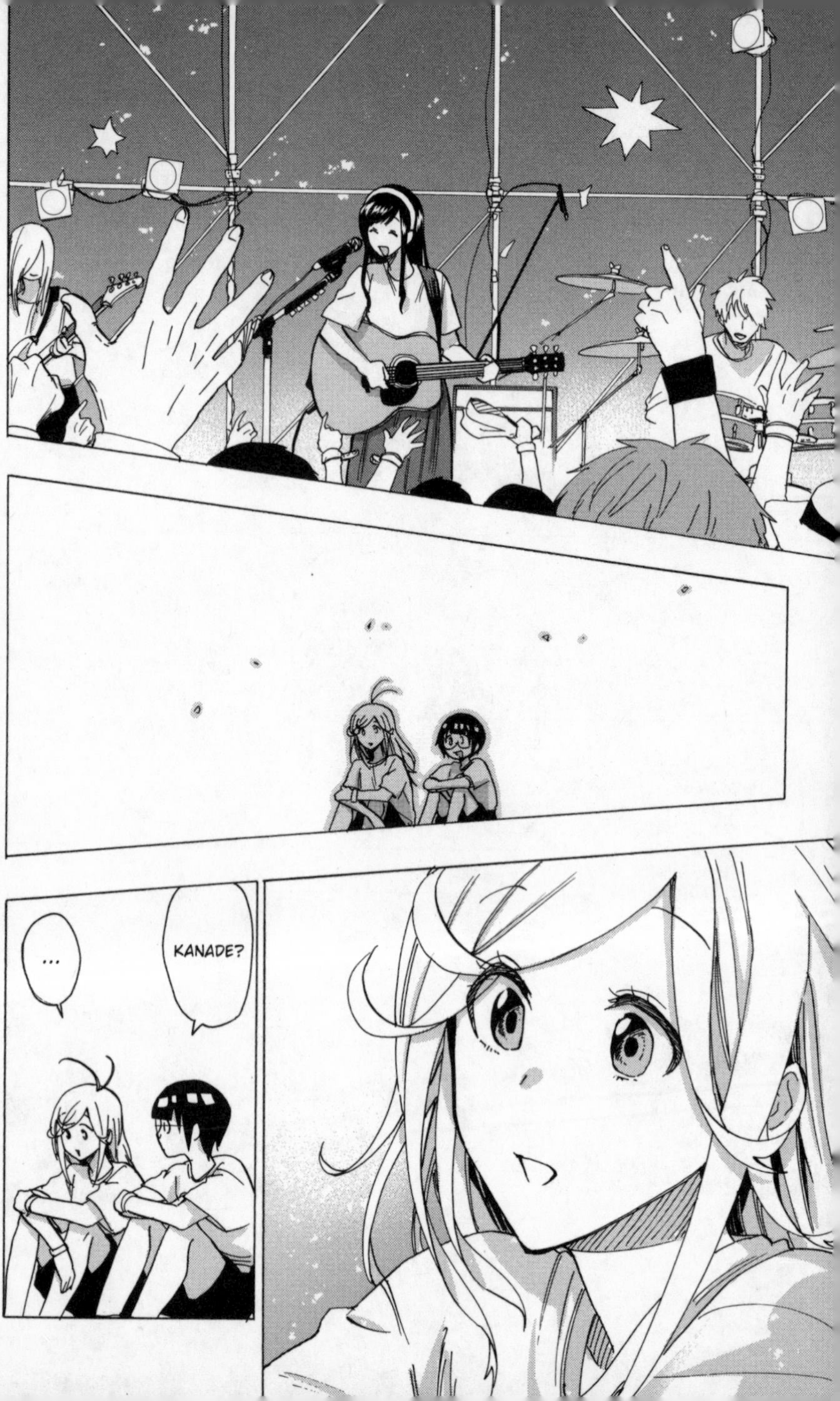
KANADE?
...

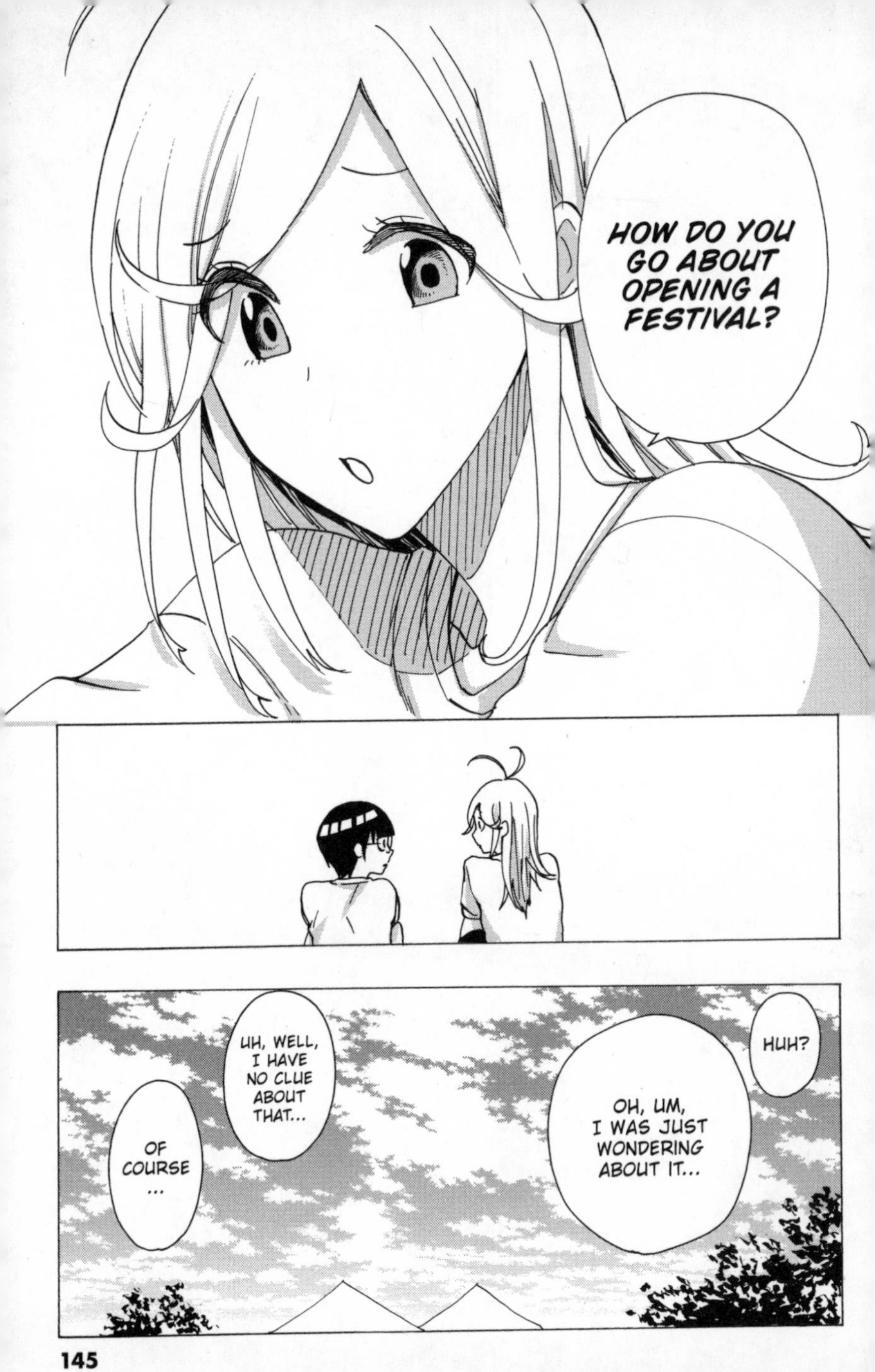
HOW DO YOU GO ABOUT OPENING A FESTIVAL?
HUH?
OH, UM, I WAS JUST WONDERING ABOUT IT...
UH, WELL, I HAVE NO CLUE ABOUT THAT...
OF COURSE...

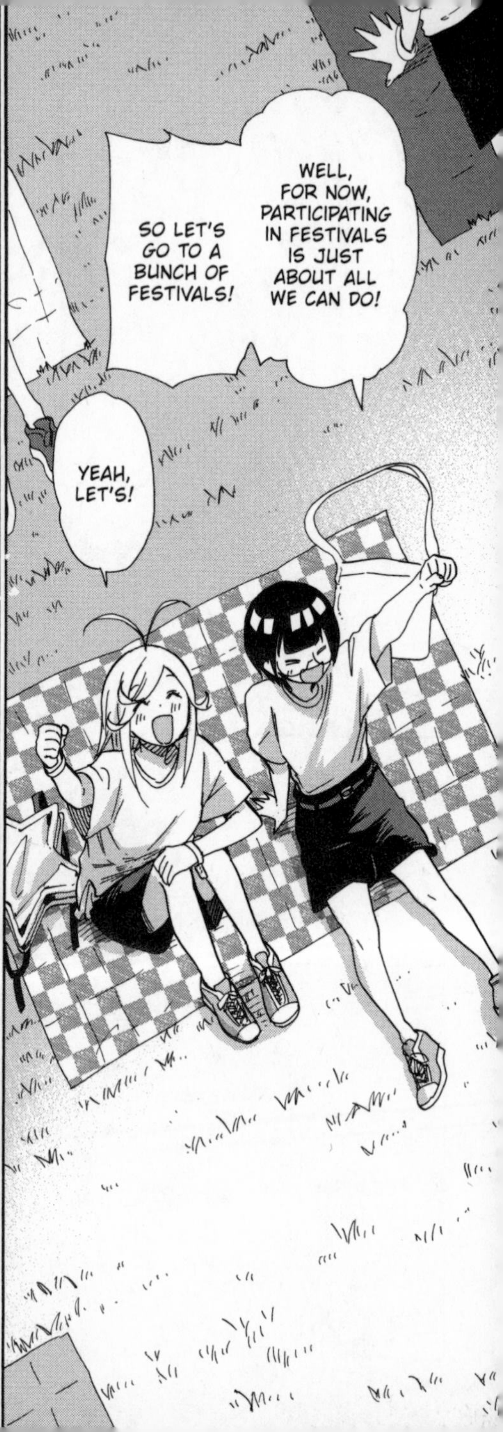
WELL, FOR NOW, PARTICIPATING IN FESTIVALS IS JUST ABOUT ALL WE CAN DO!
SO LET'S GO TO A BUNCH OF FESTIVALS!
YEAH, LET'S!
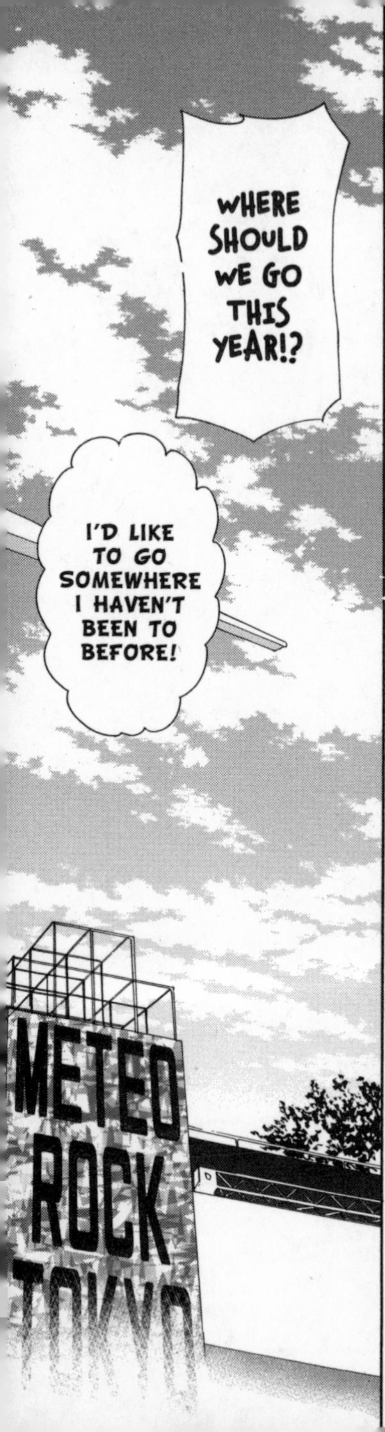
WHERE SHOULD WE GO THIS YEAR!?
I'D LIKE TO GO SOMEWHERE I HAVEN'T BEEN TO BEFORE!
METEO ROCK TOKYO

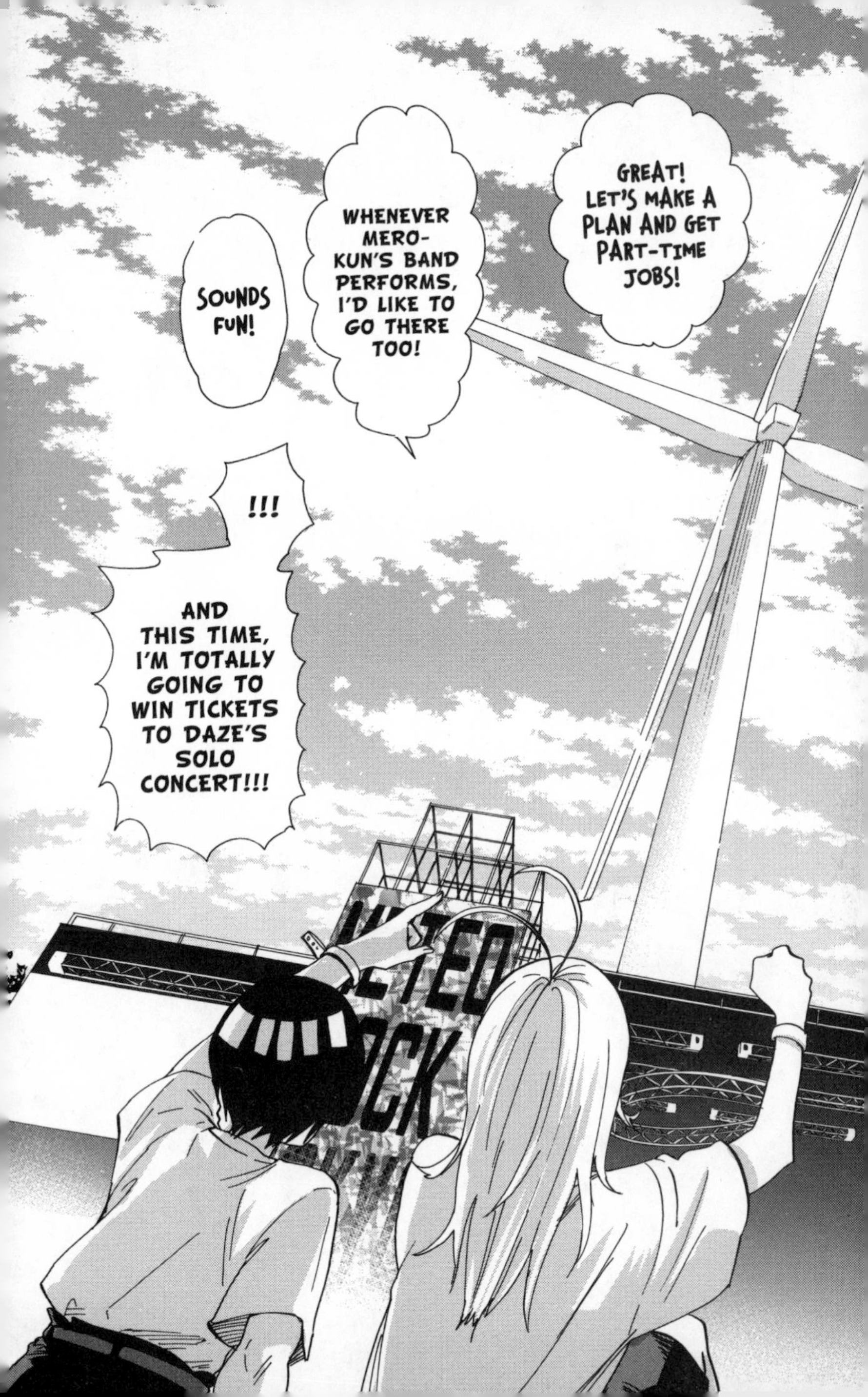
GREAT! LET'S MAKE A PLAN AND GET PART-TIME JOBS!
WHENEVER MERO-KUN'S BAND PERFORMS, I'D LIKE TO GO THERE TOO!
SOUNDS FUN!
!!!
AND THIS TIME, I'M TOTALLY GOING TO WIN TICKETS TO DAZE'S SOLO CONCERT!!!

Days on Fes

FES 22.5

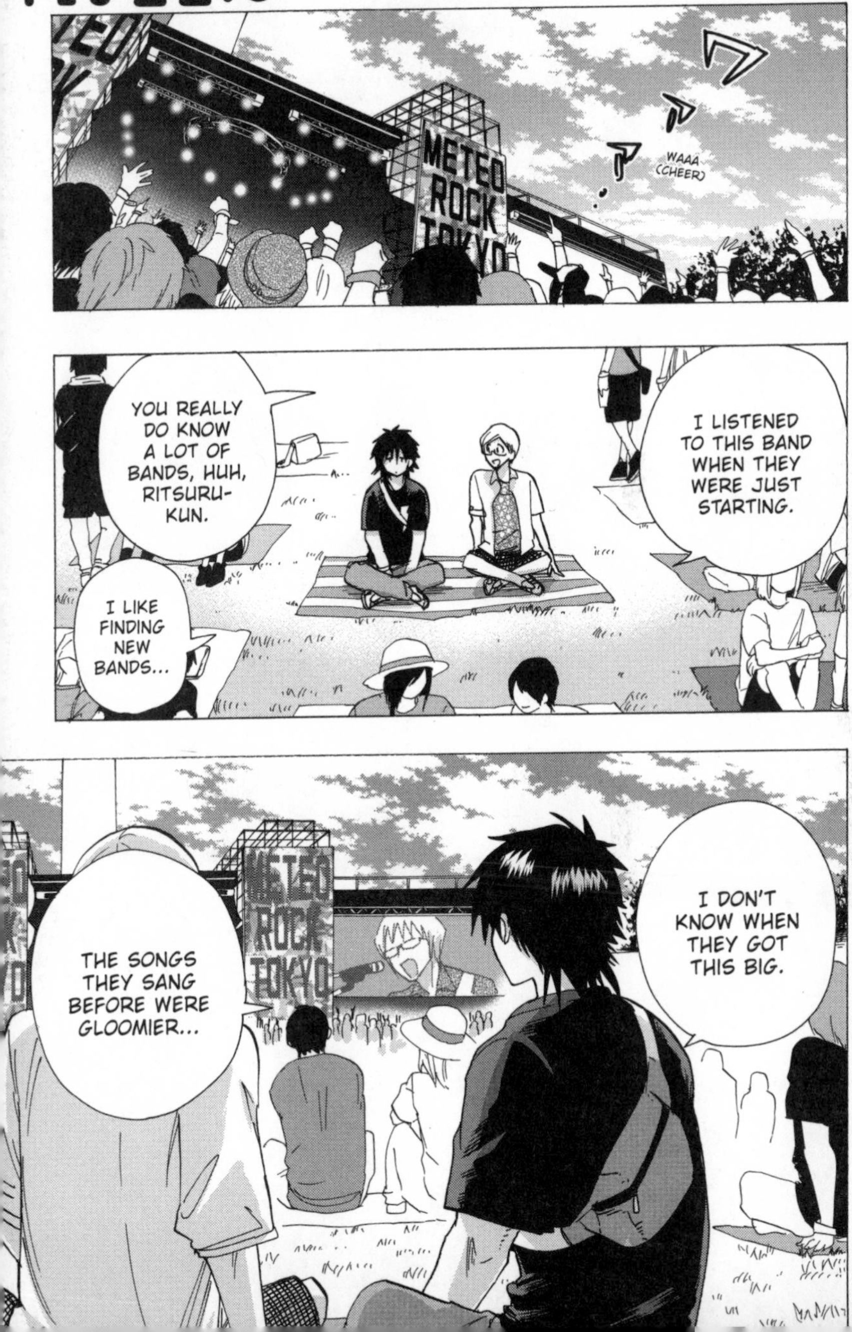
WAAA
(CHEER)
I LISTENED TO THIS BAND WHEN THEY WERE JUST STARTING.
YOU REALLY DO KNOW A LOT OF BANDS, HUH, RITSURU-KUN.
I LIKE FINDING NEW BANDS...
METEO ROCK TOKYO
I DON'T KNOW WHEN THEY GOT THIS BIG.
THE SONGS THEY SANG BEFORE WERE GLOOMIER...

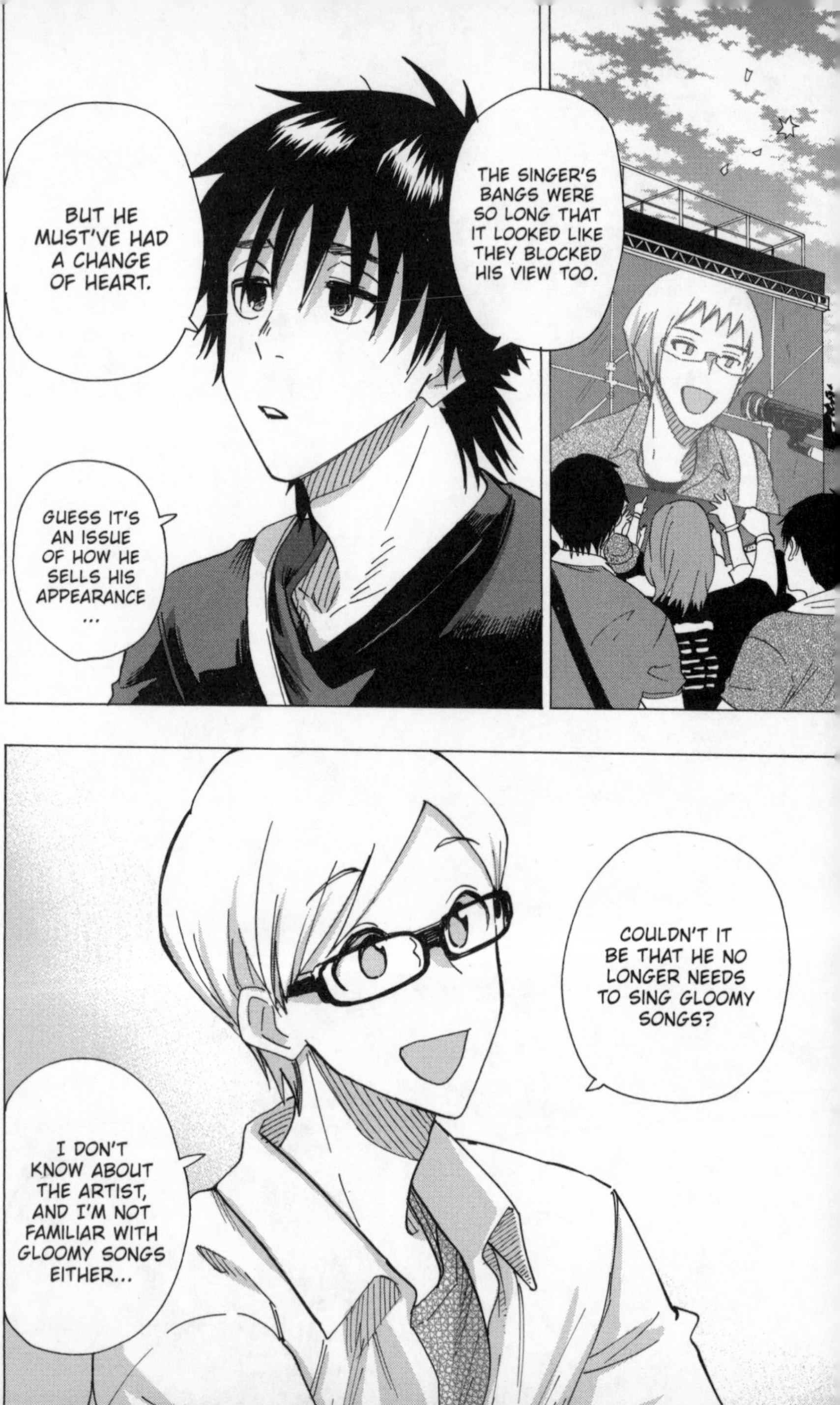
THE SINGER'S BANGS WERE SO LONG THAT IT LOOKED LIKE THEY BLOCKED HIS VIEW TOO.
BUT HE MUST'VE HAD A CHANGE OF HEART.
GUESS IT'S AN ISSUE OF HOW HE SELLS HIS APPEARANCE ...
COULDN'T IT BE THAT HE NO LONGER NEEDS TO SING GLOOMY SONGS?
I DON'T KNOW ABOUT THE ARTIST, AND I'M NOT FAMILIAR WITH GLOOMY SONGS EITHER...

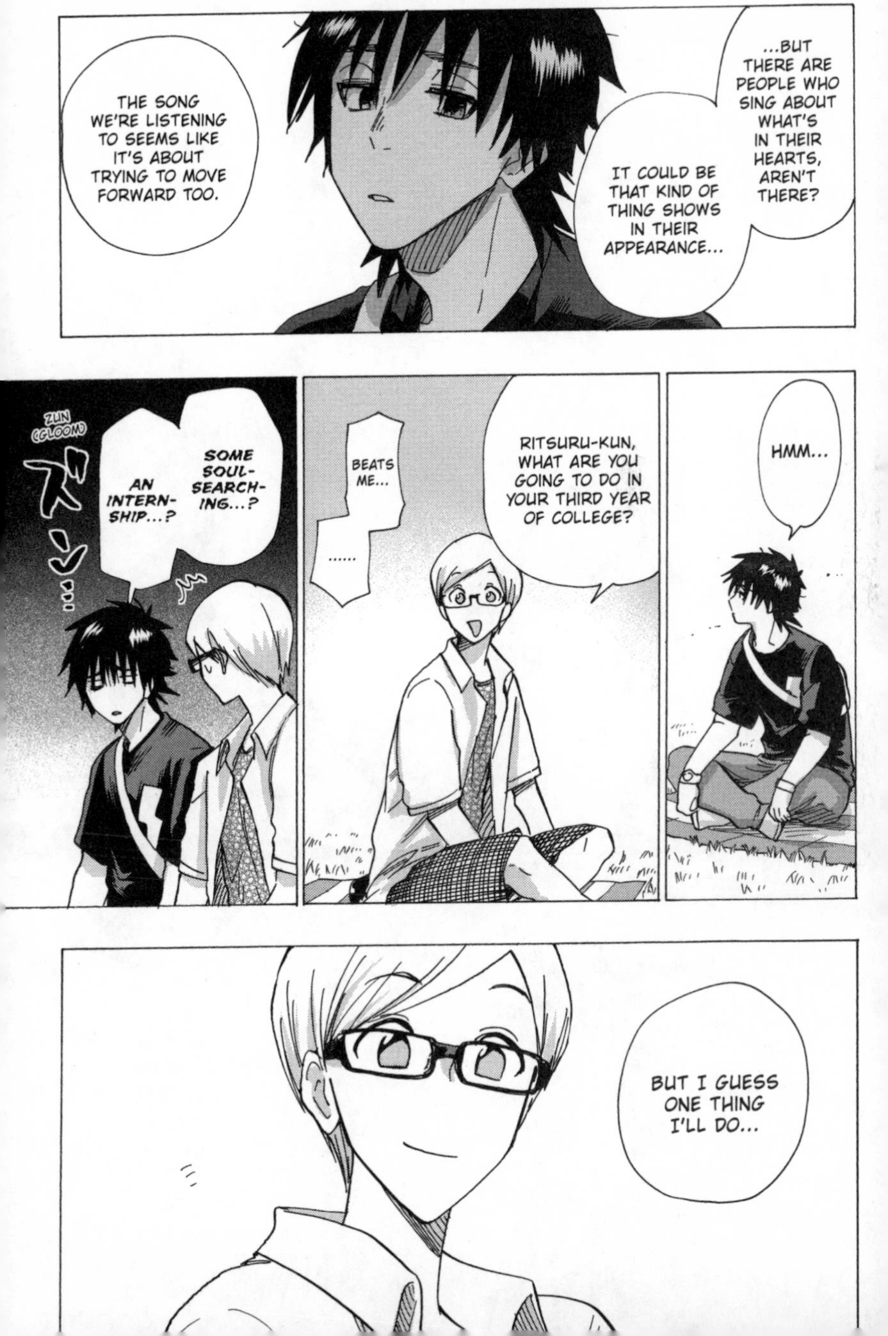
...BUT THERE ARE PEOPLE WHO SING ABOUT WHAT'S IN THEIR HEARTS, AREN'T THERE?
IT COULD BE THAT KIND OF THING SHOWS IN THEIR APPEARANCE...
THE SONG WE'RE LISTENING TO SEEMS LIKE IT'S ABOUT TRYING TO MOVE FORWARD TOO.
HMM...
RITSURU-KUN, WHAT ARE YOU GOING TO DO IN YOUR THIRD YEAR OF COLLEGE?
BEATS ME...
......
SOME SOUL-SEARCHING...?
AN INTERNSHIP...?
ZUN (GLOOM)
BUT I GUESS ONE THING I'LL DO...

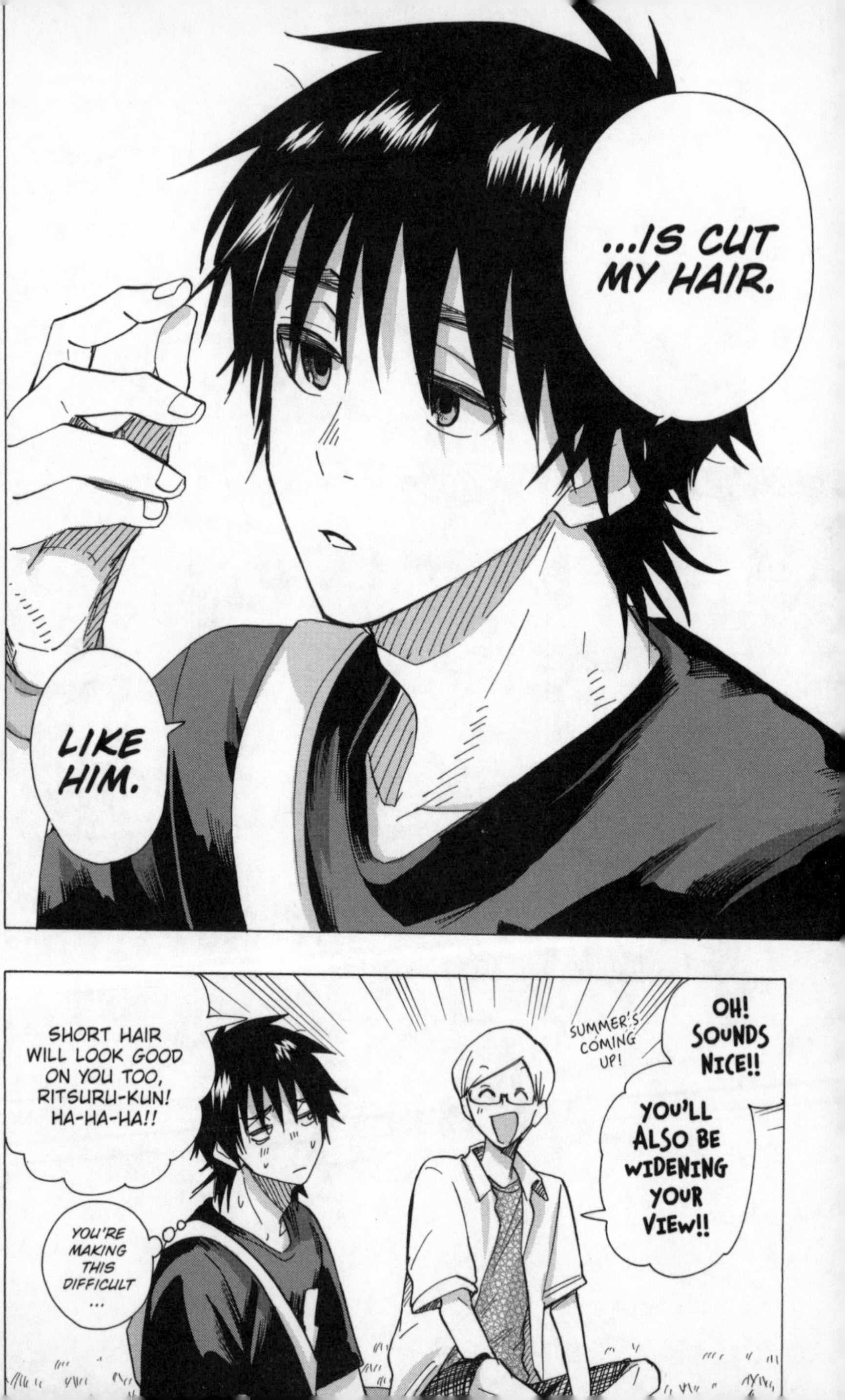
...IS CUT MY HAIR.
LIKE HIM.
OH! SOUNDS NICE!!
YOU'LL ALSO BE WIDENING YOUR VIEW!!
SUMMER'S COMING UP!
SHORT HAIR WILL LOOK GOOD ON YOU TOO, RITSURU-KUN! HA-HA-HA!!
YOU'RE MAKING THIS DIFFICULT ...

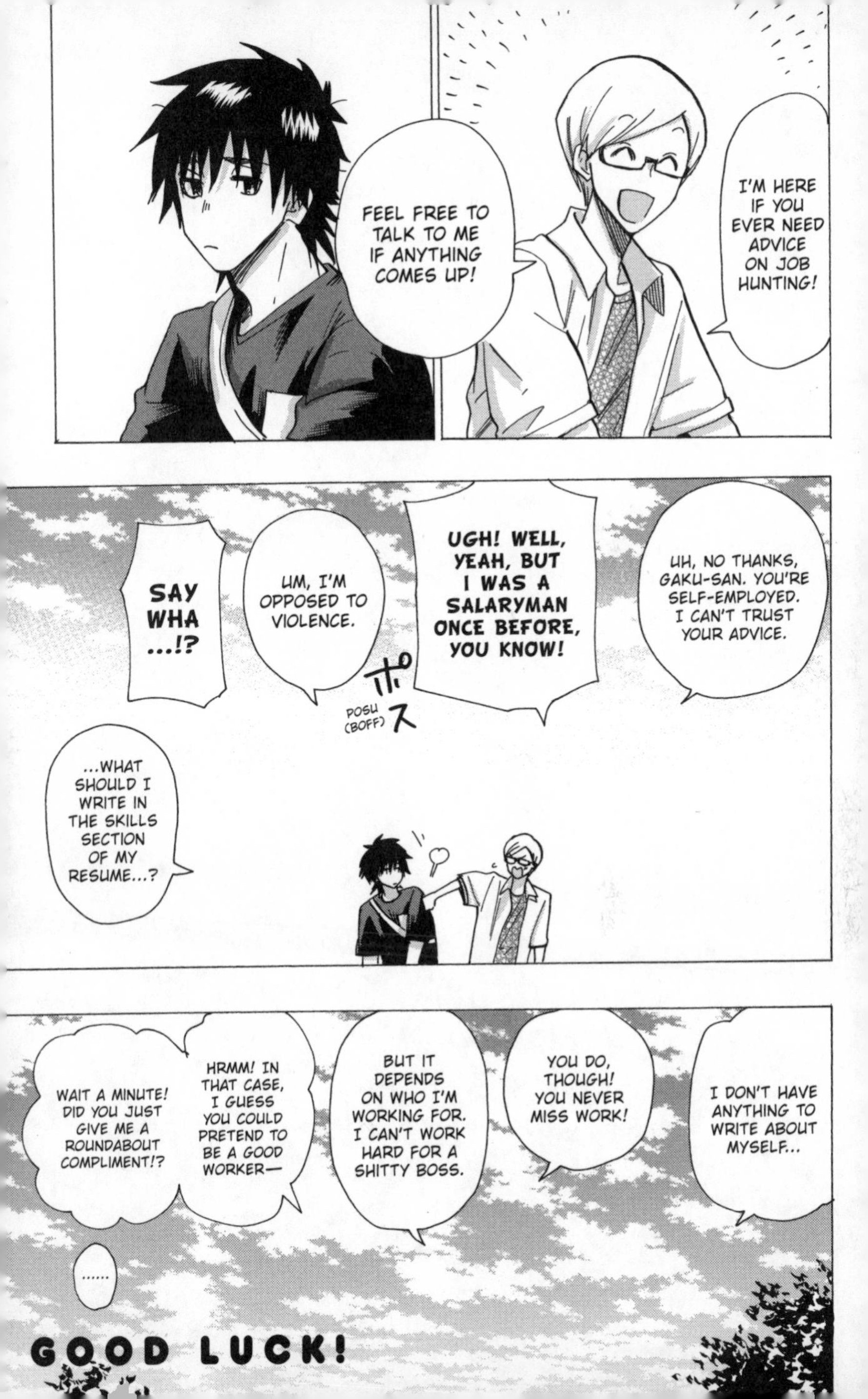
I'M HERE IF YOU EVER NEED ADVICE ON JOB HUNTING!
FEEL FREE TO TALK TO ME IF ANYTHING COMES UP!
UH, NO THANKS, GAKU-SAN. YOU'RE SELF-EMPLOYED. I CAN'T TRUST YOUR ADVICE.
UGH! WELL, YEAH, BUT I WAS A SALARYMAN ONCE BEFORE, YOU KNOW!
ポス
POSU (BOFF)
UM, I'M OPPOSED TO VIOLENCE.
SAY WHA ...!?
...WHAT SHOULD I WRITE IN THE SKILLS SECTION OF MY RESUME...?
I DON'T HAVE ANYTHING TO WRITE ABOUT MYSELF...
YOU DO, THOUGH! YOU NEVER MISS WORK!
BUT IT DEPENDS ON WHO I'M WORKING FOR. I CAN'T WORK HARD FOR A SHITTY BOSS.
HRMM! IN THAT CASE, I GUESS YOU COULD PRETEND TO BE A GOOD WORKER—
WAIT A MINUTE! DID YOU JUST GIVE ME A ROUNDABOUT COMPLIMENT!?
......
GOOD LUCK!

Days on Fes

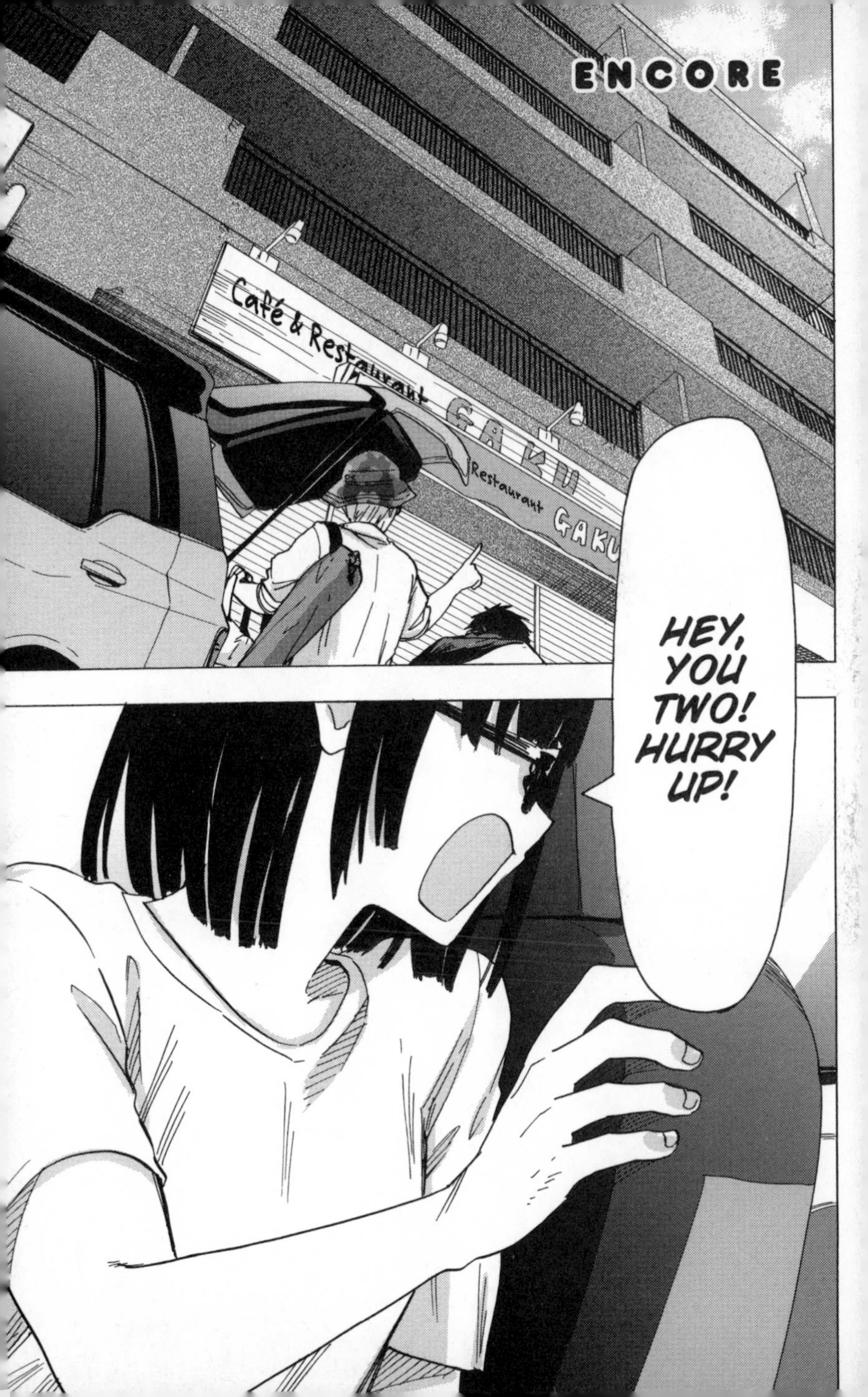
ENCORE
Café & Restaurant GAKU
Restaurant GAKU
HEY, YOU TWO! HURRY UP!

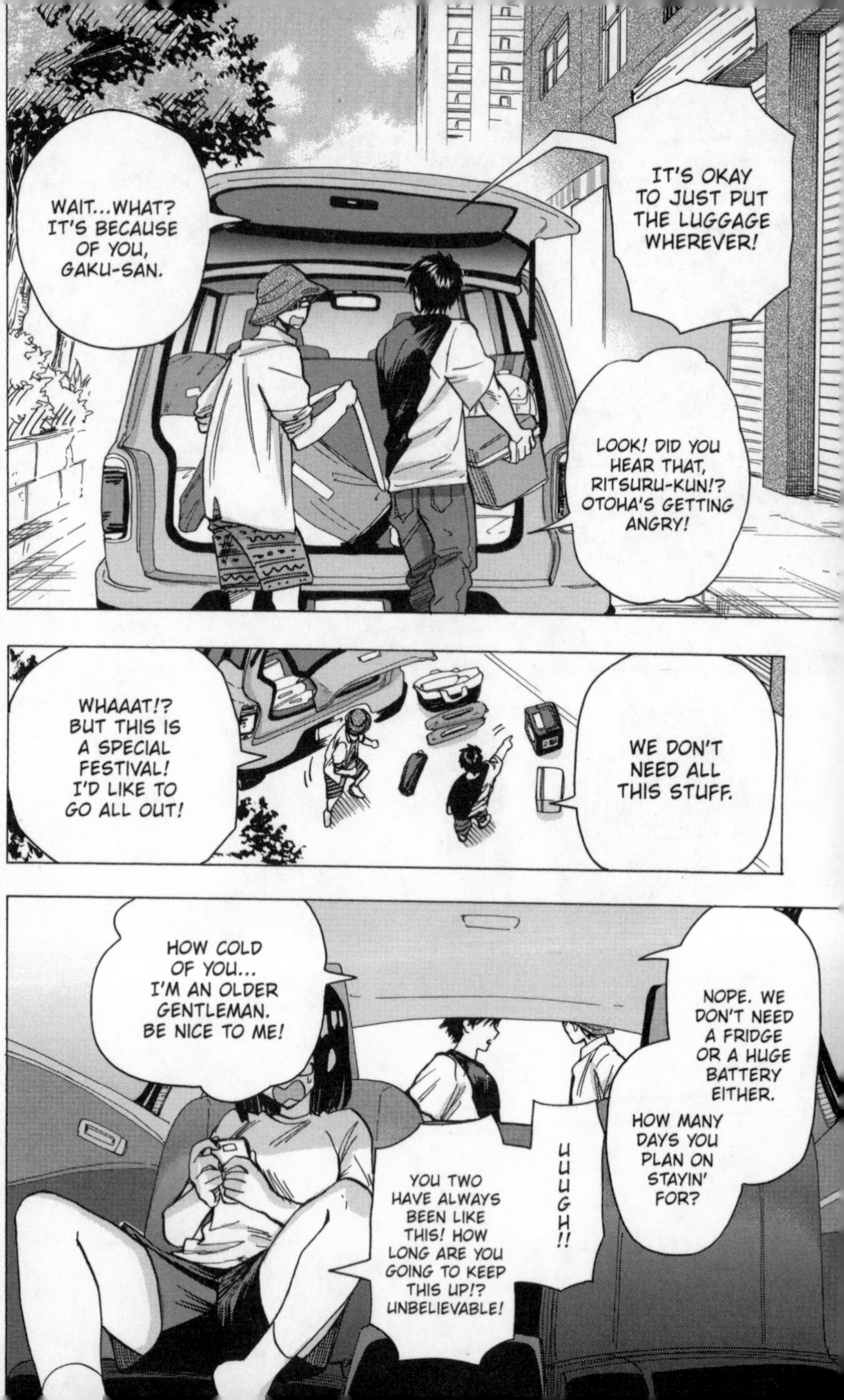
IT'S OKAY TO JUST PUT THE LUGGAGE WHEREVER!
WAIT...WHAT? IT'S BECAUSE OF YOU, GAKU-SAN.
LOOK! DID YOU HEAR THAT, RITSURU-KUN!? OTOHA'S GETTING ANGRY!
WE DON'T NEED ALL THIS STUFF.
WHAAAT!? BUT THIS IS A SPECIAL FESTIVAL! I'D LIKE TO GO ALL OUT!
NOPE. WE DON'T NEED A FRIDGE OR A HUGE BATTERY EITHER.
HOW MANY DAYS YOU PLAN ON STAYIN' FOR?
HOW COLD OF YOU... I'M AN OLDER GENTLEMAN. BE NICE TO ME!
UUUGH!!
YOU TWO HAVE ALWAYS BEEN LIKE THIS! HOW LONG ARE YOU GOING TO KEEP THIS UP!? UNBELIEVABLE!

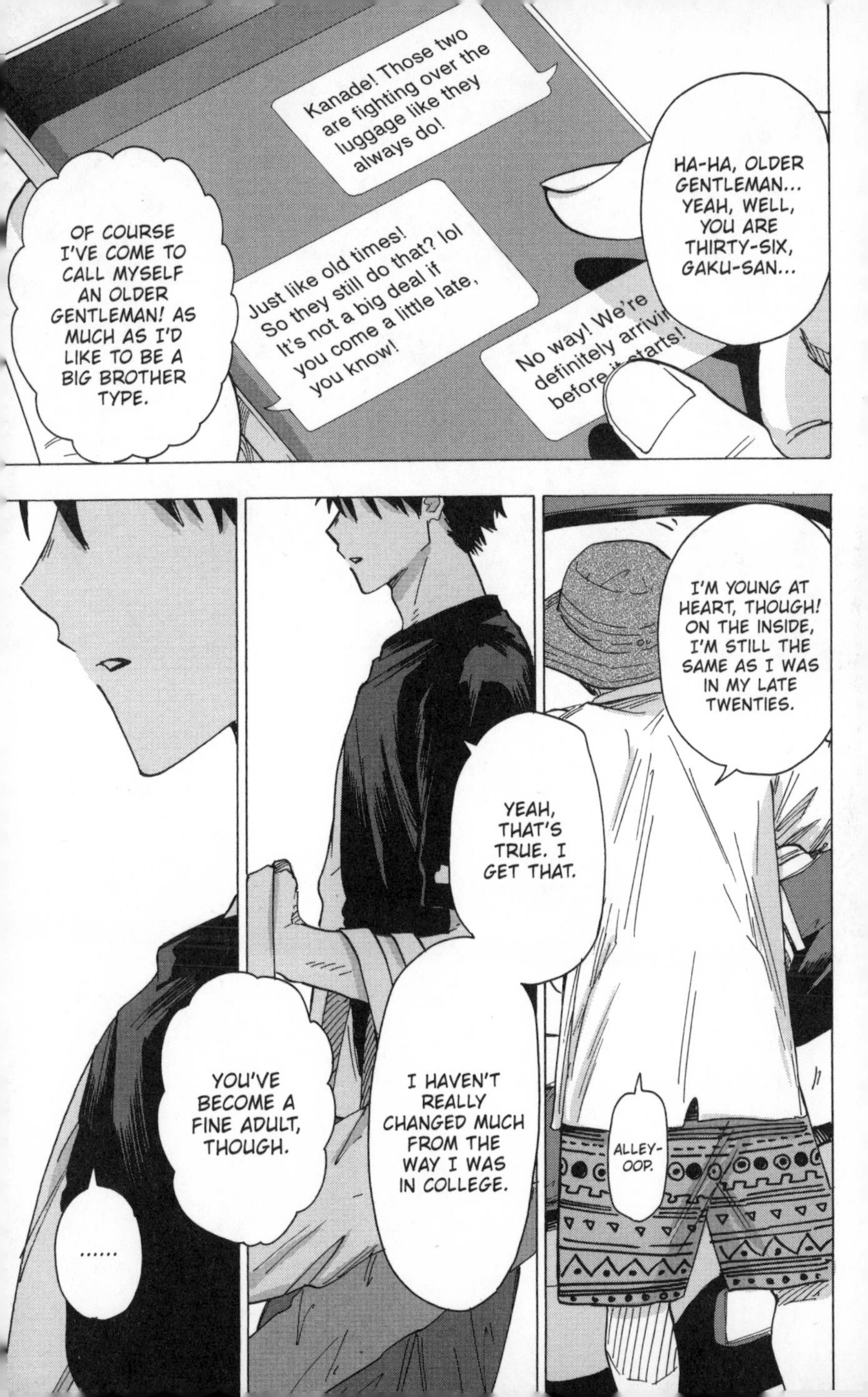
HA-HA, OLDER GENTLEMAN... YEAH, WELL, YOU ARE THIRTY-SIX, GAKU-SAN...
Kanade! Those two are fighting over the luggage like they always do!
Just like old times! So they still do that? lol It's not a big deal if you come a little late, you know!
No way! We're definitely arrivi
OF COURSE I'VE COME TO CALL MYSELF AN OLDER GENTLEMAN! AS MUCH AS I'D LIKE TO BE A BIG BROTHER TYPE.
I'M YOUNG AT HEART, THOUGH! ON THE INSIDE, I'M STILL THE SAME AS I WAS IN MY LATE TWENTIES.
YEAH, THAT'S TRUE. I GET THAT.
ALLEY-OOP.
I HAVEN'T REALLY CHANGED MUCH FROM THE WAY I WAS IN COLLEGE.
YOU'VE BECOME A FINE ADULT, THOUGH.
......

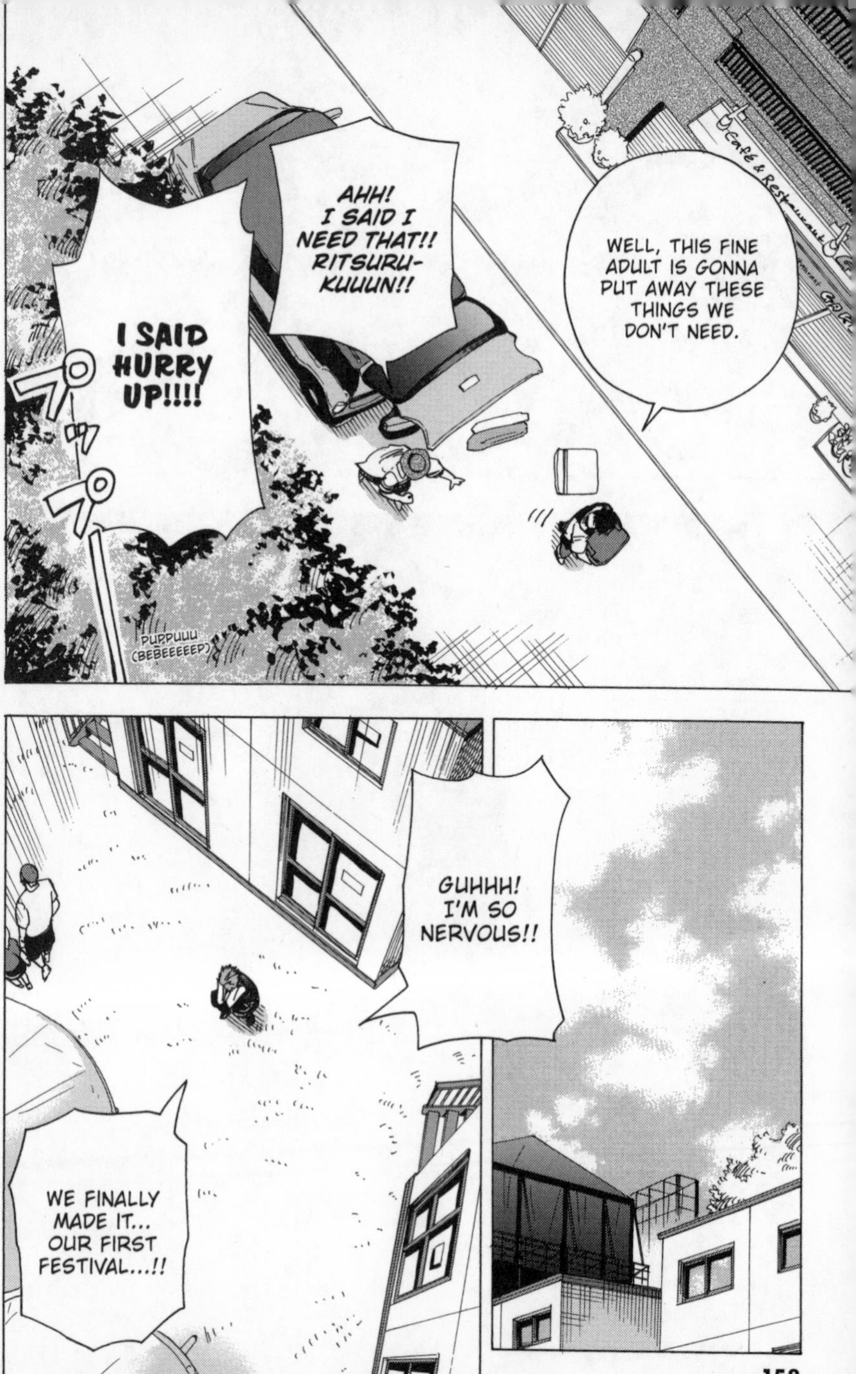
WELL, THIS FINE ADULT IS GONNA PUT AWAY THESE THINGS WE DON'T NEED.
AHH! I SAID I NEED THAT!! RITSURU-KUUUN!!
I SAID HURRY UP!!!!
PUPPUUU (BEBEEEEEP)
GUHHH! I'M SO NERVOUS!!
WE FINALLY MADE IT... OUR FIRST FESTIVAL...!!

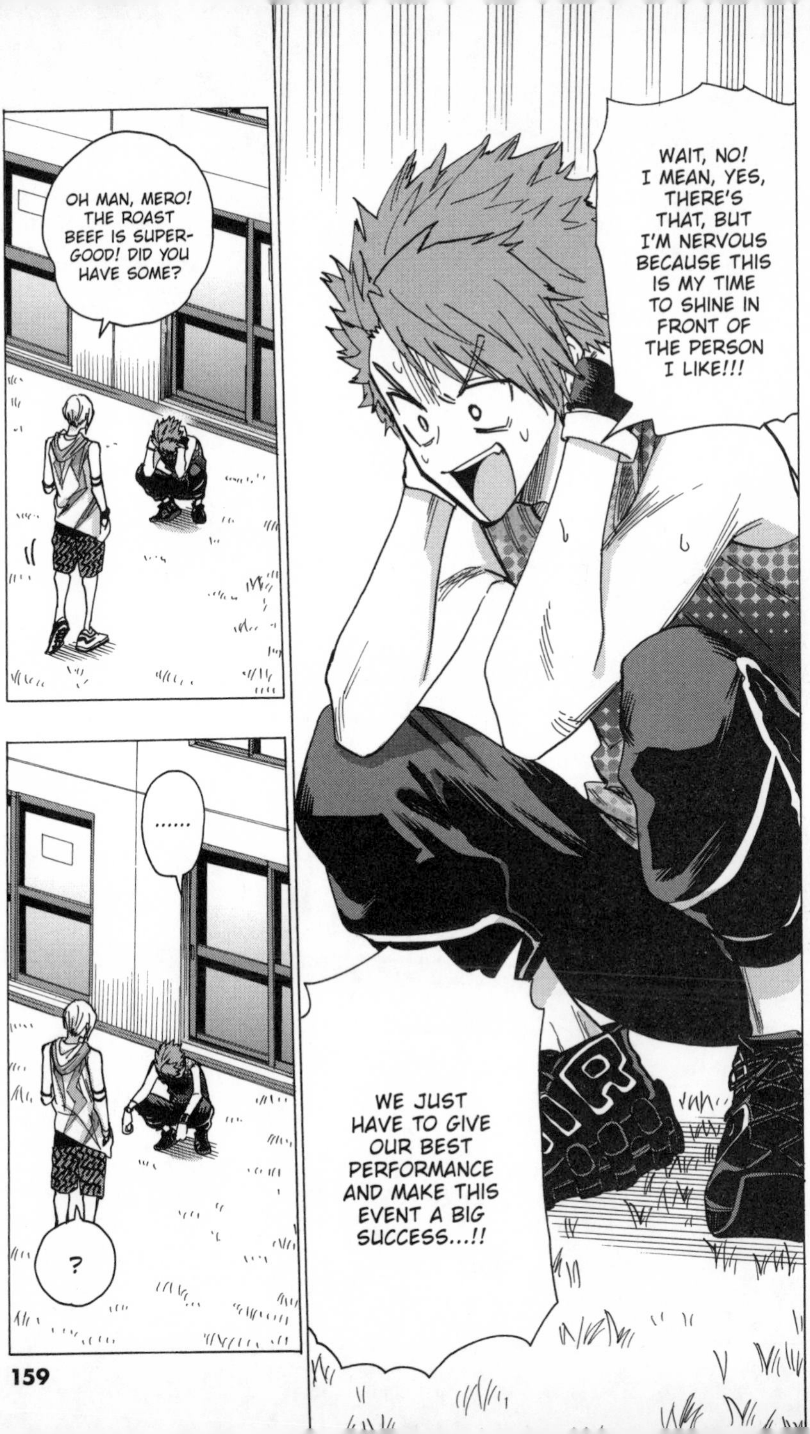

WAIT, NO! I MEAN, YES, THERE'S THAT, BUT I'M NERVOUS BECAUSE THIS IS MY TIME TO SHINE IN FRONT OF THE PERSON I LIKE!!!
WE JUST HAVE TO GIVE OUR BEST PERFORMANCE AND MAKE THIS EVENT A BIG SUCCESS...!!
OH MAN, MERO! THE ROAST BEEF IS SUPER-GOOD! DID YOU HAVE SOME?
......
?

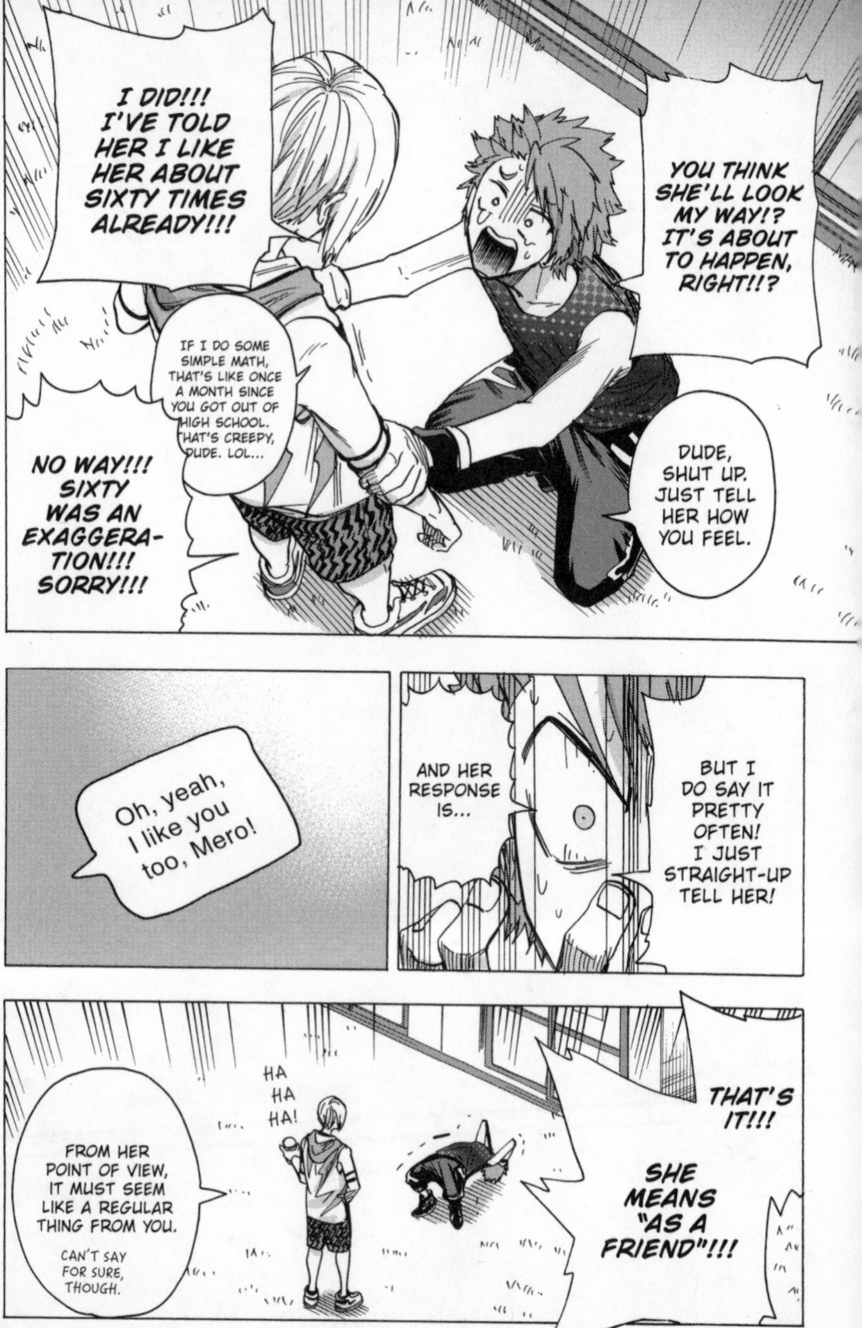
YOU THINK SHE'LL LOOK MY WAY!? IT'S ABOUT TO HAPPEN, RIGHT!!?
DUDE, SHUT UP. JUST TELL HER HOW YOU FEEL.
I DID!!! I'VE TOLD HER I LIKE HER ABOUT SIXTY TIMES ALREADY!!!
IF I DO SOME SIMPLE MATH, THAT'S LIKE ONCE A MONTH SINCE YOU GOT OUT OF HIGH SCHOOL. THAT'S CREEPY, DUDE. LOL...
NO WAY!!! SIXTY WAS AN EXAGGERA-TION!!! SORRY!!!
BUT I DO SAY IT PRETTY OFTEN! I JUST STRAIGHT-UP TELL HER!
AND HER RESPONSE IS...
Oh, yeah, I like you too, Mero!
THAT'S IT!!!
SHE MEANS "AS A FRIEND"!!!
HA HA HA!
FROM HER POINT OF VIEW, IT MUST SEEM LIKE A REGULAR THING FROM YOU.
CAN'T SAY FOR SURE, THOUGH.

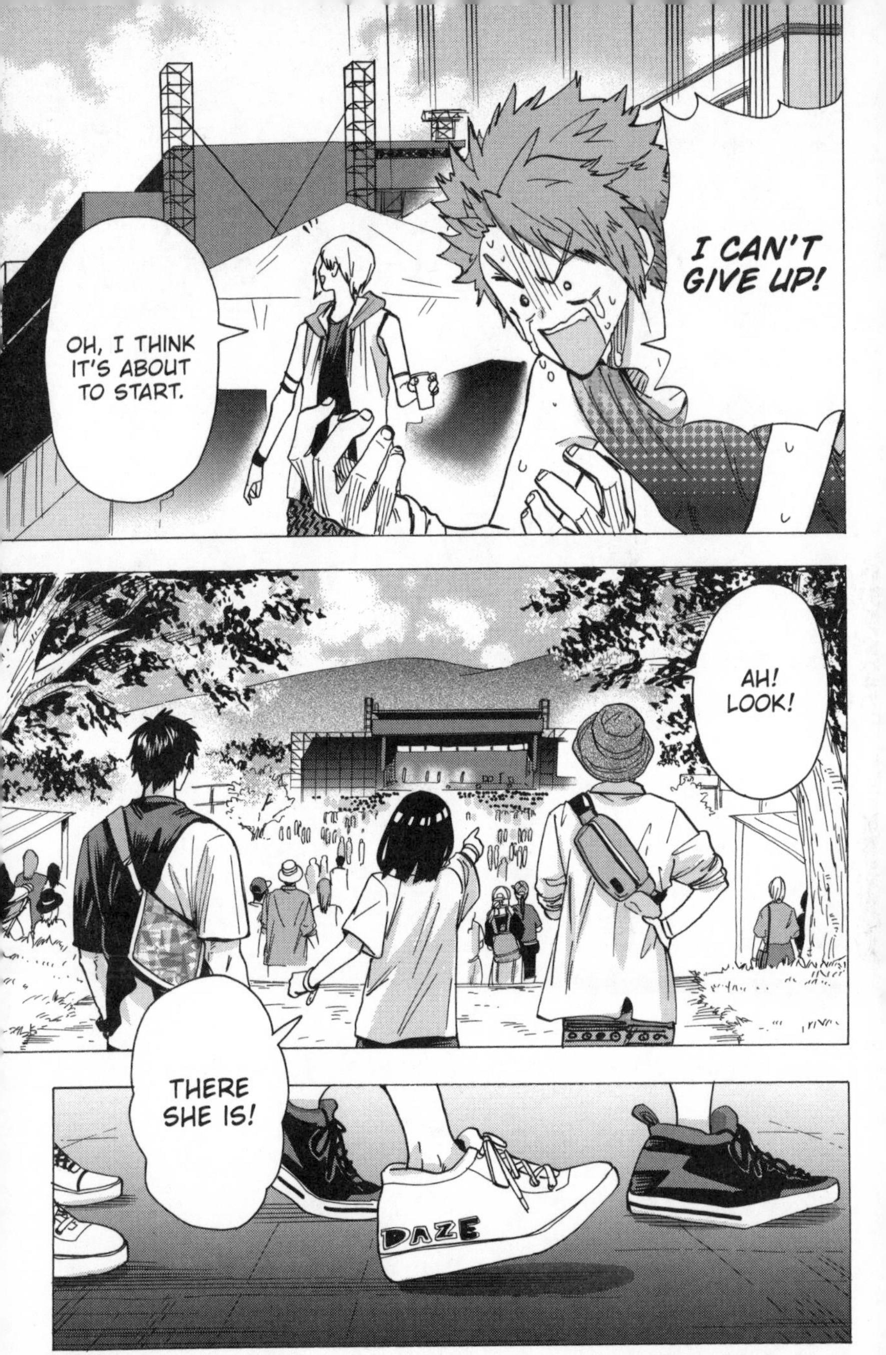
I CAN'T GIVE UP!
OH, I THINK IT'S ABOUT TO START.
AH! LOOK!
THERE SHE IS!

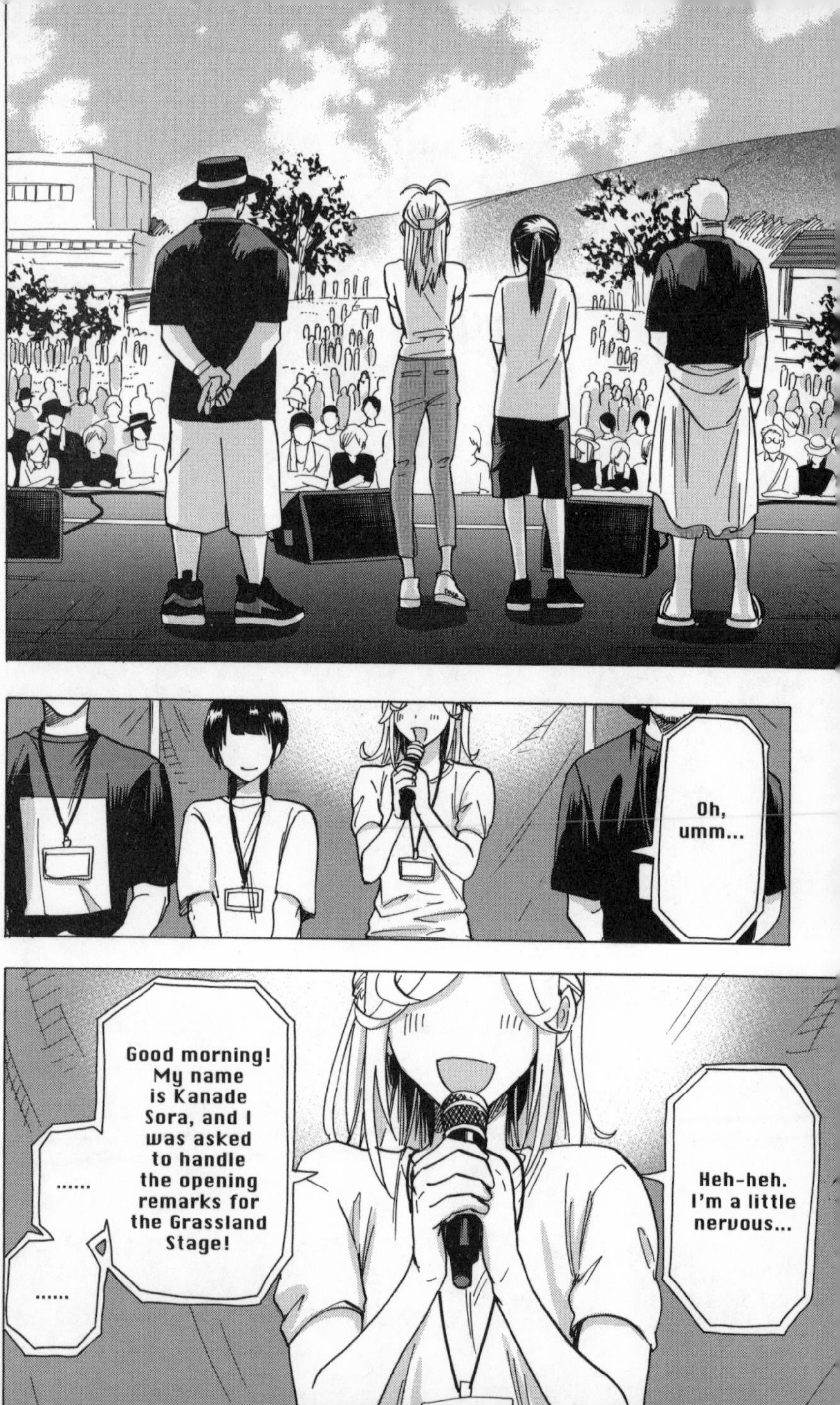
Oh, umm...
Heh-heh. I'm a little nervous...
Good morning! My name is Kanade Sora, and I was asked to handle the opening remarks for the Grassland Stage!
......
......

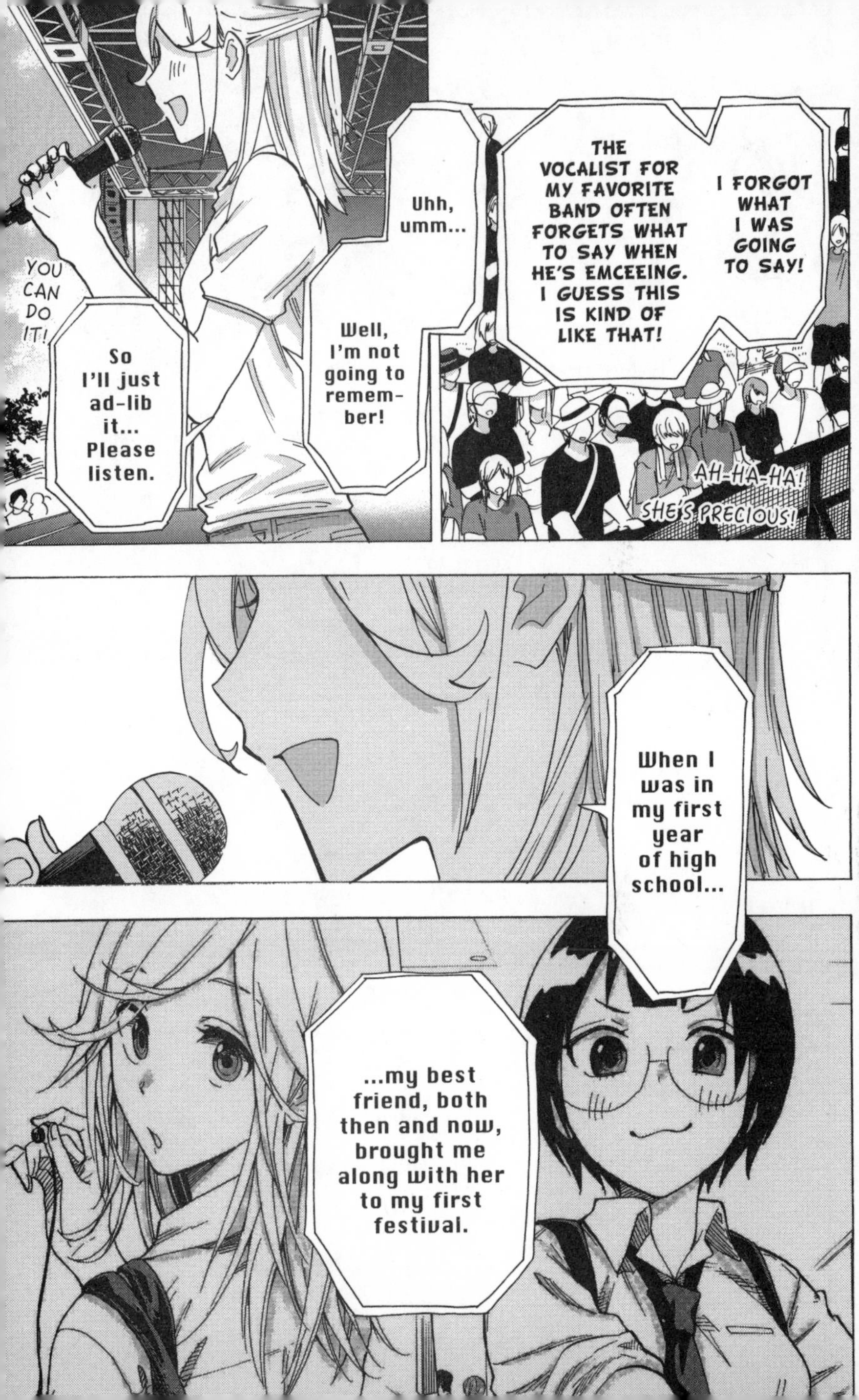
I FORGOT WHAT I WAS GOING TO SAY!
THE VOCALIST FOR MY FAVORITE BAND OFTEN FORGETS WHAT TO SAY WHEN HE'S EMCEEING. I GUESS THIS IS KIND OF LIKE THAT!
AH-HA-HA! SHE'S PRECIOUS!
Uhh, umm...
Well, I'm not going to remem-ber!
So I'll just ad-lib it... Please listen.
YOU CAN DO IT!
When I was in my first year of high school...
...my best friend, both then and now, brought me along with her to my first festival.

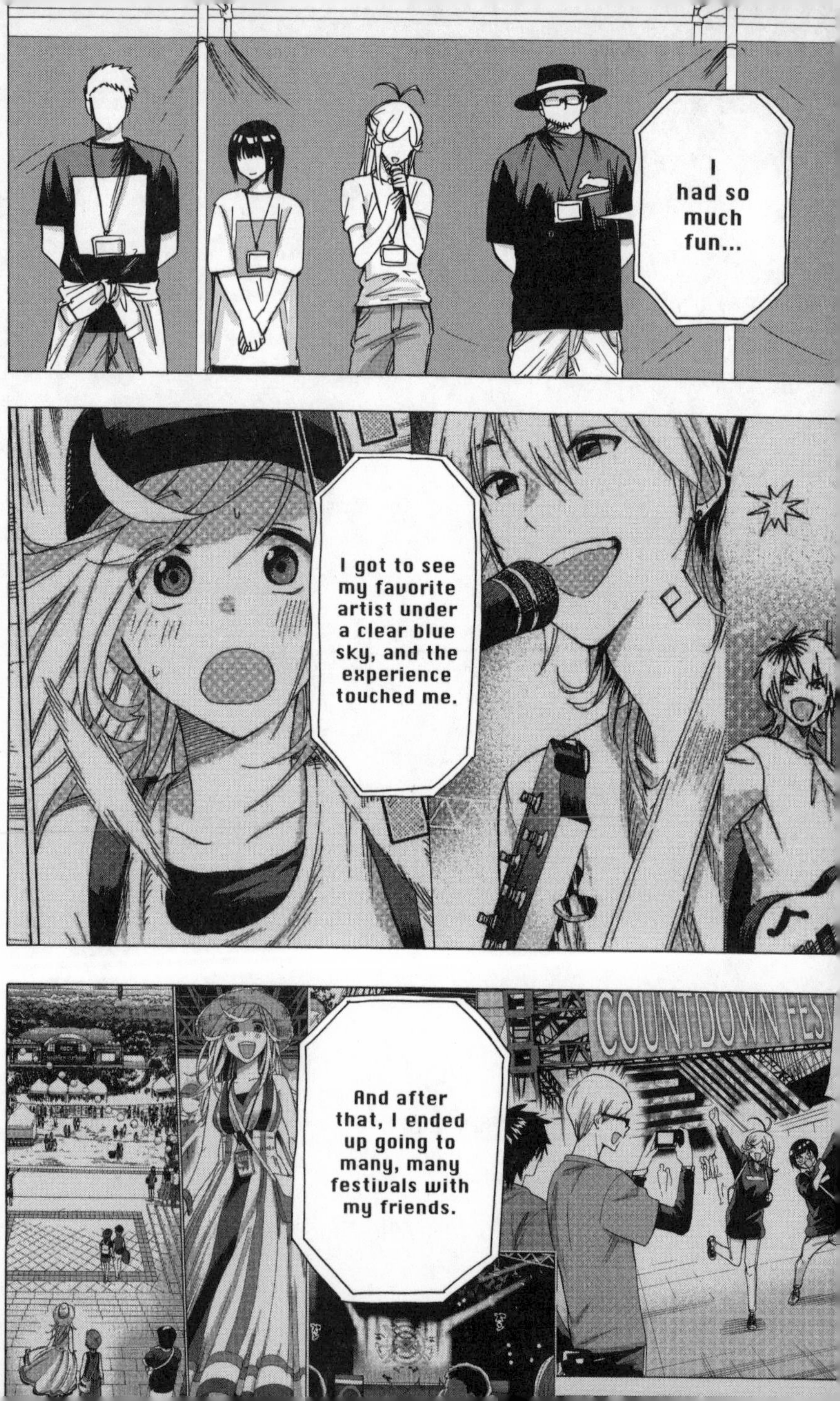
I had so much fun...
I got to see my favorite artist under a clear blue sky, and the experience touched me.
COUNTDOWN FES
And after that, I ended up going to many, many festivals with my friends.

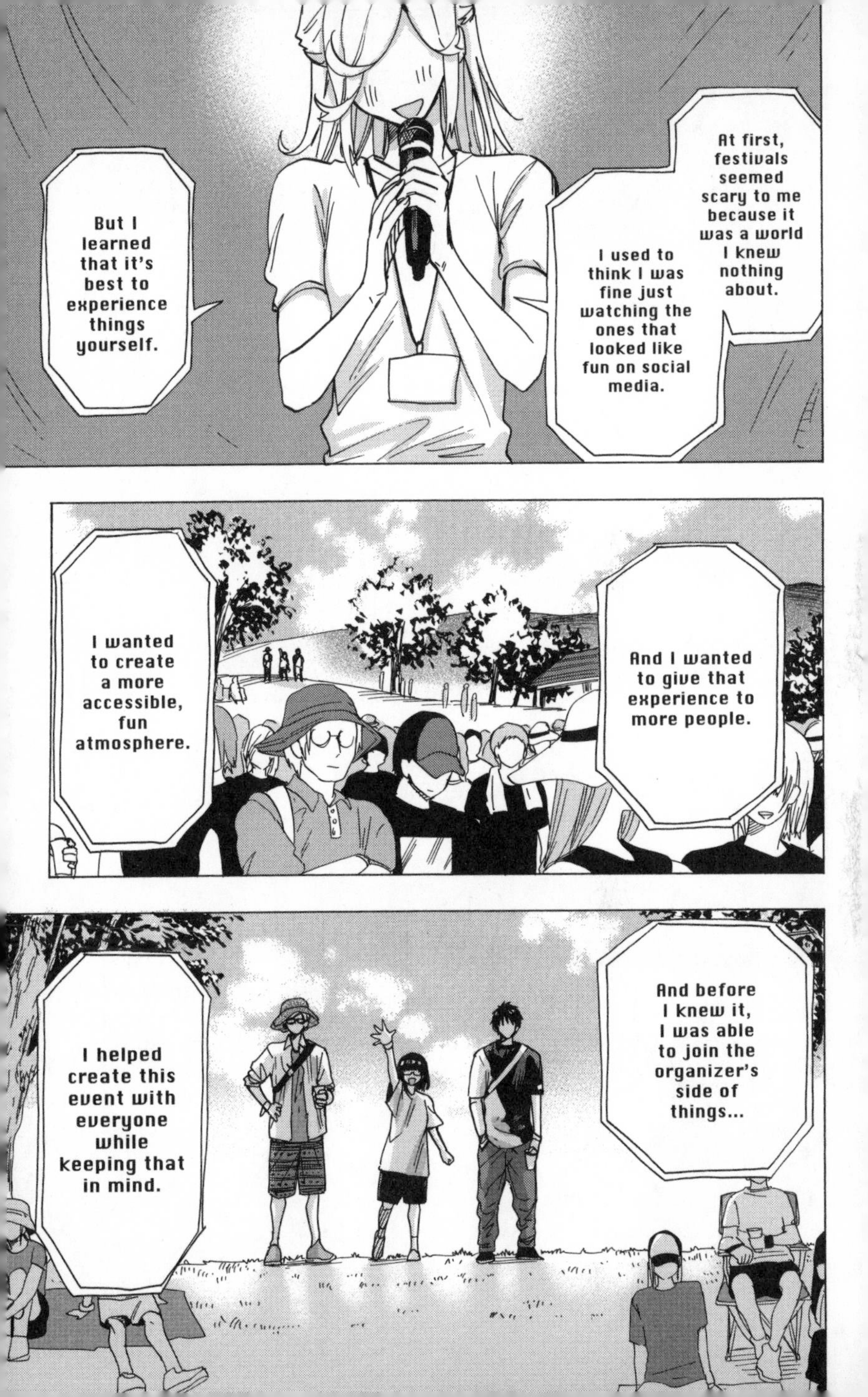
At first, festivals seemed scary to me because it was a world I knew nothing about.
I used to think I was fine just watching the ones that looked like fun on social media.
But I learned that it's best to experience things yourself.
And I wanted to give that experience to more people.
I wanted to create a more accessible, fun atmosphere.
And before I knew it, I was able to join the organizer's side of things...
I helped create this event with everyone while keeping that in mind.

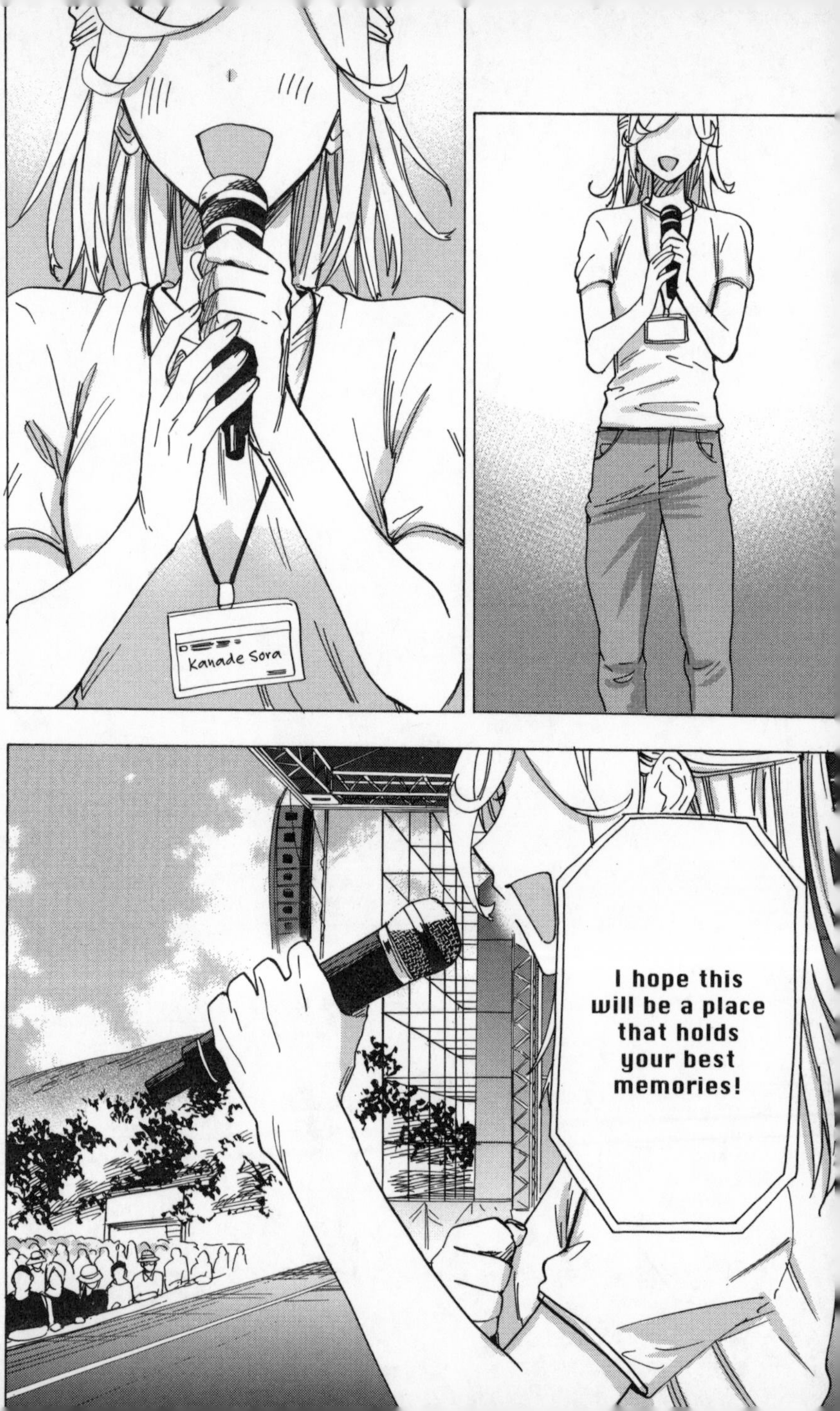
Kanade Sora
I hope this will be a place that holds your best memories!

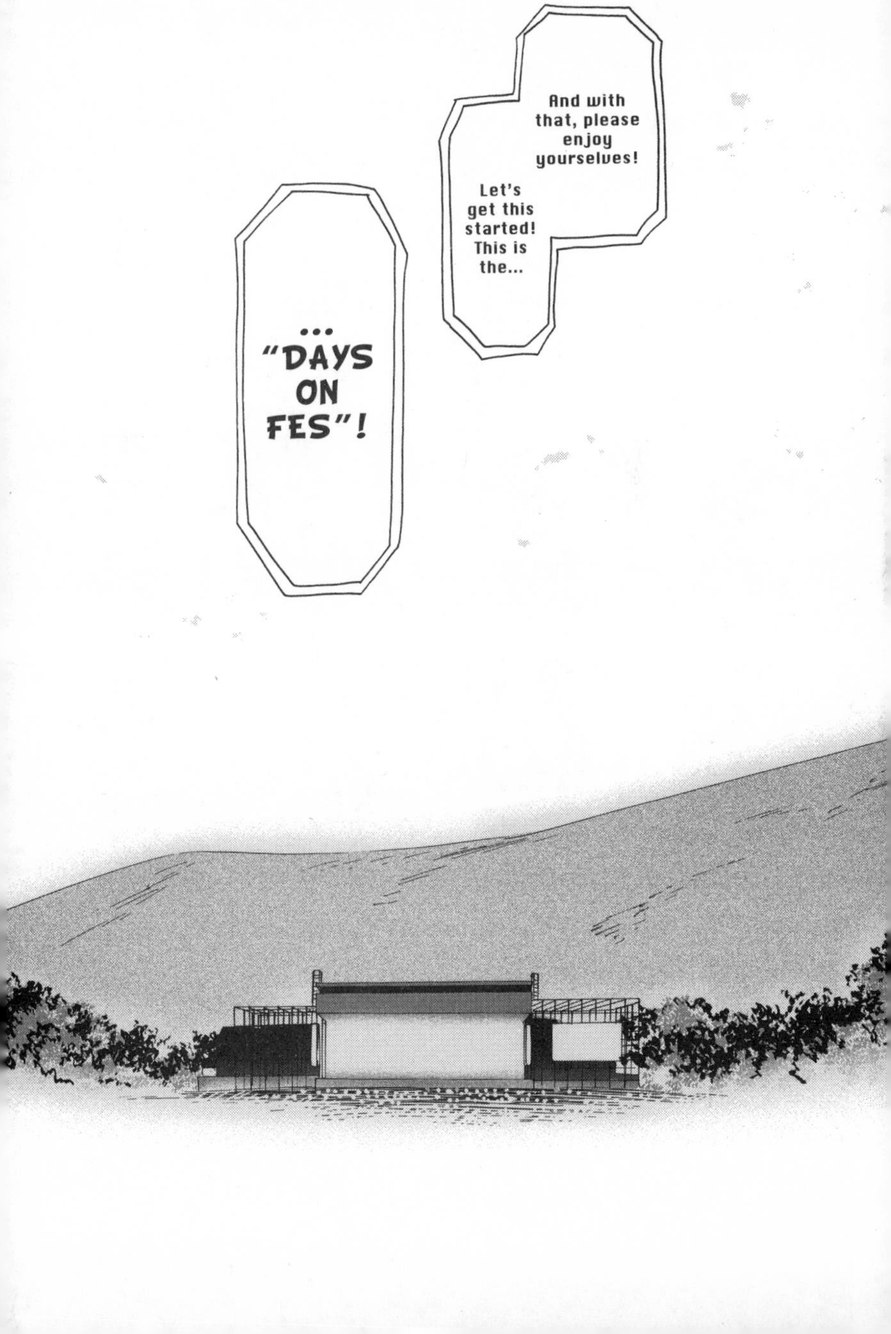
And with that, please enjoy yourselves!
Let's get this started! This is the...
..."DAYS ON FES"!

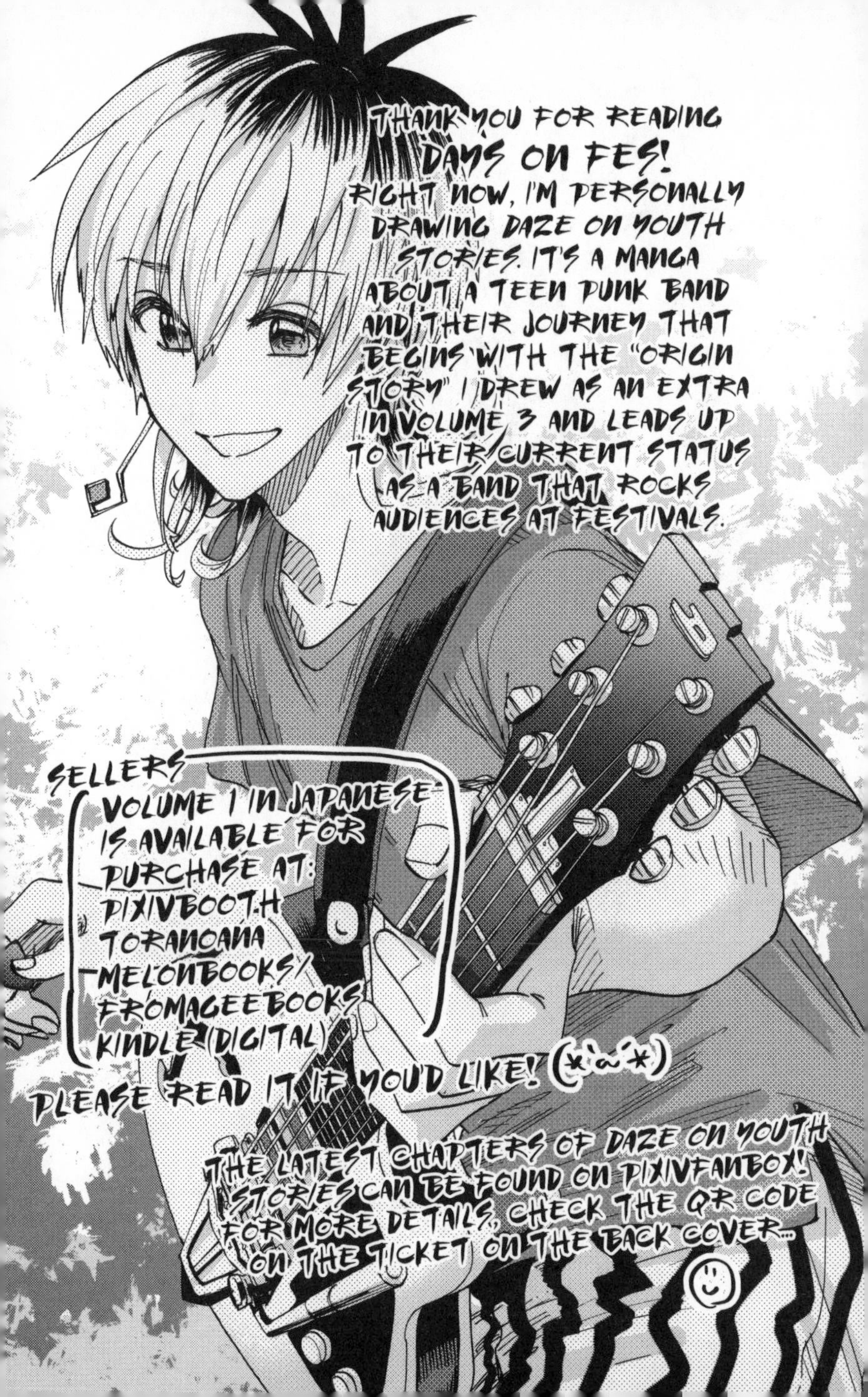
THANK YOU FOR READING DAYS ON FES!
RIGHT NOW, I'M PERSONALLY DRAWING DAZE ON YOUTH STORIES. IT'S A MANGA ABOUT A TEEN PUNK BAND AND THEIR JOURNEY THAT BEGINS WITH THE "ORIGIN STORY" I DREW AS AN EXTRA IN VOLUME 3 AND LEADS UP TO THEIR CURRENT STATUS AS A BAND THAT ROCKS AUDIENCES AT FESTIVALS.
VOLUME 1 IN JAPANESE IS AVAILABLE FOR PURCHASE AT:
SELLERS
PIXIVBOOTH
TORANOANA
MELONBOOKS/
FROMAGEEBOOKS
KINDLE (DIGITAL)
PLEASE READ IT IF YOU'D LIKE! (*´∀`*)
THE LATEST CHAPTERS OF DAZE ON YOUTH STORIES CAN BE FOUND ON PIXIVFANBOX! FOR MORE DETAILS, CHECK THE QR CODE ON THE TICKET ON THE BACK COVER...

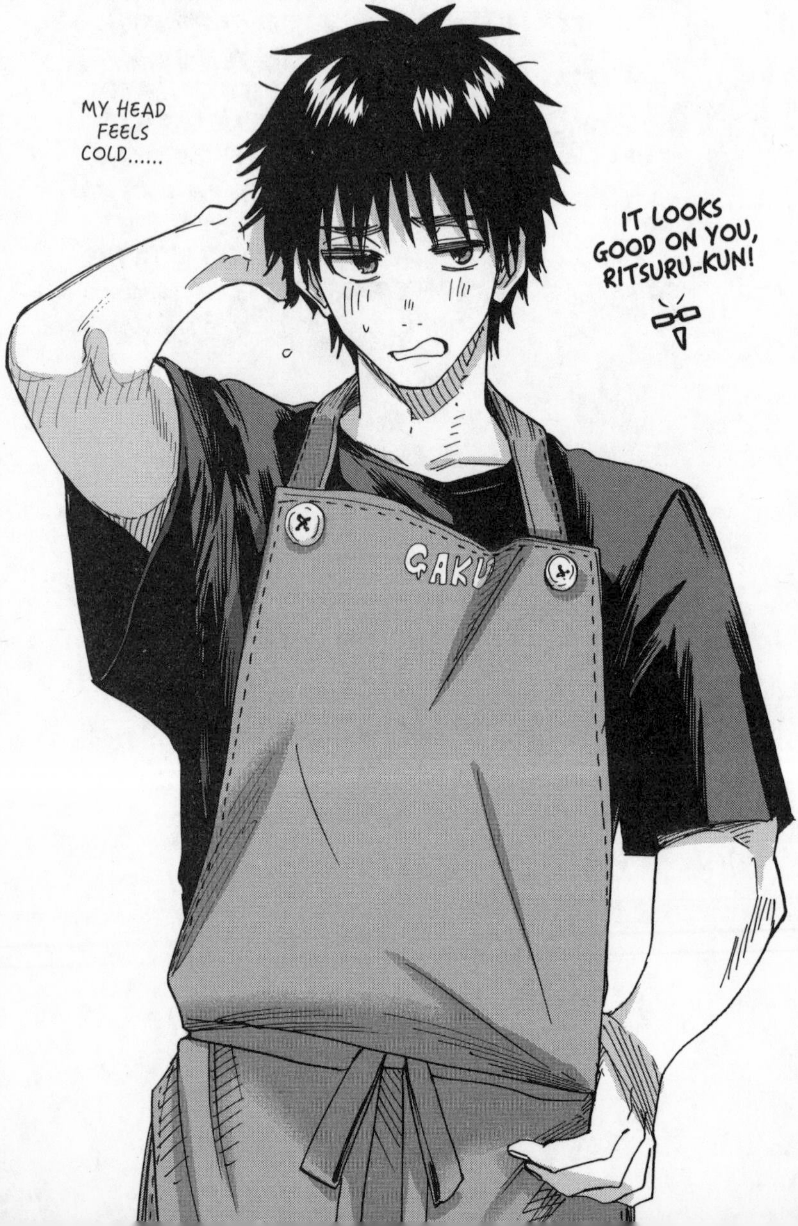
IT LOOKS GOOD ON YOU, RITSURU-KUN!
MY HEAD FEELS COLD......
GAKU

THANK YOU VERY MUCH!

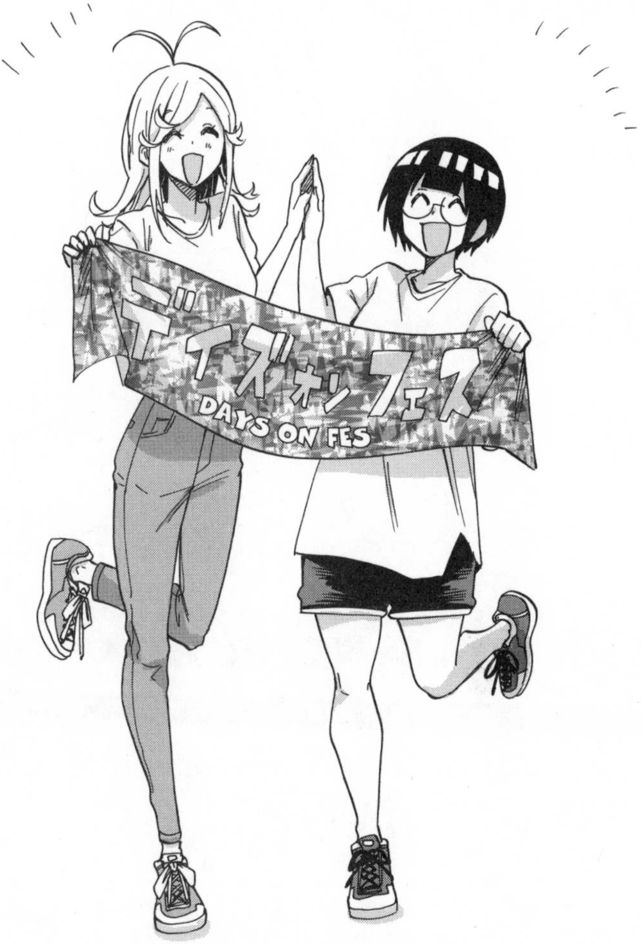
デイズォンフェス
DAYS ON FES

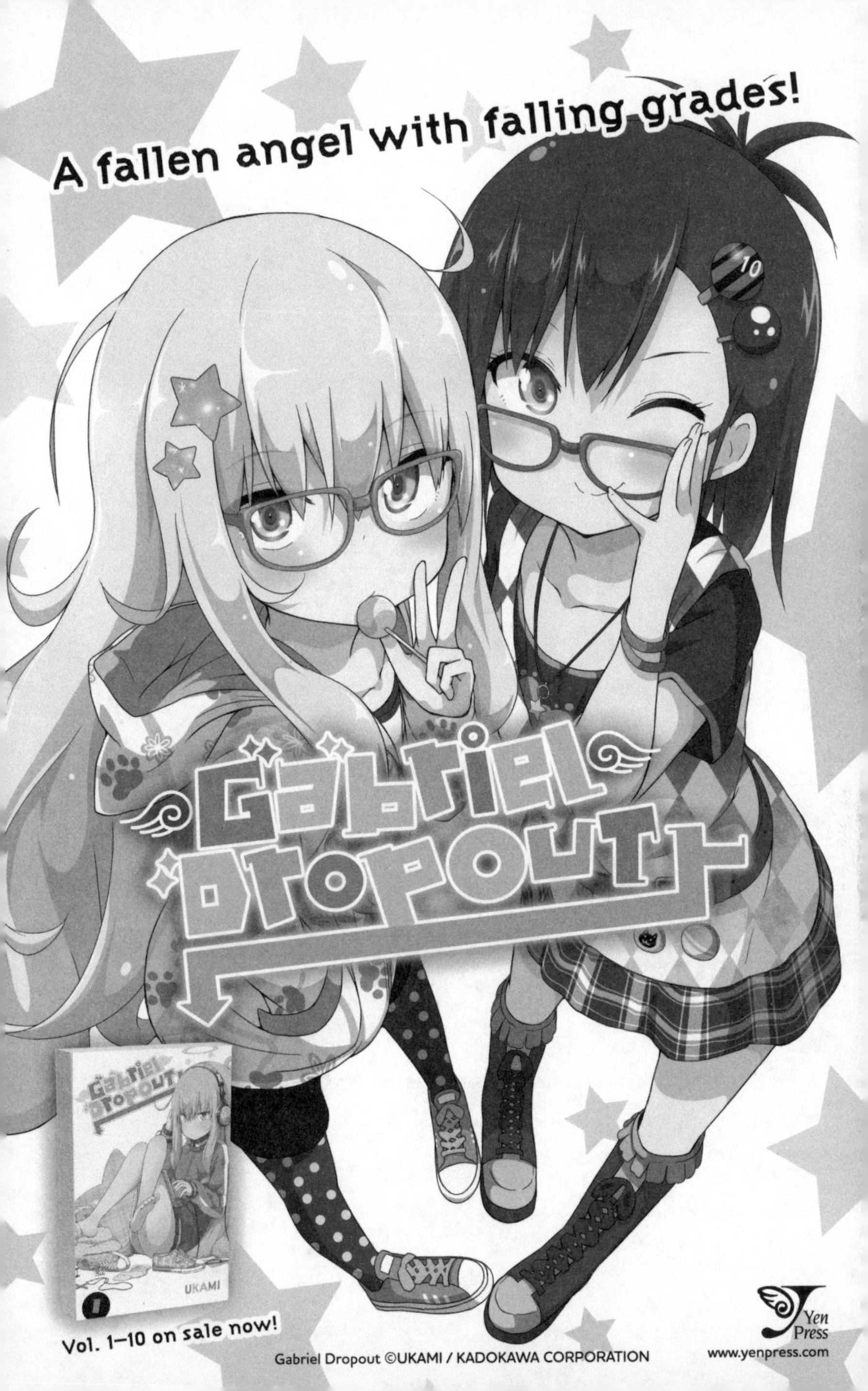
A fallen angel with falling grades!
Gabriel Dropout
Gabriel Dropout
UKAMI
1
Vol. 1–10 on sale now!
Yen Press
www.yenpress.com
Gabriel Dropout ©UKAMI / KADOKAWA CORPORATION

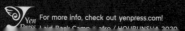

©Aidalro/SQUARE ENIX

Toilet-bound Hanako-Kun

At Kamome Academy, rumors abound about the school's Seven Mysteries, one of which is Hanako-san. Said to occupy the third stall of the third floor girls' bathroom in the old school building, Hanako-san grants any wish when summoned. Nene Yashiro, an occult-loving high school girl who dreams of romance, ventures into this haunted bathroom...but the Hanako-san she meets there is nothing like she imagined! Kamome Academy's Hanako-san...is a boy!

Yen Press

For more information visit www.yenpress.com

Days on Fes
vol. 5
KANATO OKA

TRANSLATION: AJANI OLOYE | LETTERING: ALEXIS ECKERMAN

This book is a work of fiction. Names, characters, places, and incidents are the product of the author's imagination or are used fictitiously. Any resemblance to actual events, locales, or persons, living or dead, is coincidental.

DAYS ON FES Vol. 5
©Kanato Oka 2020
First published in Japan in 2020 by KADOKAWA CORPORATION, Tokyo.
English translation rights arranged with KADOKAWA CORPORATION, Tokyo
through Tuttle-Mori Agency, Inc., Tokyo.

English translation © 2022 by Yen Press, LLC

Yen Press
150 West 30th Street, 19th Floor
New York, NY 10001

Visit us at yenpress.com ♪ facebook.com/yenpress ♪ twitter.com/yenpress
yenpress.tumblr.com ♪ instagram.com/yenpress

First Yen Press Edition: April 2022

Yen Press is an imprint of Yen Press, LLC.
The Yen Press name and logo are trademarks of Yen Press, LLC.

The publisher is not responsible for websites (or their content) that are not owned by the publisher.

Library of Congress Control Number: 2020950221

ISBNs: 978-1-9753-4001-8 (paperback)
978-1-9753-4002-5 (ebook)

10 9 8 7 6 5 4 3 2 1

WOR

Printed in the United States of America